CW00688677

I understand that the Korean economy was constructed
tive of political leadership and extraordinary efforts of t
ing smoothly. Under the conditions of rampant poverty
dealing with political forces in opposition, the leadership encouraged entrepreneurs,
upgraded labor forces, and awakened farmers through leading bureaucrats for national
development, and the people responded from their respective positions. This book
describes vividly the dynamic process of collaboration and conflict among political
leadership and the people of all social standings on the leap from poverty to a modern,
democratic nation in Korea. It will give insights to how poverty is overcome at individual and country levels, how wealth is created, and how democracy and sovereignty
in a nation are secured.

—O Won-chol, Former Chief Secretary for Economic Affairs to the
President Park Chung-Hee of the Republic of Korea

Shaped and influenced by the author's early experience of poverty and a destitute
childhood in the 1950s, this account of South Korea's economic and social transformation is deeply personal. It is also deeply relevant to today's global community at
many levels; especially for leaders seeking to understand the pathology of poverty as a
national chronic disease and formulate policies to transform underdeveloped economies. South Korea's inspiring transformation provides hope and lessons learned for
undeveloped economies on the arduous journey of poverty reduction. For those of
us working to support the cause of global poverty reduction, Dr. Chun's account is
instructive to realize that break-through poverty reduction solutions are often at odds
with the economic and development orthodoxies of the day. For this reason, this
manuscript is a must read for corporate leaders and development practitioners seeking
to develop positive impact solutions that create enduring economic and social value.

—Kim Bredhauer, Group Managing Director and CEO, Palladium

Dr. Seung-hun Chun has crafted a compelling and thought-provoking book on South
Korea's development experience. His attention to detail, careful analysis, and human-
istic approach give great depth to the myriad of factors that have contributed to South
Korea's rich and fascinating experience. Chun probes this experience with a sensitivity
that obliges the reader to action to ensure that the trials and lessons from this country's rise out of destitution do not lay idly on a page but are used to inspire solutions
to move families, communities, and countries out of poverty toward productive societies and a thriving economy. Chun's ambitions when writing this book were noble and
high and it is a worthwhile endeavor to go with him through South Korea's transformation into a modern state. The reader will similarly undergo a transformation that
will hopefully bring us closer in the fight to eradicate poverty and hunger.

—Shenggen Fan, Director General, International Food
Production Research Institute (IFPRI)

This is a fascinating insider's account of Korea's economic miracle. Even those familiar with the broad contours of Korea's transformation from fragile state to industrial
powerhouse will learn a lot from this book. Its broad scope covers not only industrial
policy but also lesser known aspects of Korean policy such as the green revolution,
labour exports, and reforestation. The book tells Korea's remarkable story from a
range of perspectives. The policy-maker's viewpoint is of course there, but the book
also contains fascinating sketches of the country's leading industrialists as well as of

some ordinary Koreans whose determination and achievements embody and explain the success of their mother-country.

—*Stephen Howes, Professor, Australian National University*

South Korea's remarkable ascent from poverty to prosperity is one of the most important stories in the modern history of the world. Global development professionals often invoke it to show what is possible. In this expansive analysis, Seung-hun Chun brings this story to life and provides the necessary detail to draw lessons for other countries seeking to learn from South Korea's success. This work from a leader and long-time practitioner of economic development is an important and valuable contribution to the global development community.

—*Raj Kumar, President and Editor in Chief, Devex*

In his book on the economic development miracle of South Korea, Seung-hun Chun vividly illustrates how a nation succeeded in moving to the centre of the world stage against a haunting past riddled with poverty, destruction and multiple foreign interventions. Dr. Chun's analysis benefits from his international experience, solid grasp of development issues and knowledge of Korean development projects since the 1960s. Nowadays China's economic growth impresses many developing nations. Yet, if there is an experience to emulate and be inspired by, it is not the giant state run by a single party machine but it is South Korea. Dr. Chun's examination convincingly argues that if leaders have an informed vision, technocrats have the capacity to devise and conduct industrial policies, and citizens and entrepreneurs are willing to work hard toward a common goal, economic growth and poverty reduction are within the reach of developing nations. For those political actors who frequently associate development with quick fixes and tangible assets such as roads and bridges, there is a crucial lesson here: without building good institutions and investing in people, their path to development will remain permanently blocked. I highly recommend this book to anyone interested in understanding the fundamentals of equitable development.

—*Dr. Gül Berna Özcan, University of London, UK, and Author of* Building States and Markets: Enterprise Development in Central Asia (*Palgrave, 2010*)

This is a long overdue book as it is written by someone who was in the trenches as a development practitioner who was involved over the key period of South Korea's development, from the initial stages to the take-off stages. It is comprehensive in its undertaking and the author has chosen to weave in human stories to reflect how the devotion of the Korean people and the centrally driven public policies were able to come together on many development fronts. What has emerged from this excellent account is the insights given to the intersection between political leadership and public ownership which had been mutually reinforcing at critical points in South Korea's development history. These characteristics run through not only in the delivery of macro policies, industrial policies, but equally in the way rural modernization was achieved through the Saemaul Undong. The underlying dynamics driving the continuous renewal of the social contract offers inspiration and concrete ideas on developmental approach that could be taken by other developing countries, African ones. There is nothing more powerful than an account grounded in tangible concrete actions taken that led to the success of South Korea.

—*Hau Sing Tse, Former Executive Director, African Development Bank*

The Economic Development of South Korea

How did a country with a dearth of natural resources and a sprawling population congested in a limited arable land transform itself into a modern industrial state within a generation? How could this have been achieved given the lingering geopolitical threats to its very survival as a state, as evidenced by the Korean War and the internecine aggressive posturing of its neighbor to the north?

This book looks at strategies, institutional arrangement, the role of entrepreneurs and workers in this odyssey, and on how those factors have worked together through effective leadership to transform South Korea's economic fortunes.

Seung-hun Chun is currently President of the Korea Institute for Development Strategy (KDS). Having engaged in development policy for South Korean government for three decades, he has been actively providing policy consultations to developing countries. He received a PhD in Economics from the University of Michigan.

Routledge Studies in the Modern World Economy

For a full list of titles in this series, please visit www.routledge.com/series/SE0432

The Economic Development of South Korea

From Poverty to a Modern Industrial State

Seung-hun Chun

Routledge
Taylor & Francis Group

LONDON AND NEW YORK

First published 2018
by Routledge
2 Park Square, Milton Park, Abingdon, Oxon OX14 4RN

and by Routledge
605 Third Avenue, New York, NY 10017

First issued in paperback 2020

Routledge is an imprint of the Taylor & Francis Group, an informa business

© 2018 Seung-hun Chun

The right of Seung-hun Chun to be identified as author of this work has been asserted by him in accordance with sections 77 and 78 of the Copyright, Designs and Patents Act 1988.

All rights reserved. No part of this book may be reprinted or reproduced or utilised in any form or by any electronic, mechanical, or other means, now known or hereafter invented, including photocopying and recording, or in any information storage or retrieval system, without permission in writing from the publishers.

Trademark notice: Product or corporate names may be trademarks or registered trademarks, and are used only for identification and explanation without intent to infringe.

British Library Cataloguing-in-Publication Data
A catalogue record for this book is available from the British Library

Library of Congress Cataloging-in-Publication Data
Names: Cheon, Seung-hun, 1946– author.
Title: The economic development of South Korea : from poverty to a modern industrial state / by Seung-hun Chun.
Description: Abingdon, Oxon ; New York, NY : Routledge, 2018. | Series: Routledge studies in the modern world economy ; 174 | Includes bibliographical references and index.
Identifiers: LCCN 2017052064 | ISBN 9780815379485 (hardback) | ISBN 9781351215749 (ebook)
Subjects: LCSH: Korea (South)—Economic conditions. | Korea (South)—Economic policy.
Classification: LCC HC467 .C464 2018 | DDC 338.95195—dc23
LC record available at https://lccn.loc.gov/2017052064

ISBN 13: 978-0-367-89495-5 (pbk)
ISBN 13: 978-0-8153-7948-5 (hbk)

Typeset in Galliard
by Apex CoVantage, LLC

To the people
who are suffering from poverty in the global
community
and our descendants
who have no experiences of poverty and war

Contents

Figures

Pictures

Preface

Addressing the African people, US President Barack Obama was quoted as saying in Ghana's Parliament during his first state visit to Africa:

> But despite the progress that has been made . . . we also know that much of that promise has yet to be fulfilled. Countries like Kenya had a per capita economy larger than South Korea's when I was born. They have badly been outpaced. Disease and conflict have ravaged parts of the African continent. . . . From South Korea to Singapore, history shows that countries thrive when they invest in their people and in their infrastructure [applause]; when they promote multiple export industries, develop a skilled workforce and create space for small and medium-sized businesses that create jobs.[1]

The aim of this book is to shed light on Korea's economic development from poverty to a modern industrial state. This writing is motivated through my recent work of international development consultancy. As a witness of Korea's economic development, having been engaged in various issues of development policy for Korean government for more than three decades, I have the fortune of visiting many developing countries for policy dialogue and witnessing the levels of squalor and pervasive poverty that has caused destitution for otherwise productive people. Initially, I found the pervasive levels of poverty in some sub-Saharan African countries and Southeast Asian countries unconscionable. However, in my quiet moments, I am reminded of my own childhood experience of living in poverty.

Like many Koreans of my generation, my childhood experience was shaped by the cataclysmic events of geopolitical tensions that unraveled on the Korean Peninsula in the mid-twentieth century. When I was 4 years old in 1950, a peaceful and happy family of young parents and two sons aged four and two was hit by a thunderbolt during the Korean War. The father was kidnapped to North Korea and the family was left to my single 24-year-old mother to care for seven family members: her mother-in-law, four brothers- and sisters-in-law, and her own two children; I was her elder son. She was barely scraping to keep the family going.

My earliest memories of growing up come from receiving food aid such as rice, wheat flour and powdered milk. I still have memories of handouts given to us in elementary school. During one such event, a friend recalls that he was given a strange looking garment. Unsure of what to do with it, he decided to use it as an earmuff during winter only to later realize that he had been covering his ears with a brassiere all along. That says a lot about a generation whose formative years were cast on the margins of subsistence and near destitution.

In my seemingly transient experience of poverty, I am reminded of just how much my destitute childhood is not very different from the conditions many people in developing countries are currently living in. Witnessing poverty in the global community as a person who experienced both poverty and abundance, I began to ask myself questions about what poverty is and how poverty can be overcome in a country.

As to the definition of poverty, for the sake of analytical convenience, the World Bank defines poverty as living below $1.90 a day, which was readjusted from $1.25 as of October 2015.[2] However, poverty goes beyond low income levels. It has a profound impact on the individual as well as the community one belongs to. Poverty literally assaults the entirety of the human lives ranging from infant mortality, poor health and social alienation to low life expectancy. Poverty's greatest irony is that those who have the least capacity often tend to be its worst victims. Beyond the individual level is the impact of the externality it has on the community. Deprivation creates the fertile ground for breeding criminal and other forms of antisocial behavior and the concomitant social unrest that can be triggered. The bonds that hold communities together become the first casualty of unrest. As an example, until the 1980s Korea was notorious for incessant social unrest due to frequent student demonstrations followed by the closure of schools and merciless repression by police force and industrial dispute in the international community. However, as income rose sustainably since the 1990s, serious social unrest no longer occurred in Korea. In this context, poverty may be said to be a social evil that dehumanizes the individual and promotes social conflict in the community, jeopardizing social stability.

No one in poverty wants to remain in poverty. One may instinctively exert efforts to avoid poverty and try to improve one's standard of living. A community, at a global or local level, tries to reduce poverty of the community and help the people in poverty. At a national or local level, governments make efforts in their own way. The international community also sets poverty reduction as a core global agenda, as is represented by the Millennium Development Goals (MDGs) until 2015 and the Sustainable Development Goals (SDGs) by 2030. Yet, there is a genuine feeling within several quarter centuries that the efforts expended thus far toward poverty reduction and economic development on the global scale has not yielded fully the intended results. Then, it leads me to the obvious question of why no major gains have been witnessed in poverty reduction at the global level. To answer this question, we need to examine the nature of poverty and how to tackle poverty.

Poverty seems to have three distinct characteristics. First, it is more like a chronic disease than anything else. Because poverty is caused by multiple, complicated factors, the cure for poverty is difficult. This argument is empirically supported by the fact that of the many new republics born at the end of World War II, few countries have become members of the Organisation for Economic Co-operation and Development (OECD) except South Korea. The lackluster outcome of the decades of poverty reduction programs by the international community in places such as sub-Saharan Africa lends credence to the fact that poverty is indeed akin to a chronic disease.

Second, although poverty is a tragedy in itself, it accompanies various composite diseases. Just as diabetes comes with other related problems such as high blood pressure, poor blood circulation and diabetic retinopathy, which add to the complications of the main condition, in the same way poverty presents a cyclical effect of problems. In a state of poverty, hungry people desperate to secure daily necessities are tempted by crime, which may lead to disintegration of the community at last. History shows that many poor countries can easily slide into fragile states, and once a country becomes a fragile state, it can hardly escape from the trap.[3]

Third, different from the handicap that causes inconvenience in living but gives no hindrance to making a living, poverty threatens the life of the individual concerned and the community as well. A poor country is also more likely to be at the mercy and whims of richer powerful countries losing its sovereignty. Domination can take the form of coercive economic and political structures of engagements and of asymmetrical legal agreements on terms that are detrimental to the interests of the poor country. Sovereignty and territorial integrity only matters to states that have the capacity to exert such claims in an asymmetrical world order. It is particularly the case that poor countries lack the means to resist domination by powerful states. The recent history of Korea provides a good example of this. After World War II, despite the fact that Korea was not the country concerned in the war, the superpowers partitioned the Korean Peninsula into the North and South. In the 1997 Korean financial crisis, the International Monetary Fund (IMF) and lending countries withdrew their whole loans without sharing any risks of their investment, and Korea suffered mass unemployment and corporate failure due to a costly money policy charged by the IMF. The history of the world is in a sense the history of the rise and fall of countries, and a major factor of the fall is poverty and the lack of power to maintain its sovereignty.

Considering the foregoing, South Korea came up against all odds and learned useful lessons in the process. Starting as one of the poorest countries, in several decades Korea has grown into a high-income country based on a democratic system. These lessons culminated into the uniqueness of Korea's development model. Korea is thus arguably the international poster child of poverty reduction.

However, there is also a school of thought that attributes the stellar economic performance of the East Asian cohort to the philosophical and ethical dimensions of traditional Confucianism. Its hierarchical structure, they say, supports the authoritarian systems that have been used effectively to the service of economic growth. While I hesitate to be drawn into the broad philosophical undertones of what informs this conclusion, I am persuaded that the Korean experience stands with the reasons as follows.

For all its grandeur, Singapore, the city-state of five million inhabitants, does not fulfill the full range of development challenges and climate that many of today's developing states are confronted with. This limited territorial and population scope of Singapore places it in an exclusive league that is divorced from the realities of the conditions that normal states should deal with on such critical issues as managing national security and formation of national consensus. Singapore has also had a rather unconventional political system that has been running on what is perceived as illiberalism incarnate in the Lee family and the People's Action Party (PAP) that has governed the country since its founding.[4]

China is routinely associated with this cohort, but this assertion obscures the fact that China is in an exclusive club of its own creation. With the Communist Party at its helm, China has broken conventions by having the Communist Party defy its Marxist traditions in running the economy on free market policies. The political space remains perniciously out of reach to most of its population of 1.3 billion. It is hard to think of any other country that can maintain the type of iron grip that the Communist Party has on the economic levers of the country while it purports to run a market economy. Its political questions aside, the huge population offers China an important factor endowment in the form of a huge domestic market. At a time when the primacy of the market is all there is, China can make up for its technology deficiency by trading market access with advanced technologies it needs from multinational corporations. While it is true that only few states, arguably, can claim to be able to emulate this strategy, which underscores its complexities, China's gross domestic product (GDP) per capita of $7,590 in 2014 has still placed it at the upper-middle-income category of states. It also remains to be seen how its institutional hybrid of socialism and market principles will play out in the long run.

For its part, South Korea after a series of chaos has since evolved into a fully functional market economy run on liberal norms undergirded by a pluralist political space notwithstanding its unique security challenges. While consulting, I have had the chance to engage with high-ranking government officials, political leaders, intellectuals and employees of international institutions related to poverty reduction and economic development.

Above all, the key takeaway is that Korea's remarkable development performance may provide an inspirational model for many of today's developing countries in their quest for poverty reduction. Particularly, those that have unsuccessfully sought economic development find a great deal of inspiration from Korea's travails, and that translates into not just optimism but a resolve to tackle the canker of poverty head-on. Rather than despair, there is a genuine interest in understanding the theoretical and technical impediments that Korea had to overcome en route to national development, with the obvious goal of benchmarking its own ongoing challenges. This, in my mind, is not to be taken lightly.

In succession, they were curious to know how South Korea tackled the various issues and obstacles on the way to national development. If poverty reduction is that difficult to achieve, how could Korea succeed with no natural resources and a large population in a geographically small area? How did it mobilize its discouraged people to pursue national development? How did it manage to change the traditional mind-set of the people to a more development-oriented one? How did it develop a highly skilled and tech-savvy human resource? How did it mobilize the enormous financial resources for development? With a small domestic market, how did it develop advanced industries in information technology (IT), automobile, steel and shipbuilding with global competitiveness and foster global corporations like Samsung and LG? How could Korea overcome the corruption chain and mistrust, which are intrinsic to the countries in poverty? Did Korea follow the same path traveled by today's developed countries toward its own development? In a fully globalized international environment, is the Korean model still applicable?

Answering these questions is one of my two objectives of this book for policymakers and practitioners to rely on as they weave their way through the complex web of poverty reduction. Hopefully Korea's travails and resulting successes will inspire them in the seemingly wild goose chase of poverty reduction.

The other objective is enabling younger generations with no experience of serious poverty to understand poverty and the price of the decent living standard they are currently enjoying. Young people and coming generations who have not lived through the tough times of Korea's lowly beginnings tend to take the performance made for granted, if not being downright cynical about the current gains. By highlighting the struggle for survival and overcoming poverty, we are bound to take a serious look in the mirror and develop a resolute understanding of the sojourn that has saved this generation and those to come from the horrendous experiences of poverty.

Many books have been written ostensibly to describe, explain or contextualize South Korea's development experience. Thus far, the written accounts can be placed within two broad categories. One set falls within the memoir category – written based on the firsthand experiences of individuals involved in the nation's public service during the heyday of national development under the late President Park. Among them are the likes of Kim Chung-yum (2011), O Won-chol (2009), Choi Hyung-sup (1995) and Nam Duck-woo (2009). The other category is what I call ex post theoretical analysis, which is more academically oriented and based on statistical indices. Among them are Lee-jay Cho et al. (2005) and Eun-mee Kim (1997). Focusing on fast economic growth in East Asia, they shed light on the role of states in economic development. Both groups are indeed very valuable intellectual assets in their own right. The former offers vivid experiences of practical policy formation and its enforcement. However, it is often limited to their personal experiences and to a specific field. The latter is very useful for academic research and provides insight and theoretical knowledge for economic development. However, it has limitations in terms of practical usage to the people who must make decisions or take actions in a dynamic and complicated real world.

This book has a couple of characteristics in its approach to the analysis of economic development in South Korea:

- First, it covers the whole process, from a poor country dependent on foreign aid to a modern industrial state and donor country. It sheds light on how a country could transform itself from a poor, fragile state to an industrialized, democratic one.
- Second, in a sense, economic development is a dynamic process of pursuing their own interests among political leadership, entrepreneurs, laborers and farmers in a form of collaboration and conflict. In this respect, rather than providing ex post analysis or interpretation, it tries to convey a vivid state of things and behaviors of major players to the environment of the days on a path toward economic development.
- Third, this book also considers that economic development is not a monotonous growth over time but a dynamic process of attaining driving forces with ups and downs. In this regard, it tries to explain how driving forces and the basis for sustainable economic growth and state building are established in a country and what their consequences are. This is the hardest phase, just like that of takeoff for a plane. Once takeoff is complete, the country is on track for sustainable growth with its own resilience.

In development economics, there are several fundamental hypotheses that explain potential obstacles for developing countries to achieve sustainable economic development. F. Fukuyama (2004) argues that institutional transferability from advanced countries to developing ones is low. In this regard, few developing countries so far have witnessed full democracy and market economy in the process of their economic development. It is also generally argued that realizing full industrialization may not be feasible in developing countries without a large population and a big domestic market to accommodate heavy and chemical industries, and recently it has been claimed that deindustrialization is happening in developing countries, which causes means that industrialization cannot be a solution for economic development in the developing world. (*Economist*, "The third great wave," October 4, 2014). In general, inclusive growth is desirable for sustainable development in developing countries. (J. Stiglitz: Price of Inequality, 2012). However, it seems too ideal for developing countries to realize it from the start beginning under serious resource constraints and with large fragile strata to manage. This book examines how these hypothetical obstacles could be overcome in South Korea.

This book does not by any means claim to provide definitive answers to all the questions about South Korea's development experience. In fact, I am prepared to concede that there are moments in this book that I cautiously dabble with between both my status as a blunt scholar and the steadiness of the civil servant in me. What this book does is to shine a spotlight on the forces of economic development and dynamic collaboration and conflict among players. May I also be charitable in my admission that a significant chunk of the narratives and events in this book are not situated within a specific theory of economics or scholarship tradition for that matter. This is by no means to be construed as an omission because it is consistent with the spirit of the very factors that shaped the uniqueness of South Korea's development experience. It gives me the confidence in saying that because Korea's development experience generally defied the economic orthodoxies of the day, it will be rather unwise to try to attribute to one tradition rather than the other. The accounts discussed in this book, for all intents and purposes, avoid such weaknesses. There are accounts of a generous presentation of activities, individuals and events. I thus avoid the inclination to tout the supremacy of one model over the other. I am principally engaged in the task of presenting the events as a seamless flow of processes during a plastic moment in history.

Traversing of the path of Korea's development reminds me of one of Shakespeare's plays. A distraught Portia speaking in *The Merchant of Venice* lamented that "If to do were as easy as to know what were good to do, chapels had been churches, and poor men's cottages princes' palaces."[5] The timelessness of Portia's lamentation for me sums up the experience and the story of South Korea's development sojourn. By confounding the orthodoxies of the day, with the benefit of hindsight, it is easy to appreciate why this phenomenal breakthrough was, quite frankly, almost often experimental, improvisational and inspired by sheer necessity at different stages of this remarkable odyssey.

Notes

1 "Remarks by the President to the Ghanaian Parliament," The White House, Office of the Press Secretary, July 11, 2009, accessed August 5, 2017, https://obamawhitehouse.archives.gov/the-press-office/remarks-president-ghanaian-parliament
2 www.worldbank.org/en/topic/poverty/brief/global-poverty-line-faq
3 Independent Evaluation Group, *Engaging With Fragile States: An IEG Review of World Bank Support to Low-Income Countries Under Stress* (Washington, DC: World Bank, 2006).
4 Lee Kuan Yew and his People's Action Party (PAP) have cast a very long shadow, and maintain a hegemonic control of the political culture of that city state, as some critics contend. Now in its second generation of leadership transition from the senior Lee to the junior Lee, the PAP basically built on the institutional structures bequeathed to them by the British colonial administration, with a rather stern authoritarian tweak to its governance process.
5 Taken from *The Merchant of Venice*, Act 1, Scene 2.

Acknowledgments

Just within my lifetime Korea has remarkably transformed from a listless failing state to a very competitive dynamic high-tech economy. From a GDP per capita of $339 in 1972 when I was a young college graduate, to $10,432 when I was retiring from active public service, I have witnessed this phenomenal transformation and along the way become a "development evangelist." Beginning in 1972 when I was a rookie civil servant at the Economic Planning Board (EBP), then to the Ministry of Finance and Economy to my retirement from the civil service in 1999, I have been involved in different levels in the development policy-making processes that transformed South Korea.

Outside of the state bureaucracy, I spent another 6 years as a consultant for state development think tanks up to 2005, until I became the co-founder of the Korea Institute for Development Strategy (KDS). My mission with the KDS has been to share this historical process with many of those looking to South Korea for inspiration and guidance in their own struggles with transforming their economies. Along with this process I have made a career of understanding the dynamics of poverty and the formulation of policies that can transform underdeveloped economies.

As president and co-founder of the KDS, a Seoul-based development policy consultancy firm, my professional focus has expanded beyond the shores of Korea. My line of work involves regular engagements with public officials from developing countries, whose enthusiasm for transforming their economies, as Korea did, is commendable to say the least. This book is in many ways a response to the chorus of calls from government officials, policymakers, and some of my personal friends across the world whose magnanimous encouragement is the culmination of my modest attempt to share the legacy of this experience in fine print.

I cannot conceive of how this project would have come about but for the invaluable contribution of the gracious people whose wisdom, experience and support made a great difference. It has been my great fortune to benefit from the expertise of Mr. O Won-chol, arguably the brainchild of Korea's industrialization, as the country's Chief Secretary for Economic Affairs under President Park Chung-hee. As a co-founder of the KDS, my professional and personal relationship with this stalwart was critical in shaping my own insight into the inner workings of the theory and praxis of development and state building as it pertains to Korea's bold leap of faith into economic development. To him I owe a great deal of gratitude.

I am also thankful to Dr. Song Hi-yeon, former president of the Korea Development Institute (KDI); Dr. Lee Yung-sae, former president of Korea Cyber University; and Dr. Shin Ki-Deok, former president of both the CJ Economic Institute and JThink (Jeonbuk Institute). The invaluable insight and contribution of all the fellows at the KDS is also duly acknowledged and appreciated. Many thanks are also due to the many academics, policymakers and political leaders across the world with whom I have had the privilege of working over a decade. While I am unable to name you individually, I acknowledge that yours has been an incredible contribution to enriching my sociocultural experience as you provided innumerable opportunities for me to broaden my narrow scope.

David Alenga, the lead reviewer and editor of the initial draft, in collaboration with his partner, Dylan Irons, put a tremendous amount of work into making sure that this book's analytical and policy relevance consistently reflect the challenges of our times, because it is a rewind of history. Ms. Moon-hi Kim and Ji-young Hwang were very resourceful research assistants, who put together the data used in this book.

Finally, the consistent love and understanding given to me by my family, although rarely explicitly acknowledged has always been deeply appreciated. Through her deep faith in God and fortitude, my mother Chun-hwa Cho (Chun) has been my spiritual backbone. The same appreciation goes to my wife Mie-ryung Kim (Chun) for her understanding, encouragement and patience during the long hours I stayed away to work on this book. My son Hongmin Chun, who is a partner for international development consultation at the KDS, has provided some of the critical balance in my personal thoughts, and my daughter-in-law Na-young Ahn has provided illustrations for this book. Indeed, my family, including my daughter Eun-young Chun (Park) and son-in-law Byung-ju Park, has been a source of energy and inspiration for this work and my mission of international development.

In a sense, this work is a tribute to my father, Chun Kwang-soo, who like many of our forebears was a victim of the dark days of colonialism and the ensuing post-colonial political turbulence. A true believer in the promise of our nation's future, he was a diligent community organizer whose conviction in the future saw him lead the establishment of a community self-help organization called the Agricultural and Fishing Villages Cultural Association in 1948. Even within the dark precincts of his era, my father was committed to the zeitgeist of colonial Korea as reflected in his passionate writings including titles such as *Human Life and Success, Independence and New Life and Executive Manual*. Up until the unfortunate episode of his kidnap and smuggle across the 38th Parallel, he published a monthly magazine, *Hwa-rang*, with the view of contributing to the sociocultural enlightenment of his compatriots. It is therefore befitting that this book be a sign of my modest contribution to my father's work toward the blissful future that he desired for Korea. May my witness provide the light to which the achievements of the present era be reflected on his blessed spirit.

In a temporary quarter at the foot of Mt. Sobek

1 Korea from the trap of poverty to a modern industrial state

1 From hopelessness to the Miracle on the Han River

The defeat of Japan by the Allied Powers in 1945 saw the liberation of the Korean Peninsula from colonialism and the birth of the new nation, the Republic of Korea (hereinafter referred to as South Korea or Korea) in 1948. However, its birth was not without complications. Driven by competing geostrategic interests, the Soviet Union and the United States were soon to rush into taking controlling stakes of the liberated Korean Peninsula in 1945. The Soviets took control of the northern half and the Americans the southern half. During this period of occupation, nascent governments were being groomed along the ideological cleavages of their respective occupation forces. Both blocs eventually agreed to place Korea under a United Nations (UN) trusteeship, arguing that Koreans lacked the capacity for self-government. The proposal was, however, fiercely rejected in the southern half of the peninsula because of fears that it was the first step in a plot to place the peninsula into the Communist bloc. After initial opposition, the north was nudged by the Soviet Union into endorsing the proposal. A planned nationwide general election under the auspices of the United Nations was rejected by the North, and South Korea was born as the only legitimate government by the UN. The North declared another government, the Democratic People's Republic of Korea (DPRK, hereinafter referred to as North Korea), supported by the Socialist bloc, the Soviet Union and China. Tip O'Neill, the late US congressman from Massachusetts, popularized the axiom "all politics is local." Yet, the moral of local politics hardly ever matters in the realm of international politics, and none more so than the history of the brutal twentieth century. So it was that weak states were subordinated to vassals and allegiances transient in a crude worship of the morality of power.

The North soon launched an unprovoked attack against the South, backed up by its Socialist alliance of the Soviet Union and China in 1950 with the goal of unifying the entire peninsula under a single communist government. This triggered a response from the democratic bloc in defense of the South in what became the Korean War (1950–1953). The end of hostilities between the two halves was reached through an armistice that is still in force today. Geopolitically the newly born South Korea became an isolated island blocked to the north by a hostile Socialist regime and over the ocean confronted by the former colonial regime Japan with no diplomatic relations. Under the circumstances, South Korea had to struggle against serious poverty and military threats to survive.

Suffice it to look at the living conditions under which the citizens of the newly formed republic in the South lived in the immediate post-war era. Three main indicators may be used to measure a fair assessment of living conditions in a country: (1) international balance of payments, (2) gross domestic product (GDP) per capita and (3) life expectancy. The first indicates how much a country is financially sustainable; the second measures the average earnings of a country; and the third refers to the health status of the people. The following three figures give a sense of the long-term trend of these three indicators in Korea with international comparisons. For the sake of discussion, let us just focus our attention on the status of the early 1960s figures for the time being.

First, regarding international balance of payments, Korea was faced with serious trade deficits during the period under review, as Figure 1.1 shows. To making a living, at least in the long run, it is important to ensure that revenue or earnings exceed expenditures, and that holds true for households, corporations and countries. According to the same figure, Korea exported $33 million and imported $344 million worth of goods, making a deficit of $311 million in 1960. In fact, Korea was importing approximately ten times more than it was exporting. Meanwhile, the

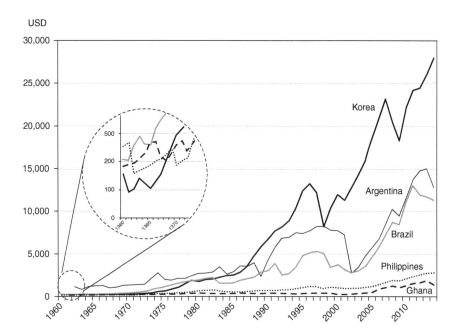

Figure 1.1 The trend of trade balance (in current USD), an international comparison

Source: Korea International Trade Association and World Bank national accounts data and OECD National Accounts data files

Philippines and Ghana were in much better position in this respect. It would thus be no surprise to learn that by this point the Korean economy was closer to the verge of bankruptcy than many developing countries until the 1960s.

Looking into trade items is even more disappointing. Agricultural and fishery products constituted the bulk of South Korea's exports, whereas import products were mainly foodstuffs, raw materials and intermediate goods, energy and chemical products – all essential goods for the livelihood of the citizens.[1] The prospects for trade imbalance looked very bleak indeed.

Second, regarding income levels in Figure 1.2, Korea's GDP per capita in 1960 was $156, lagging against Ghana and the Philippines. In many ways, it was the poster child of an underdeveloped and fragile state among the lowest income group of nations, according to the World Bank. Income levels were lower than that of most Asian countries, similar or lower than that of most African countries in those days, and much lower than many South American countries such as Brazil and Argentina.

Third, the low-income level is reflected in the low life expectancy of 53 years in 1960 shown in Figure 1.3, at a time when the average figure of the OECD (Organisation for Economic Co-operation and Development) member countries was 67.3 years. This confirms the general correlation between poverty and high mortality.

To avoid default, the deficits had to be compensated by either foreign aid or foreign loan. As Figure 1.4 shows, Korea was heavily dependent on foreign aid

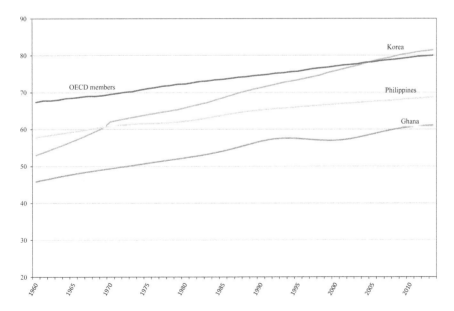

Figure 1.2 The trend of GDP per capita (in current USD), an international comparison

Source: World Bank national accounts data and OECD national accounts data files

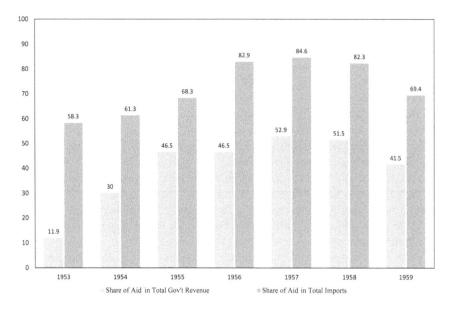

Figure 1.3 The trend of life expectancy in Korea

Source: World Bank DataBank – World Development Indicators

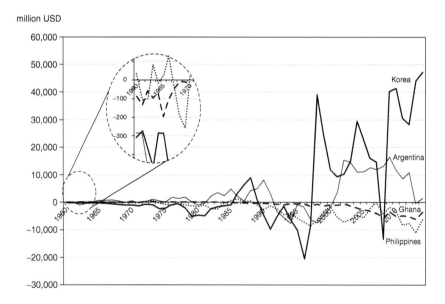

Figure 1.4 Foreign aid during 1950s in Korea

Source: Kim Jun-Kyung et al., 2011 Modularization of Korea's Development Experience: Impact of Foreign Aid on Korea's Development, (Seoul, Korea: MOSF and KDI school, 2012), 87

for subsistence. According to the figure, during the late 1950s foreign aid occupied almost half of the government's revenue. Korea was financially unsustainable. Foreign aid was a lifeline to the poor Korean citizens in those days.

The miserable status of Korea was well witnessed by international experts and journals. After an inspection tour of war-torn Korea as part of the United Nations Korea Reconstruction Agency (UNKRA), the maverick Indian diplomat V. K. Krishna quipped, "will a rose blossom in a refuse bin?" An assessment of the South Korean economy by the government of Japan published in a report titled "On the Korean Economy" in July 1961 added to the scathing international consensus that South Korea was a literal basket case.[2] A well-known scholar in Asian studies and senior consultant of USAID in the Asian region, David I. Steinberg (2001) argued in his comparison of Myanmar, Thailand and South Korea that Myanmar would be the potential economic and political leader, Thailand the second choice and South Korea not a contender among the three.[3]

Now let us turn our attention to the aforementioned three figures focusing on 2000s. Concerning the international balance of payments, the chronic deficit position that appeared almost impossible to deal with shows a stable position at an enormously enlarged scale. During the period of 1960 and 2014, exports jumped from $33 million to $573 billion and imports from $344 million to $526 billion, respectively, which resulted in a sharp switch from a deficit of $311 million to a surplus of $47 billion. Meanwhile, the Philippines and Ghana are suffering deficits of $6.6 billion and $3.7 billion, respectively. Looking at per capita income, GDP per capita in Korea surpassed the $20,000 mark in 2006. This marked the beginning of an aid-dependent country transforming into a donor country as a member of the OECD/DAC (Development Assistance Committee). Alongside the increased income, a corresponding increase in life expectancy was observed, far surpassing that of the Philippines and Ghana, and even the average of OECD member countries. This goes to confirm that the poverty reduction and economic development of Korea is not just empty rhetoric.

If as the axiom says, "a picture is worth a thousand words," the pictures Seoul's downtown Chong-gye stream show symbolically the remarkable transformation of living standards of citizens of Seoul and the Korean people during recent decades. The shabby houses in Seoul in the 1950s were completely reshaped in the 2000s, as the right-hand side picture illustrates. Its unprecedented rags-to-riches story has been dubbed the "The Miracle on the Han River," as did Robert Lucas Jr. (1993):

> I do not think it is in any way an exaggeration to refer to this continuing transformation of the Korean society as a miracle. . . . Never before have the lives of so many people undergone so rapid an improvement over so long a period, nor is there any sign that this progress is near its end.[4]

At the heart of the significant increase in the nation's output and income was the result of a sustained growth in the industrial base. Korea has grown as an international manufacturing hub in steel, electronic goods, automobile, shipbuilding

Picture 1.1 The feature of Chong-gye stream downtown Seoul: in 1950s (top) and in 2000s (bottom)

©Seoul Museum of History Digital Archive

www.museum.seoul.kr/www/theme/NR_themeMuseumView.do?arcvNo=65301&arcvMetaSeq=21243&langGubun=01&groupNo2=341&sso=ok)

and machinery goods, which supports an enormous growth of exports and thus surplus in the international balance of payments. This industrial performance is particularly appreciated in several respects by the international community.

First, full industrialization in Korea was attained in a country that has an insufficient domestic market. To fully develop the heavy and chemical industries (HCI) such as steel, automobile, shipbuilding and petrochemicals, the market should be large enough to accommodate them. In Korea's case, here was a population of 35 million when full-scale industrialization policies were launched. Second, the pace of the industrialization is also quite breathtaking. As will be discussed in Sections 5.1 and 7.3, industrialization in Korea has proceeded much faster than in Western Europe and Japan. This may be accountable to either reduced learning costs by being a late starter for industrialization, a more efficient industrial policy in Korea or both of these.

2 The start of the urge

To understand the great transformation of the South Korean economy, we need to analyze both the initial conditions for development and the corresponding development strategies based on the initial conditions of the economy. First, the country had a population of 25 million in 1960 that was growing at 3 percent per annum, partly due to a huge southbound migration from the North after the partition of the peninsula. With a territorial mass of 98,431 square kilometers, there was a population density of 254 persons per square kilometer. This was further complicated by the fact that only 22.9 percent of the land was arable. Little wonder that Korea was in good company with overpopulated city-states like Singapore, Hong Kong and Macau, and Bangladesh to a lesser degree. The sprawling population had a pernicious impact on food security, given the adverse territorial conditions and low agricultural productivity.

Second, the level of human capital is associated with the educational attainment of the population. Regarding educational attainment, of the population over 13 years old, 28 percent were illiterate and only half of the population had an elementary education in 1960.[5] "Being learned" was traditionally associated with the ruling class and in another sense was a symbol of social status. Historically this opportunity had been limited to the upper class of the people, and was later open to all the citizens. There was a major interruption in the historical desire for educational attainment during the colonial period. Much of it had to do with Japanese colonial policy that deliberately restricted educational opportunities. High human capital investment in Korea can be attributed to the Confucian-oriented culture and rewarding mechanism to education and human capital investment, which will be picked up in Chapter 8.

It was also Japanese colonial policy to bar Koreans from having access to technological and managerial work in the industrial fields.[6] The pedagogy delinked science and technology education in the higher educational process.[7] Because they were not educated and had no technology, they had to be engaged in manual work. The economic partitioning that purposefully reserved the North as an exclusive industrial zone and the South an agrarian zone under the colonial regime meant that the Koreans in the South had little access to industrial work compared to those in the North. Even with that, the Korean War (1950–1953) destroyed most of the factories that remained.

Let me spare a moment to also highlight the impact of the colonial process on the psychosocial disposition of the masses within a historical context. Koreans had lived in a centralized kingdom for thousands of years, competing for survival against China, Mongolia and other tribes in Manchuria before Japanese colonial rule from 1910 to 1945. Colonized people tend to live subserviently and go through a psychological process that Frantz Fanon describes as "making them liable to developing an imbibed inferiority complex."[8] A colonized or dominated person has less of a sense of sovereignty and over time acquires a sense of inferiority. The same can be said about their allegiance to the land and its productive capacity, which is steadily lost on them. Koreans were taught to look upon themselves with contempt and inferiority under Japanese occupation. The colonial educational system did not offer self-reliance skills, but was rather predicated on dehumanizing the colonized subjects.

Cynicism and self-disparagement were ubiquitous in the colonial era. This was a period in which sayings such as "What do you expect from *yeopjeons*?"[9] and "What can *waraji*-wearers do?" used the terms *yeopjeon* and *waraji* in a self-derogatory fashion.[10] After all, what kind of power could *yeopjeon* have in a dollar-based world? Moreover, while most of the world wore shoes, Koreans were seemingly destined to be lifelong *jipshin* wearers. The citizens also had no concept of time. The infamous "Korean time" was a popular mantra used to describe the lack of punctuality among the citizens.[11] This mind-set needs to be viewed within the context of how the depressing economic environment allowed for the lethargic mind-set to fester.

Prior to the land reforms of the 1950s, private land ownership had virtually been usurped by a privileged minority of feudal lords who owned most of the land and leased it to tenant farmers. To address this imbalance, a major land reform measure was initiated and implemented during the period of 1940–52, based on a principle of "land to the tillers." The 3 hectare ceiling on land ownership per farming household remarkably transformed the land tenure system in Korea. The land reform process drove the landlord class into oblivion and promoted social mobility across the board.[12]

Under colonial rule, over 90 percent of electricity plants, steel mills and metallurgy, chemical, metal and various machine plants were established in the North, which had abundant mineral resources and was adjacent to Manchuria. In May 1948, the North disconnected power supply to the South, plunging Seoul into darkness and causing industrial production to plummet to below 10 percent. The North incentivized Japanese technicians and engineers with high salaries to both retain and transfer their skills to locals. It also received heavy subventions from its socialist allies to revive its industrial base after a setback during the war. All the aid given to the South, on the other hand, was mainly in the form of relief and consumer goods.

In the 1960s, the North was producing large-caliber guns, ammunition, military vehicles, tanks and guided missiles on its own supported by power supply, while the South could not produce even rifle parts under a serious shortage of electricity.[13] A South Korean soldier stationed at the demilitarized zone (DMZ), where the North and South military forces stand guard, recalled the situation at that time: "When I was serving as a chief in the barracks, we had no electricity and the North did. We were in short of rice, while they were rich in rice and exported more than us."[14] Under these more favorable conditions for industrialization and economic development than the South, the North pursued national development based on social ownership and self-subsistence. The North confiscated the land and distributed its right of using it gratuitously. Meanwhile, the South opted for economic development through the market system and an export-oriented strategy. The South obtained the land for counter value and distributed its ownership rights onerously.

From the preceding review, in comparison of the circumstances for development of Korea in its early days with that of currently developing countries, there seem to be no significant differences in fundamental factors. In demographic conditions and the mental aspect of the people no fundamental differences are identified, because Korea also experienced colonial rule and serious poverty. In development potential among the Asian countries, Steinberg (2001) evaluated that among Myanmar, Thailand and South Korea, South Korea had the least potential among the three.[15] North and South Korea provide a good counterfactual analysis case, because both are the same people. North Korea was in a more favorable condition in demographics, energy and industrial base than its counterpart. The fundamental differences were in the political system and leadership. It is interesting what outcomes were produced under the counterfactual conditions in both Koreas.

Notes

1 O Won-chol, *The Korea Story: President Park Jung-hee's Leadership and the Korean Industrial Revolution* (Seoul, Korea: Wisdom Tree, 2009), 66–67.
2 *Ibid.*, 68.
3 David I. Steinberg, *Burma: The State of Myanmar* (Washington, DC: Georgetown University Press, 2001), 32–33.
4 Robert Lucas Jr., "Making a Miracle," *Econometrica*, Vol. 61, No. 2 (March 1993), 251–252.
5 O Won-chol, *Hanguk-hyeong gyeongjegeonseol 7: Naega jeonjaengeul hajaneun getdo aniji anneunya* [Korean Type Economic Construction 7: An Engineering Approach] (Seoul, Korea: Korea Type Economic Policy Institute, 1999), 195.
6 *Ibid.*, 193–195.
7 Kim Keun-bae, *Hanguk geundae gwahak gisul illyeok-ui chulhyeon* [Emergence of Modern Science and Technology Manpower in Korea] (Seoul, Korea: Literature and Intelligence Co., 2005), 450–452.
8 Frantz Fanon, *The Wretched of the Earth* (New York: Grove Press, 1963), 35–41.
9 The brass coin traditionally was used by Koreans as currency, and this term was used to demean Koreans.
10 O, *The Korea Story*, 433.

11 *Ibid.*
12 Ban Sung Hwan, Moon Pal Yong and Dwight H. Perkis, *Rural Development: Studies in the Modernization of the Republic of Korea: 1045–1975* (Cambridge, MA: Council on East Asian Studies, Harvard University, 1982), 283–287.
13 O Won-chol, *Bakjeonghuineun edtteoke gyeongjegengguk mandeulleonna* [How Park Chung-hee Made Economic Power] (Seoul, Korea: Dongsuh Press, 2006), 100–101 and 111–112.
14 *Hwangmujieseo ilgun soetmul, pocheol sinhwa* [Molten Iron From the Wasteland, the Myth of POSCO]. Directed by Kim Dong-kook (Seoul, Korea: KBS, September 14, 2009), accessed August 10, 2017, www.kbs.co.kr/1tv/sisa/docucinema/view/vod/2186813_66621.html
15 Steinberg, *Burma*, 33.

2 The travails of state building and institutional arrangement for development

1 Trial and error for state building

That the new nation was born in 1948 under a democratic mandate, confronted with the Herculean task of nation building in an environment defined by extreme levels of poverty, political and social insecurity, did not sound like a promising start. Three vital conditions are required for nation building: (1) poverty reduction, (2) social security and (3) national defense capacity. In the case of Korea, the third factor was in many ways a question of the survival of the young state, especially against the backdrop of the presence of powerful adversarial military forces from the Asian continent looming large. The US commitment to defend this tiny nation can thus be seen in this regard as definitive response to this fundamental question of state survival, thereby paving the way for the young government to experiment with the nation building process.

Poverty reduction and social stability have interlinked each other. Poverty directly undermines social security to its very core, and both have a directive causative relationship. Social insecurity incapacitates normal economic activity for poverty reduction. Most often, poverty comes together with fragility. To achieve poverty reduction, there has to be social stability, and in reverse, the latter depends on the former. The dilemma of poor countries is in the paradoxical sense that they are required to catch two rabbits simultaneously.

As Korea gained independence in 1945, it faced serious conflict that led to division of the Korean Peninsula into two parts. The North was occupied by the Soviet Union military force, and the South by United Nations (UN) forces led by the United States. The period from 1945 to 1950 was the period of desperate efforts for state building. In a state of prevalent poverty, socialism was a tasty carrot for the masses. It is said that if a young man in his twenties is not leftist, he has no heart, and if still a leftist in his forties, he has no brain. At that time in Korea, many intellectuals, young people must have had heart. The Republic of Korea was born in 1948, led by the founder and the first president, Syngman Rhee. In the meantime, armed revolt occurred several times, which was barely suppressed by military and police forces.

Syngman Rhee played a key role in deciding the fortune of the Korean people. He had foresight about the trends of the world and international politics.

Overcoming serious threat from the left, Rhee succeeded in establishing the Republic of Korea as the UN's recognized head of state, a democratic republic based on market system. After World War II, many newly independent countries were carried away by the wave of communism. Many African countries, including Ethiopia, Tanzania and many others, were among those whose embrace of communism made them miss the opportunity in their early stage to launch economic development based on a market economy. The North's Socialist regime under the Russian army expatriated landlords and claimed nationalization of land ownership. Indebted to Syngman Rhee, Korea could build the institution of democracy and market economy allied with the Western world.

In a desperate effort to secure public support, Syngman Rhee of South Korea conducted land reform in 1949. However, this caused weakening in his power base in the National Assembly, in which the landlord class had great power. At the same time, US forces were withdrawn according to the resolution of the UN on December 1948 that all foreign military forces should withdraw from the Korean Peninsula. Those two events provided a golden opportunity for Kim Il-sung of North Korea to occupy the whole Korean Peninsula, thus bringing about the Korean War of 1950–1953. The armistice agreement left Korea with a devastating wound and no outcome. Disregarding human casualty and the destruction of industrial facilities and infrastructure, to procure war expenses, the amount of money issued by the Bank of Korea increased 15 times during the period June 1950 to December 1952.

The period 1953–1961 was a time of post-war reconstruction and political instability. Because the Korean government had no financial capacity for post-war reconstruction, it had to depend largely on US aid. At that time, US aid was a lifeline for the Korean people. However, the power struggle continued even during the war, when the South was left with only a small part of its territory that put the country to be a light before the wind. The US military authority preferred an easy-to-manage politician to the hard-liner Syngman Rhee. However, Rhee succeeded in a constitutional amendment under martial law in 1952. Washington behind the scenes was uneasy with his general radical outlook. In fact, it was widely rumored that Washington preferred a more malleable person to the maverick Rhee. With the constitutional amendment again in 1954, Rhee succeeded in remaining in the presidency. In the 1960 presidential election, the ruling party was charged with unfair election practices, and angry students revolted, which led him to resign from the presidency. The minority party then took power in the next election under the new constitution of a parliamentary government system. However, with the new ruling party split, the new government could not handle policies due to political conflicts among congressmen. Disappointed with the government's inability and corruption, the student force that toppled the Rhee administration once occupied the National Assembly. Meanwhile left-sided politicians demanded dialogue with the North and claimed radical reunification. Political and social disorder accelerated. The military coup occurred before the new government had been in power for barely a year.

The Korean experience of state building witnesses that building the foundations of the new state under conditions of squalid poverty proved to be a somewhat untenable undertaking. Coming out of several millennia of kingdoms alongside the exploitative practices of colonialism without any relevant intervening political orientation process made electoral democracy sound like an abstractly alien process. All the conditions for a haphazard process were at play in ways that cast serious doubt about the ultimate ends of the process. Rather than promote good governance, it festered corruption, abuse of power, social dissonance and what have you.

Politicians and public officials also engaged in and condoned gross wrongdoing amid social disorder and economic crisis. The ideological conflict also polarized society to the point of jeopardizing national security. Political instability and corruption compounded the nation's state of crisis. An individual facing a state of crisis will do whatever it takes to overcome, just like the metaphorical sinking ship. If all the desperate people in a sinking ship rush to the deck in a bid to escape, it will not take long for the collective weight to hasten the wreck of the ship. South Korea in those days was like a sinking boat, in which the people behaved instinctively like that boat's desperate passengers.

For 12 years, the story of the Korean government was like an experiment of catching two rabbits, each respectively representing poverty reduction and national security under democratic institutions. The problem with the Korean government was that, except for foreign aid, it lacked the means for poverty reduction. The government was facing great difficulty because of having to deal with internal violence forces based on ideology and incessant military threats from the North. And under social instability, the government's poverty reduction effort was simply not effective. On the flip side, there was no way of achieving social stability in this atmosphere of pervasive poverty. For over a decade since their foundation, the first two administrations mainly focused on imminent relief for the people in famine, rehabilitation from the war and maintaining social stability in the country, which seems to be a catalog of shambolic starts.[1]

These were the conditions that created the fertile ground for a military coup d'état. The coup leader Park Chung-hee was born in 1917 when Korea was under Japan's colonial rule. Park Chung-hee's mother became pregnant with him, her seventh child, at the age of 45. The family was so poor at the time that she tried all she could to obtain an abortion. She drank heaps of soybean sauce and purposely tumbled down hills; however, the baby continued to live.[2] Park graduated from a regular school and became a teacher at an elementary school shortly after. He then became a military official for the rest of his life until he raised the coup. Cho Gap-jae (2007), who studied the life of Park leaving a work in 13 volumes on his entire life, describes Park with two words: "simplicity" and "independence." Because he grew up in a poor family in a country under colonial rule, these kind of morals or attitudes seemed to have been cemented in him. Nonetheless, this life that almost never made it into our world changed the fortune of South Korea.

The military junta he led staked its claim to power on the principal mandate of achieving national unity and to improve the deplorable lot of the masses. The junta was after all determined to make its legitimacy contingent on reforming the state in ways that would enhance its ability to deliver the critical public goods that any viable state offers its citizenry. It is worthy of note, however, that the junta had to contend with how much the usurping of the constitutional order imposed a political liability in the face of simmering domestic tension and the disdain of its major foreign donors to coups d'état. Being the fragile state that it was, General Park, more than anyone else, understood that he could ill afford to ruffle the feathers of the country's benefactors. Notwithstanding these lingering tenterhooks, the junta proceeded to embrace the challenge of national redemption by replacing the constitutional order with martial law. The martial law was effective for 2 years and 5 months until October 1963, when Park was elected president under a new constitution. The new constitution concentrated power in the executive by imbuing the president with a range of sweeping powers.

The martial law paved the way for the junta to pursue a two-pronged goal hinged on poverty elimination and stabilization of the tumultuous domestic political landscape. Toward this end, a radical plan was set in motion to neutralize all the domestic sources of political and social disorder backed by a corresponding strategic poverty-reduction and economic-development program. In other words, domestic stability paved the way for the effective implementation of economic development programs. This thinking within the military government inspired a steady buildup of a comprehensive system of mass surveillance with the express purpose of eliminating dissidents, ostensibly considered to be the prime sources of ill will against the government. Hence, the Korea Central Intelligence Agency (KCIA) was established and granted sweeping surveillance powers to snoop through the country. It disbanded the National Assembly and replaced it with the National Reconstruction Supreme Committee (NRSC) under martial law. A campaign of political lustration was set in motion with the enactment of the Cleansing of Political Activity Act of 1962. The Act sought, among other things, to proscribe the participation of individuals the military government considered as an impropriety to the nascent political culture it was developing.

A radical campaign was instituted to reform the nation's legal system to ensure that it aligned with the president's vision of a top-down regulated structure of controls. For good or bad, it is hard to argue against the fact that reform was urgently required, given that in nearly 13 years of its existence as a sovereign state, the phraseology of the nation's core laws was still crafted in English and Japanese. Led by the NRSC, 365 new pieces of legislation were either enacted or reformed for 6 months, in contrast to the 115 under the preceding regimes.[3]

To appreciate the conditions that inspired the draconian actions instituted by the leadership of the junta, it will help to get a sense of the disposition of their worldview and how they believed to be their role in that plastic moment of history. First, its resolve to wrestle down poverty was first and foremost driven by the realization that poverty constituted the number one threat to the viability of the state, much less the external threats to the burgeoning state. For the generals, nothing could precede preservation of life and social stability. The tenets of freedom and democracy, in the minds of the ruling generals, were nothing but abstract constructs divorced from the realities of the living conditions of the masses. An altruistic conception of freedom and democracy must out of necessity be grounded first in pragmatism – of which the preservation of life must be prioritized.

As indicated earlier, this line of thinking runs contrary to the mainstream, the Western liberal-normative order of state building. The premise of Western state building gyrates from the sacred cows of democratic liberal norms, which makes the military regime's chosen path inconceivable. The same narrative reigns supreme in contemporary discourses of state building by which liberal democracy is imposed on poor countries by the Western citadels of power; the same was said and demanded of South Korea by its Western benefactors. With the benefit of hindsight, we can conceivably agree that the military junta's conscious commitment to prioritize the bread and butter needs of the people over dogmatic allegiance to concepts has been all but vindicated. Having investigated the impact of democracy on growth by simultaneously considering a country's secular-historical experience of democracy and current political regime, Ma and Ouyang (2016) have shown that the relationship between a political regime and economic performance is neither linearly universal nor nonlinearly universal, but is an asymmetrical phase that depends on whether a country's accumulated stock of democracy can pass the threshold level.[4]

Moreover, against the backdrop of the pervasive state of poverty, the scope of radical measures required was of such nature that a business-as-usual mindset was incapable of making the critical difference that was sorely needed. For instance, the junta defied the dogmatic allegiance to the power of markets to effect economic development. My personal conviction is that in many instances the logic of this ominous worldview of free market fundamentalism tends to crumble when confronted with the practical exigencies of poverty reduction. I think of the blind faith in the power of the markets to address poverty reduction in the same context as expecting a patient at an advanced stage of a terminal disease to be healed naturally without any medical intervention. For most poor countries, the only entity endowed with the resources and capacity to build the institutions of state and the dividends of citizenship is the government of the day. Neither nongovernmental organizations (NGO) nor the international community can replace the government.

The market-centered approach is fundamentally handicapped in its ability to contextualize the cause-and-effect dynamics of poverty. For the government to treat the patient with advanced diseases, the government should be competent and strong enough to treat and control the patient. Another irony is the neoclassical doctrinal obsession with small government. Oblivious of the implications of having a small government in a poor country, the neoclassical orthodoxy so conveniently overlooks the importance of a strong government imbued with the structures to enforce radical pro-development policies. Like the advanced disease analogy, having a small weak government is akin to entrusting the treatment of the patient with the advanced disease to a nurse or a home doctor. Liberalization can also be viewed as requiring the convalescing patient to return to work to make a living.

In the same way, the process of poverty reduction, like the treatment of a chronic disease, is a long-term sacrificial sojourn as opposed to a short-term funfair sprint. Poverty reduction or economic development is essentially sacrificing today for tomorrow. It requires sacrificing consumption today for saving tomorrow and leisure for labor. It accompanies changes of interests and wealth among stakeholders within the community, which provokes conflict among them to be coordinated by the active role of the government. Given this background, the problem of poverty and its reduction ought to be contextualized in a far more radical scope. If poverty is perceived as the chief threat to the survival of a community, naturally its elimination should be prioritized above all else; self-preservation instincts thus makes the poverty battle a high-stakes one indeed. Essentially this is how Park's regime conceived the challenges of wrestling down poverty.

2 Public administration reform and defining the strategic imperatives

The junta introduced a unique decision-making system that allowed for dexterity to make radical development decisions. Considering the militaristic worldview of the junta, the quest to wrestle down poverty had to be treated with the same level of military precision and strategy that one would usually employ for any high stakes duel. I have personally observed a disturbing trend in many developing countries where this sort of resolute consciousness is sorely lacking, which has been colloquially dubbed the canker of the so-called NATO (No Action, Talks Only) phenomenon. Thus said, conditions of political instability sometimes constrain what can be conceivably achieved. Many of the developing country governments in politically unstable conditions would better expend their might on fighting for their very survival than take on poverty reduction. In South Korea's case, it was General Park's first mission to consolidate his power firmly through the concentration of significant powers in the executive before plunging into his war on poverty campaign. By arrogating to himself the position of the general commander (GC), he could issue a raft of presidential emergency orders by circumscribing the gridlock of Parliament. The powers also allowed him to appoint regional governors and mayors of cities until the Local Autonomy Act went into force.

That aside, a unique decision-making system was used to complement the president's sweeping powers. Its stated goal was to ensure that an indigenized leadership system is created to respond to the exigencies of economic development that the junta set about to achieve. The role of the prime minister (PM) was adjusted to make way for a system that ensured that the president could maintain a finger on the development pulse of the country. The PM was relegated to performing ceremonial and protocol functions, whereas the deputy PM (DPM), who doubled as the Minister of the Economic Planning Board

(EPB), was tasked with handling development policies and answered directly to the president. As is described in Figure 2.1, the role of field commander (FC) to support the president in the execution of development policies is assumed by the DPM and Minister of the EPB. The DPM and Minister of the EPB chair the Economic Ministerial Meeting and coordinate policies related to economic affairs. Key policy decisions are made between the president (GC) and the DPM and Minister of the EPB (FC). The reason that the PM is one step aside along the decision-making line in development policymaking is that the president was determined to stake his credibility of achieving economic development. For this reason, entrusting the PM's office with that task could in some ways be misconstrued as passing the buck – this was in contravention of his express will of pursuing enhanced efficiency through rapidity and alacrity in decision-making.

It was further distinct in that there were two principal economic advisers to the president at the top. President Park set the precedent of having two separate economic advisers, each responsible for macro-economic policy coordination and industrial development policy. Clearly, he was keen to tie his legacy and the future of the country to building a vibrant economic system. In appointing his Chief Secretary for Industrial Development in 1966, he was quoted as saying:

> hundreds of people are currently dying of famine and we are in a race to increase rice production, build petroleum, plywood, and glass plants. While I generally concur with the economic experts admonishing us to control inflation, stabilize exchange rates, and maintaining economic growth rates, the real question becomes how long can we wait to meet the urgent food needs of the people?[5]

The president believed that policy implementation was more important than policy development and spent four times more hours on monitoring policy implementation than on policymaking. For the 18 years that he was in office, he traveled 119 days on average annually, covering a total of 15,039 kilometers to check policy implementations in the field.[6] Mr. Kim Yong-hwan, Park's chief economic advisor, recalled that President Park spent nearly 20 percent of his time on preparation of development policies and 80 percent on monitoring and implementation.[7] The organizational chart of the government of Korea from the 1960s and 1970s under Park Chung-hee is shown by Figure 2.1.

South Korea's dark days were characterized by pervasive levels of corruption that permeated the public and private sectors to a cancerous degree until the early 1960s. Corruption was becoming the nation's nemesis. The military revolution cited clamping down on corruption as one of its prime goals. However, the entrenched state of corruption proved to be nothing but a malignant tumor that cannot be easily cured. It was in every sense a political circus in which politicians relied on graft to run their elaborate election campaigns and businesses were eager to buy access and privilege. The corrupt culture of the political leadership steadily seeped into the civil service.

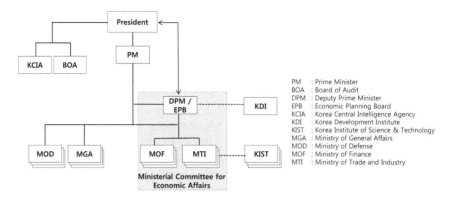

Figure 2.1 Organization of the Korean government in the 1960s–1970s

Civil servants who dealt directly with citizens, such as tax officials and customs officials, were vulnerable to corruption. A triangular cabal of politicians, taxpayers (businessmen) and tax officials soon emerged. Politicians needed money to run for office, and thus accepted bribes from businessmen in exchange for influencing tax officials in favor of those businessmen; this fleecing relationship, while benefiting this cohort, came at the cost of the exchequer. Such illicit links were pervasive in Korean society in those days. Even though the president himself developed the reputation of being a remarkably austere man who jealously guarded his integrity from the influence of big money, his own political party was eventually entangled in allegations of illegal campaign finance practices.[8] It was this sordid experience that further informed the putsch to rid the influence of big money on politics through a series of radical measures. The Board of Audit (BOA) was established to thoroughly carry out the Monitoring and Evaluation (ME) components of the government's policy. Working in collaboration with the KCIA, the BOA was on the heels of nearly all public servants. The KCIA grew into a vast surveillance machinery that reported directly to the president. Its agents engaged in clandestine neutralization of dissidents and in most cases resorted to extrajudicial processes against alleged opponents of the regime.

3 Establishment of development-priority administrative system

From the preceding section, it is also somewhat easy to find the correlation between the general's worldview and his conception of the strategies he deployed in transforming the country's economic fortunes. His was an implementation of a series of resolute strategies predicated on a combat-readiness disposition to the socioeconomic challenges that clearly had the potential to determine whether the nation survived or not. In a military strategy, the general set about defining his military targets systematically. The regime set about addressing its poverty reduction goals into specific, realistic strategies, which will be discussed in this section.

Suffice to acknowledge that the success of the poverty reduction efforts is contingent on mobilization of the required financial and human resources. Mobilization of domestic financial resources and foreign savings are an indispensable precursor to helping poor countries get out of their financial dire straits, especially constrained in their capacity to mobilize financial resources through domestic savings and taxation. To plug the state revenue shortfall, the regime pursued a systematic campaign of encouraging thrift and a culture of savings among its citizens. The goal was to build a formidable pool of financial resources through domestic savings. Public spending, in the same way, had to be streamlined to focus on a handful of specific priority sectors. By bringing the banking system under executive control, the regime could exert unfettered influence on both fiscal and monetary policies.

Coupled with the financial resources was the need to improve the quality of the nation's human resource base. Effective policy implementation cannot be treated in isolation to the quality and discipline of the human resource pool. The civil service had to be revamped and resourced to align with the national development vision the regime outlined. It became imperative to extend the reform efforts to the bureaucracy because up until then, the Korean civil service was largely administered by a cohort of foreign consultants and foreign trained indigenes. In the early days of the junta, the cabinet was entirely dominated by military appointees, but for pragmatic reasons President Park had to concede that this was an untenable process. A steady process was put in place to replace military appointees with competent civilian bureaucrats who had proven worthy of the high call of stewardship. There is a contrast between President Park's personnel policy with how the military junta in Myanmar until recently coopted and monopolized the political and bureaucratic system for the better part of six decades. The outcome is that policy process deliverables are driven by a meritocratic process rather than patronage.

Because the junta also staked its claim to power on bringing social order, it had to be accountable on this front too. But that is hard to achieve without meeting the basic human needs (BHN) that so often cause social agitation. With its militaristic mind-set, the regime also linked its public order objectives to being effectively able to rein in political agitators. On the basic human needs question, a campaign was instituted to boost the country's agricultural productivity through construction of fertilizer producing factories and high-yield seeds. The KCIA, the regime's domestic intelligence agency, was at the forefront of enforcing the government's public security agenda. The KCIA's ruthless suppression of dissent largely explains why that period of iron-fisted approach to social order often comes for critical commentary as "the periods of dictatorship." These criticisms are symptomatic of the wider debate about the seemingly irreconcilable dichotomies of democratic tenets and public security in a fragile state. An uncompromising pursuit of public security may inevitably result in the violation of civil liberties and subversion of a democratic order. The Park regime was confronted with this same dilemmatic odyssey when its Western donors raised red flags about his administration's wanton disregard of civil rights and democratic norms. In the end, the administration insisted on defying the Western order of the democratic normative structure of state building. It was deeply convinced that getting rid of poverty was far more imperative than allegiance to idealistic norms.

Let's now take a detailed look at the specific reforms made to the public administration system that ensured an alignment between the political leadership's vision and that of the bureaucrats, who were the implementing forces. Going back as far as ancient times, the bureaucracy has always been the beating heart of state activities in Korea. The ancient Koryeo and Chosun dynasties ran a national civil service examination called the Kwago, designed to measure the literary competences of candidates and recruit them as high-ranking government officials. The tradition of the Kwago was inherited in the form of the Higher Civil Service Examination (HCSE) – a gateway to high-ranking government official positions installed by the newly born Korean government. The government also established the Central Officials Training Institute (COTI) to provide continuous training for the newly recruited and incumbent officials. The officials and their spouses were provided with a pension for their lifetimes.

However, by the time the military junta had taken over the reins of power, its vigor had hit a stone wall with the national chaos. Reforms focused on recruiting talented young men from throughout the country through a transparent system, regardless of their background. A noteworthy aspect of the reforms was the expansion of the HCSE "pass quota" from the pre-revolution average of 10–20 to some 200 people annually. Once having passed the examination, examinees would go on to constitute the core of the state bureaucracy with all its perks and job security. They were faced with challenging tasks for national development, but with generous conditions of services, pensions and opportunities for a bright future. For talented young men, the HCSE became a gateway for an instant upward social mobility.

The expansion was an important prospectus for the thousands of unemployed youths who were desperate for employment opportunities. The meritocratic system of the civil service proved to be attractive for the brightest and most talented who were drawn by both the job security and the career development prospects that came along with the position. Of course, it was common knowledge that civil servants also had the social privilege of being attractive as spouses and were thus highly demanded suitors. The policy created a boom of talented youth from throughout the country preparing for the HCSE, and thus contributed to national development.

All officials within the bureaucracy went through routine in-service trainings to keep them functioning at a very competitive level. Rookie civil servants went through a rigorous training program at the COTI. Promotion to senior level positions was also contingent on going through the training programs. There were also overseas training programs funded by foreign donors for staff up until the 1980s. Until the mid-1970s, to avoid the possibility of government officials not returning to their poor homeland after their study abroad, the government prohibited government officials from study abroad if accompanied by their spouses. However, the government was very fast in adapting its policy to the new environment. Entering the second half of the 1970s, as the Korean economy improved, foreign fellowship aid for Korean citizens decreased. The Korean government complemented these programs with its own extensive fellowship program for civil servants to study abroad for a period of 2 years, and encouraged studying abroad by allowing remittance of foreign exchanges and family accompaniment. The returning cohort thus constituted a critical mass for development; their diligence, knowledge and commitment made a great deal of difference. The generous incentives that came with a civil servant position generally insulated personnel from corruption impulses amid the strict code of conduct they were held to.

Development planning system

For the first time in the nation's history, a series of Five-Year Economic Development Plans was promulgated to provide medium-term blueprints for transforming the county. It was radical in ambition and scope based on free market principles. That means, for instance, primarily unlike in a planned economy, the basic investment and business decisions are made by individual firms. Except in very rare instances, the government mainly provided the policy direction and assistance to those firms that needed strategic plans to get off the ground. One of the chief reasons for using the Five-Year Plans was to hedge against the challenges of operating in an uncertain environment by allowing dexterity to respond to emerging trends where necessary. The plan was subject to routine evaluation for the very reason that it allowed for the agility response that the government envisaged. At its core, the plans included very definitive strategic targets that were intended to be crisp and consistent with the broader goals of transforming the economy. Here an important distinction can be made with the trend in development policy circles where struggling developing countries are compelled to pursue policies of balanced and harmonized growth through the rather dubious externally induced poverty reduction strategies. Such policies in my view are not only emblematic of the jack-of-all-trades syndrome but clearly very phony, given the enormity of the resource constraints that these economies must grapple with.

   The military junta felt the necessity of establishing an agency being exclusively responsible for economic development, which came in the form of the EPB. It was created within 10 days of the coup d'état, initially under the name the Ministry of Construction, ostensibly explaining its raison d'être. It was charged with the three core tasks of planning, budgeting and attraction of foreign capital. For policy synergy, the budgetary function was taken away from the Ministry of Finance and placed within the purview of the EPB. Second, because each line-ministry's policy had to be promoted harmoniously, the EPB was expected to better perform the function of policy coordination if it had the authority to budget each line-ministry's expenditure. In addition to those measures, aiming to enhance the harmony of individual line-ministry's policies with the overall development plans, the Minister of the EPB was simultaneously appointed as the deputy prime minister so that he or she could control and coordinate other line-ministries' policies one level above them. Candidates from the top tier of the HCSE were appointed to the EPB to ensure that it had the highest caliber of staff and to ensure the integrity of the agency's work. It is worth mentioning that competent officials at the EPB were often promoted to ministers of other line-ministries. The EPB produced many ministers and vice ministers in the cabinet and members of the National Assembly of Korea. Morale was naturally very high in the EPB.

The Korea Institute of Science and Technology (KIST) and the Korea Development Institute (KDI) were established as think tanks in 1966 and 1971, respectively, to provide complementary, empirically backed research to support the government's development policies. Like the EPB, its personnel were also offered very generous conditions of service and incentives, details of which will be discussed in Section 7.3. With the government's fullest backing, these think tanks were remarkable in providing the technological development and theoretical backup for economic development. They played a very critical role in the early phase of the development process. As time went on, their dominant role was steadily challenged by the emergence of private research centers and institutes, often by large corporations with the financial clout. Within this framework, the first Five-Year Economic Development Plan (1962–1966) focused on economic recovery through export promotion and increase in food production. Yes, it was wrought with technical know-how and personnel deficiencies defects, yet it was an instrumental part of the momentum for the forward thrust of the economy in the succeeding phases.

The Second Five-Year Economic Development Plan (1967–1971) built on the momentum of the previous years and inspired the next generation of planners. The Third Plan (1972–1976) focused on fostering heavy and chemical industry (HCI), aiming to realize an advanced industrialized country. The Fourth Plan (1977–1981) made a significant transformation from being growth oriented to pursuing growth, equity and efficiency at the same time, and it incorporated a social development scheme into the major component of the national development plans for the first time. The Fifth Plan (1982–1986) also made another transformation from the one oriented toward economic development so far to that of pursuing economic and social development at the same time. Reflecting this concept, the title was changed from the economic development plan to the social and economic development plan, which was followed by the Sixth Plan (1987–1991). However, the durability of development planning ended with the introduction of the new concept of vision titled the New Economy Five-Year Plan since 1992.[9]

Resource mobilization

For all the resolve of the ruling junta to economically transform the country, it was acutely aware of the dire state of the country's finances. Again, up until this point, it relied on foreign aid to balance its books. Addressing this problem required critical systemic changes in consumption and the country's high birthrate. It was imperative to devise a policy intervention that could cut both ways simultaneously. A top-down approach was adopted to encourage citizens to embrace a savings culture by tightening their belts through a corresponding raft of tax incentives. Various savings programs like property formation saving for employees were introduced with tax incentives. A special "Savings Day" was introduced, and each year the president conferred an accolade on one person who saved the most money. In addition, citizens were encouraged to make every financial transaction through banks, which was soon followed by private business sectors.

Moreover, the government either directly controlled imports or levied heavy tariffs. To deter the human tendency to circumscribe rules, smugglers were severely sanctioned alongside a comprehensive nationwide campaign to sensitive the public against the practice. Under President Park's personal directive, smuggling, just as the consumption of ostentatious foreign goods, was not only a proscribed conduct but one that was to be placed on par with sedition. Trade in luxury goods was also proscribed, and even little children were schooled on the patriotism of buying and utilizing only locally made products. To enhance its effectiveness, a two-child family planning program was also strongly enforced. Medical insurance and social welfare schemes were deferred until economic development reached an appreciable level.

To make true its commitment to balancing the country's books and making the resources available for long-term investment in specific strategic sectors, the government took the unconventional decision of bringing the banking system under its control. Special banks such as the Korea Development Bank (KDB) were established to provide long-term credit financing; the Small and Medium Enterprises (SME) Bank for credit for SMEs; and the Korea Export and Import (EXIM) Bank for export financing in addition to its shares in major domestic commercial banks. Attention shifted to strengthening the country's fiscal capacity through the establishment of the National Tax Service (NTS) in 1966. Up until then, fiscal activities were within the ambit of the Ministry of Finance, but that was to change with the birth of the NTS as an autonomous and devolved institution.

The EPB operated the special account for financing economic development, and a significant part of the financial resources, apart from minimal defense spending and servants' salaries, was invested into the special account. The account fund was used in concentration for the construction of social overhead capital and promotion of industries and export. As an example of this is that the government provided policy loans for targeted industries and SMEs at a concessional condition below market interest rates, and the gap of interest rates was compensated by the national budget.

Notes

1 The full-scale drive for economic development and national security could not be launched until the Park Chung-hee regime took power in a military coup in 1961. However, some people argue that the democratic regime was toppled too early to have sufficient time to achieve any economic development.
2 Cho Kap-jae, *Bakjeonghui 1: gunin-ui gil* [Park Chung Hee, Series 1] (Seoul, Korea: Jaeil Printing, 2007), 26–28.
3 Cho Kap-jae, *Bakjeonghui 4: 5.16-ui 24si* [Park Chung-hee Series 4] (Seoul, Korea: Jaeil Printing, 2007), 234–245.
4 Ma Tay-Cheng and Lishu Ouyang, "Democracy and Growth: A Perspective From Democratic Experience," *Economic Inquiry*, Vol. 54, No. 4 (2016), 1790–1804.
5 Hong Eun-ju and Lee Eun-hyeong, *Korian mirakeul 3: Sumeun gijeokdeul junghwahakgongeop, jichukeul heundeulda* [Korean Miracle III: Heavy and Chemical Industry Shakes the Axis of the Earth] (Seoul, Korea: Nanam, 2015), 54.
6 O Won-chol, *Bakjeonghuineun edtteoke gyeongjegengguk mandeulleonna* [How Park Chung-hee Made Economic Power] (Seoul, Korea: Dongsuh Press, 2006), 182.
7 Kim Yong-hwan, *Imja janega saryanggwan aninga* [Aren't You Commander?] (Seoul, Korea: Maeil Business Newspaper, 2002), 282.
8 Kim Chung-yum, *From Despair to Hope: Economic Policymaking in Korea 1945–1979* (Seoul, Korea: Korea Development Institute, 2011), 566.
9 Kang Kwang-ha, *Gyeongjegaebal 5nyeon gyehoek* [Five-Year Economic Development Plan: Evaluation of Goals and Implementation] (Seoul, Korea: Seoul National University Press, 2000), 42–115.

3 Transforming the social and environmental landscape

Amid the massive task of post-war reconstruction, social and environmental concerns had to give way to the most pressing needs of the day. In terms of scale, while the infrastructural reconstruction needs certainly required attention, it was equally imperative to recognize the tenuous social and environmental conditions that fed into the nation's crises. Our very survival as humans is contingent on maintaining a sustainable balance between nature and consumption. Any action that disregards this balance is doomed to unleash catastrophes down the road. This fact notwithstanding, we must also concede that poverty, in all its diverse manifestations, in many instances lies at the heart of whether societies will have the capacity to maintain this balance with nature. A large population living on a limited landmass places enormous strain on the productive capacity of the land. Human activities such as cultivation of crops and the generation of fuel can trigger deforestation. Up until the mid-1960s, this cycle of poverty-induced environmental degradation caused by incessant pressure from human activities perilously threatened to offset the delicate balance between nature and consumption.

A sudden surge in the population on the limited landmass had taken place between the 1940s and the 1950s, comprising a first wave of massive inflows of refugees fleeing the North and a second wave of ethnic Koreans in the diaspora returning home. Both migratory waves resulted in an increase in the population by nearly four million, causing serious food shortages and unbridled pressure on the environment owing to increased human cultivation activities. The population density had increased from 218 to 254 persons per square kilometer.[1] During the period 1955–1960, the country's annual population growth rate was 2.9 percent, while in the same period the annual increase rate of value added in the primary industry was merely 1.7 percent and the annual growth rate of food products was 1.5 percent. Consequently, the per capita rate of access to food plummeted disproportionately, making the country one of the world's basket cases of food insecurity. This chapter therefore sets out to discuss how this problem came about and the resulting policy measures that were implemented to mitigate them.

Suffice it to begin with a look at the phenomenon of deforestation, as it is the most visible incarnation of the competition between humans and the environment within the context of maintaining the optimum balance of nature. Think of forests like roofs that provide protection against the elements. So even in our industrial development calculus, it is always important to place this within the proper context of its place within nature. It needs to be pointed out that deforestation in Korea has historical roots. During World War II, the colonial Japanese regime engaged in large-scale logging as part of its war efforts. Then after the North unilaterally cut electricity supply to the South, the country turned to dependence on firewood for heating during its long winter months. During the post-war reconstruction era, the forests were further depleted, as the lack of hard currency meant that the huge demand for lumber for reconstruction was sourced domestically. Illegal logging also proliferated because of the raging political chaos and the poor administration. After years of overlogging and destruction, Korea's lands and mountains were left completely bare of trees, and the country rose swiftly to becoming one of the countries with the lowest lumber accumulation rate per unit area in the 1950s.[2] It is why Korea was often described with the colors white and red – a pejorative description of the inhabitants, who were clad in white linen traveling across barren dirt grounds with no greenery. The depleted forest landscape was not only an eyesore, but also had an almost deadly effect on the lives of the people who depended on it for their survival. The environment became critically prone to floods and landslides.

On the other hand, the spate of droughts was occurring at rapid intervals leading to poor harvests. Because the water storage capacity of the mountains back then was one-tenth of current levels, there were chronic water shortages and with them a very real risk of desertification. The historical record shows that floods and droughts usually occurred at 20- or 30-year intervals, but as time passed, they occurred more frequently, at 5- or 10-year intervals, eventually occurring at

Picture 3.1 Frequent drought until the mid-1970s. Until the mid-1970s, frequent drought drove Korean farmers to despair as forest remained devastated and there were few dams

©Anonymous

2- and 3-year intervals after 1945.[3] Consequently, the imbalance between humans and nature caused by the destruction of the ecosystem was seriously threatening the sustainability of livelihoods, and the people felt helpless and frustrated.

For this reason, the prevention of deforestation became an urgent development priority, given the link between the natural habitat and man. But how was this going to be done by a poor government and a frustrated people, particularly coming, as it did, against the backdrop of the Korean War and a government that was wobbly at best? It was amid these crises that the leadership of President Park was to prove very decisive. He demonstrated his leadership through his resolve to mitigate the looming environmental catastrophe through three major policy interventions: (1) the green revolution, (2) family planning and (3) reforestation. Clearly it was necessary to pursue such radical policies to address the factors that were at the heart of the social and environmental problems of the country.

1 The green revolution and food security

As outlined in the preceding section, South Korea's chronic food security problem was a literal basket case situation. It took a massive inflow of external food aid to keep the country afloat. Indeed, a nation as desperate as South Korea was, in a literal sense, a danger to itself. Thus, it was so urgent that food security measures had to be put in place, beginning with increasing the nation's rice production. Several factors accounted for the chronic food insecurity as a direct consequence of low agricultural productivity. The incessant droughts and floods had a direct correlation with the depleted landscape of the mountains. The Korean War had also taken its toll on agricultural lands and the land reform also placed short-term constraints on productive capacity. Furthermore, chronic deficits in the international balance of payments, as Figure 1.1 shows, did not allow for the import of food. Food aid, despite being a short-term bandage on a chronic problem, was the only viable option.[4]

It is also worth noting that the government amid this crisis took modest steps to control the excessive demand for food. For instance, the government recommended that people eat wheat foods on a "Flour-Food Day" every week to reduce the consumption of rice, the staple food of Koreans. Another seemingly minor but consequential measure was implemented to discourage some unnecessary styles of rice consumption. There was an erroneous belief that the taste of cooked rice or rice cake is dependent on the frequency of the pounding process. That means the more you pound the dough, the tastier the cake eventually becomes. But this frequent pounding would inadvertently cause splashing and loss of the dough. Moreover, there were concerns that excessive pounding could also reduce the ultimate nutritional value of the cake. On average, the rice went through nine rounds of pounding, but a new government regulation ordered a reduction of the rounds to seven.

A ban was placed on making alcoholic drinks from rice. Parents were encouraged to mix rice with other grains for meals for their children's lunch at school.

President Park himself took the lead in frugality. Mr. Kim Chung-yum, one of the president's aides, recalled:

> The president took the need to conserve rice by replacing with barley to heart. During the decade I served as his Chief of Staff, I was amazed that how he always made sure to mix rice with barley, and to eat wheat flour noodles for lunch instead of rice only, as a customary for regular Korean families. I myself found it a bit difficult to eat lunch for nearly ten years.[5]

The policy of controlling rice consumption was waived in 1977 after the country had achieved its optimum rice sustenance level.

About the green revolution, the government implemented policies in four respects. First, it increased the supply of fertilizer. Given the limited arable land, the most viable solution was to increase the yield per unit of land, and supplying chemical fertilizers was by far the most convenient means to this end. Until the 1950s, over 90 percent of the fertilizer plants on the Korean Peninsula were in North Korea, and the remaining plants in the South were barely operational due to a shortage in electricity, resulting in South Korea becoming a net importer of fertilizer financed by foreign aid. Lacking the capital and technical know-how, the government had to revert to foreign help for both. Foreign credit was procured to engage foreign contractors to construct the nation's first fertilizer production plant.

Construction of the first fertilizer plant was planned in 1954 just after the Korean War, using an aid grant of $23 million from the United Nations Food and Agriculture Organization (FAO). The contractor assigned to the construction was the American firm McGraw-Hydrocarbon. According to the terms of the contract, the Korean government would cover all the costs that McGraw-Hydrocarbon would demand, and there were no penalties for missing the deadline of the construction. The government agreed to take over the operation of the plant if the plant would work successfully for 10 consecutive days. It means that just after the completion of the plant construction, no further guarantee was provided for normal operations of the plant. These details of the contract show how ignorant the Korean government was of standard contracts. That contract was altered five times after the commencement of construction, and the total costs increased by 70 percent, with the construction period extended another 2 years.[6] Even after the government took over the operation of the plant, it was not fully operational.

Disappointed after the first fertilizer plant, the government contracted the second fertilizer plant with West German company LURGI in 1958. Unlike the first fertilizer plant, which was based on "cost plus" methods, the second plant was meant to be built by fixing the total cost of construction at $27 million. Unfortunately, however, the second one also was not fully functional due to frequent mechanical failures. Thus, the government had to rebuild a facility that would use oil as a raw material rather than anthracite coal for higher productivity and less pollution. Even if the first and second plants had been fully operational, the supply would have accommodated less than 20 percent of the nation's entire fertilizer demand.

Then the Park Administration planned a third and fourth fertilizer plant with foreign and domestic investment and a foreign loan. The South Korean and US governments agreed that 45 percent of the capital ($20 million) would be shared equally by both governments, while the remaining 55 percent ($24.2 million) would be covered by American aid loans. The American investors demanded that they obtain the right to manage the plants for 15 years until they could recoup 150 percent of their investments. The investors also demanded that the investment fund needed to be recovered completely in 5 years, and interests be secured until 15 years after the investment period.[7] The question of whether to accept these obnoxious terms was referred to President Park. Confronted with a take it or leave it scenario, he grudgingly had to accede to the demands of the creditors. O Won-chol, who was present at said meeting on behalf of the Ministry of Industry and Trade, recalls how the president, confronted with this untenable dilemma, was visibly dispirited at being resigned to a pawn in machinations of international asymmetric power relations.[8]

Because of the lopsided contractual terms imposed on the government, the price of the fertilizer produced in the plant had to be set high enough to enable the recovery of the principal and high interest rates for the foreign investment in a short period. There was no way local farmers could afford such high rates. With its hands tied, the government could not help but heavily subsidize the fertilizer for local farmers. The national exchequer suffered in the process, compounded by a raging fiscal deficit. The government officials involved in negotiating the contract were roundly criticized as "traitors to the country" because of the outrageous terms under which the contract was concluded. However, the country had no alternative because saving the people from hunger was a far more urgent priority than clinging to abstract dogmas of patriotism or its lack thereof. Fertilizer production increased from 175,000 metric tons in 1966 to 500,000 metric tons in 1971.

Second, agricultural mechanization is yet another prerequisite for increased productivity. For that to happen, there needs to be readjustment of farmland, improvement of roads and providing farmers with the financial means to procure mechanized equipment. As far as fiscal circumstances allowed, there was concerted effort at mechanization. As will be discussed in Chapter 10, through the national drive of *Saemaul Undong* (new village movement), a revolutionary transformation took place in the agricultural sector, which was mainly dominated by rural communities.

The third facet of the green revolution, arguably its most challenging aspect, lay in developing high yield crop varieties. This requires extended periods of research, often without any real guarantees of success. Failure could potentially undermine the food security goals and perpetuate the vicious cycle of poverty once again. Moreover, new crop varieties require new farming technologies, which many of the nation's conservative farmers were not very amenable to. Old habits, after all, die hard! However, with the conviction that without developing high-yield crop varieties, food security may not be feasible, the Korean government dared to take its chances all the same.

Thanks to the establishment of the Rural Development Administration (RDA) in 1962, as the central clearinghouse in the development and dissemination of modern agricultural technologies, the green revolution got off to a good start. Its extension services engagements allowed it to have a presence on the ground and gather appropriate feedback from the farmers.[9] President Park personally ensured that the RDA was adequately resourced to fulfill its mission. The RDA regional offices were established in every county, and the head of the office was girt with the same official rank as the magistrate of a county. Demonstrating his strong commitment to the green revolution, the president never missed an opportunity to work together with farmers on rice planting and harvesting days and the annual tree planting days during his 18-year tenure. He understood the link between the RDA and the goal of achieving the green revolution. He thus fully supported the administrator of the RDA, and held more consultations with the administrator than with the Minister of Agriculture and Fishery, who had the RDA under his jurisdiction. The administrator and not the presiding minister had the president's ear. The first administrator remained in office for 7 years, providing consistent leadership to the agency.

Dr. Hur Mun-hoe, an expert in breeding rice varieties, was an instrumental player in this regard. With the backing of the government in 1964, he conducted a 2-year study on several crop varieties at the International Rice Research Institute (IRRI) in the Philippines. He crossbred the *Yukara* variety, which is resistant to cold and common rice diseases, with the *Japonica* variety, and then he crossbred them with the *Indica* variety. Dr. Hur had the goal of creating a "Super Rice" variety, which would be short and strong with high yields made possible by large ears. All this while, he was confronted by the real possibility of failure given the precedence of past experiences. In crossbreeding like this, there was a possibility that the new variety would be infertile, as was the cases with the liger (a hybrid cross between a lion and a tiger) and the mule (a hybrid cross between a donkey and a horse). Fortunately, however, Dr. Hur's experimental hybridization in breeding three varieties was successful, producing a new variety with new traits.

In 1967, 1,350 clones of the new variety were transported from the Philippines to the crop experimentation station at the RDA. The agency chose 15 varieties, after experimentally planting IR667 (this variety was the 667th rice seed bred at the IRRI). In 1969, one of the 15 varieties was grown in a small rice paddy on a farm. In May and June of that year, the rice showed little strength, with yellow-brownish leaves and weak stems. However, when July came with the summer weather, something surprising occurred. The hitherto weak rice crop turned healthy green with its leaves stronger. In late August, it was estimated that IR667 would yield 6.24 ton/ha. In those days, the average yield was 3.5 ton/ha. In autumn of that year, 12 kilograms of the harvested seeds of IR667 were sent to the Philippines, where they could grow rice three times year round. In March of 1970, the new rice seeds of IR667, which increased to 9.35 ton/ha, were transferred to Korea.[10]

Although the "miracle rice seed" was successful in producing high yields, it was vulnerable to cold weather, diseases and pests. The next year, IR667 was distributed across the country for preliminary cultivation under the promotional slogan of "miracle rice seeds." Unfortunately, the seeds were inflicted by a red discoloration disorder, resulting in outraged farmers confronting government officials, who visited farms to monitor the cultivation of the rice. The RDA prepared a farming schedule and technologies for the new variety, and transferred them to farmers promptly through nine provincial RDA offices and 150 offices of agricultural extension units across the nation. The RDA estimated the cultivation area of the new variety at 300,000 hectares in 1972; however, the actual cultivation area amounted only to 180,000 hectares.[11]

Indeed, the RDA played an impressive role in narrowing that gap between experiments and the field. The new system of timetables was promoted in each region, encouraging farmers to manage their time. In cultivating the new rice varieties, measures were put in place to detect and to prevent possible signs of plant disease and pests, due to increased use of fertilizers and denser cultivation of crops. Difficulties associated with the field during the extension activities were identified and incorporated in research activities. Agencies in charge of pest control and pesticide services were established. In addition, cooperative farming was promoted to concentrate farming in a single cluster, which allowed several farmers to form groups to farm rice together. This allowed the RDA to focus all its efforts on one area, and farmers to share best practices more easily, resulting in increased production of rice for the group. At the same time, the government decided to present farmers who could produce 6 ton/ha rice with KRW 100,000 as "the highest yield prize money" to increase rice yields, which is equivalent to 163 percent of the monthly salary for a division director of central government of Korea at that time. The government managed to secure KRW 28 million in total for the prize money, based on the estimation that fewer than 280 farmers would produce 6 ton/ha rice. However, 3,768 farmers became eligible for prize money, which had to be paid from diverting funds from other sectors of the national budget.[12]

It was in autumn of 1972 that Korean farmers produced more than 4.32 million tons (30 million Seok) for the first time after familiarizing themselves with the high-yield rice variety. Before 1945, the total production of rice – South and North Korea combined – did not exceed 3.6 million tons (25 million Seok). The IR667, the so-called miracle rice seed, was renamed "Tong-il rice," which means "reunification rice." Tong-il rice led South Korea's "green revolution" for more than a decade until it gave way to "Il-poom rice," which was a superior *Japonica* variety resistant to the cold and diseases. Korea could achieve the goal of self-sufficiency in rice production thanks to new technologies to farmers under the "research-extension-dissemination linkage system" developed by the RDA. This effective linkage system was adjudged as a best practice management system in the world by the FAO alongside the United States and Great Britain in 1984.[13] Thus, with the full support of President Park, the RDA succeeded in developing the miracle variety, which was an indispensable part of the green revolution in Korea.

Fourth, in line with the increase of rice production, the government encouraged farmers to produce rice by a grain-procurement policy. The grain procurement system was designed to buy rice at a higher price from the farmers during the harvest season, and sell it at lower prices to consumers during the off-season. The average rate of increase of the government's purchasing price was 24.8 percent per year from 1968 to 1975, far exceeding the average rate of increase of whole-sale prices of 15.3 percent over the same period. The fiscal deficits of the grain-procurement system were enormous, which along with fertilizer management was covered by credit from the Bank of Korea.

The policy of high grain prices was maintained until 1976, when the government no more needed to encourage rice production because its food security goals had been achieved.[14] Because of these tireless efforts, by late 1970 South Korea could achieve 100 percent self-sufficiency in rice production. Per acre yield in kilograms of rice increased from 272 in 1960 to 327 in 1970 and 451 in 1979, while barley was increased from 175 kilograms per acre in 1960 to 218 in 1970 and 318 in 1979. Due to the increase in agricultural productivity and high grain price by the government, farming household's income surpassed that of urban laborers since 1974, which in turn raised the quality of living in rural regions.[15] Rice self-sufficiency has played a significant role not only in stabilizing food supplies in Korea, but also saving foreign exchange and contributing to economic growth. It strengthened nationwide confidence and created hope for the future.

2 Family planning

Until the early 1960s, the total fertility rate (TFR) in Korea was estimated at above 6, which means that a woman has six children in her lifetime, and the rate of population growth was 3 percent, as Figure 3.1 indicates. The high TFR and population growth rates posed a major obstacle to food security and capital accumulation. It was under these circumstances that the government earmarked population control in 1961 as a major development priority. The government launched family planning programs to decrease the fertility rate and thus curb the rate of population growth. One of the major obstacles to lowering fertility rates was a deep-rooted male-preference attitude in Korean society. Influenced by the history of Confucian traditions, the preference for male children was under-pinned by the practice of having male heirs to one's estate, whereas women often married off to other families. So, couples procreated often to increase the odds of having sons.

In the same year, the Planned Parenthood Federation of Korea (PPFK) was established, and the Family Planning Program was launched with the support of the United Nations Fund for Population Activity (UNFPA). A law prohibiting the import and production of contraceptive pills was repealed. A Ten-Year Family-Planning Program 1962–1971 was initiated as an integral part of the national development planning system. Its target was to lower the natural population growth rate to 2 percent by 1971 and 1.5 percent by 1976. For the decrease in age-specific fertility rates, the program encouraged eligible couples to adopt

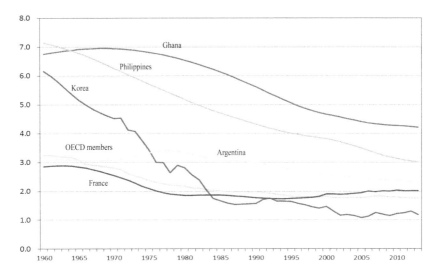

Figure 3.1 The trend of TFR in international comparison, 1960–2014 (unit: person)
Source: World Bank

family planning methods such as the intrauterine device (IUD), oral contraceptive pills, condoms, vasectomies and so on. To implement the policy, there was a boost in the recruitment and training of family planning workers including doctors, nurses and field workers; increased public awareness and targeted counseling for eligible couples; and increasing the supply of oral pills, IUDs, condoms and clinical services. The target of the program was to have 45 percent of married couples of child-bearing ages practicing family planning – 35 percent through the government budget and 10 percent through their own resources. The training of family planning personnel, including doctors, nurses and field workers, was provided by the PPFK and the Korea Institute of Family Planning (KIFP).[16]

In the early stage of the family planning program, the focus was placed on distributing contraceptive pills and devices through health centers or having personnel visit individual homes to offer family planning materials and promote the necessity of family planning. Starting from 1964, the government started to make determined efforts to reduce population growth by staffing 1,400 township (Myeon) offices across the nation with family planning personnel and providing contraceptive devices for 300,000 people. For this project, approximately 2,000 family planning and health workers were recruited and resourced. The family planning program also received support from the UNFPA and the United States in technical cooperation and material assistance.[17]

Although the family planning program achieved limited success initially, it was still dogged by challenges. It initially came up against the long-held Confucian norms of valuing the succession and prosperity of family. Government officials as well as local influential persons were also not very enthusiastic about the family planning program. It was much more difficult to promote in the rural areas, where the success of the policy largely depended on obtaining the endorsement of a reluctant cadre of local influential leaders. In urban regions, it also faced a serious problem. The hustle and bustle of urban life meant that it was nearly impossible to find spouses at home for staffers to distribute contraceptive materials.[18]

Yet the birth control policy gained momentum in 1969 and was expanded in the 1970s. In 1973, 36 percent of fertile women made use of contraceptive devices, and 30 percent terminated pregnancies through abortive surgery. Accordingly, the TFR declined from above 6 to 4 in 1973.[19] Entering the 1970s, the government took further measures to enforce family planning programs more effectively. First, it encouraged the public to pursue family planning programs as part of the *Saemaul Undong*. Accordingly, promotional materials for family planning were distributed more effectively in urban areas. In addition, medium-sized companies and large corporations were advised to provide their employees with family planning services. Labor unions were encouraged to educate workers and their families about family planning, and the Ministry of Defense supplied military personnel and their families with family planning education and contraceptives.[20] Second, the government addressed the cultural and institutional factors that support high fertility rates. The issues of demography were included in the curricula of junior and senior high schools and universities. The Ministry of Education revised textbooks to include the potential threats of high population growth, and with the support of the UNFPA distributed reference materials for demographic issues to all school levels.

The government introduced various incentives to establish the institution of the nuclear family. In 1974, the Ministry of Finance altered the tax code so that families with fewer than four children could benefit from a tax deduction, and in 1977, the ministry decided to provide that incentive for families with fewer than three children. In addition, it made sure that companies benefited from tax reduction regarding family planning projects, and families whose female members underwent sterilization operations after giving birth to one or two children were eligible to own public houses. The government took direct measures to undo the prevailing male-preference culture. It revised the Family Law to allow daughters the right of inheritance and launched public campaigns to increase the status of women.[21]

The strengthened efforts of the family planning program produced considerable results in the 1970s. From 1961 to 1978, more than 700,000 people received contraception-related services through family planning programs. Moreover, more people came to prefer sterilization operations to temporary tools such as contraceptive pills or devices. In 1979, more than half of fertile women made use of contraceptive tools, and thus the TFR fell below 3.[22] As was seen in Figure 3.1, the fertility rates in Korea have markedly declined. In no more than two decades, the TFR declined from 6 to below 2.1. The drastic fall in fertility rates can be attributed to a couple of factors. The success of the family planning program owes much to effective implementation of the program itself, but also to rapid urbanization due to industrialization, the increase in women's economic participation ratio and the rise of educational attainment due to continued economic growth.

This rapid decrease in South Korea's birthrates was almost unprecedented in the world. Although many Western countries succeeded in reducing their birthrates much earlier, the rate of the decreases was far more gradual than that of South Korea and other developing countries. For instance, it took almost 120 years for the United States to reduce the birthrate of 7 per woman in 1820 to the birthrate of 2.1 per woman in 1937. In the case of France, birthrates began to decline in the late eighteenth century, and the trend continued in the nineteenth century. In the cases of Scandinavian countries, which were latecomers in Europe, the decline in the birthrates was a little steeper, but the rate of drop in the birthrate in South Korea was twice that of Scandinavian countries.[23] By contrast, it took 60 years for South and Central American countries to attain that goal. Just two other countries — Singapore and China — succeeded in reducing their birthrates in a period on pace with South Korea. However, we need to consider the fact that both countries were exceptional, in that Singapore is a city-state and China prohibited the birth of more than one child under socialist laws.

This remarkable decline in fertility rates and population growth rates accompanied an equivalent change in the structure of the population. Consequently, the proportion of the eligible working population has increased sharply, and the workforce increased far more rapidly than the population for several decades. Those increases in the workforce, due to the structural change in the population, were also triggered by the change in women's role in the economy. More and more women participated in economic activities, and with the drop in birthrates, gender discrimination in education decreased with traditional biases against women weakened. The percentage of people having a university degree in 1960 was 0.4 percent male and 0 percent female, which in 2000 jumped to 12.5 percent male and 7.5 percent female, respectively.[24] The fall in TFR came with a decline in population growth and an increase in the ratio of the working population, which helped accelerate economic growth by ensuring food security, increased savings rates and capital accumulation.[25] However, just two decades later, in the mid-1980s, the TFR continued to drop to below the replacement level of 2.1, and that trend has led to the lowest birthrate in the world, causing South Korea to be concerned about population decline and an aging population.

3 Forestation

Once a forest has been depleted of its trees, restoring it is difficult to do, because trees take more than 20 years to reach maturity. Korea's forests were left devastated during the chaotic years at the end of Japanese rule, the years after liberation from Japan and the Korean War. Previous governments tried reforestation but to no avail.[26] Forest depletion accelerated because of the lack of financial resources and management experiences, frequent floods and damage by harmful insects. The government's efforts to encourage people to plant trees by providing them with foreign aid wheat flour failed miserably because the people continued to use trees as fuel in the winter season. To make matters worse, because a piece of wood meant immediate cash in those days, illegal logging continued briskly. A witty description of the trend went as follows:

> As young men who were born in South Korea, we had no work other than cutting down trees secretly in *Jirisan* or smuggling in *Goheung* or *Yeosu* for making a living. We had no other workplace. Thus, villagers would not consider those felling trees secretly on the mountains as criminals. In fact, they sympathized with those people.[27]

It was almost impossible to stop the illegal logging menace. The government tried to closely monitor the illegal logging by mobilizing local government officials, which turned out that it simply added to the officials' pocket money with no fruits. Thus, even Jirisan, which was called "the lung of the Korean Peninsula," was in danger of becoming a barren mountain. And as large-scale logging persisted, it brought with it annual droughts and floods as discussed earlier. The vicious cycle was being perpetuated despite the best intentions of the authorities.

Starting in February of 1963, prior to President Park's visit to West Germany, with the enactment of the Temporary Act for Promoting the Restoration of Green Forests, the government had already launched a massive sand reclamation

Picture 3.2 A Korean traditional kitchen in 1967: The women of a farm household are heating the rooms and cooking using a traditional wood furnace

©Anonymous

and tree planting initiative relying on compulsory labor. Civil servants, students and those who had not yet undergone military conscription were mobilized to implement the campaign. The results were very disappointing, however, because the mobilized people simply pretended to be engaged in the tree planting activities while idly passing time. Upon his return from West Germany, President Park then gave serious thought to reinvigorating his tree reforestation goals. His efforts were twofold. On the supply side, he initiated strong enforcement of tree planting and protection, and on the demand side, the provision of alternative fuel and energy sources and of alternative opportunities for the people subsiding on slash-and-burn farming.[28]

Active enforcement of tree planting

A major turning point in the country's reforestation drive occurred during President Park's state visit to West Germany. What he witnessed during the trip instilled in him the need to urgently address the country's depleted environment. While in West Germany he witnessed green, well-grown forests and a picturesque agro-forestry landscape.[29] Tree planting and the protection of trees are two of the only viable ways to prevent deforestation. Due to the poor fiscal condition of the country, financial investment in tree planting schemes was not a plausible option. The best would be to encourage voluntary tree planting activities and individual initiatives to protect the forests. The Korean floor heating system of *ondol* (like the hypocaust of Ancient Rome) consumed significant amounts of lumber, tree branches, leaves and roots.

This practice damages soil texture because leaves act as nutrients for the soil. Thus, the land could not be reforested through conventional methods of planting trees. Instead, the land had to undergo anti-erosion or sand reclamation processes before trees could be planted. In the 1960s revisions were made to the country's laws and regulations to streamline the administration of forest assets. The Reforestation Act in 1961 laid the statutory framework. Starting in 1962, the Five-Year Reforestation Plan was implemented under the First Five-Year Economic Development Plan. Until the mid-1960s, the first part of the plan focused on land reclamation efforts to prepare the land for tree planting.[30] With the nation financially reeling, the government resorted to passing the Temporary Act of Forest Reclamation in 1963, whose performance turned out to be unsatisfactory as was mentioned earlier. To oversee forestation administration, the Korea Forest Service (KFS) was created under the Ministry of Agriculture and Fishery in 1967.[31] Although planting trees was important, it was equally important to develop the proper tree species conducive for the mountainous terrain. Collaborative research programs between industry and academia were set up to develop a new tree species planting program toward this end. Also, the ratio of fast-growing "rapid-growth trees" to slow-growing "long-term trees" was set at 7 to 3 to encourage rapid reforestation. In 1967, Dr. Hyun Sin-kyu developed Hyun-aspens after an extended period of research at the Korea Institute of Forest Genetics. As fast-growing trees, Hyun-aspens were planted throughout the country.[32]

President Park, while on a tour of the Pohang Steel Corporation (POSCO) in 1971, reportedly told Park Tae-jun, the then head of the corporation, as follows: "Each time I return to our country from abroad, I look at Yeongil Bay, and realized that the first entrance to our land is absolutely barren. I cannot stand looking at it. We need to carry out a large-scale project to control erosion in Yeongil, and I want you to spare some time to direct that project." Park Tae-jun replied: "Your Excellency! At present, whatever good project I pay attention to, POSCO will suffer thus." "That's right," President Park replied. "So, the head of the Korea Forest Service should be the ideal position for this."[33]

That is how the president gave serious thought to strengthening the KFS with the appointment of Sohn Soo-ik, a barely 40-year-old bureaucrat, to be the figurehead of the institution in 1973. President Park told Sohn Soo-ik at the appointment ceremony, "We have seen great progress in *Saemaul Undong*. Unfortunately, we haven't seen such progress in reforestation and controlling mountains. I want you to make progress in those areas." From that occasion on, Sohn devoted himself to reforestation with the slogan "Mountain, Mountain, Mountain! Tree, Tree, Tree!" displayed in his office. Meanwhile, in March of that year, he initiated measures to ensure that the KFS would be incorporated into the Ministry of the Interior instead of the Ministry of Agriculture and Fishery. Those measures were taken so that the KFS could function better in controlling illegal activities on the mountains with the help of the Ministry of the Interior, which had provincial government officials under its jurisdiction.

Immediately after being appointed head of the KFS, Sohn Soo-ik established the First Ten-Year Plan for Mountain Reclamation and Reforestation in 1973. The plan called for a massive reforestation campaign by encouraging citizens and organizations to participate in tree planting campaigns. The plan sought to completely replant all the mountains with trees.[34] Dr. Im Gyoung-bin of the Forestry Department at Seoul National University led the efforts to identify tree varieties to be planted and support the nationwide reforestation projects. Led by the example of President Park, the Korean public, including civil servants, soldiers and students, sowed grass seeds on Sand Reclamation Day (March 15) and planted millions of trees on Arbor Day (April 5).[35] President Park's interest in reforestation shone through everywhere. Sohn recollected as follows:

> At the beginning of 1975, I accompanied the President in his 150-minute-tour of *Kyungbu* Expressway, and my hands hurt badly because I had to write down 50 instructions he gave me. Each instruction took about three minutes to write. The President seemed very knowledgeable about all the details regarding reforestation projects because he instructed me in detail.[36]

Owners of mountains became legally obliged to plant trees on their land. If the owners neglected it, the administration may plant trees on the mountains and ask

Picture 3.3 Twenty years of tree planting by Lim Chong-guk from 1956. Over 20 years from 1956, Lim Chong-guk planted three million trees by himself, and changed a 1.48 square kilometer patch of scrubland into a deep forest to be inherited by descendants

©Chosun Daily

the owners to reimburse the cost of planting trees. Of course, the owners found it in their interest to comply with this directive or risk the penalties.

> It was typical in those days to hear the owners of the mountains brag about how many trees they had planted. That was almost a fierce "competition." Everybody was determined to dedicate themselves to planting trees for the successful reforestation of their lands.[37]

For example, in 1956 when everybody was too poor to manage their living, farmer Lim Chong-guk started to plant trees by himself: 150,000 trees every year for 20 years with a total of three million trees on 1.48 square kilometers of wild land in Changsung Chollanam-do. People used to mock him pitifully.[38] To promote tree planting, revenue-sharing schemes between villages and absentee landowners were promoted to incentivize tree planting. Under this scheme, villagers cultivated trees on the absentee owner's land, and received a percentage of the profits made by selling the trees for commercial use. The performance-based incentive scheme was introduced for sand reclamation works for farmers, to maximize the sand reclamation and tree planting efforts.[39] A total of 24,000 villages were encouraged to grow seedlings in the seedbeds (990 square meters per village), and seedlings produced by the villages were purchased by the government. Provided with the seedlings, the government persuaded all the villages to plant trees and carry out projects to control erosion.

Regarding how the citizens were devoted to planting and raising trees, at that time Ko Kun, former Minister of the Interior, recollected as follows.

> In 1972, we planted trees in 27,000 places all over the country, which amounted to 13,000 hectares. In total, we planted 310,000,000 trees. We checked every tree in the field, through which, we checked whether trees took root and how well they grew, constantly monitoring the healthy conditions of every tree. In other words, we checked and managed all 310,000,000 trees.[40]

That was probably why South Korea succeeded in restoring forests, given the painstaking efforts of all the Korean people.

Large-scale projects to control erosion in the Yeongil area, in which President Park showed great interest while talking to Park Tae-jun, were carried out thanks to President Park's initiative. The Yeongil area, 4,538 hectares of land, was surrounded by high, bare mountains without a single patch of grass. Because the region was characterized by a gneiss terrain where it was extremely difficult for trees to grow, planted trees could be washed away by rain. The region was formed by the eruption of the foreshore under the seawater, and thus, large amounts of salt prevented trees from growing by depriving them of water. That was why almost 50 projects to control erosion, which were carried out from the Japanese colonial era to 1973, failed to produce significant results.[41,42] However, the erosion control projects in the Yeongil area were begun in 1973 and completed in 1977. The then head of the forest department at the Kyungbuk provincial government recollected how much interest the president had in the project.

> On April 17, 1975, the storm was so severe. President Park visited the fields in a Jeep provided by the Marine Corps. It took three hours, although the distance could be covered by a couple of minutes by helicopter. The Jeep moved violently and so Governor of *Kyungbuk* Province got a bruise on his head.[43]

After an initial survey of the site and trial and error, work began to prepare the land for sand reclamation. There were several steps in the soil reclamation process. First, walls made of stone, gravel and cement were built on the sides of the mountains, much like the steps of a pyramid. This was to prevent soil washing off when it rained. Then the soil had to be imported and placed over the pyramid steps, so that trees such as alder, acacia and pine could grow.[44] The erosion control projects in the Yeongil area involved 3.6 million people per year, and they turned the barren land of 4,538 hectares into green lands almost miraculously, as the picture of Yeongil region shows.

On April 5, 1977, President Park went further and ordered that the government institute a "Day of Growing Forests" in the autumn, so that the people

Picture 3.4 Yeongil region before tree-planting and 5 years later: Thanks to a five-year desperate struggle the area was changed from a land of difficulties (upper) to the land of miracles (below) with shapely trees

©Anonymous

could monitor the growth of the trees they had planted in the spring. Accordingly, the first Saturday of November was designated as the "Day of Growing Forests," and large numbers of citizens participated in the efforts to fertilize forests, inspect trees, protect the trees from harmful insects, remove shrubs and prune tree branches to great success. The combination of these measures helped to complete the reforestation project 4 years ahead of schedule. Just as mothers nurse their babies, so Koreans breed trees, and eventually the wasteland became heavily wooded.

Alternative energy to address deforestation

To protect forests effectively, it was necessary to provide the people with alternative fuel sources. A government-led initiative was implemented to replace wood with coal as a source of fuel. In January 1962, Lee Jung-hwan, acting president of the Mineral Resources Corporation, conferred with Park Tae-jun about the need to develop a credible alternative means of meeting the country's energy needs to shift from consumption of wood. His reasoning was that, if the reforestation program were to succeed then, it was imperative to have alternative fuel sources.[45] To this end, he proposed that the government increase his agency's staff from 25 to 220 and invest KRW 300 million each year for 5 years, so that they could mine 1.5 billion tons of anthracite coal reserves instead of the mere 30 million tons it currently ran.

Despite feeling buoyed by the strength of the arguments in his proposal, Lee at the end of his meeting was crestfallen by what he saw as Park Tae-jun's indifference to his proposal. Surprisingly, 2 days later, without prior notice, President Park visited the corporation accompanied by Park Tae-jun, who instructed Lee to forthrightly restate his proposal to the president. After listening to Lee's proposal, the president ordered that the government increase the staff to 220 and the annual budget to KRW 300 million (which was 15 times the previous year's budget of KRW 20 million). That decision was unprecedented in that there had been no case where the government increased an agency's staff and budget by such a huge margin.[46]

Thanks to this measure, the Mineral Resources Corporation carried out extensive geological surveys and developed mineral resources. Thus, by 1966, when the first Five-Year Economic Development Plan ended, South Korea's minable anthracite coal reserves amounted to 1.6 billion tons, which was more than 50 times those of early 1962. Consequently, anthracite coal has been used up to today as an energy resource. Mining large amounts of anthracite coal led many briquette manufacturers to spring up all over the country.[47] Therefore, the government could provide alternative energy sources, which was the other challenge to restoring forests. That was the result of President Park's determination, Park Tae-jun's insight and an expert's conviction.

But that could not be achieved in isolation to the sprawling illegal logging menace. The KFS under the Ministry of Agriculture and Fishery was thus moved to be under the jurisdiction of the Ministry of Interior (MOI), to leverage its vast resources and capabilities to enforce the anti-deforestation legislations. The forestry commission was also confronted with a chronic problem with the practice of slash-and-burn farming practices. Clearly, there was no conceivable way of achieving the reforestation goals in isolation to such farming practices. Nomadic farmers operating in the hinterland were the worst offenders. So, in 1966 the Act to Regulate Slash-and-Burn Farming was promulgated to curb this problem. Among other things, the act called for the relocation of nomadic farmers from vulnerable areas and all those affected were granted government support.[48]

Based on the census of the nomadic farmers conducted in 1973 and 1974, the government launched a 4-year financial assistance program for nomadic farmers in the mountains in 1974. Government assistance in relocating farmers included subsidies to pay for moving expenses and construction costs for a new house, loans to purchase livestock and a provision with employment opportunities in public works projects. With the relocation of 2,300 households in 1977, and of a few more farmers after being spotted by aerial reconnaissance planes, the nomadic slash-and-burn farming for hundreds of years was ended – a relic of Korea's poverty.[49] However, protection of the forest was not limited to mountains. In urban planning, the government introduced the Green Belt Regulation System in 1971, which restricts development of the urban region designated to preserve the green environment. This contributed significantly to preserving the green environment in urban regions.

Meanwhile, research was conducted to improve the efficiency of wood-burning furnaces, which led to the introduction of a furnace that consumed 30 percent less wood. During 1974–1976, the government improved the furnaces of about 6.7 million rural households, achieving a savings of 3.3 million tons in forest fuel. Also, forest management techniques were strongly promoted by the government, such as periodic thinning and trimming of trees, which produced a considerable amount of additional fuel, helping to alleviate the fuel shortage problem in rural farming villages.[50]

By 1977, the energy shortage in rural farming villages was resolved benefiting from a strong drive for rural electrification by the government. Coal and oil started to replace traditional sources of energy fuels. With the introduction of job opportunities to farmers, cutting trees for fuel became an unprofitable venture. A farmer recollected those days as follows:

> If we go to the mountain and gather fuel in one day, we will get about three days' worth of firewood. On the other hand, if we go to a *Saemaul* factory, we can earn a wage, with which we can buy briquettes for five days. So, everybody has no choice but to replace firewood with briquettes.[51]

With a supply of alternative energy, farming villages near urban areas replaced firewood with coal and petroleum as fuels, and consequently, rural fuel problems were completely solved by 1977.

Thus, the first 10-year plan to regulate mountains and restore forests ended in 1978, 4 years earlier than planned, and the country's mountains were green and covered with trees. The FAO in 2005 recognized South Korea as a world leader in afforestation together with Germany, the United Kingdom and New Zealand.[52] The case of South Korea succeeding in restoring lush forests while developing its economy is remarkable given that world leaders in forest management, such as the United Kingdom and Germany, devastated their forests during periods of economic growth. Lester Brown, the president of the Earth Policy Institute, said in his *Plan B 2.0* (2006) that forestation of Korea was a success of the world, and as Korea did, we could make the earth green again.[53] That was the result of the collective commitment of the Korean people to plant and foster trees under the leadership of President Park. In a sense, Korea's success in restoring forests can be said to be of far greater value than the country's economic development. Fukuda Takeo, then prime minister of Japan, was reported to have said to Kim Chung-yum when he was Korean ambassador to Japan: "Korea reminded me of naked mountains. A restored forest is more difficult to achieve and valuable than any other economic achievement such as Korea's rapid economic growth, the increase in exports, and improved employment."[54] The FAO's assessment of the country's deforestation gave a very bleak pronouncement of its prospects in 1969. Thanks to the remarkable transformations that occurred in the country's landscape, it moved from being a basket case to a success story in reforestation by 1982.[55]

Notes

1 Whang In-joung, *Integration and Coordination of Population Policies in Korea, Asian Survey* (Oakland: University of California Press, 1974), 985.
2 Kim Chung-yum, *From Despair to Hope: Economic Policymaking in Korea 1945–1979* (Seoul, Korea: Korea Development Institute, 2011), 244–245.
3 *Mindungsan-ui gijeok, sallianokhwa* [The Miracle of a Bald: Forest Recreation], Internet Broadcast. Directed by Chang-joon Lee (Seoul, Korea: KBS, August 3, 2008), accessed August 7, 2017, www.kbs.co.kr/1tv/sisa/docucinema/view/vod/2177606_66621.html
4 O Won-chol, *The Korea Story: President Park Jung-hee's Leadership and the Korean Industrial Revolution* (Seoul, Korea: Wisdom Tree, 2009), 431–432.
5 Kim, *From Despair to Hope*, 217.
6 O Won-chol, *Hanguk-hyeong gyeongje geonseol 1: Enjinioring eopeurochi* [Korea Type Economic Construction 1: An Engineering Approach] (Seoul, Korea: Korea Type Economic Policy Institute, 1995), 138–141.
7 *Ibid.*, 170–173.
8 *Ibid.*, 177.
9 Kim Sok-dong et al., *Modularization of Korea's Development Experience: The Green Revolution in Korea: Development and Dissemination of Tongil-Type Rice Varieties* (Seoul, Korea: Research Data Alliance & Northern Agriculture Research Institute, 2012), 171–172 [in Korean].
10 Lee Wan-joo, "Saero sseuneun daehanminguk 70-nyeon (1945–2015) [19] Tongilbyeowa jageupjajok" [70 Years of Using Tongil Rice and Self-Sufficiency in Korea], *Chosun Ilbo*, July 9, 2015, accessed August 7, 2017, http://news.chosun.com/site/data/html_dir/2015/07/09/2015070900337.html
11 *Ibid.*
12 *Ibid.*
13 Kim et al., *Modularization of Korea's Development Experience*, 24–25.
14 Kim, *From Despair to Hope*, 215–216.
15 Kim et al., *Modularization of Korea's Development Experience*, 21–26.
16 Whang In-Joung, *Social Development in Action: The Korean Experience* (Seoul, Korea: Korea Development Institute, 1986), 128–131.
17 Cho Lee-jay and Carter Eckert, *Hanguk kundaehwa, kijok ui kwajong* [Modernization of the Republic of Korea: A Miraculous Achievement] (Seoul: Chosun News Press, 2005), 399.
18 *Ibid.*
19 *Ibid.*, 400.
20 *Ibid.*
21 *Ibid.*, 400–401.
22 *Ibid.*, 401.
23 Griffith Feeney and Andrew Mason, "Population in East Asia," *Population Series 88–2* (Honolulu, HI: East-West Center, 1998).
24 Cho and Eckert, *Modernization of the Republic of Korea*, 415.
25 *Ibid.*
26 Kim, *From Despair to Hope*, 266.

27 *The Miracle of a Bald*, KBS.
28 Moon Gap-sik, "Gyeongbugosokdoro jogyeongeun bakjeonghui daetongnyeongui jakpum" [Kyungbu Expressway Landscape Is the Work of President Park Chung-hee], *Premium Chosun*, June 25, 2015, accessed August 10, 2017, http://premium. chosun.com/site/data/html_dir/2015/06/24/2015062402603.html
29 *Ibid.*
30 Kim, *From Despair to Hope*, 266.
31 *Ibid.*, 246.
32 *Ibid.*, 253–259.
33 Lee Dae-hwan, "Ttaelgam ttaemune beolgeoke doen mindungsaneul pureuge mandeun baktaejunui myoan" [Park Tae-jun's Idea for Reforestation], *Chosun Ilbo*, September 15, 2014, accessed August 10, 2017, http://premium.chosun. com/site/data/html_dir/2014/09/14/2014091400755.html
34 Kim, *From Despair to Hope*, 251.
35 *Ibid.*, 247.
36 Moon, "Kyungbu Expressway."
37 *The Miracle of a Bald*, KBS.
38 Lee Han-su, "60 nyeon jeon han sanaiga simeun namu, eoneusae 300man geuru supeuro" [Trees a Man Planted Trees 60 Years Ago Made Forest of 3 Million Trees], *Chosun Ilbo*, May 24, 2017, accessed August 7, 2017, http://travel.chosun. com/site/data/html_dir/2017/05/24/2017052402254.html
39 Kim, *From Despair to Hope*, 254.
40 *Ibid.*
41 *The Miracle of a Bald*, KBS.
42 Moon, "Kyungbu Expressway."
43 Moon Gab-sik, "Hanuui sikseonkkaji bakjeonghui daetongnyeongui hanmadi" [A Word From Park Chung-hee Changed the Taste of Korean Cows], *Chosun Ilbo*, June 25, 2015, accessed August 10, 2017, http://premium.chosun.com/ site/data/html_dir/2015/06/24/2015062402641.html
44 Kim, *From Despair to Hope*, 264.
45 Park Tae-jun was a member of the National Reconstruction Supreme Committee in charge of trade and industry affairs.
46 Lee, "Park Tae-jun's Idea for Reforestation."
47 *Ibid.*
48 Kim, *From Despair to Hope*, 247.
49 *Ibid.*, 261–262.
50 *Ibid.*, 255–256.
51 *The Miracle of a Bald*, KBS.
52 Moon Gab-sik, "114nyeon jeon oegukini barabon mindungsan Joseon" [114 Years Ago, Foreigners Saw a Bald of *Joseon*], *Premium Chosun*, June 25, 2015, accessed August 10, 2017, http://premium.chosun.com/site/data/ html_dir/2015/06/24/2015062402663.html
53 Lee Kye-min, *Korian Mireokeul: Sumun Gijeokdeul. Sup-ui yeoksa, saero sseuda* [The Korean Miracle III: Rewrite the History of Forests] (Seoul, Korea: Nanam, 2015), 183.
54 Kim, *From Despair to Hope*, 267.
55 *The Miracle of a Bald*, KBS.

4　Impact for export and job creation

1　Exporting national factor endowment

During a visit to Bangladesh nearly a decade ago, I was engaged in a discussion with some Korean expats about the issue of tackling poverty there. They quipped that after living there for years, they could hardly fathom the prospect of breaking the poverty cycle in Bangladesh. Aside from its seemingly cynical undertone, it was clearly a frank observation based on the conditions on the ground, especially for an expat. However, as an active witness of Korea's development experience, I was somewhat convinced that, even if we could not wave a magic wand to trigger transformation, there still could be a way out of this silo of poverty, granted a good mix of the right policy disposition and grit are leveraged. Again, like Portia surmised in Shakespeare's *The Merchant of Venice*, cited earlier in this book, the real question was how to do it. So, I will attempt to describe how Korea went about to answer the how of this question in the economic sphere.

In radically reforming the bureaucracy and tackling the country's environmental problems, President Park was simultaneously keenly aware that none of these measures could be treated in oblivion to the bread and butter questions of his long-suffering compatriots. The primitive and rudimentary conditions under which the colonial and indeed much of the pre-colonial era had been functioning made turning fortunes around overnight nearly an untenable situation. Yet the scale of the nation's myriad of challenges was not lost on him.

All he really had to work with was a desperately discouraged citizenry whose state of collective sense of apathy was legendary. In his heart of hearts, he could perhaps empathize with a people whose sense of possibility was so eviscerated by the realities of the misery of their daily subsistence. Want of job opportunities has a direct correlation with developing the ethics and skills of a productive professional. This lack of opportunities for personal development truncated access to social mobility and its attendant dividends of capital accumulation. Being the seasoned soldier that he was, President Park could have conceivably understood that he was toying with the fringes of mission creep.

We see in Figure 4.1 a summary of the incarnations of the reinforcing correlation of the factors that condemns a typically poor country into a perpetual state of fragility and poverty. (For the time being, disregard the "impact" part of the

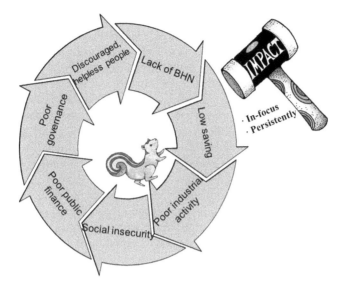

Figure 4.1 Vicious cycle of poverty

Trying to get out of the cycle of poverty is just like a squirrel trying to make progress by running in a squirrel cage: the cycle merely turns around endlessly. To find a way out, the Korean government persistently focused impact on a critical point of the chain.

Source: © Na young Ahn

figure.) Poor people are generally deprived of basic human needs (BHN), which causes low savings, poor investment and little industrial activity, which in turn causes social insecurity and poor public finances, which also leads to poor governance, resulting in people being discouraged and feeling helpless. The vicious cycle of poverty and fragility, which feed off each other, poses a true dilemma. Due to the intertwined nature of poverty and fragility, it is difficult to find a clue to the solution of the problem. Trying to get out of the cycle is just like a hamster trying to make progress by running on its wheel. This is why few countries in poverty and fragility have succeeded in becoming advanced states.

Clearly, it was just inconceivable that South Korea, which was confronted with a myriad of dilemmas, could delude itself into believing that it had all the answers to the bleak choices that fate presented to it. Yet it would have still been irresponsible to resign to fate. The Korean government saw that it was impossible to resolve its problems by tackling all the issues at the same time. If they were ever going to end this vicious cycle, it was imperative to find a way of striking a critical blow at the heart of their problems. Let's now concentrate on the "impact" part of Figure 4.1 again: if an impact can be made on the critical point persistently, then a momentum will be created to disentangle the vicious cycle.

This approach to exodus from poverty and fragility seems alien to the mainstream poverty reduction strategies pursued by many developing countries under the auspices of the World Bank. By and large, the World Bank–led poverty reduction strategy papers tend to pursue balanced, harmonized development. It is often premised on a very simplistic view that all the problems of poverty can be tackled and improved at the same time. However, countries blighted by the scourge of poverty often have very limited room for maneuver within the capacity and resource constraints they must work with. My contention is that this speaks to the fact that there is very little to show for after years of such policies being implemented in the developing world.

What was the critical point in Korea's vicious chain? The imminent and immediate symptom of poverty was deplorably low income levels in the country. The economy was also burdened by chronic balance of payment deficits due to poor capacity to export. The country was in the throes of a major balance of payment crisis. Chronic deficits hamper a country's capacity to engage in international trade, which results in shortfalls in essential commodities such as energy to run the domestic economy. Widespread shortages can become a powder keg for social unrest, especially for a country as dependent on foreign aid as South Korea was. Therefore, improving the chronic international balance of payments in trade was a fundamental prerequisite for the survival of the fragile nation before poverty elimination came into the picture. The critical point, as conceived by the Korean government, was surmised in its "export promotion for job creation" dictum. As Figure 4.1 depicts, there was an undercurrent of pressure to awaken the sleep-walking Korean people to the potential benefits that can be accrued from reorienting their lethargic mind-set.

Therefore, the core is in awakening the consciousness of the people by creating jobs and opportunities for earning income through export. Then, it will trigger a trickling effect. First, incomes will be boosted and vital skills acquired along the way, which also opens the door to further opportunities for upward mobility. Second, they can increase savings for investment and improvement in the balance of payments (BOP) at a national level. With the improved BOP, they can secure more energy and new materials for higher economic growth. Third, this will invigorate entrepreneurship for start-ups and business expansion, and more investment and trade for higher economic growth. With higher earnings, people will work more diligently because of the renewed appreciation of the importance of money. Thus, poverty can be reduced, and we can now gather the momentum for poverty reduction and sustained economic development. Therefore, the core of South Korea's poverty reduction strategy was mobilization of Korea's full national capacity to spur export and job creation under the chronic deficits in the international balance of payments and widespread poverty.

Viewed retrospectively, the policy appears logical and straightforward by today's standards. Yet it is easy to forget what exporting meant for an undeveloped economy – it meant the wholesale transfer of natural resources to foreign buyers. How was export policy going to be a realistic policy posture for a country as resource-deprived like Korea was? It was certainly a daring effort to place export at the very top of the national development agenda – an unprecedented move. The chief economic adviser to President Park, O Won-chol, recalls that as a fragile and desperately poor country, the idea of manufacturing goods for export was a great discovery.[1] In fact, few developing countries in the world designated export promotion as a core development strategy in the 1960s.

South Korea prioritized export as a development policy not because it had any valuable resource deposits or vibrant industries. Moreover, the policy was driven by proven empirical evidence about its prospects but out of sheer necessity. Think of it in terms of how desperation drives ingenuity in the best of times and in the worst of times triggers a blind leap of faith into the abyss. Once the resolve was conceived and set in motion, the remaining question was, what kinds of commodities could be exported?

2 Governance and export promotion

Notwithstanding the espoused desire to plunge into exports, the elephant in the room was what to export. The dilemma was not made any easier by the fact that this was a resource-poor country, with the added burden of lacking the capacity to export. In fact, the only reality on the ground was a country with a sprawling population that had to be fed. Traditionally Korean women generally kept very long hair, which was a symbol and dignity of women. So desperate were the conditions that women used to cut their hair and sell it on the market. Middlemen bought this hair and processed it for producing wigs that would be exported. Another reminder of the desperate conditions was the production of leather from rat skin. During the 1950s and 1960s, rats were a major nuisance to farming, threatening to cause crop losses. The government launched a national campaign to catch rats. As a primary school pupil, I was obliged to submit tails of rats caught at home. Some ingenious merchants made coats with rat leather for export. There was a point along this history that South Korea was reputed for leading in the export of rat leather products, accruing nearly $360,000 per annum for the country.

In a way, this was rather an opportunistic way out of the living hardships. So much for a country under such conditions to be so obsessed with exporting as a national development priority. Laying aside any inklings of cynicism, this could be clearly qualified to be the biggest joke of the day if not a pipe dream. For export promotions to be successful, two vital ingredients are required. One is how to drive export, and the other is what to export. The latter will be discussed in the next section. Regarding the former, various support systems for export were put in place.

First, the government set up annual and medium-term export targets and incorporated in the Five-Year Economic Development Plans alongside annexed annual action plans. The export target was very ambitious because President Park declared his so-called nation building on export agenda. During the early period of export promotion from 1964 to 1970, an annual export growth target was set at around 40 percent as the standard, while setting the $1 billion exports mark as the target in 1970, up from $121 million in 1964. The $1 billion export may mean that at this stage, the hardships faced by the nation would be eased thanks in large part to the growth of the economy. To meet the expectation of President Park, every minister, provincial governor and ambassador vigorously competed to achieve high export quotas within their respective jurisdictions. Of course, it was in their interest to use these schemes to curry favor with the strongman rather than incur his wrath.

Second, the government introduced strong incentive packages including a favorable exchange rate policy, tax benefits and financial support for exporters. Set with the goal of promoting export, a uniform exchange rate system was adopted in 1964, and the Korean won (KRW) was devalued to the US dollar (USD) by nearly 100 percent in favor of export, which made Korean products cheaper and doubled the cost of foreign products. In financial terms, the short-term export credit system was streamlined as early as 1961. Financial support was extended in the form of direct subsidies for exports, as well as automatic export loans provided at preferential interest rates. The essence of the new system was the automatic approval of loans by commercial banks to those with an export letter of credit (L/C).

The tax benefits provided to exporters included reduction or exemption of taxes on income and investment. In addition, an export-import link system in which import quotas were proportionally given to exporters according to their export performance was utilized to strengthen export incentives. Furthermore, many free trade zones were established, and customs procedures and the administrative services were simplified in those zones to cut the red tape. Overseas marketing was supported by the Korea Trade Promotion Corporation (KOTRA) with the provision of market information and trade services. These measures enabled Korean exporters to make inroads into foreign markets. Of course, this incentive system was made possible thanks to a robust fiscal policy that ensured improved domestic revenue mobilization activities through tax administration reform, as will be detailed in Section 9.3.

Third, these export promotion policies were thoroughly monitored by the president. To ensure actual implementation of export promotion policies, he personally monitored export promotion every month through chairing the Monthly Export Promotion Meeting. The meeting routinely convened all the export-related cabinet members and high-ranking government officials on the one side and business leaders and representatives on the other. During such meetings, business leaders directly presented their challenges to the president and concerned cabinet ministers were tasked to provide prompt responses. The meeting was like the supreme operation conference for exports. These meetings ran for 2 hours, usually from 10 a.m. to noon, and were held every month from 1965 to 1979.

Fourth, a select group of companies was earmarked to spearhead the export promotion drive. The goal as espoused by the government was to consolidate the role of exports as the bedrock of the nascent economy. This lofty aspiration notwithstanding, the country had to contend with real challenges – not least that it was a poor underdeveloped country with no history of export to talk of. In other words, "brand Korea" would be nothing but an ominous presence on the international stage. Undeterred, the government was willing to confront the challenge head-on beginning with a streamlined policy outline that saw the designation of general trading companies in 1975. The requirement of the general trading companies was exporting over 2 percent of the nation's gross exports, earning an average revenue of $1 million and trading in 30 or more countries. In addition to general incentives for export, tax incentives and easy access to credit were provided to the companies. The general trading companies thus acted as the central command post for exports until its official dissolution in 2009.

The icing on the cake was the recognition conferred on high achievers in the export industry. A National Export Day was consequently designated to recognize and reward the achievements of the country's industrialists, academia and civil servants whose collective efforts bolstered each year's export goals. By demonstrating its solid commitment to the export drive, the government had essentially spurred the nation's industrialists to further action. Because of these policies, the annual export growth rate from 1964–1970 was 41.9 percent, while from 1971–1979 it was 39.8 percent. The average growth rate of exports during these 16 years was 40 percent per annum – an incredible feat indeed. Total export revenue had also increased from $100 million in 1964 to $1 billion in 1970, then continued on an upward trend to hit the $10 billion mark by 1977. The performance of exports repeatedly exceeded ambitious targets. Compared to similar major export nations, South Korea's figures were quite telling. For instance, West Germany needed 11 years to achieve the $10 billion mark whereas Japan did so in 16 years. Progressively South Korea's export industry had come of age in a manner that was nothing but stupendous.

The government's militant approach to the question of poverty elimination through an export-led development policy ought to be seen within the context of the high stakes it had to contend with. Given that the viability of this nascent state was all but the most urgent obsession of the leadership, it is hardly surprising that the nation's energy was channeled into surmounting the odds. President Park was famous for repeatedly admonishing the citizenry that "Anything is possible. We can do it." Beyond the changes in the material sphere in the successful export drive, a significant transformation had also come along in terms of the psyche of the nation. Not least was the wobbly and unpromising start the nation had from the Korean War and its consequent destabilization.

3 Export of labor forces

Amid the sprawling population conditions, the government for the first time began to steadily consider the possibility of exporting labor to supplement its product exports. After thinking this through, a decision was made to establish the Korea Overseas Development Corporation in 1965 with the explicit mandate of facilitating the export of Korean labor abroad. Labor export in the early stage of development went through major four phases. The first phase was from

1963 to 1977, which was characterized by the dispatching of a contingent of manual laborers and nurses to work in the sweltering mines and hospitals of West Germany. The second phase was the use of teenage garment workers from 1964 to 1970. For all its worth, the income they earned in foreign currency could be rightly termed as labor export. Third, the period of 1966–1970 saw the deployment of Korean soldiers to join the American war effort in Vietnam. Despite being a purely military campaign, the troop deployment also brought in a substantial financial gain in the form of hard foreign currency. Fourth, when the oil shock hit the Middle East construction boom in the 1970s, Korea dispatched many workers to participate in construction projects in the region from 1973 to 1978.

Mine workers and nurses to Germany[2]

Up until the early 1960s there had been cases of Korean laborers migrating to West Germany; most went there through private arrangements. But it took the initiative of a diplomat at the mission in Bonn to start the formal process of labor migration. This diplomat is said to have acted on his own volition to negotiate an arrangement with Bonn to allow for the deployment of Korean laborers. When the South Korean ambassador got wind of the deal, he was exasperated and rebuked the diplomat for coming up with such an ill-conceived plan. The ambassador opposed the suggested plan because he felt that having Korean workers in the country would mean a lot of troubles for the embassy.[3] This tells that even under the omnipotent military government high-ranking government officials used to fall on prudentialism, a clear symptom of underdeveloped countries.

Confronted with urgent capital needs, the government turned to the West German government for help, to which Bonn agreed to provide a DM 150 million loan ($35 million). Of the amount being offered, half was in the form of a commercial loan, requiring a payment guarantee by the third-party banks. Hardly any financial institutions were willing to hedge their funds for a country in such financial dire straits. As the process of sealing the loan agreement appeared to be reaching a dead end without the collateral, an unusual breakthrough came in the form of an unorthodox idea. The story is told of a young Korean man who studied in West Germany discussing the issue of the collateral with his German alumni. It was then that the idea of sending Korean workers to work in West Germany so that their wages could be held in trust as a form of collateral was discussed. Through his contacts in the Korean bureaucracy, this young man brought this possibility to the attention of the government. So, to secure the loan, the government in a way mortgaged its people to work in West Germany, for which their wages were used as collateral for the loan.[4]

In 1963 a recruitment advertisement was published calling for mine workers and nurses to be dispatched to West Germany. Forty-six thousand young men applied for 500 open positions for miners. Anxious to make the final roster, many of the applicants who did not have prior mining experience resorted to desperate measures to increase their chances. It is alleged that some of the interviewees deliberately bruised their palms with briquettes prior to the interview to create the false impression of having previous experience to boost their chances of being selected. Following several rounds of recruitment interviews, on December 21, 1963, the first batch of 367 miners departed for West Germany. They were slated to work for 3 years. Then from 1966, several batches of nurses and nursing assistants were also dispatched to West Germany. Thus, by 1977 a total of 7,936 miners and 11,057 nurses and nursing assistants had working stints in West Germany.

Kwon Yi-jong, one of the miners dispatched to West Germany recalled his living conditions this way: "I was doing hard manual labor in Seoul, and I had to sell my blood to buy some food. Being able to work in West Germany was an opportunity of a lifetime."[5] As one of the world's poorest countries, South Korea had record inflation rates that ranged around an annual rate of 42 percent and a staggering unemployment rate of 23 percent. These were days of extreme poverty, where folks literarily scavenged the dumps of the city to subsist. The few fortunate ones who were recruited as mine workers in West Germany had to endure the drudgery of a daily trip of 1 kilometer deep into the mines, while inside they traversed a total distance of nearly 3 kilometers across the mine pits under temperatures of 40°C.

Instead of the usual German greeting of "Guten Morgen" (Good morning), the miners became accustomed to the unorthodox form of using "Glück Auf" (Good luck).[6] There was a tale of living day by day – a stark indication of the extremely dangerous working conditions that they faced nearly every day of their time in the mine pits.

Picture 4.1 Korean workers digging coal in West Germany from 1963 to 1977. 7,936 Korean workers dug coal in West Germany from 1963–1977, working 1,000 meters underground

©ehistory.go.kr

www.ehistory.go.kr/page/view/photo.jsp?photo_PhotoSrcGBN=PT&photo_PhotoID=3720&detl_PhotoDTL=28574)

The conditions of the nurses were not very different. Most of them were assigned duties of washing corpses and other menial tasks. Um Keum-ja, who served as a nurse in West Germany in 1970, recalls that

> one patient was going to die. The doctor, stumping with his feet, shouted for me to bring something but I didn't understand what he was saying. The patient's condition was urgent, so after running about in confusion the entire time, I went home and cried.[7]

But again their work ethic and professionalism endeared them to their employers, which is why they were described as the "Korean angels" by a local newspaper – a testament to their sacrificial services under very difficult conditions.

The patients who were moved by the "Korean angels" included influential members of Parliament like floor leader Dr. Leo Wagner, who submitted a recommendation to the West German government to strengthen its bilateral relations that would lead to helping Korea alleviate its pervasive poverty. This culminated in the official state visit of President Park to West Germany. The visit was steeped in a rich tapestry of symbolism and history, given that it marked the beginning of the first-ever visit of a Korean head of state to Europe. It came against the backdrop of cooling in relations with Washington and of intensified international pressure on the military government from its major donor countries. The dedication of the young nurses provided a critical diplomatic avenue for the government, especially in its hour of need.[8]

President Park visited the site of the Korean laborers during his visit to West Germany. Appalled by the shape of his young compatriots colored with black coal, President Park responded in an emotional speech saying "Compatriots, what I'm I seeing here? I am crying bloody tears . . . I am a criminal! I am guilty of making the youth of Korea suffer this extreme torment!" Moved by the contrition and empathy of the president, the assembled audience held each other, and burst into a chorus of crying and wailing. At the end of it, President Park pledged the following: "We face this torment because of our poverty, but let us not pass down this poverty to our children!"[9]

The workers clearly took the message of the president to heart by clinging to a great deal of thrift and frugality. Seok Suk-ja, a nurse who was part of the 1973 cohort, was quoted as saying "The starting salary was 750 Deutsche Mark (DM). Of which 20 Marks was for stipends and 30 for boarding costs, and the rest of the 700 is remitted to their parents in Korea." Han Jung-ro had a similar story, saying "The most interesting part was wiring the money to our parents. It would be pointless to do such a hard work, if we didn't have that joy . . . that was so joyful."[10] Many of them also took on overtime and part-time work to earn extra money to enable them transfer more funds back home. With the money remitted by their daughters, their parents could finance the education of other siblings. The girls played the role of family nurturers. The total remittances to Korea during the 10 years running from 1965 to 1975 amounted to $101,530,000. This figure represented nearly 2 percent of the country's total exports.[11]

Female garment workers[12]

The labor export evolution in South Korea went through a seminal period in the late 1960s to early 1970s as an important source of low wage employment for female workers. This sort of work is still prevalent in low-income developing countries. The dire conditions of poverty often compelled young female members to participate in income generating activities. Tradition and culture made the weaving and garment industry an imperative option for young females seeking a viable source of employment.

The low wages of developing countries drive the outsourcing of these low-skilled jobs from rich industrial economies. South Korea was thus an obvious destination for outsourcing the production of garments. A new opportunity was thus opened for young girls from destitute homes to earn incomes to support their families. To secure a work order, the wage rates had to be lower than other competitive countries. If compared to the existing wage standards of the first half of 1964, for instance, you will note that Japan's hourly wage was 56 cents against Korea's and Taiwan's hourly wages of 20 cents. But even with that, Taiwan had a relatively superior labor force, which further strained competition. The Korean government consequently decided to devalue the Korean won against the US dollar from 130 to 255.

As the exchange rate readjusted, the price of oil and other imported goods became expensive. With a great deal of initial hesitation, Koreans had to endure these changes on the ground. This depreciation shaved off as much as 10 cents per hour from the wages of the workers. It created the fertile conditions to incentivize the entry of the foreign garment production industry into the country. For all their labor, the average wage was 10 cents per hour and $20 per month. Word of the skills, diligence and productivity of the Korean laborers soon spread abroad, bringing with it an increase in the number of manufacturers outsourcing their production to Korea. Despite being a low-wage employment sector, the employees were generally better paid relatively by Korean standards. During the 1960s, the garment industry was the leading export industry, and thus made great contribution to the improvement in international balance of payments and the national exchequer.

The export volume of $300 million in 1967, which was mainly supported by the growth of the garment industry, was particularly significant in that the amount is equivalent to the annual foreign aid Korea received from the United States to balance its books. With this export performance, it thus set the course of weaning itself off dependence on foreign aid and steadily breaking the vicious cycle of poverty. The female workers not only earned money but also provided their parents in rural sectors with accessibility to the outside world through bringing in radios and other electronic devices for their parents on festive days. The women of the 1960s can be rightly called patriots who kept the nation afloat when it was clearly needed.

These young ladies were a source of profound national pride, especially coming, as it did, against the traditional background of marginalization that women were subjected to in this largely patriarchal society. It was not out of place to reduce women to servitude, as the culture has a long history of preference for male children. Many poor households had their daughters work as domestic servants to save food for the family. But they were still extremely devoted to their families and demonstrated an uncanny level of courage. Despite the conditions of hardship, many had an acute entrepreneurial spirit and solid intellectual depth, even for their tender teenage years. Yet still they exhibited a strong yearning for personal development, with many working the grueling long day shifts and then spending the night studying.

For all its gains, that industry was not sustainable in the long run, chiefly for two reasons. First, as wages steadily increased, they affected price competitiveness. Wages could not keep pace with the cost of living, and so the incentives were no longer very attractive, triggering a high turnover in the industry. Besides, all the foreign manufacturers really cared about was their bottom line, and were thus unwilling to incur extra costs in the form of higher wages. The exodus process to alternative cheap labor destinations was thus just the next natural order. There were quite a few countries willing to offer cheaper labor even if their production quality was a bit lower. Second, there was the question of sustaining the labor supply. As conditions started to improve, especially on the financial aspect for these highly skilled young ladies, despite their low level of education, there was a steady decline in interest to work in the factories. The year 1970 marked a significant period in the history of the country when the wage levels of females had risen to the second highest in Asia, behind only Japan. This transformation had taken place within 7 years, from mid-1964 to 1970.

Participation in the Vietnam War[13]

The next phase of the labor export was the deployment of young men overseas. Viewed within the context of the labor export, the deployment of active young men to battle was nothing but the natural sequence in the treadmill. It also helped deal with the dilemma of what to do with youth who were neither in school nor firmly placed within the labor market. Then the Vietnam War beginning in 1966 and the Middle East construction booms proved to be a productive avenue for reaping financial gains for both the nation and its youth. The 1960s into the mid-1970s saw the scepter being transferred to the nation's male youth. As a generation, they were called to carry the responsibilities of providing for their kith and kin, much like the female laborers did in the garment industry. The number of young South Korean young men entering the battlefield of Vietnam beginning in 1966 had reached nearly 400,000. This figure constituted both military and civilian workers, mainly composed of young men in their early twenties. They came from all walks of life and saw an opportunity to better their economic lot by engaging in the war effort overseas.

The government found itself between a rock and a hard place when the US government officially requested for the deployment of Korean soldiers to the war effort in Vietnam. For its part, the Korean government found no compelling justification to deploy its troops to a war abroad, but for historical reasons there was little wiggle room, given that the request was coming from the United States. The request ought to be seen within the context of the military alliance between the United States and South Korea, and how that was a major factor in the decision. However, the dispatching of Korean troops was previously proposed by President Syngman Rhee in 1957, which was not accepted by the United States. In his first summit meeting with the United States, President Park also made a similar offer in 1965.

Despite its initial request to deploy its troops, the timing of the American request troubled the South Korean leadership. President Park was in distress after receiving the official request from the Americans. First Lady Yuk Young-soo confirmed that the president stayed up mulling the request and smoked all night in a visibly distraught state. President Park accepted the troop deployment in exchange of financial compensation. He saw in the deployment an opportunity to use the funds to invest in modernizing the hardware of the Korean army and the establishment of the Korea Institute of Science and Technology (KIST). He envisioned the establishment of KIST as the precursor to making science and technological research the cradle of the country's future economic development, and indeed a worthy return for the sacrificial efforts of the nation's youngsters. On the government's planned troop deployment, his political opponents denounced the plans as a misguided effort by the government "to send Korean youth to a foreign war as raw cannon fodder." To this, President Park is quoted to have retorted, "where in this world is there a parent that would send one's children to fight in a foreign battlefield!"[14]

There was a high demand for military supplies and manpower to support the logistical process of the war effort, which opened a window of opportunity for Korea to benefit financially from contributing military forces. However, the required huge military supplies were largely outsourced to Japan by the Pentagon. Because it had no capacity of manufacturing military supplies, Korea could not enjoy the benefits although it deployed troops to Vietnam; the benefits went to Japan. It was almost as though the labor was performed by the Koreans whereas Japan reaped the windfall.

With two reasons to join the war and risk their lives, volunteer applications flooded in to such an extent that only the lucky military officials and higher ranks were chosen. One of the reasons was that the experience of war engagement would add credit to their future career, and the other was that they could make money to buy a house. During war operations, Korean soldiers did a good job with modern weapons. The Korean military authority on site reported that many of their weapons were lost, but brought them to Korea to upgrade the armament of Korean soldiers. The military authority of the rich Americans was generous with their poor, able war friends. Soldiers bought many electronic goods with their salary from post exchange (PX) to send to their parents through their fellows returning home, and their parents sold them to their neighbors, making profits. Among many military supplies, the Korean government successfully lobbied the US government to include kimchi in the ration of the Korean troops.

But the Korean companies contracted to supply the kimchi lacked the required canning technology; consequently from the point of departure to docking, all the kimchi stock went stale. The excitement of receiving a ration of kimchi soon turned into disappointment when the troops got hold of it. General Commander Chae Myung-shin addressed the soldiers saying: "With our technology, we can only make kimchi like this. If we say we cannot eat this, after 2–3 weeks we can receive tasty canned kimchi, which is made in Japan. Should that happen, the benefit will not go to your parents laboring on the fields but rather to Japanese people." Then, the soldiers responded, "Oh, no! The kimchi cabbages were sown in our home country, so the profit should go to our parents. How can it go to the Japanese?" The soldiers ate the spoiled kimchi as if it were OK.[15] Kimchi exports from Korea continued all the same. Consequently, the hard currency earned because of the troop deployment from 1966 to 1970 was more than $650 million thanks to the gallant contribution of these young men. In a way, this sum contributed in spurring South Korea to achieving the much desired $1 billion export mark in 1970. Indeed, this is the price of the sweat, blood and tears of its long-suffering people under very trying circumstances.

Participation in the Middle East construction works[16]

The 1973 Yom Kippur War and the collusion of the Organization of the Petroleum Exporting Countries (OPEC) triggered a major panic in the international oil market, resulting in the first oil shock of 1973. As a net importer of oil, the Korean economy took a major hit as a direct consequence. By 1974, oil prices had spiked to $11.25 per barrel from $2.50 per barrel at the end of 1972. The second oil shock in July 1979 nearly tripled oil prices to $32 per barrel.[17] These developments came against the backdrop of Korea just beginning its major investments in industrial development through foreign capital and labor exports. Immediate threats to the forward progression of the industrial development process were coming to the fore, thanks to the panic induced by the oil shocks.

Consumer prices had suddenly increased by 72 percent and wholesale prices reached 99.9 percent during the period of 1973–1975. These high inflationary rates were significantly higher than the recorded rates of other developing countries.[18] It also brought with it a balance of payments crisis. The current accounts deficit increased from $388.9 million in 1973 to $2.227 billion in 1974. This was hardly surprising given South Korea's status as a net importer of oil and the dependence of its industries on imported energy resources. It was thus staring a crisis in the face.

About the same time, the government ought to create an opportunity from the crisis created by the oil shock on the economy. The oil-producing Middle-Eastern states such as Saudi Arabia and Iran went through a massive construction boom because of the financial windfall from the oil price hikes of the 1970s. Sensing an opportunity, President Park's chief economic advisor, O Won-chol, came up with the idea of exporting the Korean labor force to the region to tap into the construction opportunities there. His reasons were quite compelling.

The Middle East was not a particularly attractive destination for outside migrant labor, especially given the hostile climatic conditions, its rigid social and religious conservatism and its low wages. However, Koreans possessed some skills in construction obtained from the Kyungbu Highway project. Disregarding these risks, President Park instructed the cabinet to map out ways that would ensure that the Middle East market would provide the pull effect to draw the country out of the financial doldrums created by the oil shock.[19]

However, widespread skepticism was aroused. The hot, desert climate was a harsh environment alien to Koreans. Besides, many of the world's leading companies had already established firm footholds in the region. These big shots had the technological, capital and equipment superiority over the Korean rookies. Naturally, it placed them in a position where they had strong insider networks and contacts with the senior elite and the regions ruling monarchies, which in many ways gave them a quasi-monopolistic hold on key industries. Overseas construction projects were also regarded as a high-risk endeavor.

Moreover, up until then, very few Korean enterprises had ever experienced large-scale overseas construction projects. It was a sensitive move, coming against the real fear that should any Korean firm bungle a project in the region, then it would ultimately undermine the long-term goal of making forays into the lucrative Middle Eastern market. Widespread skepticism greeted the initial thought of going into the Middle East region with its alien mores and climatic conditions, but also the international business acumen of Korea came into question. Faced with this strong skepticism, President Park asked Chairman Chung Ju-yung of Hyundai Group for his opinion. Chung turned the argument on its head by saying:[20]

> In Korea, rainfall used to hinder construction works, so it will be good if we had rainless days in the Middle East. For construction, we need sand, gravel and cement. If we go there, we have a lot of sand and gravel, and all we need is to take the enormous cement from our country. If there is no water, we can use desalinated water. If it is hard to work because of the daily heat, then we can work at night.

His view was a clearly radical approach to balancing the benefits and trade-offs coming out of that region. He spurned advice from his family and associates and took the bold move of launching moves into the risk of doing business in the Middle East.

Swift actions were taken to support construction companies as they sought to advance into the Middle East market, beginning with the establishment of a special task force team to support the quest of Korean construction firms to make forays into the region. The Korea Institute for Middle East Economy, under the auspices of the Economic Planning Board (EPB), was leading the charge in this budding venture. A systematic plan was instituted to provide regular research to furnish local firms seeking to enter the region with the most salient information to enhance their success.

However, it did not prove to be smooth sailing despite the best efforts that went into it. Construction companies faced enormous liquidity and credit difficulties in ways that did not make them viable contenders for implementing large-scale projects. Under the circumstances, the Minister of Construction requested help from the Minister of Finance to enable domestic banks to provide Korean construction companies that win bids with credit guarantee without collateral. To this, the minister responded that they would rather make such offers on an individual basis as opposed to unconditional offers to all companies. Finally, this issue was settled with the intervention of President Park, who forced the hand of the Minister of Construction by saying that considering the conservative attitude of banks, it is likely that selective payment guarantee may prove to be an impediment to the advancement of construction companies to the Middle East. Thus, the path was opened for banks to provide credit guarantees without collateral for high-risk overseas construction businesses.

Despite the extremely challenging climatic and working conditions, South Korean companies and their employees gave a very good account of themselves. Strong entrepreneurship by businessmen like Chung Ju-yung and diligence and professional work ethic of laborers endeared them to the folks in the region. Surprised at the discipline and diligence of the laborers, rumors circulated in some of the Middle Eastern countries that they were conscripts masquerading as civilians. It was understandable given that the construction process was a grueling around-the-clock operation. I daresay this observation was not entirely farfetched if you consider that nearly every able-bodied male Korean must go through the mandatory military service program. Moreover, it is entirely plausible that some of them may have gone through the battlefield experience of Vietnam. They also accumulated construction skills honed from working on construction of the Kyungbu Highway.

The work ethic of the South Korean construction companies and workers became the subject of several anecdotal references. The most stunning is the so-called torchlight legend effect in the Kingdom of Saudi Arabia. The story goes that Samhwan Construction Inc. was responsible for the implementation of the first beautification project in Jeddah. One day, about a month after the project had begun in September 1974, the mayor of Jeddah requested that the project be completed by December 20 when the annual hajj was set to begin. Samhwan responded to this demand by beginning to work at night using torch lights. The use of numerous torches had the effect of creating a scenic landscape. Having never seen such a sight, this procession soon became the talk of the town among the residents of Jeddah. One day, King Faisal happened to come across this procession. Deeply impressed by what he saw, he ordered that more projects be given to these people who worked so hard and with such earnestness. Saudi newspapers picked up this story, which has since become known as the "torchlight legend."[21]

In 1976, Hyundai Engineering & Construction Co. Ltd. obtained a $940 million contract to construct a port in the Saudi city of Jubail, which is equivalent to half of the national budget of Korea. The project was the largest scale work that companies of developing countries cannot dream of. The path to the contract and its implementation was adventurous. The Saudi government had a short list that included nine world-class construction enterprises. Hyundai joined the bid late. The scope of the Jubail harbor work included construction of the bank revetment (7,900 m) and breakwater (1,680 m) and a rock wall to build the landing stage for vessels. The rock walls varied in scale from 6 meters deep and 550 meters long to 14 meters deep and 2,350 meters long.

The most difficult part is construction of a landing stage capable of accommodating 300,000-ton oil tankers, which requires a rock wall of some 30 meters in depth. Thus, a 30-meter deep OSTT (Open Sea Tanker Terminal) capable of simultaneously housing four 300,000-ton oil tankers should be constructed some 12 kilometers off the coast. Hyundai had no experience of under-the-sea construction work at all. The actual construction involved wedging some 660 concrete piles 1–2 meters in diameter in water 30 meters deep. As will be referred to in Section 6.3, Hyundai succeeded in the contract, and over the 2-year period in which the OSTT project was completed, some 1.1 million cubic meters of concrete mix and an average of 1,500–2,000 cubic meters of concrete casting were used daily. This amount in turn required the use of 500 8-ton trucks every day. All in all, 104,000 tons of steel were used to produce the steel structure. This project used 200 full-time technicians and managers from the fields of civil engineering, architecture, machinery and facilities including skilled workers from 100 different fields daily, which is a historic performance.[22] With the exception of the personnel assigned to the production and transportation structures in Korea and in terms of total labor devoted to Saudi Arabia, a total of 2.5 million persons worked on these projects.[23] This was an incredibly exceptional feat to be carried out by a country such as Korea under the kind of conditions it had to work. The world derided Hyundai when it submitted the bidding, and the world was surprised when Hyundai completed the construction work.

The entrepreneurship demonstrated by several businessmen was possible in the environment of diligence and hard work of the laborers. One of the laborers dispatched to Saudi Arabia recalls the situation this way:

> I was recruited in competition against 5 other candidates. My sole reason for going to that hot desert terrain was for financial reasons so that I could marry. For the opportunity to earn money, I had to bet even my life. The temperature there was 48 to 50 degrees Celsius. Work started at 6 AM, and I used to work for 13–14 hours to receive allowances for overtime work.

Hardship and diligence were not limited to blue-collar workers, but to white-collar workers as well. At that time, several general trading companies were established to facilitate trade between Korea and the Middle East. The only medium of communication between Korea and Saudi Arabia was telex. A staff working for a general trading company recalls:[24]

> Due to the 8-hour time difference between the two regions, I had to come to the office at 1 or 2 AM daily to respond to the telex. My counterparts on

the other side of Saudi Arabia used to ask, "Are you working for living, or are you living for working?"

Faced with great demand of construction works in the Middle East by entrepreneurship and hard work, there arose a shortage of skilled technicians. Due to the sudden growth of demand in skilled labors, Korea could not have enough skilled technical personnel to match the huge Middle Eastern demand. The few available ones attracted enormous competition from recruiters. To address this problem, a special course was instituted in the technical high schools to foster artisans for the overseas construction market. The second-year students in the special course had been trained through rigorous program of day and night sessions running 800 hours of work. Two thousand artisans were dispatched to the Middle East through this program.

Thanks to the active support of the government, construction companies and laborers chalked up a great deal of success in the Middle East market. Korean companies started from road construction and later entered more sophisticated technical civil engineering projects such as the construction of harbors and major plants. In all there were nearly 2.5 million Korean laborers who participated in the Middle Eastern construction boom. The "oil dollars" accounted for 75 percent of Korea's foreign exchange reserves at its peak.[25] The revenue breakdown was $89 million in 1974, followed by $751 million in 1975, then in 1976 a whopping $2.429 trillion, in 1977 $3,387 trillion and $7.982 billion in 1978.[26] Here is a classic case of Korea's sojourn, dispatching its young men to toil in the sweltering heat of the desert to rake in hard currency. This was coupled with the contribution of the teenage women in the garment industry to provide for their households, and in an instant the economic lot of the country was transformed.

Notes

1 O Won-chol, *The Construction of Pyramid-Type Export-Oriented Industries* (Seoul, Korea: Korea Type Economic Policy Institute, 2003), 13–14 [in Korean].
2 O Won-chol, *The Korea Story: President Park Jung-hee's Leadership and the Korean Industrial Revolution* (Seoul, Korea: Wisdom Tree, 2009), 78–91.
3 Cho Kap-jae, *Bakjeonghui 6: Han unmyeongjeok inganui naseong* [Park Chung-hee Series 6] (Seoul, Korea: Jaeil Printing, 2007), 6, 269–270.
4 Korea Engineering Club, *Joguk geundae juyeokdeul* [The Heroes of "Quantum Jump"] (Seoul, Korea: Quiparang Press, 2014), 102.
5 *Geullwik aupeu! Dogil-lo gan gyeongje yeokgundeul* [Glück Auf! The Economic Forces That Went to Germany]. Live Broadcast. Directed by Sang-wook Park 박상욱 (Seoul, Korea: KBS, 2013), accessed August 7, 2017, www.kbs.co.kr/1tv/sisa/docucinema/view/vod/2151999_66621.html
6 *Ibid.*
7 *Ibid.*
8 Paik Young-hun, *Joguk geundaehwa-ui eondeokeseo* [On the Hill of Modernization of My Fatherland] (Seoul: Mind and Thinking, 2014), 77–86.
9 O, *The Korea Story*, 84–85.
10 *Padokgwangbu 50junyeon teukjip – padok geu hu, 50 nyeon* [50 Anniversary of Dispatch of Korean Mine-Workers to West-Germany]. TV Special (Seoul, Korea:

MBC, December 16, 2013), accessed August 7, 2017, www.imbc.com/broad/tv/culture/mbcspecial/vod/

11 *Glück Auf*, KBS.

12 O, *The Korea Story*, 431–450.

13 O, *Economic Construction 7*.

14 Kim Sung-jin, *Bakjeonghuireul malhada (geu-ui gaehyeok jeongchi, geurigogwaingchungseong)* [Speaking of Park Chung-hee: His Political Reform and Excessive Loyalty] (Seoul: Life and Dream, 2006), 270.

15 *Choecho haeoepabyeong beteunamjeon* [First Overseas Deployment in the Vietnam War]. Internet Broadcast. Directed by Lee Sang-ik (Seoul, Korea: KBS, 2013), accessed August 7, 2017, www.kbs.co.kr/1tv/sisa/docucinema/view/vod/2160942_66621.html

16 For details, please refer to O, *Economic Construction 6*, 431–484, and *Samak-eseo geumeul kaeda* [Dig Gold in the Desert]. TV Documentary. Directed by Lee Hee-jung, KBS, October 12, 2013, accessed August 7, 2017, www.kbs.co.kr/1tv/sisa/docucinema/view/vod/2192548_66621.html

17 Kim Chung-yum, *From Despair to Hope: Economic Policymaking in Korea 1945–1979* (Seoul, Korea: Korea Development Institute, 2011), 434.

18 In OECD countries during the same period, wholesale prices increased by 49.3 percent, and in four Southeast Asian countries they rose 80.6 percent. See O, *The Korea Story*, 323–326.

19 O, *The Korea Story*, 342.

20 *Suchul 100eokbul, hangang-ui gijeokeul iruda* [The Han's 10-Billion-Dollar Miracle of Exports]. Directed by Lee Chang-joon (Seoul, Korea: KBS, 2013), accessed August 7, 2017, www.kbs.co.kr/1tv/sisa/docucinema/view/vod/2167130_66621.html

21 *Ibid*.

22 *Ibid*.

23 *Ibid*.

24 *The Han's 10-Billion-Dollar Miracle of Exports*, KBS.

25 Moon Gab-sik, "Icheojin aegukja chungdong geullojadeul chulcheo" [Middle Eastern Workers are Forgotten Patriots], *Chosun Ilbo*, September 1, 2015, accessed August 7, 2017, http://news.chosun.com/site/data/html_dir/2015/08/31/2015083103351.html

26 O, *The Korea Story*, 370.

5 Path to industrialization (1)
Paving the way to industrialization

1 Industrialization and economic development

Exporting labor is by no means a sustainable approach to spurring economic growth and with that achieving significant gains in poverty reduction. As readers could perhaps glean from the preceding chapter, it is mostly industries that are disproportionately clustered within the so-called 3D (dangerous, dirty and difficult) that have openings for cheap labor exports. So, when considered from the long-term perspective, the nation's policymakers, given these nagging realities, had to confront the lingering question of what it would take to achieve real long-term sustainable development. Agriculture and developing a manufacturing industrial sector were two immediate but rather remarkably diametrically opposed options from which it had to choose. Because the nation was still reeling under tenuous food security challenges, the reasoning was that the future of the nation could not be conceived in disregard of agricultural development. Moreover, the agricultural sector was by far the only viable industry. Conventional wisdom would thus dictate that when confronted with dilemmas, your instincts should lead you to placing your best foot forward. Of course, historically, industrial development was largely carried out on the back of primitive accumulation of capital through the agricultural sector.

Whatever choice was made had to be tempered with how to deploy the required means to bring it to fruition. These choices had to be viewed against the backdrop of the prevailing sentiment of the time. The most resonant development narrative in the development field, be it academia, donors or by extension the Multilateral Development Banks (MDBs) was the unflinching belief in the policy of balanced or harmonized growth. It was also argued that for a very poor country such as Korea, the most feasible development path out of poverty was to vigorously pursue agricultural development. This argument in and of itself had some degree of traction – after all, a country that could be barely feed itself would do itself a great favor by learning to prioritize the bread-and-butter issues of its hungry populations.

This view of the development conundrum reeks of an overly simplified reading of a complexly intertwined phenomenon. There was also a great deal of conflation of disparate social, economic and political matrices. On this occasion, as in several other instances, the government chose to turn conventional wisdom on its head. Based on its own internal assessment, which skeptics would have called very foolhardy, a conscious decision was made to opt for industrialization instead of investing in agricultural development. Call it a pragmatic decision that was informed by the exigencies of its long-term sustainability needs; the government reasoned that there was no way agriculture could provide a viable path for economic growth to a nation with a sprawling population confined to a small arable landmass. Only 22.9 percent of the country's total land was arable. Besides, there were no natural resources to speak of. Furthermore, the agricultural sector tends to be subject to decreasing returns of scale unlike the manufacturing sector. Conversely, the manufacturing sector, given the right amount of capital and technological investment, can facilitate an unlimited productivity capacity. These considerations did eventually put to rest any doubts about the resolve to pursue industrial development.

On the substantive question of how to bring that about, neoclassical economic theories generally contend that the invisible hand of the market and other related market forces foster the organic growth of industries. Based on that premise, artificial interventionist measures to spur the development of industries can be counterintuitive to say the least. It is an argument rooted in the history of industrial development in Western Europe. History in some ways bears this fact out. It is true that the advent of small firms in segmented and small markets coincided with the era of rudimentary transportation and communication systems. As the Industrial Revolution ushered in a dispensation of rapid mechanization in mass transportation and rapid communication systems, it opened opportunities for markets to expand and with it the exponential growth of firms. What this did was introduce a new era of competition where the economic foxes of economic efficiency ate the lame ducks of inefficiency by unleashing large-scale production. Under such conditions, governments can reasonably take a back seat and let the market sort things out.

The obsession with the market's omnipotent capacity to ensure the growth of industries and enterprises still reigns supreme in the corridors of the Western-led development cooperation mind-set. It is a thinking that has obvious and significant implications for many of today's developing countries and their bid to develop resourceful industrial bases. There seems to be a tone-deaf overlook of the circumstances confronting contemporary developing countries and how that patently differs from those that Western economies had to deal with in their own early march toward industrial development.

A good example is the asymmetric environment that defines the conduct of business in the current era of unbridled globalization. Take the case of a budding enterprise in a developing country and the primitive conditions with which it must operate coming up against a giant multinational enterprise and the long years of experience under its belt. Such a firm is compelled to skip the early stage of competing with its local peers to gain the maturity it needs to enter the next stage of taking on the so-called Goliath enterprises. Children cannot be reasonably expected to skip the stage of puberty and maturity that comes with adulthood, yet there is always a willful blindness about recognizing this for developing countries. To mitigate this situation, South Korea's policymakers were resolutely determined to allocate government a premium role in the market to facilitate the creation of its own solid industrial base. It was essentially turning the neoclassical logic on its head.

Even with this aspirational goal, developing a formidable manufacturing industrial base can be a very challenging endeavor for developing countries. It will generally take the presence of five factors to achieve industrial development: skilled labor, capital and technology, raw materials, entrepreneurship and a market. In South Korea's case, it had very little skilled labor to speak of, understandably because of the limited job opportunities by which people could accumulate the required skills and experience. Capital could hardly be in the equation given that the citizens were barely subsisting, and the least said about technological endowments the better. The peninsula's security and geopolitical uncertainty offered no real incentive for entrepreneurism to flourish. The domestic market did not inspire any form of confidence, as folks were literally living on the breadline and could barely come up with any disposable income to facilitate consumption.

Moreover, the peremptory impositions of the Cold War worked with the geographic conditions to keep the country isolated. The North was a de facto no-go area, and coupled with the fact that diplomatic ties with Japan had been severed, South Korea was also technically out of reach. Under such circumstances, industrial development did not appear to be a viable option. There were real concerns about how such a country could become a manufacturing hub within its own region, much less becoming competitive far afield. There was also an ingrained widespread perception among the Korean masses that manufacturing goods for export required skill sets that were innately or exclusively that of Japanese or Western industrial nations.

In confounding its critics as well as its own skeptical domestic population, the government of Korea could resolutely pursue its aspiration of building an industrial development program, enhance the growth of a vibrant export base and ultimately wrestle down poverty. How these goals were achieved simultaneously and concurrently will remain the core theme of this book.

Figure 5.1 illustrates comprehensive steps of the evolution of development in the garment industry. At the very bottom is the basic processing, such as dying and sewing using imported garments. From processing, it needs to move upward to garment manufacturing for higher value added, then to synthetic fiber and finally the incorporation of petrochemicals for the same reason. Throughout the whole process, research and development (R&D), and machinery and plants are required to design and manufacture the products. The final products rely on petrochemical products as its main raw material. Manufacturing final consumption goods is called light industry, and manufacturing raw materials of steel, petrochemicals and machines is called heavy and petrochemical industry. Therefore, starting from the light industry, industrialization generally reaches maturation with the development of heavy and chemical industries. Once started, it should be rapidly accelerated.

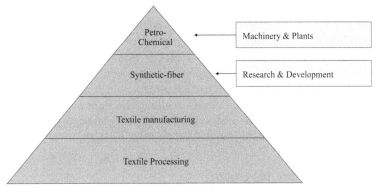

Figure 5.1 Industrial pyramid
Source: O Won-chol (2009), *The Korea Story*, p. 53

Female manual workers generally tend to dominate the first stage of the textile processing industry.[1] Once at this level, a country may want to rapidly accelerate its ascent because generally the low level has a very marginal level of value added, which naturally offers negligible economic returns. Sustaining or even enhancing upward mobility requires significant capital investment and technology. Industrialization is the process of stepping up the ladder of the industrial pyramid. An economy qualifies to be declared an industrialized state once it reaches the top of the pyramid. Only a handful of economies have achieved that exalted status. It is especially so among the clear majority of the post-colonial states born after World War II.

President Park, as development minded as he was, predicated his development plan for the country on the establishment and nurturing of enterprises to facilitate the country's rise on the industrial pyramid. German economist Walther Hoffmann proposed the use of quantitative grades to denote the different levels of industrial development in 1935 under the so-called Hoffmann coefficient. A country with a grade of 6.5–3.5 was said to be in the first stage of industrial development. At that level, the country is presumed to have already established its textile and food industry. In the next stage of growth, which is 3.5–1.5, a country is said to have moved up to the second rung of the development ladder. Then comes the 1.5–0.5 stage, characterized by the presence of machinery and metal industries. The final stage is below 0.5, which is the part that fits the bill of an industrial state.[2]

Taking cognizance of the fact that the development from the first to fourth industrial state is a revolutionary change, Walther Hoffmann (1931) called it the Industrial Revolution. The Hoffmann coefficient of South Korea in 1960 was 4.26, which means it was at the first stage, where industrial development was almost at its infancy.[3] To support industrialization, it is imperative to ensure the five factors of skilled labor, capital and technology, resources, entrepreneurship and market are conducive for industrial development. However, having all these conditions is not always a given, as experience has shown time and again. Those conditions will be enhanced in the market by independent efforts of economic agents if the market for trading goods and services is established. The most important thing is to establish an efficient market in which there is a free flow of goods and people. Getting that requires building the right infrastructure. This chapter will deal with these two issues, and the following chapters pick up the rest of the issues of labor, technology and development financing.

2 Laying down the pavement

Facing seemingly insurmountable odds in its quest to get a head start in poverty reduction, this fragile state had to figuratively drill through a hill to create a road. This drilling had to take place in two areas – externally and internally. The external drilling was to unclog the road with the rest of the world, beginning with neighboring Japan. To put this into perspective, China was the main trading partner of the Koreans, but that was to change with the partitioning of the peninsula. Thus, South Korea was territorially cut off from accessing an important traditional trading outpost. Without diplomatic relations with neighboring Japan, South Korea was effectively isolated within this region.

The second part was a literal one. There was an urgent need to address the country's chronic dearth of infrastructure, a task not made any easier by the mountainous terrain across the peninsula. That such massive infrastructure investment requires hefty capital and technological investment was not lost on the idealistic policymakers at the helm of affairs. For a country virtually on its knees to conceive of such ambitious moves was seen at the time to be misguided, to say the least. That was to be the case nonetheless.

A memorable meeting was held on December 8, 1964 in Bonn, West Germany, between President Park and Chancellor Ludwig Wilhelm Erhard, the man credited for championing the post-war reconstruction campaign of West Germany. President Park had arrived hat in hand to West Germany to arrange for a concessional loan of $30 million (approximately DM 140 billion). According to Paik Young-hun, the official interpreter at the bilateral meeting, President Park had this to say to his German counterpart: "Your Excellency, believe us. Soldiers do not lie. We are a divided country like Germany. We will rebuild our economy just like the Miracle on the Rhein River and repay this loan."[4] To this, Chancellor Erhard replied:

> Your Excellency, I visited South Korea twice when Syngman Rhee was President. I observed that Korea has a mountainous terrain, which is not conducive for economic development. Excavate the main artery of the land. Germany is also mountainous. In 1932 the Bonn-Cologne Autobahn (freeway) was constructed and Adolf Hitler expanded it to the whole country in

1933, which became the driving force of economic development through the country. Your Excellency will take the historic road. Although a failure in the political arena, Hitler paved the way for economic development. He constructed the Volkswagen plant and the steel plant. Your Excellency should also construct highways to increase automobile transport and then also consider the construction of steel plants. Please also bear with Japan in terms of diplomatic relations. Leaders must look to the future rather than the past.

Then President Park continuously wept as he appealed for the financial support. Then Chancellor Erhard said "Don't cry, please! It will be considered."[5] President Park took to heart three of the key areas Chancellor Erhard admonished him to consider. Impressed by what he saw in West Germany, he also resolved to open the country's industrial arteries through construction of highways and a steel plant.

Normalization of diplomatic relations with Japan

Most importantly, Park was determined to restore diplomatic relations with Japan notwithstanding the hostile domestic sentiments toward the idea. Economic imperatives made the normalization of diplomatic relations with Japan an important foreign policy concern. Beyond the obvious geographic factors, it had to be viewed within the context of the tenuous geopolitical dynamics of this corner of northeast Asia. The geopolitical imperatives weren't just the driving force, but it was almost entirely in the best interest of Seoul to consider a thaw in Tokyo-Seoul relations. To the North of the 38th Parallel was Pyongyang and its ideological allies in the Soviet Union and China, and without Tokyo Seoul had to reckon with continually living in a cocoon in its own neighborhood.

Japan regained its pre-war status as a dominant economic power by taking advantage of its alliance with Washington. Beyond the sticky diplomatic questions, both states alongside the United States shared a formidable economic and political framework – their common adherence to the liberal economic ideologies. Despite the burden of the colonial relations, there was a real economic incentive for Seoul and Tokyo to collaboratively work toward achieving desired mutual interests, especially in bolstering their manufacturing sectors. A few preconditions, if met, the Korean side indicated its willingness to meet Tokyo halfway despite domestic opposition to thawing relations. That included an official apology for the 35 years of colonial exploitation and a corresponding financial compensation for the injuries of the period in question. Exploratory steps were initiated toward finding ways of meeting each other halfway. During the first bilateral meeting in 1951 Tokyo was reluctant to acknowledge any wrongdoing, however, which would in effect incur financial liabilities. It resulted in a major deadlock in the normalization attempts. It remained so until fresh attempts were once again reignited in 1965.

Economic exigencies compelled the Park administration to abandon its initial confrontational stance and adopt a more pragmatic approach to its dealings with Tokyo. A new sense of urgency was injected into the negotiation process. As the principal ally of both Japan and Korea, Washington was also in support of overcoming the diplomatic hurdles between the two states. Domestic public opinion was starkly opposed to a rush to normalizing ties without meeting the condition of expression of genuine penitence from Japan. Negotiations resumed on March 24, 1964, after a 14-month hiatus. There was palpable nationwide opposition to the bilateral negotiations. Beginning with a slew of student protesters chanting "We are against the humiliating Korea–Japan Summit," it soon galvanized action from civic groups and opposition parties.

Public opposition swelled into a massive public demonstration of nearly 12,000 college students on the streets of Seoul on June 3, 1964. Feeling uneasy, the government declared martial law and deployed troops across the city. Schools were closed to preempt any attempts by student activists to congregate and rally against the negotiations. Dissidents were rounded up and jailed without due process.[6] The regime's survival became seriously threatened. So, opposition was quelled by force, paving the way for the negotiations to proceed. Then diplomatic relations between the two countries were officially restored in June 1965.

Yet the stickiest issue remained the question of liabilities claimed against Japan. They negotiated a comprise that Korea would receive reparation for damages for the entire 36 years of colonization, a $300 million grant and $200 million credit assistance to be received through scheduled annual meetings from 1966 to 1975. The funds were to be invested in the import of raw materials and agricultural development.[7] The outcome of the negotiations did not satisfy many within the Korean public, especially on some specific questions. Whatever the conditions might be, the Korea–Japan negotiations could never satisfy everyone. Japan adamantly refused to concede any moral wrongdoing, and the sum paid was absurdly small if valued in terms of the bloodshed of the victims of Japan's imperial aggression in Korea. The Korean government also barred individual claims against the Japanese government as one of the conditions for the agreement. It was undercutting the legitimate claims of wrongdoing suffered by individuals and families under the vicious colonial project, a decision that did not sit well at home. Furthermore, there was an irascible public sentiment toward the government's kowtowing to the Japanese government's unwillingness to offer a formal apology; a tough sell, in every conceivable way.

The successful negotiations eventually heralded a new dawn in Korea–Japan relations. Viewed objectively, it marked a critical stage in South Korea's active engagement with the rest of the world, and with it the commercial impetus to its economic development. Korea invested much of the money for national development as opposed to spending on individual claims. The reason behind this decision was to ensure that the money would leave a lasting collective national legacy rather than individual settlements that may not have a significant impact on the economy. Viewed as a sort of blood money, the government reasoned that the fund should serve the public interest instead of settling individual claims, and be used to avoid the risk of dissipation through mismanagement. For the usage of the fund, Japan argued that South Korea should import consumption goods from Japan because Korea could not conceivably engage in industrial-scale production. To this, Seoul countered that it would import producers' goods to facilitate economic development. Thus, 26.5 percent of the fund was allocated for import of producers' goods, 4.4 percent for construction of the Soyang River Dam, and 23.9 percent for the construction of an integrated steel plant, Pohang Steel Co. (POSCO). The Philippines and Indonesia also received reparations from Tokyo, but their leadership chose the easy path of short-term gratification and sometimes literal ostentatious comfort for the elite rather than making the necessary long-term investments in development.[8]

The inflow of the funds was a figurative form of much-needed rainfall on a dry land. It also paved the way for the inflow of foreign capital into the economy. There was also an important dimension to the thawing relations with Japan that went beyond the monetary compensation. The new opening for economic exchanges provided opportunities to learn and acquire new technologies, capital goods and managerial know-how, and boosted the so-called phenomenon of learning by doing. Limitless opportunities were consequently opened for succeeding generations through this singular decision of the government. A significant portion of the fund was used primarily on national projects such as the new steel plant. The initial plan was supporting development of the agricultural sector, which was replaced with construction of the steel mill as a national edifice.[9] When cooperation projects were underway using the claim fund, the Korean government faced failure in securing an international loan for construction of a steel plant. Being determined to construct the steel plant, President Park decided to use the remaining claim fund from Japan for the steel mill plan.

Construction of Kyungbu Highway

As Chancellor Erhard of West Germany rightly admonished President Park during their meeting in Bonn, highway infrastructure constitutes an indispensable conduit for economic activities. It can be compared to the economic artery of the body in terms of how it allows for the circulation of blood through all parts of the body. Even at the height of the Cold War, the issue of highways came up during Soviet Premier Nikita Khrushchev's infamous visit to the United States in 1959 to meet President Dwight Eisenhower. Premier Khrushchev visited Los Angeles and witnessed how the spider-web-shaped highways provided a smooth traffic flow for the different ranges of vehicular traffic plying the multiple routes. Being so impressed by the highway network in the United States, Premier Khrushchev wishfully said that the only things to import from the United States were highways, Disneyland and Jacqueline Kennedy.[10] He developed a new appreciation for the role of highways as major arteries of economic development.

Having returned from the trip to West Germany, President Park became so fixated on how to replicate the remarkable German Autobahn in Korea. After mulling over the issue for a year, he quietly devised ways of constructing similar freeways in Korea. To secure justification for highway construction, the Korean government entrusted the World Bank in 1965 to conduct a study of Korea's transportation system. Contrary to the expectation of the Korean government, the World Bank consulting report in 1966 tacitly made no mention of the importance of highways in the nation's infrastructure vector. It is hard to fault the experts, considering the rudimentary capacity, poor equipment and construction technology, and low demand for rapid transportation in the country.

However, contrary to the international experts' counsel, the government went ahead to announce plans for the Kyungbu Highway construction project in 1968. According to the plan, the highway was envisaged to connect Seoul and Busan – a distance of 428 kilometers. The most viable option for financing the project was through procuring foreign loans. But that was not forthcoming because many of the leading creditors did not consider the project to be an economically viable investment, in addition to the fact that the government lacked the required technical capacity to embark on such a grand project.

Back then, only a handful of individuals owned cars, and most of the existing fleet were imported secondhand cars. Opposition party leaders even went as far as to describe the construction as a ploy to provide paved roads to enable the rich elite to travel conveniently on their weekend picnics in the countryside. In fact, maverick opposition leaders Kim Young-sam and Kim Dae-jung took the extraordinary action of lying on the construction sites, daring the construction crew to "run over me and trample me under your feet if you want to continue the construction."[11] Later, both became presidents of Korea and enjoyed the outcome of the highway.

Amid massive opposition and public outcry, the groundwork for commencement of work on the construction of the Kyungbu Highway finally took place on February 1, 1968. The project was executed just like a military operation, and President Park situated himself as the commander of the operation. Before the official announcement of the project, he sketched out the scheme of the road line on the map and ordered an evaluation of the cost of the lands that the highway would traverse. Then, he summoned Kim Jae-kyu, the Minister of Construction, and mayors and governors of provinces along the route of the highway to finish purchase of the land within a week, adding that the unit price of the land ranges KRW 170–180 per 3.3 square meters, but the budget would be KRW 300. The projects then commenced after paying the landlords.

Thirteen local construction companies were awarded the contract including Hyundai, whose Chairman Chung Ju-yung took charge of 40 percent of the construction sector. For auditing and supervision, young engineering military officials were mobilized. The construction sites were literally mountains, rivers and rice paddies that offered no realistic construction prospects. To meet the completion schedule, the construction crew worked day and night. Poor safety practices as a direct result of large-scale construction inexperience resulted in several fatal accidents on the site. Chung Tae-soo, the deputy manager of Hyundai Construction Co. recalls: "During the project, I slept only 24 days at home for a year. My wife can testify to it. Most employees worked that way."[12]

In the end, the Kyungbu Highway was formally completed and launched to pomp and pageantry on July 7, 1970, to link Seoul and Busan. In all, it took a

Figure 5.2 Kyungbu Highway. The route of the Kyungbu Highway as shown on the map of South Korea

Source: © Korea Road Agency

period of 2 years and 5 months to complete the entire 428-kilometer stretch between the two metropolises. The original estimate of the construction cost was KRW 35 billion, which was increased to KRW 42.9 billion due to frequent changes in construction design and increased cost in raw materials. Funding for the project was procured from revenues from gasoline taxes, traveling taxes, sales revenue from grain loan and squeezing of the national budget. The total construction cost of KRW 42.9 billion was equivalent to 23.6 percent of the total national budget in 1967. However, the unit cost per kilometer was just KRW 100 million, representing one-eighth of the cost of the Tomei-Meishin Expressway in Japan.[13]

Picture 5.1 President Park Chung-hee at the opening of Kyungbu Highway. President Park Chung-hee is praying for the repose of the departed 77 souls during the Kyungbu High Way construction work

©ehistory.go.kr

Thus, the Seoul-Busan Highway was thus completed at a relatively lower cost in the shortest period using only Korean technology and at a cost of 77 casualties.[14] The World Bank later rescinded its initial stance on financing projects in Korea after the country had confounded the skeptics by completing the project in record time. From initially questioning the financial feasibility of the project, the World Bank was now resigned to supporting future programs.[15]

Thus, the ultimate economic impact of the highway construction was enormous. Since its opening in 1970, the highway represented a symbol of the nation's steps toward modernity, and in many ways was an unprecedented feat. It opened other vital economic areas of the country by promoting inter-regional mobility of goods, services and people in ways that exceeded the initial projected gains.[16] The highway further allowed for greater openness of the country, as people could then travel for tourism and cultural openness. In addition, the logistical efficiency of industries was boosted greatly because most industrial complexes were placed within 15 kilometers of the highway. On the cenotaph at Chupung-ryung are inscribed the names of the 77 people who sacrificed their lives for the construction of this highway.

3 Industrial policy and development of small and medium enterprises

Strategic support to industrial development

In the previous section, we read of how the country's post-war conditions were aptly described as a literal wasteland and incapable of supporting industrial growth. South Korea's industrial development process can further be described through the traditional agrarian process a farmer goes through before cultivation. It begins with preparing the land for cultivation, sowing seeds, allowing for watering the seeds either through irrigation or rain, the growth of the plant, management and harvesting. In a metaphorical sense, paving the way for industrialization can be likened to preparing the land before sowing the seeds, but instead of seeds we have industries that are set up and guided to grow to maturity.

Here too, the government had to deviate from the neoclassical orthodoxy in building its industrial base. There was the usual talk of the omnipotent power of the markets to set things going. In fairness, prior to the government's intervention, some firms had already exogenously grown here and there. For instance, the corporate behemoth that Samsung has become today came against a humble background as a rice mill in 1936 under Japanese colonial control; then after several twists and turns the company evolved into a textile and sugar manufacturing firm in the early 1960s. So did Hyundai, which started off as a micro-construction company. There was also a series of minor players engaged in plywood, rubber shoes and textile production, albeit on a small scale. They lacked the commercial acumen to make any real dent in the wider economy in ways that could enhance poverty reduction through employment creation. In an open economy, start-ups have a hard time growing endogenously and becoming formidable enough to compete on the global stage. The start-ups based on the very meager local market often lack the requisite capital and technology, skilled personnel, raw materials and market. The risks and uncertainty can be dauntingly overwhelming. Without some form of external assistance, most will certainly go under in no time. This is the challenge confronting the growth of enterprises in contemporary developing countries.

I like to think of local start-up firms as babies in a family. It takes a man and woman, at least in the traditional sense, to have a baby. The real work begins after a baby is born, when it requires around the clock nurturing and nursing from its parents throughout the growth cycle. This cycle is also punctuated with the possibility of ailments due to their developing immune systems. Even in puberty, parents must still be around to provide guidance to their wards to keep them from straying. This sort of parenting amounts to a worthy investment in the future of a child – one can hardly dispute the possible dividends that accrue in the long term. Parents will be saving themselves the grief of an ill-bred child growing into a misguided adult. Procreation is made complex for couples who go past their reproductive prime. Even if they do procreate, there are possible medical complications for mother and child. The physical drain that comes with parenting may just be too exhausting for aging parents.

It is the same way that my analogy of parenting, especially for aged parents, succinctly describes just how developing countries strive to develop industries. Industries or enterprises in a national economy cannot be born of their own accord. As a baby is born through the procreative process of a man and a woman, with the birth pain of labor by the woman, so should enterprises in developing countries be born and nurtured to grow through the combination of private entrepreneurship and government backing. Enterprises cannot grow by themselves. It requires government's support of incubating, securing financial accessibility and exploitation of markets, as babies require their mother's care in early infancy. I further say, just like a baby is the future of a family, so are enterprises the future of any economy seeking to thrive. On this premise, there is something to be said about the government taken the utmost onus of bringing this about.

We see that role of effective parenting along the full life cycle of a child fully expressed in how President Park's administration steadily steered the full course of moving the country from a start-up state toward a blossoming industrial hub. The government of Korea under the oversight of President Park pursued a stepwise strategy for the development of industries and enterprises, as Figure 5.3 illustrates.

The first stage started with the setting up of target industries to receive resourceful nurturing. Based on an analysis of resource endowment and of national demand for industries, the government established a comprehensive long-term strategy for industrial development. Setting up target industries is far from being comprehensive at an early stage. In the infant stage of industrial development, focus was given to the development of import-substitution and consumption-goods industries. Over time, it transitioned from import to export promotion,

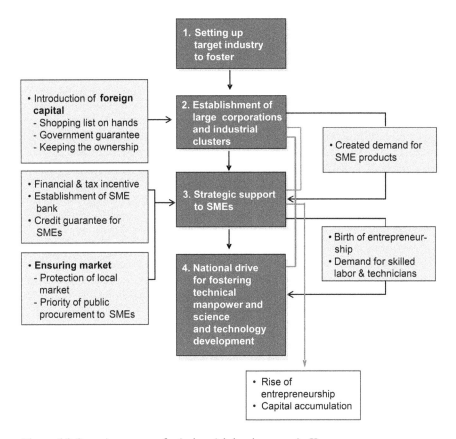

Figure 5.3 Stepwise strategy for industrial development in Korea

Source: Chun et al. (2008), *Building the Foundation for the Development of SMEs in Ghana*, Ministry of Strategy and Finance and KDI, 2008, 55

from labor-intensive to capital and technology-intensive industries, then from light to heavy and petrochemical industries, respectively.

This stage was characterized by the fostering of garment and low-end electronic goods, which were later replaced by steel, machinery, petrochemicals, automobiles and shipbuilding, high-end electronic goods and semiconductor chip industries. The Ministry of Industry and Trade (MIT), in collaboration with the planning and budgeting authority of the Economic Planning Board (EPB), drafted the plan that highlighted the target industries. The plan was then elaborated and incorporated into the regular national Five-Year Economic Development Plans. With this plan, two principal objects were achieved: (1) providing a comprehensive guide for the government's investment and support policies and (2) inducing private sector investment in the target industries. It goes without saying that back then the private sector was inclined to channel its investments in accordance with the government's future development plans.

At the second stage, large corporations and industrial clusters were established in a close cooperation between the government and the private sector. Through the first stage, the private sector understands the direction of industrial development the government is going to foster, and they adjust their plan for investment in those industries. Long-term, large-scale investment is difficult to take place without the support or commitment of the government. Policy changes pose significant threats to long-term investments by private firms. It explains why collaboration between government and the private sector remains an indispensable facet of economic development. This fact has largely been at the heart of the industrial policies of East Asia, particularly in Japan and South Korea. This captures the treacherous sojourn of the nation's powerful corporations. At this stage, the government engages in establishment of large corporations, financing schemes, preparation of industrial clusters and protection of the market for those corporations.

The first step for large corporations and industrial clusters is to take legislative processes to guide and support a specific industry. The Korean government established acts regulating individual industries: among some of the notable examples are the Machinery Industry Promotion Act (1967), the Shipbuilding Industry Promotion Act (1967), the Temporary Measure for Textile Industry Facility (1967), the Electronics Industry Promotion Act (1969), the Petrochemical Industry Promotion Act (1970), the Steel Industry Fostering Act (1970), the Nonferrous Metal Smelting Act (1971) and the Textile Industry Promotion Act (1979). The legislation defined the regulations on entry, government policy review committees, the establishment of R&D institutions and the establishment of specific business associations.

The policy review committee was usually constituted of government officials, private experts in the specific field and business representatives. Most policies were prepared within the committee through close dialogue among the public and private sector representatives. To avoid excessive competition among local firms in a small market, the government typically reserved permission for entry to a specific industry by law. Overcompetition in the small market may result in the scrambling of firms with no international competitiveness. To avoid this, the government controlled the entry of firms. For instance, the assembly plants of automobiles, like Hyundai Motors and Kia Motors, were established through permission of the Ministry of Industry and Trade under the auspices of the Automobile Industry Supporting Act.

Second, financing is a prerequisite for start-ups and fostering industries. In most cases, it requires large and long-term investment that the private sector couldn't offer. It had a lot to do with a severe dearth in domestic financing capacities, which tended to lag the demand. It was at this point that the Korea Development Bank (KDB), established in 1954, was set up as a state lender to serve this niche of long-term financing for industrial development. The government was also keen to attract significant foreign capital to supplement its pool.

Yet faced with the reality of the extraordinary risks and high stakes in Korea, foreign investors were generally put off. A desperate government, undeterred by the challenges, resorted to what was quite frankly considered to be desperate policy measures, the notable one being acting as the guarantor of the foreign loans domestic companies procured from foreign financial institutions. While providing the private sector with the latitude to invest in target areas, it briskly stepped in with public funds to supplement the areas where the private sector investment could not conceivably make inroads.

This interest in foreign investment notwithstanding, the government ostensibly was keen to restrict entry to specific industries and technological fields. Koreans also had to maintain controlling stakes in all domestic industries. In fact, several multinational automobile firms attempted to build their own plants in Korea, which were kept out to protect domestic enterprises, as was discussed in Section 7.4 for automobile parts. It was within this protective shield that the likes of Hyundai Motors, Hyundai Heavy Industry and Samsung Electronics could thrive. Chapter 9 will provide an exhaustive discussion of this matter.

Third, Korean firms also received government backing through the establishment of industrial clusters or complexes. A plan was set off toward this end with adequate legislative backing including the creation of public corporations to manage these industrial complexes. A case in point is the automobile industry, which benefited from the establishment of the Ulsan Industrial Complex to serve Hyundai Motors and other manufacturing firms to supply parts and intermediate goods. The industrial clusters or corporations thus established required continued support by the government.

Fourth, the domestic market was also protected by import restrictions. The newly born, less competitive companies could not compete with multinational automobile firms on price and quality. In the early days, the government restricted import of foreign cars, and in later days when direct restriction became inappropriate, sometimes it imposed invisible restrictions such as watching the owners of luxurious foreign cars by the tax authorities. However, these invisible restrictions were completely released soon due to trade friction in later days. There were also times when domestic corporations had to resort to low pricing as a way of leveraging entry into the international market. Were that to happen, they were offered a compensatory differential of high domestic prices to enable them to go beyond the breakeven mark. Every effort was put in place to secure not just the birth but the survival of domestic enterprises in the ruggedly competitive international market.

The third stage of industrial development is strategic support to small and medium-sized enterprises (SME). In fact, at the second stage, in the case of the automobile industry we merely established the assembly line. A typical automobile consists of 20,000–30,000 parts working jointly to enable optimum functionality. Going by this, these different parts produced by the SMEs ultimately determine the competitiveness of an automobile. In a sense, the establishment of large corporations might be easy compared with SME development. The former may be constructed with introduction of foreign capital without local technological capacity. Yet in our case, the establishment of large corporations at the second stage created a market for SMEs. A resulting spillover effect was the birth of more industries and an invigoration of domestic entrepreneurial spirit. This issue will be fully taken up in the next section. The rise of large corporations and SMEs paved the way for employment creation through the demand for skilled labor and technicians. How to foster SMEs will be discussed in the following section.

The fourth stage is national drive for fostering technical manpower and science and technology development. Like the baby metaphor used in the opening stage of this section, this boils down to whether the baby is sufficiently nourished and supported enough to grow into a functional and capable adult. By the way, the establishment of enterprises and industrial clusters do not by any means constitute a conclusive panacea to the problem. The real elephant in the room is often whether such industries are sufficiently competitive enough to merit their continued operation. In this context, the critical void to fill was the continued flow of competitively world-class standards of labor alongside the corresponding state of technology. This became the fixation of the government at the fourth level of its industrialization drive. Consequently, a robust campaign was unveiled to train and recruit a credible pool of technicians and skilled labor to address the shortage of the technology field. For an exhaustive discussion of these elements, please see Chapter 8.

Thanks to the four steps taken in a stepwise manner herein discussed, this once-upon-a-time land of industrial barrenness evolved into a hub of major global corporations. As has been explained, their success was never an isolated act of fortune but the product of a consistent government initiated and directed stepwise process. In response to the confidence placed in them, the nation's entrepreneurs rolled up their sleeves to make the most of the opportunity to become internationally competitive entities. A highly skilled and disciplined labor force led the charge on the ground in ways that were remarkable in every sense. It seems that the government's anchor, survival instinct of enterprises, and devoted labor force worked together to create a momentum for industry to take root in what was otherwise a wasteland of despondency. And as my caring parent aphorism, I would like to say, at last, the aged parent succeeded in raising healthy children.

SMEs for industrial development

SMEs, together with big corporations, function to enhance the vitality of a national economy. See the national economy as a vast ocean, home to diverse species of flora and fauna of all sizes and shapes coexisting within the maritime ecosystem. Large corporations often tend to be the focus of most economic discussions, in ways that sometimes are oblivious of the critical role of SMEs in enhancing the competitiveness of an economy at the grassroots level. SMEs are vital for competitiveness of a national economy at a grassroots level. Therefore, countries with strong base of SMEs might be prosperous for a long time. SMEs produce parts and intermediate goods such as automobile and electronic parts and some final products like garments and miscellaneous items. SMEs occupy a dominant part in the number of enterprises and employment. Without a strong base of SMEs, neither large corporations nor a national economy can be prosperous. That is why most developing countries are eager to foster SMEs, even though they cannot afford large corporations.

However, SMEs in poverty countries are resigned to operating in very adversarial conditions. One of major difficulties has to do with accessibility to financing, often with ridiculously high interest rates as well as unproductive threshold operational standards. According to World Bank data (2014), the median of the lending interest rates in 23 sub-Saharan African countries is 15.7 percent, while that of the OECD (Organisation for Economic Co-operation and Development) member countries is 2.52 percent.[17] It suggests similar conditions in Korea decades ago, when domestic firms had to contend with domestic interest rates above 20 percent per annum and were still expected to compete against big foreign firms who benefited from interest rates below 5 percent. SMEs also faced the usual problem of a poorly skilled labor pool, lack of access to modern technology, inefficient administrative protocols and above all a bizarre regulatory landscape. Naturally, those circumstances stymied entrepreneurship for start-ups and hindered any realistic growth of SMEs.

It smacks of the same faulty premise of the neoclassical economic orthodoxy of market-centered growth. In a business environment with a small market, with rudimentary technology and entrepreneurship skills, will the market eventually produce SMEs competitive in the international market? How can we conceivably expect anything out of SMEs coming from developing countries operating under the sort of chaotic regulatory and financial system outlined earlier to thrive without realistic state intervention? Unconvinced by the dogmatic impositions of the market, the Korean government went out of its way to actively intervene in supporting the growth of SMEs. There was a consensus that the establishment of a conducive ecosystem was an indispensable part of fostering industrial development. It explains why the second stage of the industrial development process as described in Figure 5.3 was largely dedicated to the fostering of SMEs, after laying the foundation for the large corporations. The establishment of the large corporations provided a good medium to feed the burgeoning SME environment that produced manufacturing parts and intermediate goods.

There is a trend in some developing countries to pursue the development of SMEs without due regard for establishing the supporting ecosystem. Skipping this critical step works to undermine whatever good intentions might be for establishing them in the first place. As explained earlier, the ecosystem creates the platform for large corporations and SMEs to feed off each other in a productive, cyclical process. The government of Korea's answer to this policy dilemma was the establishment of the sort of target industries discussed in the preceding section. Rather than building SMEs, large corporations such as Hyundai Motors, POSCO and Samsung Electronics are products of this policy move.

Taiwan, another Asian high flyer, pursued a reverse policy. It started with prioritizing the creation of SMEs over large corporations. Perhaps it can be explained by the differences in market size and resource endowments between Taiwan and Korea. As for Korea, industrial development based on large corporations was necessary and feasible, and as for Taiwan domestic market size may not allow economies of scale industries based on large corporations. Of course, that is not to say SMEs in Taiwan did not need large corporations for their markets. In fact, that space was filled by large corporations from Japan and multinational corporations (MNCs). In Korea, prior establishment of large corporations provided a good ecosystem for SMEs.

SME management in South Korea was crafted on a robust support policy framework initiated by the government. The policy framework hinged on four principal factors: finance, market access, technology development and human resource development. The SME assistance policy was based on an axiom that "SMEs are like seeds."[18] Horticulturists know well that it takes a great deal of diligent management from the moment of sowing a seed to harvesting it. We are talking about watering the seed, applying fertilizer, weeding and pruning. The government's policy was to SMEs what horticultural processes are to the seed. Blue chip enterprises received a special designation alongside a strict selection and enforcement regimen.

The first task in SME support was how to secure financial access. Due to asymmetry of information, banks were reluctant to provide finance to SMEs. The government instituted a series of measures to address this problem. One such measure was to bring the banking sector under total control of the state, to allow for the state to determine the allocation of financial resources to specific target industries. The second was the establishment of financial institutions to serve the specific needs of SMEs in 1961 under the so-called SME Bank. Under the statute establishing the SME bank, the Minister of Finance was obliged to obtain the consent of the Minister of Trade and Industry (MTI) when appointing the head of the bank. Also, the authority of audit and inspection of the bank was given to the MTI, and its officials participated in the management committee of the bank.

These arrangements aimed to shorten the distance between banks and SMEs, which was until then an enormous development hurdle.[19] Through the bank, the government provided policy loans at a very preferential interest rate in favor of SMEs, whose deficits were compensated by the national budget. Surely in providing policy loans to SMEs, the "selection and concentration" principle was strictly applied. The Korean government thought that only blue chips with potential of international competitiveness deserved the government's favor. To reduce risks of lending by banks and to facilitate finance to SMEs, the Korea Credit Guarantee Reserve Fund (1961) and Korea Technology Credit Guarantee Fund (1989) were established. Supported by these funds, SMEs in Korea could have access to banks more easily without collaterals.

Regarding market availability, several methods were employed to achieve its object.[20] As stated earlier, the establishment of large corporations and industrial clusters created significant market opportunities for SMEs. In addition, the government protected the domestic market from foreign competitors through import regulation and high tariffs. It also barred large corporations from encroaching into the designated business areas reserved for SMEs. In public procurement, SMEs were given priority. KOTRA provided services for corporations to make inroads into overseas markets.

As to technological services, the government helped SMEs break a technological bottleneck by establishing various science and technology institutes including the Korea Institute of Science and Technology (KIST), the Korea Institute of Industrial Technology (KITECH) and the Electronics Technology Research Institute (ETRI). Concessional loans were provided for R&D and various tax and financial incentives to encourage enterprises to boost their R&D interests and programs. All these SME assistance policies were based on the principle of "selection and concentration." Resources and capacity were very limited, and if they were dispersed it would produce few outcomes. Limiting targets to support is politically difficult to enforce. However, as farmers incessantly pull out weeds and weak vegetables to provide a better environment for healthy ones to grow well, so did the Korean government in fostering SMEs.

Let us look at the criteria for selecting beneficiary SMEs. According to the Mining and Industrial Census of Korea in 1963, the total number of SMEs in the manufacturing sector was 18,068. Among them, 90 percent were those with 30 employees or fewer, and the number of those above that level is only 1,973 out of 18,068. The government selected 600 firms out of the 1,973 to support. The reason was that those with more than 30 employees could have potential for international competitiveness. Among those, blue chips were chosen for actual target SMEs to support. Again, the government chose 450 enterprises classified into business categories to foster them as export enterprises. Divided by three stages, 150 firms at each stage, the government provided every effort for them to exploit the export market. Within a year and a half, the plan targeted to foster 450 export enterprises in total. Those enterprises were registered in the Division of Commerce and Industry of cities and provinces and the Korea Federation of Small and Medium Business. The enterprises put up a signboard at their gates – "Enterprise Designated as Manufacturing Export Items." Mayors and governors were to make report on the export performance of those designated SMEs within their jurisdictions.[21]

These SME policies are enforced within the legal and administrative system. Examples include the SME Basic Act (1966), which provided an overall policy framework. Administrative responsibilities were assigned to the Small Business Administration (SMA) and the Small Business Promotion Corporation (SBC). President Park took a personal interest in prioritizing the development of SMEs as a core national development policy. At each local government level, the Department of Commerce and Industry was established and granted the responsibility of administrative services for SMEs. These agencies were all well financed, effectively empowered and filled with personnel with the skills to execute the job. Individual entrepreneurs were encouraged to establish business associations to represent the collective interest of each industry.

Prior development of large corporations had positive as well as negative consequences to SME development and to the Korean economic structure. On the one hand, prior development of large corporations provided a stable market for SMEs, so that the industry could be developed smoothly. However, on the other, it triggered imbalance in development between large corporations and SMEs. Manpower and fund were absorbed by large corporations developed in advance, and large corporations were in a superior position over the SMEs in business relations because the former provided market for the latter. The former forced a lower price against SMEs, and occasionally disconnecting business relations with the latter, which drove the latter to the risk of bankruptcy. Under this environment, SMEs could not share equal opportunities for their growth with large corporations. Thus, SMEs were destined to be shriveled, and polarization of economic power proceeded in favor of large corporations in a small number.

However, through extraordinary resolution, the government had established a foundation for the smooth growth of industries and enterprises. As an aged couple in a poor family tries to have a baby through unusual efforts, and treasures the baby in rearing, so the government cared for its local enterprises. This remarkable transformation of South Korea drew the attention of the international community. As a tribute to this, the cover story of the June 1977 edition of *Newsweek* magazine reported: "The Koreans Are Coming!" It said, "Barely in 25 years after the tragedy of the Korean War, Korea reached the stage of graduating the level of developing countries . . . Koreans are working hard to realize industrial structure and the standard of living as Americans and Japanese." It added that, "The only people in the world to outpace the diligence of the Japanese are the Koreans." Indeed, it testifies that hope is being created from the country of no hope.

Notes

1 O Won-chol, *Hanguk-hyeong gyeongje geonseol 1: Enjinioring eopeurochi* [Korea Type Economic Construction 1: An Engineering Approach] (Seoul, Korea: Korea Type Economic Policy Institute, 1995), 278–279.
2 Walther Hoffmann, *Stadien und Typen der Industialisierung: Ein Beitrag zur quantitativen Analyse historischer Wirtschaftsprozesse* [Stages and Types of Industrialization: A Contribution to the Quantitative Analysis of Historic Economic Processes] (Jena: Fischer, 1931).
3 O Won-chol, *The Construction of Pyramid-Type Export-Oriented Industries* (Seoul, Korea: Korea Type Economic Policy Institute, 2003), 5 [in Korean].
4 Paik Young-hun, *Joguk geundaehwa-ui eondeokeseo* [On the Hill of Modernization of My Fatherland] (Seoul: Mind and Thinking, 2014), 105–110.
5 *Ibid.*, 108–110.
6 Hong Eun-ju, Lee Eun-hyung and Yang Jae-chan, *Korian Mireokeul 1* [The Korean Miracle I] (Seoul, Korea: Nanam, 2013), 132.
7 *Ibid.*, 133.
8 *Ibid.*, 133–134.
9 Park Tae-jun, "The Memoir of Park Tae-jun," *JoongAng Ilbo*, August 31, 2004, Korea.
10 Seol Bong-sik, *Bakjeonghuiwa hangukgyeongje* [Park Chung-hee and the Korean Economy] (Seoul: Chung-Ang University Press, 2006), 108–109.
11 Hong Yeong-sik, "Gyeongbugosokdoro gyehoeke 'dallil chado eopneunde . . . buyucheung yuram gil'" [To the Kyungbu Highway Plans "There Are No Cars to

Use It . . . It's a Sightseeing Route for the Rich], *Korean Economic Daily*, July 6, 2010, accessed August 10, 2017, www.hankyung.com/news/app/newsview.php?aid=2010070687671

12 *428km-ui ttamgwa nunmul, gyeongbugosokdoro* [Kyungbu Expressway: 428 Kilometers of Sweat and Tears]. Directed by Kim Dong-kook (Seoul, Korea: KBS, 2013), accessed August 10, 2017, www.kbs.co.kr/1tv/sisa/docucinema/view/vod/2173199_66621.html

13 Kim Chung-yum, *From Despair to Hope: Economic Policymaking in Korea 1945–1979* (Seoul, Korea: Korea Development Institute, 2011), 293.

14 Kim Chung-yum, *Hanguk gyeongjejeongchaek 30nyeonsa: choebingukeseo seonjinguk munteokkkaji* [From Poverty to the Threshold of Advanced Countries: A 30 Year History of Korea's Economic Policies] (Seoul, Korea: Random House, 2006), 288–289.

15 *Ibid.*, 304–305.

16 Seol, *Park Chung-hee*, 110–111.

17 Data for 23 countries out of 48 sub-Saharan African countries are from the World Bank. http://data.worldbank.org

18 O Won-chol, *Hangukhyeong gyeongje geonseol 2* [Korean Type Economic Construction 2: An Engineering Approach] (Seoul, Korea: Korea Type Economic Policy Institute, 1995).

19 This system was phased out in the process of liberalization of the Korean banking industry. Chun Seung-hun et al., *Building the Foundation for the Development of SMEs in Ghana* (Seoul, Korea: MOSF&KDI, 2008), 174.

20 *Ibid.*, 58.

21 O, *Economic Construction 2*, 123–126.

6 The advent of industrial titans

Great achievements often transcend individual efforts or fidelity – a fact repeatedly reinforced in the South Korean odyssey. For all his accomplishments as the architect of the country's development, President Park's foresight and leadership were complemented by that of countless known and nameless individuals. We are talking about entrepreneurs, civil servants and a host of everyday people. Among many industrial magnates, several stand out, including Chairman Chung Ju-yung, founder of the Hyundai Group; Chairman Lee Byung-chull, founder of the Samsung Group; and Chairman Park Tae-jun, the icon behind POSCO. Mr. O Won-chol, President Park's chief economic advisor, also deserves special recognition for his role as a dedicated architect of the nation's industrialization policies right in the heart of the bureaucracy. Even though seldom discussed, there was a legion of ordinary folks whose contribution at the grassroots level was as definitive as that of the titans. Within the limited scope of this book, however, the unique contributions of the aforementioned individuals are discussed. Indeed, that is not to be viewed as a diminishment of the varied contributions by the entire nation.

1 The entrepreneurial cohort

Chung Ju-yung[1]

This section traces the story of the humble beginnings of Chairman Chung Ju-yung (1915–2001) as he made his way to the pinnacle of corporate success. The eldest child in a large family of six siblings, the young Chung entered primary school at the late age of 10. Desperate to escape the grinding poverty of his family, the youngster fled home four times after leaving elementary school before finally settling in Seoul. Years later he recalled with contrition some aspects of his youthful adventure, such as when he stole his father's savings to finance one of his escapes to Seoul. It was money his peasant father had accumulated from selling the family's cattle in anticipation of preparing for Chung's elder sister's wedding. While in the city, he took up menial jobs at factories and construction sites. His was that of an ambitious youngster facing insurmountable odds in a very sprawling city.

The youngster learned an important life-changing lesson during his sordid days of sharing a room with other day laborers at a decrepit, bedbug-infested dormitory. The bedbugs were an awful nuisance to the dormitory residents at night, especially coming off a long day's labor. Some resorted to sleeping on tables instead of the floor to avoid the bedbugs, but this did little to prevent the bugs from crawling up the tables. Some of the residents came up with what was supposed to be a strategy for keeping the bugs away. They placed aluminum pots filled with water under the legs of the table. It was reasoned that the bugs would fall into the water and drown, thereby allowing the residents a good night's sleep. It seemed to deter the bugs for the first couple of days, but then the insects came up with a novel response. Surprisingly, the bedbugs crawled up the wall all the way to the ceiling, from where they would drop down to the table. Amazed by the ingenuity of the bugs, Chung reasoned to himself that "if bedbugs can achieve something by working that hard, humans can do much more."

Two years after leaving home, Chung landed a job as a delivery man for a small rice shop in Seoul. Unlike his employer's son, he distinguished himself as a shrewd employee who worked in the best interest of his boss. Moved by this exceptional level of commitment, the boss decided to bequeath the shop to this promising young man. In keeping with his work ethic, the shop continued to thrive until 1939 when the Japanese colonial authorities imposed ration quotas for rice production to serve its war effort. The new restrictions all but bankrupted the shop and momentarily pushed Chung out of business. He bounced back with the acquisition of an automobile repair shop. But that venture too was short-lived because of a fire outbreak, leaving him in debt to his creditors. Galvanizing himself for a second stint in business, he borrowed money from a friend to restart his automobile repair business. The business was successful until a decision by the colonial administration to take it over as part of its large-scale war effort pushed him out of business once again.

Following Korea's liberation after World War II, Chung embarked on a third attempt at developing his garage business. Thanks to the economic boom, his shop was expanded, allowing him to hire 80 employees within a year. He saw an opportunity in the lucrative post-war construction boom, and decided to tap into it by establishing a construction company. Among his breakthroughs was a contract to construct the US military base in Seoul. The outbreak of the Korean War saw him abandon his projects and flee to the coastal city of Busan, alongside the throngs of internally displaced persons.

While in Busan, opportunities opened to him in the construction business. It is said that, amid the war, a lieutenant of the US Army came looking for a building contractor. A visibly excited Chung immediately approached the lieutenant to present himself as a contractor. "I can do any kind of construction," he told the lieutenant through an interpreter. The lieutenant quipped, "can you build a base camp for 10,000 troops in 30 days?" Without hesitation, Chung responded, "Of course, I can."[2] Then the contract was awarded to him. He resorted to extraor-dinary measures to meet the delivery schedule of the contract. For instance, he sanitized the classrooms of closed schools, painted them and laid boards on the floor to make a base camp. Because of the demanding schedule, he could only afford 3 hours of sleep a day throughout the duration of the project. Within 1 month, Chung successfully constructed a temporary base camp to house 10,000 troops.

Impressed by his work, he was awarded another contract to complete the spreading of a lawn at the designated United Nations (UN) troop cemetery in 1952. Getting such a job done in the mid-winter season was an arduous task to say the least. Then Chung came up with an ingenious idea. He uprooted barley from a nearby field and replanted it on the site. The military officer in-charge commended him saying, "Good idea. Excellent work!" after seeing the desolate cemetery morph into a green barley field. Henceforth, he was promised future construction projects of the US Army 8th Infantry Regiment.[3]

After these groundbreaking successes, Chung returned to Seoul in 1953 to officially launch what became known as Hyundai Construction Co. Spurred by the mega-construction boom of the post-war era, his company enjoyed phenomenal growth that eventually heralded it to the top of the industry by 1960. His business empire further grew following the advent of President Park's military government and its ambitious economic development policies. In 1966, his company won the bid to construct Thailand's Tifaany Naratewat Expressway, making it the first of Korea's overseas project. In 1967, Hyundai Motors was established and successfully produced a small-sized sedan, and in 1972, successfully manufactured "Pony," Hyundai's maiden indigenously produced car. In the same year, Hyundai initiated a groundbreaking ceremony for the Hyundai dockyard and successfully won the contract for Saudi Arabia's Jubail Industrial Port construction project, the world's largest deep-sea construction project.

The construction of the Hyundai ship dock appears to be by far the most legendary of Chung's odysseys. It started with the failure of President Park to broker a major deal with Japan to construct a modern ship dock. He then passed the buck to Chung to work out a financial mechanism to fund the project. It started with a fruitless mission to London to secure a $43 million loan from Barclays Bank. The indefatigable Chung only had two sheets of paper to make his sales pitch. The first was a picture of the Mipo Bay in Ulsan and the second was a rough sketch of the ship dockyard. Chung knocked on the door of Barclays Bank of England. However, Barclays officials did not even take the trouble to review his scanty documents before wittily turning him down. Furthermore, the French bank became even colder after a visit by Japanese Ministry of Finance officials to Paris. It was rumored that the Japanese had lampooned Hyundai's lack of experience and capacity to execute a mega-project of such scale.[4] The concerns of the creditors were somewhat justified given the sum that was requested, coming against the backdrop of the request from a construction company from an underdeveloped country without any proven track record in said project. Realistically speaking, there was just no way to convince them to travel with a stranger into the bliss of the sunset. Unfazed, he pressed on with his quest to secure the loan until a positive turn was achieved in securing the international loan, as is discussed in Section 7.3, for the shipbuilding industry.

Chung was directly involved in overseeing the dramatic changes in the various projects, including the coveted Jubail Port construction project. As was discussed in Section 4.3, that project was the largest port construction project in the world at the time. It is striking that up until the moment when it entered the bid, Hyundai had neither the construction experience nor any real sense of the operational cost of constructing the ballast oil-tanker offshore terminal. It had no idea of how to go about estimating the costs and preparing the bid. Worst of all, it was coming up against nine other Western construction companies with proven track records in the industry.

Hyundai entered the bidding process at the very last minute and yet managed to win the contract. It offered the lowest cost of $931.14 million alongside a construction schedule of 38 months, cutting short the construction period by 8 months. However, the Saudi Arabian government delayed the process of a formal contract because it needed a technical review of Hyundai's proposal. A French company, the second lowest bidder at $1.4 billion, approached Chung, and proposed, on condition that Hyundai abandon the contract, an offer of a cash payment of $200 million to make Hyundai a subcontractor. Chung immediately rejected the offer and opted to press on with the project. Hyundai partnered with

Picture 6.1 Jubail harbor in the Kingdom of Saudi Arabia. The scope of the Jubail harbor work included construction of the bank revetment (7,900 m) and breakwater (1,680 m), and a rock wall that varied in scale from 6 meters deep and 550 meters long to 14 meters deep and 2,350 meters long

©HYUNDAI Engineering & Construction

an American company for technical cooperation, and thus allayed the unease of the Saudi government. In the end, Hyundai delivered the biggest construction project of the century.[5]

Progress of the construction project was somewhat adventurous. Construction of the steel structures was planned to be done at a site off the Arabian Gulf coast. However, Chung decided to have them constructed in Korea and to transport them by barge to the Arabian Gulf across the Indian Ocean. This idea was dismissed by international experts as a reckless adventure and an unprecedented move. In addition, two barges were remolded vessels for demolition for scrap iron. It was a great task requiring over 19 voyages, however it was done without marine transport insurance to save cost. Chung knew that if a hurricane came, the barges and structures would float on the sea. The project was eventually completed within the stipulated period to the surprise of the world.[6] This seminal moment marked the advent of South Korea and Hyundai as titans of the global construction export industry.

Another example of Chung's creativity and instinct for risk-taking behavior is the Seosan reclamation project. The project was to secure 155,370,000 square kilometers of land through building a 7.7-kilometer dam on the west coast of Korea. The most difficult part was constructing a 6.4-kilometer dam (A-district).[7] Starting from both sides, the dams met in the middle to block the sea water. When the distance from both dams approached 270 meters at high tide at 8 meters per second, the power of the rapid stream was so tremendous as to wash away a vehicle-sized rock. A block of rocks weighing 20 tons woven with wire through drilled holes was also swiftly swept away by the force of the flowing water. Prominent civil engineers with several decades of experience were at their wits' end.

Then Chung brought up a 226,000-ton large oil tanker with a length of 332 meters, which was imported for scrap metal. Filled with seawater, the oil tanker was sunk in between the dams. Even though the force of the flowing water was strong, it could not toss away the massive tanker, thereby all but salvaging the project from imminent ruin. The dams were thus smoothly connected and the bank to block the seawater was completed. The tanker was set afloat again after the seawater was emptied and dragged to the original position.[8] Hyundai Electronics was established in 1983, followed by Hyundai Petrochemical in 1992, thanks to the entrepreneurial acumen and foresight of this lowly runaway boy who dared to elevate his sights beyond poverty.

From these humble beginnings, his visionary work culminated into developing one of the world's leading automobile plants, one of the world's largest shipyards, and a giant conglomerate including a petrochemical and construction business. This can all be credited to the pioneering visionary of his resilient spirit, innovativeness, creativity and decisiveness in the face of seemingly insurmountable challenges. Chung said, "For me, whatever work I start, I have 90 percent conviction of success and 10 percent confidence of my capability. Besides that, I did not have even 1 percent doubt about the work." His contribution was not only limited to the business sector. He was an instrumental part of enabling Seoul to win the bid to host the 1988 Summer Olympics. He is also remembered for being an ardent believer in the reunification of the divided Korean Peninsula. So was it that at the height of the Asian financial crisis of the late 1990s he crossed Panmunjom, the unification village between the two Koreas, bringing with him 1,001 cattle to North Korea, opening the door for economic exchange between the divided Koreas. He attributed this generosity in terms of filial piety and in terms of a desire to recompense for all the grief he brought his peasant father during his boyhood truancy.[9]

Despite being an owner of a conglomerate, Chung would often disparagingly describe himself as a rich laborer rather than an industrial magnate. For instance, there was a point during the construction of the Kyungbu Highway when he picked up a rock-drilling machine to personally complete a task that his laborers couldn't satisfactorily do. He was also renowned for being able to inspire others, bringing out the best in his staff, and rewarding loyalty. A good example is with the 17th president of the Republic of Korea, Lee Myung-bak (1941–). Hyundai was carrying out a highway construction project in Thailand in 1966 when the young Lee, a recent college graduate, was appointed to be in charge of the project's financial reports. The Thai construction workers, apparently incensed by the poor working conditions they were made to labor under, erupted in a bloody riot. Many of Lee's colleagues took to their heels at the sight of the rampaging mob, but he stood his ground. Lee resolved to defend the cash safe box in the office from looting even at the risk of being lynched by the charging mob. After enduring the brutal assault from the lynch mob and surviving the effects, Lee witnessed a meteoric rise through the ranks of the company. Moved by his dedication, Chung promoted the 27-year-old Lee to the position of executive director 3 years after the bloody incident. Then, by age 34 he was promoted to managing director and reached the position of president of the company by the time he turned 35. Altogether his was a meteoric rise through the ranks of the company spanning nearly 10 years to reach the pinnacle of the company's leadership hierarchy.

An interesting exchange occurred between Chung and the renowned academic Peter Drucker in October 1977. Chung, being an elementary school graduate, had a great deal of respect for Drucker the scholar, but it turned out that Drucker was rather keen on eulogizing Chung and his business acumen. Drucker was quoted as saying,

> If I was confident that I could earn money, I would do it rather than be a professor of business administration. I found that entrepreneurship does not come from the brain rather than from the heart and human nature. I respect your courage to fight against uncertainty, vision for the unseen future, and driving force.[10]

In many respects, he is remembered for his cordiality and the amicable rapport he shared with his staff. It was typical of him to indulge in fun activities such as wrestling, singing and embracing his staff during company time-outs. Clearly, his entrepreneurial accomplishment epitomizes the heart of the dramatic transformation of the Korean economy. No one can take away his stellar achievements in pioneering the country's shipbuilding industry, the automobile industry and the Middle East construction era. His desire to translate his business successes in the political arena suffered setbacks when his presidential ambitions failed until his demise in 2001 at the age of 86. Former Prime Minister Ryu Chang-sun recalled in his tribute to Chung, "Out of pity for Korea, heavens sent the great entrepreneur to Korea. He emerged at the right time when the country was really in need of him."[11]

Lee Byung-chull[12]

Lee Byung-chull (1910–1987) was the second son of a feudal family and a graduate of Waseda University in Japan. He started his first business at the age of 26 in 1936 thanks to an inheritance of a parcel of land. His first business, Cooperative Rice Refinery, was launched in the city of Daegu.[13] Seeking to expand his budding business, the youngster procured a bank loan to acquire land that he leased to tenant farmers. Within a year, he rose to become the major shareholder of the business with 6.6 million square meters' worth of land. The venture was soon to suffer major setbacks following credit defaults.

Following this false start to his entrepreneurial endeavor, he embarked on a trip to Japan during the tumultuous days of Korea's liberation from Japan in 1950. Like Chung Ju-yung, he also reportedly learned a life-changing lesson during this brief sojourn. Walking through the alleys of a Tokyo suburb, he stopped by a barber shop. Then he asked the barber casually, "How long has this business been operating?" To this, the barber responded, "Since I am the third generation, it would be for about 60 years. I wish my son could succeed, but. . . ." The context of this conversation was being held about the same time Japan had just been defeated in World War II. It provided him occasion to reflect on not just what he had just heard from the barber but also the broader demeanor of the Japanese people. For a nation that had been brought to its knees, he found the calm and optimistic disposition of the Japanese people as they went about their daily routine as a symbol of resilience amid adversity. He found inspiration in that and resolved to lick his wounds and saddle up for another bout with destiny.[14]

Lee galvanized himself for a second stint after the failure of his maiden adventures into business. He went to Seoul and established Samsung trading company, only for the Korean War to erupt 3 years later. He fled from Seoul to Daegu, where he continued a small-scale business venture. With the goal of building a manufacturing business, he decided to make inroads in sugar manufacturing. His first sugar business was introduced to a Japanese plant. However, due to the lingering political friction between the Syngman Rhee administration and Japan, the main technicians and engineers that had to set up the plant were not permitted entry into the country. Lee resorted to local expertise in assembly, installation and test operations, which was successful. Spurred by this success, apart from the main frame of the plant, he sourced all the other machines and parts locally.

Finally, in 1953 domestic sugar hit the market at one-third the price of imported sugar.

Notwithstanding the low price, local consumers were initially hesitant to embrace his products, resulting in poor sales. The domestic sugar product was victim to the old stereotype that domestic products, while cheap, have a serious quality deficiency that put off many prospective customers. However, as time goes on, this mistrust resolved and domestic sugar could not meet demand.[15]

Lee's next venture came in 1954 – a wool mill that also received a cold reaction from the market. Samsung became the banter of many jokes. Some of the typical ridicules went like this: "it's stupid to compete against England with its nearly 400-year tradition in the wool industry," or "Samsung's lucky streak in the sugar industry has caused Lee to become delusional about his expansion aspirations."[16] Undeterred, he pragmatically put together foreign capital and domestic assets to bolster his business. Lee tried to maximize the use of domestic technology while leveraging the advantages that foreign technologies offered, such as was the case with West Germany's superior machine technologies. The manager of the German company contracted to construct the plant also argued that based on his experience in India and Turkey, it required 60 German technicians for a period of 1 year to complete the construction work. However, with the help of only several German technicians in core parts, Lee completed the construction in 6 months. Then, the production line got off the ground by early 1956, resulting in the company successfully riding the tide of the ensuing export waves beginning in the 1960s.

Bewildered by Lee's business onslaught, an executive from the US woolen machine manufacturing company Fighting Co. complained to Lee thus: "why do you use American aid money to buy European machines despite the good quality of US machines and engineers?" Lee responded, "Your machine is suitable for mass production of one type of product. We need a variety of products in a factory. Most construction work of the factory including machine assembly and installation will be done by Korean experts." Then the executive retorted, "If products are on the market from a factory made by Koreans themselves within three years, I will fly into the sky."[17]

Lee took a major leap in the establishment of Samsung Electronics in 1968, starting as a joint venture with Japan's Sanyo, which was 11 years behind LG Electronics, its major local competitor. It was initially set up to assemble and manufacture black-and-white television sets using Sanyo's core parts and technology. The factory site was little more than a 1,653 square meter, single-story building, and folks used to say that Samsung products had three characteristics: expensive, fragile and loud.[18] The start of one of the largest information technology (IT) companies was indeed, shabby. The 1970s witnessed Korea's emergence as a player in the heavy chemical industry. This phase ushered in Lee's quest for a foothold when he took bold steps into chemical fiber and other related petrochemical fields. Thus, Samsung steadily progressed from sugar and woolen mills to fertilizers, electronics, petrochemical, shipbuilding and then eventually took bold leaps to the high-tech areas of aviation, semiconductors, computers, and genetic engineering. What is now viewed as today's largest IT company had a very modest beginning.

Stripped to its bare bones, Lee's decision to enter the semiconductor business would have been viewed as a foolhardy move. The engagement of Samsung in semiconductor chips started with acquiring a 50 percent stake at $500,000 of the Korea Semiconductor Co. in 1974 at a time when the company was in serious financial doldrums.[19] Up until the 1970s, employees of the Samsung Group described the semiconductor company as a place of exile, which was the most reluctant place to work for. Then vice chairman Kim Kwang-ho recalls his reaction when he was assigned there. There were about a thousand employees there who either idled around or were left to weed around the premises of the company.[20] Senior management had already quietly cast doubt about the financial viability of the business. Government agencies, including the Economic Planning Board (EPB), the Ministry of Finance and the Ministry of Trade and Industry held the same opinion about Lee's plan for a semiconductor chip business. Their assessment was clearly not unfounded.

The semiconductor business has an inherently high amount of risk in the production cycle. It was at a time when the company did not have the funds to make the required huge investments in equipment and technological innovations. It also had to contend with another critical challenge in the form of recruiting professionals with the right expertise at a time when the global market was dominated by the titans of the United States and Japan. Lee was faced with the same conclusion that it had no economic viability from the repeated reviews by Samsung's technical team and management. The Korean government also held Lee back from his plan. The verdict was clear: the business required huge investments that the Samsung Group could ill afford. However, the tenacious Lee unilaterally declared to launch a semiconductor chip business."[21]

Considering the situation confronting his semiconductor ambitions, in May 1982 Lee embarked on a mission to exhaustively research the industry for himself. Toward this end, he met many domestic and international experts in the semiconductor industry to map out a comprehensive way forward for his plan. At the end of a year-long endeavor, in March 1983, he formally announced: "Henceforth, Samsung will launch a business of VLSI (Very Large-Scale Integration)."[22] Call it a declaration of sorts. Convinced that the company's existing business pool could not guarantee long-term prospects, Lee at the age of 74 took the wild course of wagering his entire personal estate into developing the semiconductor business.[23]

Following the so-called Tokyo Declaration, Lee devoted himself to the semiconductor business, convening meetings of his staff to check the progress two to three times monthly. A decision was made to make the 64K DRAM the first item to be developed, which was produced only in the United States but not in Japan at that time. Lee set a seemingly unrealistic target of 6 months for the completion of the plant.[24] Alarmed, insiders tried to reason with him that Lee was thinking of the construction of textile or sugar factory he had done. On average, it took 18 months to complete such mega-construction projects in advanced countries.[25] To the complainers, Lee insisted:

> If we delay, a semiconductor chip becomes less valuable than a stone in a construction site. Reducing the construction period is the only way to receive the right price for our products. If the plant is completed, we must produce 64K DRAM within six months. If the semiconductor business fails then Samsung and the entire country will die.[26]

Then, in December of the same year, Samsung announced the development of the 64K DRAM by itself, becoming the third country in the world behind the United States and Japan to do so.[27] The Japanese derision that it would take at least 20 years for Samsung to develop the 64K DRAM became a fable. In the next year, it produced 256K DRAM, and in 1992 overtook Toshiba of Japan. Samsung thus emerged as the top DRAM producer in the world.

These achievements, however, came against the backdrop of consecutive losses for 13 years, resulting in an astronomical deficit of KRW 115.9 billion between 1984 and 1987 for Samsung; under the circumstances, it was rumored that Samsung was at risk of bankruptcy collapse.[28] The details of the losses were largely development costs for prior occupation in the market. However, Lee remained steadfast, and admonished his staff not to be deterred by the poor performance. Thanks to his determination and support, Samsung staff could devote themselves in fostering technicians and in developing new technology and new products.

For Lee, being a septuagenarian, opting to pursue such an ambitious move into the semiconductor business was considered an incredibly reckless decision. But he justified it thus:

> Absent natural resources, South Korea's economic growth can only be sustained through the promotion of technology-intensive industries. While the value of 1 ton of steel is KRW 200 thousand, the value of 1 ton of a car is KRW 5 million and 1 ton of computers is KRW 300 million, while the value of 1 ton of semiconductors KRW 1.3 billion. Now all over the world, there is going to be a rush into the semiconductor market. Whoever dominates the semiconductor market will dominate the world. Korea and Samsung's future is embedded in the hi-tech market.[29]

Not so long ago, while undergoing treatment for gastric cancer, he recalled just how successful he has been at whatever business he set his sights on achieving. He concluded that it will amount to greed if he expects to have any further achievements. Intel made a sarcastic remark: "Chairman Lee is a megalomaniac."[30] He ordered the construction of a third plant to be built in Giheung in February 1987. But senior Samsung executives objected to this order, and rightly so. Back then the price of memory chips had declined sharply due to low-pricing policies by Japanese chip companies and the slump in the market in 1986. As a direct consequence of the poor market conditions, several US enterprises cut off production of DRAM. Several American market analysts described the crisis as "the second Pearl Harbor attack." Moreover, the late-starter Samsung was in more serious trouble, with accumulated deficits of KRW 200 billion. It was rumored that Samsung was likely to declare bankruptcy because of its semiconductor chip business. However, Lee's view was different. He tried to get his staff to see what lay ahead by saying: "We have the biggest opportunity ahead of us. We need to maximize and make the most of it."[31] After 6 years of Lee's direction, Samsung launched construction of the third plant.

Lee eventually died of lung cancer in November 1987, aged 88 years old, just about the time the semiconductor market was beginning to pick up globally, by which time Japanese semiconductor manufacturers had already halted their investments during the recession, and several US manufacturers had closed their DRAM businesses. Consequently, Samsung could not meet market demand even with its first and second lines operating at full capacity. It had thus forfeited the revenue that was due during the lag of transitioning to the third construction line. After Lee's death, a window of opportunity was opened for Samsung Electronics alongside other US competitors. It particularly made sense as it sought to rise from the shortcomings of its first and second waves of making a forceful foray into the market.

Lee Byung-chull held true to his belief that the company was all about the people. The good old man often says, do not hire people that are not sure, but once you hire them place your trust in them. He stands tall among the nation's illustrious development stalwarts. He was known to be so keen on prioritizing the nation's overall development over personal financial success. A good example of this is that he built a manufacturing industry rather than making profit from imports when the country had just emerged from the ruins of a destructive war, and in defiance of opposition of his staff and the government, he dared to invest in the semiconductor industry.

Lee made a core business principle of keeping a distance from politics. President Park's 1961 coup d'état, with its espoused goal of ridding the country of its ills and fostering economic development, was a bit unsettling for businesses. As soon as they took power, the military junta embarked on a populist lustration campaign aimed at the business community. Lee was among the list of businessmen scheduled to incur the wrath of the junta. It took a great deal of tact, according to Park Tae-jun, then chief of staff to President Park, for Lee to escape the revolutionary fervor. He is said to have calmly but resolutely encouraging President Park to look beyond the narrow constrictions of the impulses to exact revolutionary vengeance in the interest of the nation. He is reported to have addressed the president thus:

> Since the purpose of the revolution is to eliminate poverty and raise the national economy, it is necessary for businessmen, who are the driving force of economic growth, to pursue their business activities freely. Economic development is not possible in the climate that businessmen are treated as criminals.

Park Tae-jun, who was present at the said meeting with the president, recalls how impressed he was with Lee's resoluteness and the soundness of his admonishment.[32]

Since then, he made it a point to stay clear off political entanglements except for official meetings convened by the president for leaders of industry. Instead he was given to bolstering the technological prowess of his companies. It was this commitment that inspired the creation of the Samsung Advanced Institute of Technology in 1986. Regarding the reasons behind his successful business endeavors, Lee responded saying, "I spent 80 percent of my time nurturing and developing the talents of my staff."[33]

Park Tae-jun[34]

The country's auspicious industrialization drive cannot be treated in isolation to the critical role of the Pohang Steel Corporation (POSCO). It was at the forefront of feeding the development of the country's heavy and chemical industries, which incidentally also unleashed the shipbuilding, automobile, machinery and construction industries. In the same vein, POSCO owes its birth and growth to the tenacity of its founder and longest serving CEO, Park Tae-jun (1927–2011). Born in Kyungnam Province in 1927, he and his family immigrated to Japan in 1933 to join his father who had gone ahead of the family in search of employment. His father worked as a laborer at a railway construction site. To avoid being drafted into the Imperial Japanese Army during World War II, the young Tae-jun enrolled in the College of Engineering at Waseda University.

After Korea's liberation, he was among a group of returnees from Japan who forged a very strong bond with the future President Park during their days in the military. Thus, Tae-jun became a close confidant of President Park, becoming his chief of staff following the coup d'état of May 16, 1961. After serving President Park for a while, he was given the option of choosing between a military position and a political appointment but rejected both options, expressing interest in pursuing higher education in the United States instead.

The story is told that it all started in early 1964 during a farewell banquet organized in his honor by President Park, as he prepared to depart for his academic work in the United States. At the banquet, President Park brought up the issue of a letter from Mr. Ono Bamboku, then vice president of the ruling Liberal Democratic Party of Japan. The letter concerned details of the ongoing secret negotiations aimed at normalizing diplomatic relations with Japan. As part of the process, Seoul was required to designate a presidential envoy to lead its negotiating delegation with Tokyo. The envoy had to meet three core conditions. The individual had to (1) be the president's trustworthy confidant, 2) be fluent in Japanese and 3) have a firm understanding of the nuances of Japanese culture. Preferably that individual ought to have spent time studying in Japan. Without a second thought, Tae-jun was told by President Park that he was "the only one that meets all the criteria."[35]

So rather than heading for the United States as initially planned, Tae-jun was chosen to head this diplomatic mission. On commissioning, President Park gave him a thick envelope as he gleefully said to him: "I feel sorry for your wife that I have to push you to work long hours. You don't even have a house. So, you at least deserve to have a house."[36] So thus began his mission as Korea's lead nego-tiator. This was the first time the young man could purchase his own home after 10 years of marriage. All this while, he had lived in 15 different rented houses. He lived in the house he purchased for 36 years until it was sold in 2000. The KRW 1 billion proceeds from the sale of the house was donated to a charity called the Beautiful Foundation. Tae-jun held a conviction of giving back to society as much as one gets from society.[37]

Following the successful completion of his mission as presidential envoy, he was appointed CEO of the Korean Tungsten Company.[38] Meanwhile, the gov-ernment was pursuing an integrated steel mill construction project. In Novem-ber 1967, at the age of 40, he was appointed as chairman of the task force to promote the construction of the mega steel mill. President Park admonished him saying,

> a steel plant is an important precondition for the success of our quest for industrialization; highways and an integrated steel mill are prerequisites. I will oversee the Kyungbu Highway, and you will be responsible for the steel plant. No one can accomplish this task but you![39]

Then on the night of April 1, 1968, before leaving with his crew of 39 con-struction workers, he said to his wife: "From now onwards you can think of me as a deadbeat spouse. I am out on this mission even at the risk of my life." At dawn on June 15, 1968, before the crew set off to officially begin working on the project, Tae-jun addressed them saying: "This plant is being financed with the compensation from Japan which is the price for the blood of our fore-bears." To drive the point home more forcefully, he added, "if we fail, this will be an indelible blight on our history and our people. If that happens then we should each drown ourselves in the Yeongil Bay." With these words, he and his men took on the challenge to construct an integrated steel mill in the wildness of Pohang. He kept the workflow steadfastly and barely slept for more than three hours a day. It was routine for him to patrol the site to keep his sleepy engineers on their feet.

In fact, up until then the project had taken off in April 1968 in anticipa-tion of securing the required funding through an international loan agreement through the mediation of the Korea International Steel Association (KISA). The funding arrangement soon ran into difficulties. Facing a looming set-back, the government had to resort to financing the project from the Japanese reparation fund, deviating from the originally designated target of the fund.[40] Under the terms of the agreement reached between Tokyo and Seoul over the funds, the primary use of the funds had to be investments in agricultural development. Most importantly, it required the prior consent of Tokyo before the disbursement of the funds.

Faced with this tension, Tae-jun had to hold a series of negotiations with senior Japanese officials, including the chairman of the Japan Iron and Steel Federation, Mr. Iwanamy, to resolve this impasse. It turned out that the major obstacle was Mr. Ohira, the Japanese Minister of International Trade and Industry. An unyielding Mr. Ohira subjected Tae-jun to a dressing down in Economics 101 regarding Seoul's decision to divert the funds. Tae-jun recalls Mr. Ohira sternly saying to him, "the first step of industrialization is agricultural self-reliance. First, you need to establish fertilizer plants and factories for agricultural equipment." There was no breakthrough in getting Tokyo to accept that decision. He once again rejected Seoul's request at a second meeting.

Tae-jun reasoned that he had a better chance of countering the steely Mr. Ohira's economic arguments with equally forcefully counterarguments rooted in economics. For that to happen, he had to substitute his practitioner hat for a scholar's hat. He set about on extensive research to explore the basic tenets of building a feasible economic justification for Seoul's rationale to invest in the steel project instead of agriculture as stipulated by the agreement. This quest took him to Japan's national archives to dig through the historical evolution of Japan's own economic development. Japan, he discovered at the national archives, had

> built the Yahata Steel Mill in Meiji 30 and increased its capacity in preparation for the Russo-Japanese war. At that time, Japan's GDP per capita was below $100 of current rate. South Korea, is in a state of warfare with the North and the GDP per capita of South Korea is currently $200, twice the rate of Japan back then.

It was the discovery of this startling revelation that sent him back knocking on the doors of Mr. Ohira a third time. The soundness of the argument this time got Mr. Ohira to budge.[41]

Some may consider this an entirely counterintuitive process, given that President Park had actually set out to implement this project without conducting the required prior empirical study. Yet when confronted with an unyielding official, he was compelled to conduct his own homework, as it were, before getting the required green light to proceed. Again, President Park took the advice of the West German chancellor about constructing the steel mill as gospel truth, without delving into its other components. Finally, in September 1969, a feasibility study team for Korea's maiden composite steel plant project, headed by Akasaka Shoichi, director-general of the Economic Planning Agency of Japan, touched down to commence work. The team was scheduled to go to the coastal city of Pohang by chartered plane. However, due to a heavy downpour, the team had to travel by train on a 5-hour journey.

The delegation was somewhat dismayed upon arrival at the sandy terrain upon which the proposed mill was going to be constructed. Yet the delegation came up with a positive assessment report for the planned project earlier than expected. Mr. Akasaka justified the team's decision as follows:

> the heavy downpour of that day might be divine providence. Through a 5-hour conversation with Park Tae-jun, I became very convinced that if Park leads, we will surely succeed. He is a very forthright, honest, genuine, highly motivated and an individual who will give his life to steel.[42]

This is how Pohang Steel Co. (POSCO) was launched.

As the overseer of the project, Tae-jun was said to have seriously prioritized his staff's welfare. As a testament to this, it will be recalled that even before the loan had been secured to finance the construction project, he took the decision of constructing affordable housing units for the staff. It was financed from a domestic bank loan that allowed for the houses to be constructed on 661,000 square meters of land at the project site. It triggered a massive uproar in the National Assembly, with critics calling him a real estate speculator. Unperturbed, he went ahead to designate 50 percent of the Pohang Housing Complex and 65 percent of the Kwangyang Housing Complex as green zones. In the summer of 1992, Dr. Victor A. Sadovnichii, then president of Moscow University, visited POSCO. Amazed at the housing complex, he asked, "Who owns those houses in the forest? How were these beautiful houses built?" Upon hearing that the houses are owned by the employees through a scheme that provides them long-term low-interest loans to afford the mortgage, he was stunned. His response was, "the utopia of a society that Comrade Lenin envisaged has been realized here."[43]

Based on the trust President Park vested in him, Park Tae-jun approached the task of the POSCO E&C construction with a sense of mission and devotion that was unparalleled. His stellar achievements in this area includes, first, how he so scrupulously managed to successfully oversee the construction work at a minimum cost in record time and to competitive standards. It is worth noting that there was a great deal of political and factional interest in managing the foreign funds, a very slippery road that could have undermined the effective implementation of the project but for such capable leadership at the helm. Project procurement and logistics was one of the core areas that was very susceptible to graft and misappropriation, but thanks to the backing of President Park, POSCO could hold its ground by resisting any attempt at cutting corners or granting unwarranted favors. His entire life was a commitment to the motto "Business for the Benefit of the Nation."

His uncompromising attitude to shoddy work was on display during an event in 1977. While on a routine inspection tour of a power ventilation installation, he discovered that the bolts had not been properly fastened. In response, the staff conferred and came up with a better way of fastening the bolts. He was still very cross that the staff were not diligently discharging their responsibilities. In a drastic move, he ordered that the poorly constructed equipment be demolished in the presence of all the staff. Several hours of labor, resources and equipment had suddenly been reduced to rubble. The object here was to challenge the staff to rise beyond their lax attitude and embrace a radical commitment to excellence. Thankfully, the staff did not miss this point.[44]

Second, Tae-jun prioritized technological development. Before launching the construction of the steel mill, he started the construction of the Steel Training Institute in October 1968 and completed it the following January. Starting with the dispatch of nine personnel to the Kawasaki Steel Mill, a total of 600 trainees received technical training from foreign countries that have expertise in the steel industry, including West Germany and Australia, at a total cost of $5 million. The trainees often went to extraordinary lengths to acquire the required expertise, even crossing the line at times. In some cases, Korean trainees adopted canny methods to access restricted areas, such as floor plans of the host country's steel mills.[45] We can only imagine the nervousness they had to go through by acting like industrial spies.

Third, Park demonstrated genuine interest in the socioeconomic uplift of the local communities where he operated. It included the establishment of a scholarship foundation, schools and the Pohang University of Science and Technology (POSTECH). In the case of the latter, POSTECH started as an in-house college, setting its sights high on becoming a world-class institute of academic excellence and setting out to recruit a new president. Mr. Kim Ho-gil was recommended by a senior executive for the position. Kim Ho-gil described his initial discussions with Park Tae-jun about the offer this way:

> If I take the role, the university may start below POSCO, but POSCO will be below the university in the end. Decisions about arrangement of the campus may be up to you, however, the recruitment of professors and management of the university should be completely entrusted to me. Your acceptance of this condition does not mean that I consent to your offer, but I will put it into consideration.

Upon hearing word of the meeting, the said POSCO executive who recommend Kim Ho-gil for the appointment was taken aback and reprimanded him for being "insubordinate before the Tiger Chairman." Out of the blue, Tae-jun cancelled the remainder of the scheduled interviews with the other candidates and ordered the executive to "catch Kim under any condition!"[46] Tae-jun was unrelenting in his devotion to the steel mill, so much so that it rubbed off on his staff in terms of their motivation to achieve a spirit of excellence.[47] At its public listing, POSCO's staff was granted 10 percent ownership in stock options. In his uncompromising leadership acumen, he opted not to own any of the company's shares. Indeed, this was a rare feat by corporate standards. Park's was that of a life of unblemished personal integrity.

His seminal role in the success of POSCO was even acknowledged internationally. In one such instance in London, he met Dr. John W. P. Jaffe, who was head of the steel industry department of the World Bank in 1968 when POSCO was established. It was his so-called expert analysis that resulted in the KISA loan intended for South Korea being diverted to Brazil instead. Dr. Jaffe argued then that POSCO was a premature baby that lacked the ability to survive, much less thrive.[48] Sensing his pound-of-flesh moment, Tae-jun explained to Dr. Jaffe that

> the capacity of the Brazilian steel mill is 4 million tons and that of POSCO is soon projected to surpass 12 million tons. Both mills were constructed at the same time. What do you now think of the analysis you made 18 years ago?

In a quibbling response to the question, Dr. Jaffe said, "I wrote an honest and fair report. Even if I write it again, the result will be the same. The only thing I overlooked at that time was just 'you.' I didn't know the fact that Park Tae-jun is POSCO."[49]

When Deng Xiaoping was said to have discussed his interest in constructing a steel mill like POSCO in China with Mr. Inayama, he got a very unequivocal answer. "It is impossible," Mr. Inayama said. A curious Deng asked for the reason. Mr. Inayama asked rhetorically, "Is there anyone in the whole of China equal to Park Tae-jun?" This also mirrored the opinion of Mr. Arikashi, the leader of the Japanese technological advisory group to POSCO. "Mr. Park is a person who can touch our heartstrings. The achievement of POSCO is riddled in mythological elements. Therefore, it is an event that cannot happen twice in history."[50]

After successfully completing the construction of the Kwangyang Steel Mill in October 1992, Park Tae-jun went to the tomb of the late President Park Chung-hee to pay homage. He is said to have uttered the following words: "25 years after receiving His Excellency, the President's order, I respectfully report to the spirit of His Excellency the President that I have successfully completed the great historical work of constructing POSCO." That the two shared an unshakable bond is reflected in the level of veneration that Park Tae-jun expressed to his senior colleague in the service of the people.

O Won-chol[51]

O Won-chol was one of the leading figures in crafting the framework for South Korea's modern development sojourn. He served as President Park's Senior Secretary for Economic Affairs with oversight responsibilities for the Ministry of Trade and Industry (MTI) and the presidency between the 1960s and 1970s. He was literally at the helm of the industrial policies that saw the birth of the heavy and chemical industries (HCI), among other pioneering economic development policy initiatives. Beyond just being his confidant, President Park reportedly colloquially used to refer to him as "O, the National Treasure" in tribute to his exceptional dedication as a skilled technocrat.[52]

Born in 1928 in the North Korean Province of Hwanghae, he enrolled at the Kyongsong Technical College in Seoul soon after Korea's liberation. The Kyongsong Technical College had just been restructured to become the College of Engineering of Seoul National University, where he majored in chemical engineering. When the Korean War broke out in 1950, the young O enlisted in the Korean Air Force after passing the Engineering Cadet Officer examination in December 1950 and was later commissioned as a second lieutenant in 1951. The military provided both the opportunity and the background for him to hone his engineering skills thanks to his involvement in a host of military construction projects. He served in the military until becoming a reservist at the rank of major in 1957.

His first stint in civilian employment was at South Korea's first automobile manufacturer, the Sibal Auto Company, from 1957 to 1960. He became a distinguished engineer and rose to become a plant manager overseeing the development of the country's first indigenously designed vehicle. At that time, the firm was on the brink of collapse, prompting him to take up a new role as plant manager at another automaker, the Kuksan Motor Company. Even with that, his promising start at the firm was interrupted by the impact of the political upheavals that followed the Revolution of April 19, 1960.

Barely a week after taking up his new role, O was summoned by the Military Revolutionary Committee where he was immediately appointed – without prior consultation of course – to become director of the research department in the Commission of Planning and Research. This unit was a subcommittee of the Supreme Council of National Reconstruction (SCNR). Another swift promotion soon followed, when he was propelled to head the Chemical Industry Division of the Ministry of Trade and Industry. It was at this position that the burgeoning technocrat cut his teeth as a shrewd policymaker, a position that gave him the chance to offer critical input into the First Five-Year Economic Plan announced on January 13, 1962.

It was during these seminal days of his stint as a technocrat that he became deft at contending with the idiosyncrasies of policymaking in an underdeveloped country. He famously described the process of rudimentary policymaking for fragile economies as requiring a "micro approach" and an "impact policy" process. One of his most reputed signature policies was the "Zoning Strategy for Industrial Complexes" framework. It called for the prioritizing of individual firms in the construction of industrial complexes before opening to external industrial developers, among other things. These were the ideas that informed the planning and execution of the construction of the Petrochemical Industrial Complex at Ulsan.

When the government unveiled its export-oriented development strategy in 1964, he was tapped to be chief of the MTI department in charge of light industries. That was the country's main export product. This new position thrust him into the very heart of what became the core of the country's development strategy – exports. Another promotion followed in 1968 to head the Planning and Management Office, and another swift elevation to Deputy Minister of Mining, Manufacturing and Energy occurred in 1970. He continued to maintain keen oversight of the development of the petrochemical industry, culminating in the construction of the Ulsan Petrochemical Industrial Complex in 1972. It is this accomplishment that earned him the accolade of being the founding father of South Korea's petrochemical industry. So are his other accomplishments in developing effective policies to facilitate the development of such industries as steel, iron, automobiles, electronics and shipbuilding.

The 1970s was a decade of unusually high levels of tension between the two Koreas, which almost put them on the brink of full-blown war. As both sides competed for economic supremacy, they were also keen to outdo each other in the political and military spheres. Driven by the geopolitical exigencies, President Park found in O a complete vanguard to lead his economic charge, hence the decision to appoint him as Chief Secretary for Economic Affairs in 1971 with a special focus on building the country's defense industry. O impressed upon President Park a policy hypothesis that hinged on achieving supremacy over the North by developing a framework that linked the HCI to national defense. This was about the time he was laying the finishing touches on his infamous Korean-type Economic Development Model. O argued that as a small and open economy with no capital and technology, the usual or conventional way of economic development through the process of primitive accumulation of capital and agricultural development may not work effectively in South Korea. Such being the case, Korea pursued active prior-industrial development attracting foreign capital. To realize full industrialization in a small domestic market, Korea used this policy framework of industrial policy to accommodate large-scale HCI.

Accordingly, he began to draw up a concrete plan for the construction of the HCI, which subsequently became known as "A Theory for Industrial Structure Reorganization." It was largely in part influenced by the imperatives of the economic policies of the 1960s that hinged on the promotion of light industry. By the turn of the decade, however, the economic imperatives of that era soon had to be restructured toward a more HCI orientation. For this policy orientation to take hold, detailed research, planning and effective implementation measures had to be instituted, and that is precisely the type of leadership O offered. This indeed influenced President Park's landmark announcement in January 1973 of a development policy reorientation toward HCI. The "Implementation Committee for Heavy and Chemical Industrialization" and its planning body were established that May. Then, from February 1974, O held two positions simultaneously: Senior Presidential Secretary for Economic Affairs and head of the "Planning and Implementing Group for HCI." From then until the president's assassination on October 26, 1979, he was responsible for many outstanding achievements in the development of South Korea's industrialization.

As part of the HCI policy framework, O first and foremost was central in the development of the six pillars of the HCI: iron and steel, chemicals, machinery, electronics, shipbuilding and nonferrous metals. Then came the construction of major industrial complexes including in Ulsan, Yonchon, Changwon, Kumi, Okpo and Onsan. The industrial complex concept, which first consisted of a collection of industrial projects and then grew to include residential areas as well as a host of public sector projects, such as harbors, educational institutions, inspection centers and various training centers for skilled workers and technicians, were formulated during this period.

Second, while overseeing the development of the defense industry under the auspices of the national military modernization project dubbed the Yulgok Plan, O worked to bolster the country's defensive capabilities by overseeing a massive procurement of vital arsenals that could not be indigenously developed but were vital for the army. The nascent civilian nuclear industry also saw a major facelift under his stewardship. Third, he was literarily in the eye of the storm generated by the oil shock of 1973. As the senior official with direct responsibility for the economy, O had to devise appropriate policies to ensure the country's economy could weather the storm. His policy responses included, among other things, seeking overseas market opportunities for Korean corporations. He is most noted, however, for leading the quest to make forays into the Middle East construction boom of the 1970s and the development of the plant-engineering industry. Fourth, along those same lines, O was instrumental in restructuring the country's vocational and technical educational system to rapidly boost the nation's pool of technicians, engineers and other vocational experts. This move came against the backdrop of the increasing demand for skilled tradesmen because of the overseas construction boom of the 1970s. It was during this period that massive investments went into the country's R&D sector culminating in the establishment of clusters such as at Daedok, which currently stands out as South Korea's leading hub for advanced scientific research.

Even though his mission at the helm of the nation's economic policy-making process ended with the end of the Park regime, we can glean from a couple of the sensitive documents retrieved from President Park's desk that he was poised to take on other crucial national projects but for the demise of his boss. As was referred to in Section 7.3, one of the said documents contained an order to terminate the country's budding nuclear weapons program, alongside a "White Paper on the Construction of an Administrative Capital" and the "National Land Plan for 2000s." We are told that all these programs were ostensibly to be overseen by O once the HCI projects were successfully executed. Several critical factors explain why these policies were earmarked as the next stage of the industrialization process.

To begin with, Seoul, the national capital, and other major metropolises started to steadily attract a tide of migration to the neglect of the hinterland. Without any serious interventions, this trend would pose a demographic challenge down the road. Moreover, the sweltering factories undergirding the manufacturing drive were not only belching plumes of industrial pollutants but were also randomly and inefficiently scattered. O's policy response was to relocate several factories located inland toward the coastal areas to limit their adverse impacts on land. It was also his brainchild to relocate the capital city from Seoul to Sejong City as part of a comprehensive development plan.

Suffice it to mention an anecdotal description of his passionate commitment to duty. Although the backdrop to this story is tragic, it is still somewhat illustrative of the character of O as a distinguished technocrat and a dignified personality. The story is told of a 1977 ceremony to officially unveil the country's indigenously produced weapons, of which the president was the guest of honor. As fate would have it, one of O's subordinates was the victim of a fatal accident at this auspicious and historic event. As if the scandal of failing this important test was not bad enough, President Park ordered the chief of the hospital to which the victim was rushed to "save the life of the officer at all cost."[53] However, the officer tragically succumbed to his injuries. A few days later after the funeral, President Park demanded that heads must roll for this fiasco. Clearly, as the overseer of the project there was no denying that the buck ended on O's desk.

O was summoned by the president to discuss culpability. President Park said, "Since the funeral is over, someone has to take responsibility." In a rather awkward response to the president's remarks, O suddenly burst into singing a famous Korean War folk song, "Over the bodies of fellow soldiers, Forward! Forward! . . . Farewell to the *Nakdong* River. We'll advance!" Initially taken aback, the president somehow rescinded his demand for punitive justice in recognition of the selflessness devotion to duty. He was also able to remonstrate from O's disposition that besides just being an innocent accident, the fall of one soldier on the battlefield was by no means the last word.[54] In recognition of his meritorious service to the country, O received two state honors in 1964 and 1972. The first medal, dubbed "Kunjong," was conferred by the President in recognition of his distinguished contribution to developing the country's then budding export-industrial policies. South Korea had exceeded the $100 million export revenue target in 1964 thanks to O's distinguished contribution. The second medal was to acknowledge his achievements in bolstering the country's petrochemical industry.

Despite the president's unequivocal backing, O in the course of his duties had inadvertently stepped on several toes in the bureaucracy. There were voices within the circle of the government's economists lashing at him for undermining the country's economic stability by his excessive investments in the HCIs and the defense industry. He was also chided for siding with the government's position of overruling the independence of the central bank and the banking industry in general. Complaints about him eventually reached the presidency, so President Park suggested shuffling him to the Ministry of Science and Technology to calm the rancorous critics. O's retort was definite, when he said, "Your Excellency, I'd like to work only for you. The day I cannot work for you is the day I retire." True to his words, he resigned from office immediately after President Park's assassination on October 26, 1979.

Since then, O has devoted himself to writing books and contributing articles to local media outlining his years of experience at the heart of the country's industrial development. He published a seven-volume series on South Korea's economic development and industrialization under the title of *Korean Type Economic Construction* (in Korean) from 1995 to 1999, and an English version entitled *Story of Korea* in 2009, particularly focusing on President Park's leadership. These books are valuable intellectual assets for understanding South Korea's economic modernization and industrial development. He remained passionately committed to sharing South Korea's poverty reduction and economic development experiences across the world, and transferring the lesson from the experiences to succeeding generations to come. Kim Chung-yum paid glowing tributes to O, saying, "Thanks to his creative engineering approach, South Korea could put import substitution industries, competitive light industries, heavy and chemical industries and defense industry on the right track in a stepwise manner within a short period."[55]

2 The grassroots as industrial warriors

In this remarkable odyssey of poverty reduction, we would do well to look at the contribution of ordinary folks at the grassroots as well. While it might be beyond the scope of this book to provide a detailed point-by-point account of their life experiences, it is still possible for analytical purposes to highlight important aspects within this grand project. As has been repeated several times in this book, it is an account of a generation. In a sense, South Korea's development story is the sum of efforts and struggles of individual Koreans to overcome poverty and not to bequeath their poverty to their children.

Park Jung-sung: the sailor who crossed all the five oceans in 43 years[56]

In February 1964, an old and raggedy cargo ship called *Rungwha* was set to sail from the harbor of Tokyo to Hong Kong. This 2,700-ton ship was about to be retired at the time of this voyage. Unsure of the seaworthiness of the ship, the Japanese sailors refused to board, leaving just a crew of 28 that consisted of desperate peasant Koreans, including the captain, to embark on the impending treacherous voyage. It was rumored that the sailors would surely not return alive. Yet these poor folks went ahead, despite the obvious risks.

Two months after setting sail, the *Rungwha* crew finally radioed the Tokyo harbor about the imminent arrival of the ship. They had defied the odds, or better still, risked their lives just to accomplish what was considered an obviously dangerous mission. To the surprise of onlookers at the Tokyo harbor, the ready-to-be-retired ship was neatly reconstructed, like a ghost ship resurrected. Upon their return, one of the sailors was quoted as saying: "To secure our continued employment, we had to show that we are working very well. We returned home, keeping the ship while risking our lives."[57] As seemingly insignificant as this story might appear, it clearly underscores the level of desperation of Korean laborers back in the day to take up whatever job was available irrespective of the attendant risks.

Park Jung-sung's father was a civil servant when the Korean War broke out. The family fled Seoul to Busan to seek refuge from the war. Like most Koreans, the family was barely subsisting in the post-war condition of devastation. At 21, the youngster watched helplessly as his father died of a stroke, plunging the already impoverished family into further despair. He then was enlisted in the military in 1970 for a 3-year service period. Following his discharge from the military, he found work as a sailor for a fishing trawler company. It was to mark the beginning of his eventful life on the world's high seas. The company he worked for operated a fleet of seven light vessels that went as far as to the Indian Ocean to catch tuna. For the most part, the vessels had crews of 20 sailors roaming the open seas. The experience was a strenuous battle against the waves under very treacherous conditions.

Unfortunately, the company went bankrupt barely a year after Park joined. Upon his return, the young sailor tied the knot with Sun-duck Kim, a neighbor. The newlyweds promised themselves to work together "to earn money and live happily."[58] Fortune beckoned again, and the young sailor found a new job that saw him set sail again. His second son was born while he was on the high seas. He delayed naming the son until he docked 1 month later. His children could barely recognize him after his year-long voyage. In many ways, the story of Jung-sung's voyages is a complex tale of the sacrificial labor of a generation, whose it was to burrow through the difficulties fate had bequeathed to them. To get to grips with these complex layers, I will attend to a few of his high and low points as a desperate sailor.

Word of the success of the *Rungwha* mission provided an important reputational boost to Korean sailors. Their dedication and commitment consequently attracted keen interests across the maritime industry. An American scrap metal processing company called Schnitzer, seeing the change of the ghost ship, established Lasco, a marine shipping company employing only Korean sailors.[59] At that time, when the monthly salary for low-grade local government officials was KRW 5,000, a sailor could earn as much as KRW 37,000. A year's wages could enable one to purchase a house. It was a popular refrain among Koreans that "boarding a ship saves a family."[60] There was therefore a strong incentive to take on all types of risks to guarantee continued employment. Such voyages typically involved high risks of pirate attacks and on occasion sailing through treacherous militarized seas to deliver cargo.[61]

Let's start with a critical phase in the twists and turns in the story of this lowly sailor. He was on a routine voyage when the Iran-Iraq war broke out in 1980. His vessel had a rice cargo loaded in Bangkok destined for the Iranian port of Amirabad (Almiya) at a time when hostilities between the belligerent forces were in full swing. After traversing the seas as missiles were firing overhead, the crew finally arrived at port only to realize that there were no assigned tallymen to offload the cargo. They had to stay at port for about a month as the war raged on. From there the vessel headed for Tokyo after offloading another cargo in Durban, South Africa. They had barely settled in Tokyo when duty called for another delivery of rice from Bangkok to Iran. To avoid paying a war allowance to the crew, the ship owner had the ship anchored on the outer block of the port in Iran. After all, the crew could not receive war allowances.[62] Loading ironstone in West Germany, miscellaneous items in England and cosmetics in France, the ship set sail for the Caribbean. Once departed from a harbor, it takes 2–4 weeks to reach the next harbor.

Tragedy struck Park's vessel in 1978 while they were sailing in the Pacific Ocean. A Korean sailor fell 30 meters to his death while attempting to close the door of a corn reserve. As the senior man of his compatriots, Park took it upon himself to properly prepare the mortal remains of his deceased colleague for cremation. Hard as he wished the family of the youngster would have been able to bid befitting farewell to the deceased, he was constrained by the conditions of the sea and the operators of the vessel. A devastating cyclone struck the vessel in the same year on Christmas when the vessel was approaching the Caribbean. The crew battled the violent wind that was threatening to sink the vessel as the high waves tossed it about. At one point the ship's engine momentarily went still. Amid the panic to salvage the vessel, one of the ship's crew lost an arm. This was but one of the countless times Park had witnessed young sailors sustain debilitating injuries working on foreign commercial vessels.

Beginning with the so-called *Rungwha* ghost ship, Korean sailors have worked on foreign vessels since 1964. It was about the same time that major maritime nations such as Japan, Greece and the United States were in urgent need of crews to man their fleets. Korean sailors were drawn by the open recruitment process in transnational merchant vessels, especially given that they had limited work opportunities domestically. Since the initial dispatch of 28 sailors in 1964, Korean sailors remitted $167 million home over a 10-year period. In 1977, when the country's exports reached the $10 billion mark, 13,462 sailors made remittances of $88 million; and in 1988 when total exports were $50 billion, sailors contributed $516 million.[63] By 2014, over 9,700 Korean sailors had perished at sea. To hold the victims in memory, President Park Chung-hee established the Martyr Crews Memorial Tower at Taejongdae in Busan in 1979 and wrote the epitaph with his own hands.[64]

Park Jung-sung sailed the ocean for 43 years from 1970 to 2013. According to official estimates, he sailed on board 35 ships. For all his toil, he and his wife could only manage to save to purchase an apartment for themselves and a second smaller apartment for their son and a small shop that they leased out. He had mixed feelings about the impact his extensive sailing experience has had on the relationship with his son. "I feel sorry. I have many regrets," is how he describes his supposed inability to be around for his son.

> My only memories of him are the times I scolded him. However, that was by no means my intention. All I ever did say to him was 'study hard!' I just thank Sun-duck who has been the best steward of the house all these years.[65]

Ahn Young-ok: the scientist who chose his country[66]

In 1966 Choi Hyung-sup, who was appointed to head the newly created Korea Institute of Science and Technology (KIST), embarked on a broad recruitment campaign for fellows. In collaboration with the Battelle Memorial Institute in the United States, a call was made for applications from Korean scientists across 500 locations abroad. Out of 800 applicants, 75 were short-listed for interview, and Choi personally interviewed each one of them in the United States and Europe in October 1966. He made it a point to forthrightly stress the following to his interviewees:[67]

> The research environment is guaranteed. Everyone works as a research center head. Everyone will be guaranteed a stipend to live comfortably. However, there is a condition. Those who hope for the Nobel Prize should not apply.

> Don't think about writing a thesis. Don't think about earning money except in research. We must develop technology to keep our country from starving.

It was along this recruitment campaign that he met Ahn Young-ok, the son of Ahn Kuk-hyung, a famous Korean liberation fighter. The younger Ahn was the youngest of three children, and had enrolled at the Department of Chemical Engineering of Seoul National University. It was there that he became the recipient of the American Officer's Wives Association scholarship, and at the behest of his father went to study in the United States in 1955. He embarked on the journey to the United States with the help of a loan from his elder brother. It was not until 12 years after departing Korea did he even entertain the thought of returning, thanks to his meeting with Choi Hyung-sup. His was by no means an isolated case, given that from the end of the Korean War until 1967, of the 7,958 students who studied abroad, only 973 had returned to Korea. Following Choi's interview, 18 researchers were selected from the doctoral applicants and master's degree level with career experiences in industry, and Ahn Young-ok was among the 18.

His was a promising start in the United States, after a bachelor's degree at the University of California, Berkeley, and a master's degree at Ohio State University, leading to a well-paid job at Union Carbide. However, he returned for a doctoral program at the urging of his elder brother. As soon as Ahn graduated from university, he was employed as a researcher by the DuPont Institute, which was considered a dream job. He was to join a roster of 1,300 doctoral-level researchers and nearly 3,500 junior-level researchers. Given the competitive remuneration he received, he could afford a very decent life for his family.

It took his interview with Choi in a Washington, DC, hotel room in October 1967 to alter this otherwise comfortable course of his life of stability in the United States. "Return and let's establish an institute together," was Choi's sales pitch. Clearly, that didn't sound like a reassuring piece. Then looking at Choi's perforated socks, Ahn replied, "Let me consult my wife." After mulling through the details, his wife tacitly consented to the possibility of her husband risking their middle-class life in the United States for what was like going with Choi into the sunset, which was certainly very unusual by every stretch of the imagination.[68]

In February 1969, Ahn and his family returned to Korea after 14 years. He was appointed research director of his field at KIST. Choi Hyung-sup kept his promise to Ahn, except that it came with a slight twist of sarcasm. For a researcher just coming from an institute replete with legions of doctors assigned to each department, having a single doctor assigned to head a department at KIST would have sounded like a bad joke. It was not just for the basic sciences but also for the very important aspects of applied science. Yet under these conditions, he is still credited for pioneering important technological developments, such as Freon gas, which is used in air conditioners and in insulation materials of semiconductor chips. The research of his fellow researchers culminated in the establishment of POSCO, and the research of optical fiber was linked to the development of the telecommunications industry. Lee Yong-tae established an electronic traffic control system, the foundation base for an e-government, and the first PC manufacturing company in Korea in 1980.[69] The government's initiative to attract brains from abroad was ended because it no longer had to worry about brain drain, thanks in no small part to the cohort that chose to return to lay the foundations for the country's technological breakthroughs. Of the 25 founding members of KIST, four passed away within 10 years due to being overworked.[70]

Choi Hoe-seok and Chung Ok-ryun: the miner-nurse couple who spent all their youth laboring[71]

The story of the infamous expedition of Korea's labor export started with the departure of the first cohort of 123 individuals on December 23, 1963. Bound for West Germany, the laborers enplaned at Gimpo Airport, with a brief layover in Tokyo, then flew across Anchorage destined for the West German city of Düsseldorf. The laborers were scheduled to join other migrant workers in West Germany's dangerous coal mines. The first day of work was like hell. The miners typically greeted each other "Glück Auf!" (Good Luck!), just because one was never guaranteed coming out of the pits alive. The machine carried them underground 1,100 meters in a moment, and moved another 3,000 meters in a horizontal direction.

While deep in the mines, the machines emitted suffocating toxic dust. The front was hardly visible, and it was hard to breathe.[72] By 1977, there were 7,936 Korean miners toiling under these hazardous conditions. Choi Hoe-seok was one of them. The son of a local elementary school principal, he was the fifth of six siblings who lived on the breadline. He recalls being a naughty kid growing up, and with very little prospects as a youth, he decided to enlist in the military. His decision to enlist was partly at the urging of his elder brother, who felt that rather than wasting his youth, the military would offer the best use of his time.[73]

Once his military service was over, again his eldest brother told him, "just go to West Germany," to take advantage of the miner recruitment program. But Hoe-seok was a few kilograms shy of the minimum weight threshold of 61 kilograms for recruits. Determined to make the weight cut, he followed his brother's advice of eating 30 egg yolks to provide a short-term weight boost. The applicants for mineworkers in West Germany were that desperate.

Since the age of 22 in West Germany, Choi remitted KRW 45,000 every month, which is three times larger than that of the school principal's monthly salary that his father earned. He also gifted his father a 99 square meter house to commemorate his 60th birthday. Before the first remittance from his troublemaker son, the father shed tears without saying anything. His eldest son said to his father, "the top troublemaker in our family did the best filial duty." As he enplaned to depart for Germany on October 12, 1970, an ecstatic Hoe-seok recalls saying to himself that "I've never earned any real money in my life, but this is a chance to become a good son." He certainly felt very fulfilled as he looked back.[74]

Hoe-seok's spouse, Chung Ok-ryun, was yet another individual from a very humble background who rose to give a good account of herself. Ok-ryun grew up as the youngest daughter in a family of seven children. Overwhelmed by the pressure of taking care of all her children, her mother felt that getting Ok-ryun to marry would lessen her domestic burdens. Preferring to get an education to better her lot, she eventually trained as a nurse and worked in a local hospital before joining the exodus of migrant workers to West Germany. Her pay in Korea was KRW 20,000 per month, and that in West Germany was DM 600, which is equivalent to KRW 54,000. Her mother said to her seventh daughter filling out the application form for West Germany, "just get married." The daughter replied, "I don't want to hear you. I will definitely go." On July 31, 1971, Ok-ryun arrived in West Germany, and on the next day she was assigned to the surgery room of gynecology and obstetrics at Ahlen Hospital. The hospital strongly requested that the mayor send Korean nurses. They appreciated Korean nurses who worked hard and well.[75]

Hoe-seok met his future wife in 1971 during a visit to Ahlen to celebrate Christmas. They got engaged 4 months after their first meeting and married that same year. To support his family, Hoe-seok had to take on extra hours in the dangerous conditions and pushed himself to the limits. He was always eager to step in for any absent colleague under the searing temperatures of 42°C, which often left him dehydrated.[76]

Because three shifts daily were not enough to compensate for his trouble in the past, Hoe-seok worked 14-hour days in hell. However uncomfortable and dangerous it was, he always agreed to step in for an absent colleague. At a temperature above 42°C, he couldn't even takeoff his work suit out of fear that splints of coal would penetrate his body. Because all his internal water evaporated as swiftly as he took it in, he could hardly urinate. On one occasion, when he went to the entrance to get his equipment he just dropped to the ground; he happened to face a collapsed wall and from the side of the heap of rocks he could see the boots of his colleague. He ran to the emergency phone, shouting, "Tod! Tod! [Death! Death!]" In 3 years, he made this call three times. The men who dared to drill to get 1 meter deeper into the mine were usually Koreans. There were persons who even claimed, "Crack my fingernails with this hammer," so they could rest due to injury. In the morning, to prepare breakfast, it was necessary to massage the fingers for more than 10 minutes just to be able to stretch them. However, after 40 years, Hoe-seok said, "If we think of money, the hard life we had to take was not really hard."[77]

The pressure of working in the nursing homes also took its toll on the nurses both physically and psychologically. Because they felt so sorry for the elderly, their psychological state was affected adversely. Caring for tall, heavy elderly people, which included cleaning up their urine and feces, caused the physical health of nurses to decline as well. However, just like their male colleagues, many of them worked long shifts and spent their off-days working in other hospitals. The couple decided to remain in Germany after finishing their 3-year contract. Hoe-seok found work at a company manufacturing lenses on the recommendation of his wife's acquaintance. Ok-ryun continued working as a theatre nurse where she endeared herself to one of her previous patients. It marked the beginning of a healthy relationship with the family. Their financial conditions were significantly boosted during this period.

The couple had a son in 1976 and a daughter a couple of years later. Choi returned to Korea with their son in 1979, where he was joined by his wife and daughter the next year. It was only after the children were grown that he could tell them the story of their difficult experience of working in the hazardous mines of West Germany. Through their hard lives in mining, the Korean youth made remittances worth $100 million, and in the meantime, 29 youths lost their lives in mining accidents in Germany. Choi Hoe-seok and Chung Ok-ryun recall about their lives, "[We] have not been lonely because we found love early. No one at that time was not unyielding and no one had lived in comfort. Truly we have lived vivid and discerning lives. It was hard though, but pleasurable."[78]

Kim Jin-han: the export titan[79]

Although 30 years had passed since its independence, South Korea remained a very obscure territory for many people across the world. With such obscurity, there was no way of talking about a national brand for such a nation seeking to make forays into the international export market. Yet coming out of the oil shocks of the 1970s, that is precisely what the government chose to do – export. For that to happen, it had to have a network of competent merchants to rally the campaign. Thus, it designated general trading companies to serve as points of export front.[80] "Korea? I understand that when war broke out in Korea, we sent humanitarian aid there," the postmaster general of Egypt stoically quizzed Kim Jin-han, then chief of the overseas sales division of Taehan Electric Wire Co. As if that was not enough, he went to upset Kim by asking "will you really produce a communication cable?" Egypt was by then earmarked as the gateway to the African market in 1970s.

The Egyptian government had opened an international bid for procurement of a copper telecommunications cable worth about $4 million. Among the bidders were established industry names such as the American Essex, France's Alcatel, Italy's Pirelli, Finland's Nokia and Germany's Siemens. Emitting cigarette smoke, the postmaster general added, "We only have used the American and European cables, well. . . ." Kim tried to conceal his wounded feelings with a smile on his face. Determined not to let this deal go under, he mounted a strong sales pitch to the Egyptian official and even went so far as to offer an enormous bargain for the Taehan cable. With this arrangement, Taehan could get a foot in the door as the most preferred bidder because of price competitiveness. Even with this arrangement, the Egyptian government was still far from convinced that Taehan, without any proven record, would be able to deliver.

A few months later, a message came from Egypt requesting sample products and a delivery performance certificate. In fact, Taehan Electric Wire had no record of delivery of the specific goods at the time. Kim immediately dispatched a drum of 200-meter cables instead of simply 1.5 meters. As for a performance certificate, with the delivery certificate from a public corporation, the name of the model cable was stealthily inserted on the list and translated into English. After reviewing the samples, the Egyptians and competing firms were amazed at the excellent performance of the product. Its performance had exceeded the stated level on the certificate and it had passed the on-site protocol tests with ease – and with it, Taehan won the contract.

As expected, the Egyptian market provided the launching pad for Taehan to enter the wide African market. The firm was now a steady contender alongside American and European companies in the African market. Entering the early 2000s, the American and European companies retreated from the African market, and Taehan held 40 percent of the market and remained the dominant force in that area.[81] At that time, the volume of the communications cable market in Africa was $30 million per annum, of which Taehan occupied $12 million.

Kim then set his sights on Libya, which was embarking on a grand canal construction project in the early 1990s. It involved construction of a waterway stretching deep into the Sahara Desert and other cities across the country. Until then, Italy's Pirelli, by dint of historical and proximity ties, had enjoyed a near monopoly status for nearly 30 years in Libya. Italy was just a mere 12-hour sailing distance from Tripoli, whereas sailing from Busan took a month on average. To make a real dent, it was important for Taehan to overcome this geographic disadvantage. Faced with an urgent delivery, Kim hurriedly impressed on headquarters to consider air freight to achieve a timely delivery of the order, urging that "trust" at the end of the day is far more valuable "than money." So, two Korean Air cargo planes and one chartered Hong Kong Air cargo plane were mobilized, and all the goods for the first delivery were delivered in time accordingly. Because Libya was under UN sanctions, the planes had to land in neighboring Tunisia instead of Tripoli. The goods were then off-loaded and ferried by trucks across the border into Libya through the night to meet the delivery deadline. The company thus incurred financial losses, which prompted the head of the Libyan procurement agency to call Kim a "brother." Pirelli's near monopoly in the Libyan communications cable market had been reduced by half thanks to Kim's deftness.[82]

Thereafter his cable business moved down to South Africa. He acquired a South African cable company called M-Tech in 2000. In a market dominated by two European telecommunications companies, the newly acquired M-Tech emerged to rank on top. Up until then, he had sold a cumulative $100 million in Egypt, $50 million in Libya, and the South African subsidiary M-Tech had experienced a major turnover and generated a surplus the following year. He retired from the company in 2010. Thirty years have passed since he began his overseas marketing business for a company manufacturing leather gloves in 1980. For this he sanguinely said,

> I am in debt to families in Korea for my long overseas exploits. I have spent 30 years fully engaged in exports. It nearly cost my life along the way. But through it all, I was driven by the commitment to my family and my country. It was an immense pleasure to do all I did.[83]

Behind the enormous expansion of Korean exports, there were Korean salesmen who thread every nook and cranny of the globe, often separated from their families and risking their lives.

Notes

1 Cho Sang-haeng, *Jeongjuyeong, huimangeul gyeongyeonghada* [Chung Ju-yung, Managing the Hope] (Seoul, Korea: By Books, 2012); Park Sang-ha, *Igineun jungjuyeong, jijianneun ibyeongcheol* [Winning Chung Ju-yung, Not Losing Lee Byung-chull] (Seoul: Muhan, 2010).
2 Park, *Winning Chung Ju-yung*, 81–83.
3 *Ibid.*, 81–83.
4 O Won-chol, *The Construction of Pyramid-Type Export-Oriented Industries* (Seoul, Korea: Korea Type Economic Policy Institute, 2003), 368.
5 Hong Eun-ju and Lee Eun-hyeong, *Korian mirakeul 3: Sumeun gijeokdeul junghwahakgongeop, jichukeul heundeulda* [The Korean Miracle III: Heavy and Chemical Industry Shakes the Axis of the Earth] (Seoul, Korea: Nanam, 2015), 304–308.
6 *Ibid.*
7 Hyundai Seosan Farm Co. introduces the status of the Seosan reclamation site on its homepage, www.hdfnd.co.kr/
8 This remarkable method of construction drew attention of *Newsweek* and *Time* magazines. Hong and Lee, *Korian mirakeul 3*, pp. 304–308. "The *Seosan* reclamation has become a huge source of food which produces 54,000 tons of rice per annum."
9 Korea Engineering Club, *Joguk geundae juyeokdeul* [The Heroes of "Quantum Jump"] (Seoul, Korea: Quiparang Press, 2014), 331.
10 Lee In-yeol, "Nodongja Chung Juyeong-ui 100nyeon" [100 Years of Laborer Chung Ju-yung], *Chosun Ilbo*, March 28, 2015, A26, accessed August 9, 2017, http://news.chosun.com/site/data/html_dir/2015/03/27/2015032704352.html
11 Lee In-yeol and Yun Hyeong-jun, "Sangsangeul mandeuneun bul gateun dojeon" [A Fiery Challenge Changing Imagination to Reality], *Chosun Ilbo*, November 25, 2015, A2, accessed August 9, 2017, http://news.chosun.com/site/data/html_dir/2015/11/25/2015112500515.html?Dep0=twitter&d=2015112500515
12 Min Seok-ki, *Hoam Ibyeongcheol* [Hoam Lee Byung-chull] (Seoul, Korea: ReadcrsBook, 2012), and Park, *Winning Chung Ju yung*.
13 Lee reportedly said he embarked on this business consciousness of the Japanese perception of Koreans as a people who have no sense of working cooperatively.
14 Park, *Winning Chung Ju-yung*, 79–80.
15 In 1953 when the company was established, imports of sugar were 23,800 tons and its dependency ratio on imports was 100 percent. This was reduced to 51 percent in 1954, 27 percent in 1955 and 7 percent in 1956. Refer to Min Seok-ki, *Ho-Am Lee Byung-chull*, 87.
16 Min, *Hoam Lee Byung-chull*, 92.
17 *Ibid.*, 95.
18 Korea Engineering Club, *Heroes*, 457.
19 The remaining 50 percent share was owned by a small venture enterprise in the United States.
20 Hong and Lee, *The Korean Miracle III*, 263–264.
21 Min, *Hoam Lee Byung-chull*; Park, *Winning Chung Ju-yung*, 79–80.
22 Korea Engineering Club, *Heroes*, 463–466.

23 *Ibid.*, 464–469.
24 *Ibid.*, 468.
25 *Ibid.*
26 *Ibid.*, 464–468.
27 Hong and Lee, *The Korean Miracle III*, 400.
28 Park Sang-ha, *Winning Chung Ju-yung*, 136.
29 Korea Engineering Club, *Heroes*, 465–466.
30 *Ibid.*, 466.
31 Min Seok-ki, *Gyeongyeongui Jeongdo* [The Path of Management] (Seoul, Korea: ReadersBook, 2012), 59–60.
32 Park, Tae-jun, "The Memoirs of Park Tae-jun," *JoongAng Ilbo*, August 31, 2004.
33 Kim Yoon-hyeon, "Rimembeo Ibyeongchul Samseong Geurupui changeopju" [Remembering Lee Byung-chull, Samsung Group Founder], *Chosun Ilbo*, January 22, 2010, accessed August 9, 2017, www.chosun.com/site/data/html_dir/2010/01/22/2010012200890.html
34 For details, please refer to Park Tae-jun, "The Memoir of Park Tae-jun," *JoongAng Ilbo*, and Seo Gab-kyung, *The Steel King: The Story of Park Tae-jun* (Seoul, Korea: Haneon,2011) [in Korean].
35 Park Tae-jun, "The Memoirs of Park Tae-jun," *JoongAng Ilbo*, August 2–December 9, 2004.
36 *Ibid.*, August 16, 2004.
37 *Ibid.*
38 When Korea's foreign exchange earnings were nearly $40 million in 1961, the tungsten company alone earned $15 million. Despite its extraordinary contribution, the company was saddled with chronic deficits.
39 In the end, President Park opened the Kyungbu Highway in 1970, and Park Tae-jun completed the first phase of construction of the POSCO steel mill in 1973.
40 At that time, the fund was under execution with the agreement of both governments, and the remaining amount was $100 million.
41 Park, "The Memoirs of Park Tae-jun," September 1, 2004.
42 *Ibid.*, October 22, 2004.
43 *Ibid.*, September 30, 2004.
44 *Ibid.*, November 2, 2004.
45 *Ibid.*, September 15, 2004.
46 *Ibid.*, October 5, 2004.
47 *Ibid.*, November 23, 2004.
48 *Ibid.*, November 16, 2004.
49 Lee Dae-hwan, "Pocheol geonseolhyeonjand cheot bangmunhoe 'jecheolsoga doegineun doeneun geoya?'" [Park Chung-hee Upon Visiting the POSCO Construction Site for the First Time: "Is It Going to Become a Steel Mill?"] *Chosun Ilbo*, November 24, 2014, accessed August 9, 2017, http://premium.chosun.com/site/data/html_dir/2014/11/23/2014112302204.html
50 Park Tae-jun, "The Memoirs of Park Tae-jun," *JoongAng Ilbo*, October 21, 2004.
51 O Won-chol, *The Korea Story: President Park Jung-hee's Leadership and the Korean Industrial Revolution* (Seoul, Korea: Wisdom Tree, 2009), 796–803; Korea Engineering Club, *Joguk geundae juyeokdeul* [The Heroes of "Quantum Jump"] (Seoul, Korea: Quiparang Press, 2014), 15–45.
52 Korea Engineering Club, *Heroes*, 16.
53 This story is not publicly known through official documents but only to a few people who were present at the event. This is based on a presentation by O Won-chol at a KDS workshop in 2013.
54 O, *The Korea Story*.
55 Korea Engineering Club, *Heroes*, 18.

56 Lee Cheol-won, "Odaeyang hechimyeo dalleo beol-I 43nyeon . . . baetnom-eun geuroke ganangwa ssawotta" ['Daehan Nation, Our Story': The Sailor Fought Poverty], *Chosunilbo*, April 3, 2015, Accessed August 9, 2017, http://news.chosun.com/site/data/html_dir/2015/04/03/2015040300105.html
57 *Ibid.*
58 *Ibid.*
59 *Ibid.*
60 *Ibid.*
61 *Ibid.*
62 *Ibid.*
63 *Ibid.*
64 Lee Dong-hun, "Bakjeonghui daetongnyeong seugo bimunkkaji sseun busan taejongdae sunjinseonwon wiryengtap" [Park Chung-hee Established the Martyr Crews Memorial Tower and Wrote Its Epitaph], *Chosun Ilbo*, July 14, 2017, accessed August 9, 2017, http://pub.chosun.com/client/news/viw.asp?cate=C01&mcate=M1003&nNewsNumb=20170725392&nidx=25393
65 *Ibid.*
66 Lee Cheol-won, "Nobelsang daesin gisul gaebalhae joguk sallija-neun mal-e kkumui yeonguso tteona gwiwuk" [Let's Save the Fatherland Instead of Gaining the Nobel Prize . . . Leave the Institute and Return to Korea], *Chosunilbo*, May 15, 2015, accessed August 9, 2017, http://news.chosun.com/site/data/html_dir/2015/05/15/2015051500303.html
67 *Ibid.*
68 *Ibid.*
69 Korea Engineering Club, *Heroes*, 425–449.
70 *Ibid.*
71 Park Jong-in, "Byeongwon-e bachin cheongchun . . . doneun huimang, sarangeun guwoniyeotta" [The Youth Dedicated to Hospital—Money Was Hope and Love Rescue], *Chosun Ilbo*, April 24, 2015, Accessed August 9, 2017, http://news.chosun.com/site/data/html_dir/2015/04/24/2015042400278.html?related_all
72 *Geullwik aupeu! Dogil-lo gan gyeongje yeokgundeul* [Glück Auf! The Economic Forces That Went to Germany]. Live Broadcast. Directed by Sang-wook Park (Seoul, Korea: KBS, 2013), accessed August 7, 2017, www.kbs.co.kr/1tv/sisa/docucinema/view/vod/2151999_66621.html
73 Park Jong-in, "The Youth Dedicated to Hospital," April 24, 2015.
74 *Ibid.*
75 *Ibid.*
76 *Ibid.*
77 *Ibid.*
78 *Ibid.*
79 Park Jong-in, "Urineun jeongmal samakeseo nalloreul pallatta daehanminguk suchul dolgyeokdae" [The Export Titan: We Sold Stoves in the Desert], *Chosun Ilbo*, June 5, 2015, accessed August 9, 2017, http://news.chosun.com/site/data/html_dir/2015/08/11/2015081101807.html#08
80 *Ibid.*
81 *Ibid.*
82 *Ibid.*
83 *Ibid.*

7 Path to industrialization (2)
Heavy and chemical industries push the needle

1 Economic solutions to national security crises

That this barely subsisting country was setting its sights on competing in the international exports market alongside an aspiration for industrial development has been the punchline of its modern history. For this to happen, there had to be a corresponding collective reorientation of the possibilities on the horizon in ways hitherto unknown. Yet this had to be tinkered with in the looming realities of the sticky and captive geopolitical undercurrents of the region. For every rational analyst, it was easy to see why any gains under this cloud of geopolitics could easily be undone by an outbreak of hostilities. In fact, for most parts of the 1960s that was an ever-present reality. For instance, in 1966 alone the de facto demilitarized zone (DMZ) was the scene of nearly 37 transgressions by Pyongyang. These incidents surged to 447 in 1967 and 542 in 1968. Then still, a clandestine guerrilla band of 31 armed North Korean agents infiltrated to within 500 meters of the Blue House. All these incidents underscored the very tenuous nature of the security conditions created by the unresolved geopolitical vestiges of the Korean Peninsula.

President Park remained very uneasy about the South's relatively weaker economic base. There was an understanding that economic vitality almost certainly cannot be disentangled from military capability. The different policies of both Koreas at its independence further enlarged the gap between the two. The North retained 868 Japanese engineers and technicians on their territory after liberation. These technical remnants of the colonial state were to help ensure the continuation of the industrial plants and factories of the colonial government. As in most parts of its early history, Pyongyang also benefited from continued political and technical advice from a legion of Soviet experts, with the notable one being G. M. Malasanov.[1] Unlike the North, South Korea couldn't wait to see the backs of all Japanese experts after liberation. The consequence was as expected a disruption in the operations of the few remnants of colonial industrial structures. In the 1960s, the North produced military weapons and submarines, while the South could not manufacture even a rifle.

Moreover, things didn't look promising for the South, as the Cold War system was entering a phase of détente. The Nixon White House, with Henry Kissinger at the heart of the Nixon doctrine, served notice to Seoul in 1969 of plans to withdraw one infantry division from South Korea. This was followed by Vice President Spiro Agnew announcing the same year that US troops in Korea would be completely withdrawn in 5–6 years. Then a year later Nixon announced his now famous visit to the People's Republic of China. Given these circumstances, Seoul had every reason to be shaking in its boots.

Based on an internal South Korean review, Seoul was lagging Pyongyang in military capabilities on a ratio of 3 to 1. In addition to personal weapons such as rifles, the North Korean defense industry was producing large-caliber guns, ammunition, military vehicles, tanks and guided missiles on its own. What South Korea had was nothing but rifles of World War II vintage handed over by US forces. Moreover, left to its own devices Seoul had an uncharacteristically strategic deficiency in every respect.

Pyongyang intensified its military provocations against the South in the wake of the normalization of diplomatic relations between Beijing and Washington, because of the emerging détente between the East and the West. The gains of the Viet Cong in Indochina provided an important moral boost to Kim Il-sung's belief in a military solution to the problem of the division of the peninsula. North Korean agents infiltrated the South and made several unsuccessful attempts on the life of President Park, with one of them resulting in the death of the first lady. Another security scare occurred with the discovery of underground tunnels that were found in Yonchon in 1974, in Chulwon in 1975 and in Yanggu in 1990. North Korea dug the tunnels across the DMZ in an undoubted attempt to put many of its troops behind South Korean lines in the event of a war. All these were informed by the premise that Washington, which was now pursuing a policy of disengagement, would not commit itself to another war on the Korean Peninsula.

Third, the global economy was undergoing a great transformation in ways that were inimical to the core of the South Korean economy's production capacity. While protectionism was being strengthened throughout the world, China and other countries, which had recently jumped on the bandwagon of economic development, were fueling industrialization, intensifying competition in the world markets. The greatest potential threat was posed by China, a nation with a population of 1.3 billion that could build a vast domestic market and push for industrialization with low wages. The government understood that without urgent action, it would certainly be a matter of time until their products drove South Korean products out of world markets. That was the reason why South Korea, which was besieged diplomatically, militarily and economically, had to hasten to develop technology and upgrade its industry. Otherwise, its survival could be in jeopardy. South Korea would find its past achievements degenerating into ruins and its fate faltering, like a candle flickering in the wind.

Faced with a national security crisis, Seoul adopted a two-track strategy of an amiable policy toward North Korea and capacity building for self-reliance in national defense. Regarding the former, the South launched secret negotiations with the North, which led to the July 4 South–North Joint Declaration. The declaration called for easing military tensions on the Korean Peninsula and mutual efforts toward the reunification of Korea. President Park was reported to have said that these intermittent moments of goodwill could lay the foundation for confidence building and decrease the risk of war. His intention was to exploit this moment of lull in conflict to aggressively shore up Seoul's defense capacity.

As part of this policy, President Park in 1970 directed Kim Hak-yeol, then deputy prime minister and the Minister of the Economic Planning Board (EPB) to oversee the buildup of the defense sector. Manufacturing military weapons is a precision machine industry. Until then, Korea was incapable of a machine industry, much less precision machines. Bear in mind that developing a formidable defense industry required massive capital and financial investments. As stated earlier, military and economic capabilities have both causality and a correlational relationship, at least in the medium to long term. Against this backdrop, President Park summoned O to discuss how to boost the country's export. His specific goal was to achieve a $10 billion net export revenue. To this, O floated the idea of establishing a foundation for developing a heavy and chemical industry (HCI). In practical terms, this meant it would have to climb the ladder of the industrial pyramid in Figure 5.1 and complete its industrialization as advanced industrial countries did, such as the United States, Germany and Japan. He recalled a briefing he had given the president on the North Korean economy a few months prior.

> I briefed him on the state of the North Korean economy, with exports assumed to be in the $500-million to $600-million range in 1976 – a level South Korea reached in terms of per-capita exports in 1970. Maybe President Park felt that North Korea was exporting more than he had originally thought. When he asked about what South Korea should do to export $10 billion, President Park perhaps thought that South Korea would not be assured of clear-cut dominance over the North, even if it raised its exports to the level of $5 billion in the 1980s. He apparently wanted to raise the volume to $10 billion so that Kim Il-sung would not dare to challenge South Korea when it came to their race for supremacy. That was the only reasoning I could think of regarding the president's goal of $10 billion in exports – an ambition that he thought he could not attain unless he built a full-fledged heavy and chemical industry.[2]

There are four preconditions for developing an HCI: financial capital, manpower, economies of scale and marketing capabilities. First, as to the financial capital requirement, when the government's HCI plan was on the drawing board, its estimated cost was $10 billion for capital investments. That was an enormous amount of money for a developing country, considering that for 1972 alone Korean cumulative export revenue stood at $1.8 billion. When it had the pressing task to feed its people, how was the government expected to raise such an amount to make such a long-term investment? The most viable financing option was to procure external capital, but even with that, few foreign investors were willing to take a huge risk in making investments in the face of mounting uncertainty about Korea's HCI.

Second, HCI requires a steady supply of highly skilled technicians and workers and a research and development (R&D) capacity. It is one of the few industries that demands a high level of accuracy and precision. For instance, the manufacturing of rifles and guns demands precision permitting a margin of error no greater than 1/100 of a millimeter. But the smallest margin of error available in the nation at the time was 1/10 millimeter. In other words, the domestic industry could not produce rifles and guns, because technicians and workers were incapable of doing the high-precision craft. Besides, it requires the development of science and technology and R&D capacity for continuous development. Despite having an abundant labor flow, it was a very unskilled pool that was just unsuited for the HCI. Korean workers were not so attentive to their work and not so careful with the final touches; sloppy work was anathema to the HCI, which demanded strict adherence to specifications of the blueprint. Many of them were perceived to be easily distracted after a few initial hours of work.

Few incentives were given to skilled training, with techniques and skills not valued in the Korean occupational value system. Skilled workers came third after the literati and farming classes and before the merchant class in the traditional four-tier value system. What Korean workers learned was simple work using agricultural tools such as hoes and A-frame carriers. It was widely held both among Koreans and foreigners interested in Korean affairs that precision work did not fit Korean workers. When Kim Hak-yeol, then deputy prime minister, asked a visiting Japanese delegation for Japan's assistance in building what he called four core plants in Korea, the delegation leader was reported to have said that developing a machinery industry in Korea would be like growing roses in a desert. Instead, he recommended a shipbuilding industry that required less precise skills.[3]

Third, a small domestic market would pose a serious problem when it came to economies of scale. Construction of industrial plants in the field of economies of scale would require a huge scale of facility investment. In a small economy like Korea, if a plant was to be built for economies of scale, it would result in overproduction and a surplus inventory. On the contrary, if a smaller plant was built to meet the small market demand, the downside would raise the production cost, making its products more expensive than imports. Usually, countries with HCI including steel mills and automobile industries tend to have vast populations. South Korea's population was merely 35 million at that time. For instance, the country's first-ever attempt at an integrated steel mill in 1962 occurred at a time when the domestic demand was at a mere 116,000 tons per annum, while the international standard was 3 million tons. It was no different when it came to petrochemical production. A naphtha-cracking plant would have to have a production capacity of 300,000 tons or more; in terms of ethylene, Korea's domestic demand was at 30,000 tons. The World Bank and a legion of other foreign experts advised the government to abandon the idea of constructing a steel mill, and opt instead for importing steel, which would be less expensive. Eventually the steel mill plan had to be shelved in the face of opposition from the World Bank and the country's donors. It also had to suspend its plan to construct a large shipyard when Japan refused to finance its construction, claiming that it would not be feasible at all.[4] The international consensus by well-meaning experts and multilateral agencies was a damning rejection of the idea as inconceivable, given the country's adverse conditions.

Then finally the elephant in the room was how to market the brand "Made in Korea." If perceptions are indispensable to a successful brand, then clearly there was nothing to inspire confidence in anything Korea-related. Moreover, major international brand names already held a hegemonic stranglehold on the global HCI market and could scarcely welcome new entrants. They had pockets deep enough to follow the prevailing market practice of providing purchasers with credit or permit them deferred payments. The multinational corporations (MNCs) had both brand power and global sales networks as well as capacities to provide credit, while Korean heavy and chemical industries yet to be born had none of that. Against this backdrop, there was real doubt whether Korea could build heavy and chemical plants with economies of scale and compete against MNCs based in advanced countries, which were dominating the world markets with abundant financial resources and internationally well-known brands. Simply put, Korea did not look prepared for an HCI.

President Park, despite all the obstacles, was determined to launch an HCI in his belief that nothing else would guarantee sustainable development and national security for South Korea. He had to take extraordinary measures in preparations because the hindrances were anything but ordinary. First, he thought that he needed to stabilize the domestic political landscape, and thus he set about to concentrate power in the executive to facilitate swift and effective decision-making. For this purpose, he issued a special presidential decree on October 17, 1972 (the October Yushin modeled after Japan's Meiji Restoration) for a revision of the constitution, which stipulated the election of the president by an indirect vote and strengthened presidential power to appoint one-third of the National Assembly members.

The restructuring of the political system was followed by two other decrees on January 12, 1973 – the Decree of State Building of HCI and the Decree of Orienting the People Toward Science – a measure designed to conduct the envisioned HCI development successfully and to strengthen economic power sufficient for securing national security. The three decrees were cornerstones for an HCI. In making them, he was pinning the nation's fate on the HCI project. He wanted to concentrate national resources on industrialization at the expense of procedural democracy. Clearly, notwithstanding whatever noble intentions informed these decisions, opinions are divided on its import. Critics contend that these were part of a long litany of ruses for an arbitrary power grab by the president.

2 Defending the Motherland[5]

As stated earlier, the deputy prime minister was tasked by the president to oversee the revamping of the nation's defense capabilities. Dr. Harry Choi of the Battelle Memorial Institute was contracted by the deputy prime minister to advise the government on building a formidable defense manufacturing industry. His report proposed the establishment of five core plants: a composite steel mill, a foundry, a special steel plant, a dockyard and a heavy machinery plant. It is worth highlighting that while Dr. Choi's recommendations were welcomed, they did not constitute an entirely new concept. President Park was at various points interested in steel mills and other large-scale industrial plants. Some of these projects were already well underway, albeit at limited capacity as will be discussed later in this chapter. The reason for his interest in these industries had a lot to do with the fact that steel is required to produce weapons, automobile technology for tanks and dockyards for warships. Because the composite steel mill project was in progress, the remaining four were called the four core plants for building the defense industry.[6]

The plan of establishing the four core plants was reported to the president and was approved in June 1970. The required funds for the construction of the plants were to come from a loan from Japan. A task force consisting of officials from the EPB, the Ministry of Trade and Industry (MTI), the Ministry of Defense, and the Korea Institute of Science and Technology (KIST) – dubbed the Heavy Industry Propulsion Team – was thus established. Upon the recommendation of the team, the Agency for Defense Development (ADD) was established the same year to oversee R&D in the defense industry. In early 1971, a field survey was conducted for about 500 private industrial facilities to check the industrial capacity for the production of weapons. Being fully aware of the keen interests of President Park, Deputy Prime Minister Kim Hak-yeol became a committed overseer of the project. However, the four core plants project stalled from the beginning due to Tokyo's reluctance to fully cooperate. The feasibility study team headed by the director-general of the Heavy Industry Bureau of the Ministry of Trade and Industry of Japan visited Korea, and concluded that the project was infeasible due to the lack of capacity for HCI coupled with Korea's lack of any history of technology development.

Deputy Prime Minister Kim also encouraged businessmen to invest in the projects. However, very few businessmen had interests in the defense industry because it required huge investments coupled with unusually very high risks and uncertainty. After receiving a briefing on the progress of the project at the EPB in November 1971, President Park was disappointed. Chief of Staff Kim Chung-yum recalls, "On the way to the Blue House after the meeting, President Park said with a sigh of grief, "after being entrusted with the project for one year yet no progress has been made."[7] Coincidentally a breakthrough was to come about that same day, even as he was so crestfallen. After arriving at the office, Kim Chung-yum received a call from O Won-chol, who explained that because the EPB-backed defense industry project was going nowhere, he thought he could suggest some alternative policy solutions. O was invited to be granted an audience with the president, where he made what was almost a passionate sales pitch to the chief executive as follows:[8]

> Enterprises are concerned about profits. Without securing long-term profitability they will never invest. The reason why it is hard to obtain international

loans and to secure the interests of businessmen is because the plants have an exclusive military purpose. This offers little prospects for making profit during peace time. They can also hardly attract highly skilled technical manpower. Every weapon are parts in disassembly. Every viable defense industry would need to have as its other goal a strong heavy and chemical industry that can have the dual utility of convertibility to weaponry during war. This is linked with the profit motive of the private sector. The four core plants plan needs to be reexamined with respects to economic feasibility and international competitiveness, and then consider financial procurement. In this regard, we can make use of good civilian factories which are already in operation. Manufacturing of parts of weapons under specific classification can be allotted to selected factories with processing capacity of precision machines according to their expertise. The ADD can control their quality through routine regulation. Instead, it is necessary to ensure that such companies run 70 percent of their business on the production of civilian goods.

Up until this point, the president was mulling giving up on the project until O's presentation gave him a renewed confidence in staying the full course. He then conferred with Chief of Staff Kim, who concurred with the proposal. After further deliberation, the president apparently called out to his chief of staff, saying:

From now onwards, I will personally take charge of developing the defense industry as well as the heavy and chemical industry which is the foundation of the former. Let O work at the Presidential Secretariat. Tell the Minister of Defense and the Chief of the ADD to start developing weapons right now! Make sure to tell them that this is a presidential command.[9]

At the president's request, O was accordingly appointed as the Chief Secretary for Economic Affairs II, with specific responsibility of counseling the president on the defense and heavy and chemical industry. This was a clear testament to the president's commitment to national security.[10]

Mr. O recalled the events as follows:

On my appointment to the second chief economic secretary, President Park's instructions clearly indicated the urgency of the issues at hand and that we needed to produce weapons necessary for the armament of 20 reserve divisions with light equipment in advance. For that purpose, he requested that a special design room of military weapons be established in the Blue House and he would directly supervise the making of weapons prototypes. As the commander gives order in a military operation, President Park stood on his feet whilst issuing his instructions, and I received his instruction standing straight and stiff. I felt how tense the President considered the situation.

With the president at the helm, the plan took off briskly.[11] O set the deadline for production of prototype weapons at the end of that December, of which the

ADD was given only a little over one month for its manufacturing. Then in line with the strict orders, the prototypes were commissioned and displayed at the Blue House that December 16 to pomp and pageantry. Then on April 3, 1972, a historic demonstration of weapons made in Korea was held with dignitaries of the president, and VIPs from the government and chief of staff of the army. The weapons included carbines, hand grenades, grenade launchers, 3.5-inch and 66 mm antitank rockets, and an antipersonnel mine. All the weapons were successfully built and showed great power. On the next day, a presidential order was passed down that large-caliber guns for soldiers in active service as well as military equipment for 2.5 million reserve forces be localized, and large-scale plants for their production be constructed at the rear location for security consideration.

Further advancement of the defense industry came under the aegis of the Yulgok Project (1974–1996). The first phase of the development plan period was 1974–1981, involving an investment of KRW 3.14 billion. To finance the project, a defense tax was introduced as an object tax. With this background, the Changwon Machinery Base was born as a core base of the nation's defense industry. In 1977, a total of 88 machinery plants were in this base. Several US congressmen visited the base and expressed satisfaction with its course. In 1978, the Military Committee of the US House of Representative dispatched a delegation to offer a final review of the US policy of withdrawal of troops from Korea. O recalled thus:

> After the tour of the *Changwon* complex, the delegation became serious. After seeing the huge arsenal stockpile, they were perplexed. They were worried about the possibility of transferring military facilities to the Communist bloc. Before their departure from Korea, the delegation announced that "Since South Korea has already built the capability to defend itself, it coincides with US interests to have South Korea as an ally. This will be reported to the (US) government."[12]

In the summer of 1977, after the huge investments in the defense industry, a ceremony was held to showcase the latest advances in the country's weapons capabilities. The occasion brought together foreign dignitaries, senior government officials and representatives of opposition parties. Then a boisterous President Park announced that "I think that now our military forces are much stronger than, and far superior in equipment and training to, North Korea."[13] One thing to note is that in promoting the defense industry, the Yulgok project and HCI, Park kept his word of personally overseeing every aspect of the policy, thus bypassing the EPB and the Ministry of Defense. This was a departure from the established norm of delegating development initiatives to the deputy prime minister and the EPB. It is further somewhat unusual for the president to arrogate the responsibilities of the deputy prime minister, given that he was among one of his most trusted aides. In the absence of any verifiable explanation, we can only speculate that the president was driven to take such actions because he felt so strongly about the nation's defense needs and thus felt the need to directly manage every aspect of it. In any case, the buck of national security ultimately stops at his desk, irrespective of who is in charge. He was somewhat determined to ensure that the project was not in any way held back by administrative procedures of the defense ministry or EPB, which can explain why he took such unorthodox measures. There is also a second hypothesis that the president took all the unsuccessful attempts on his life very personally because there was credible evidence that the assassination attempts were the direct order of his personal foe, Kim Il-sung, for which he saw it as a personal obligation to return in kind every covert attempt on his life. As a battle-tested military general, you can expect nothing less from him.[14]

3 Place your bets

In December 1972, President Park convened a meeting of all his top officials to a conference in the Blue House, where O briefed them on the president's HCI plan. The plan earmarked six industrial sectors for development: steel mill, machinery, shipbuilding, electronics, petrochemicals and nonferrous metals. The projects to be launched under the plan included an integrated still mill for Pohang Steel Co. (POSCO), an auto assembly plant for Hyundai Motor Co., the Gumi industrial complex for electronics, the Ulsan and Yeocheon petrochemical complexes and the Changown machinery complex, with construction of some of them already underway.

As was referred to in the previous section, the country was confronting four major challenges in its HCI bid, with funding being the biggest of them all. O summed up the meeting as follows:

> It took about four hours until he said, "Thank you for listening to my briefing." As the room remained totally silent, President Park took his turn. Sitting upright with his hands on his lap, he said to O in a solemn and quiet voice, "Mr. O, how much will this cost?" To which I responded, "If domestic funds and foreign borrowings are put together, it would amount to about 10 billion in U.S. dollars." The president began to move his head up and down slowly, and then looked up toward the ceiling in deep thought. He was apparently comparing the amount with the country's annual total exports at the time, which stood at $1.6 billion. Then, he turned to Nam Duck-woo, Minister of Finance, who was sitting behind him, and asked, "Minister Nam, can you arrange the necessary funds?" It turned out to be a rhetorical question. Nam responded saying, "The amount of funds we need is too enormous . . ." Nam was equivocating in replying. President Park said in a solemn and dignified voice, "I am not starting a war, am I?" The President seemed to be by himself. Usually on such occasions you would find the ministers vigorously argue amongst themselves. But not on that day. As President Park sat stoically, with his eyes seemingly gazing upon something others could not see, none of us dared utter a word. Instead, silence prevailed in the conference room, until the decision was eventually made to launch the $10-billion project.[15]

President Park's question regarding the "war" needs elaboration for better understanding. In historical terms, at the onset of the Meiji Restoration, Japan was confronted with the same dilemma. Up until the return of the Meiji emperor in 1868, Japan was all but a perilously backward country, tearing itself apart with legions of dubious feudal lords. It lacked a properly disciplined standing army and relied on a very primitive technological system. The consequence was that Japan became subservient to the great powers of the day, whose whims and caprices bound Japan into trade treaties that worked against its interests. The Meiji emperor understood that for Japan to regain its rightful place in the community of nations and fully restore its territorial integrity, desperate measures had to be taken.[16] It was then that the emperor made the conscious decision of investing more than half of the nation's annual budget in preparing for both the Sino-Japanese and Russo-Japanese wars. It involved extreme belt-tightening by the Japanese people. The president thus used the Japanese analogy to illustrate why it was imperative for the nation to make important sacrifices in preparation for long-term gains. Unlike the Japanese case, the sacrifice the president was ostensibly alluding to was for the Korean people to build a sound base for job opportunities and to build the country's military capability in anticipation of defense against aggression.

The message he apparently wanted to get across to the participants was that South Korea would have to overcome any obstacle it might encounter in building a HCI for a strong economy if the country was to have supremacy over North Korea.[17] After the meeting, President Park met with Finance Minister Nam privately and once again impressed on him to take all measures to ensure the required funds were procured for the project. For Nam, the president's obsession with the project was a solid command for which he realized that, in his own words, "I have to resign if I was found to be derelict in my duty."[18] Raising domestic funds for HCI was easier said than done, given that South Korea had no financial market to speak of at the time.

Besides, there was no domestic credit or capital market, only local savings banks that offered short-term loans to businesses. Driven by these constraints, Mr. Nam came up with the idea of a National Investment Fund (NIF), which was to be created with parts of savings deposits of banks, insurance premiums and other public funds.[19] The law enacted for the NIF required banks to put 10–39 percent of deposits into the fund, insurance companies 40–50 percent of their premium revenues into the fund, and public funds 90 percent of their reserve into the fund. These directives were implemented in oblivion to the interests of the firms in the financial industry; moreover, firms under a free market system are supposed to make investment decisions on their own. Economists and banking experts criticized the government for driving the banking industry backwards. The rationale behind the creation of the fund was that capital gains from the operation of HCI plants would be returned to the people. During 1974–1979, the NIF financed 61 percent of HCI investment requirements.[20]

As to the question of improving the country's manpower and R&D capacity, the government's policy was already geared toward realizing this objective through the economic development programs that were launched in the 1960s. Each of these issues will be taken up in Chapter 8.

Regarding the issue of economies of scale, the scale of plants needed to be adjusted to reflect the unique characteristics of individual industries. In determining the scale of an HCI plant, it was decided to have as large a capacity for production as the market permitted at the time, with an eye for expansion that would follow when demand picked up. A forecast for future demand is critical in determining an investment's viability. Multilateral development banks, donor countries and foreign financial experts conducted a demand forecast based on the past trend and provided feasibility studies, with the conclusion that the domestic market was too small to accommodate HCI, in which an integrated steel mill and an auto assembly plant were included. The Korean government always had to argue against feasibility studies for HCIs and mega-projects by multilateral development banks and international experts. In defiance of their opposition, however, President Park committed himself to building an HCI because it was the only way for Korea to sustain growth in exports and reinforce national security.

As it turned out, demand surpassed most liberal forecasts by even the standards of the most optimistic Korean experts. President Park and his government were vindicated when demand took a path different from its past trend just at the time the Korean economy began to take off. The usual forecasting did not consider the possibility that demand would be on a completely different path as the economy took off.

Regarding the issue of the competitiveness of Korean HCI products on the global market, the government thought that the international competitiveness of parts and intermediate goods was critical. On this specific issue, the government launched programs for industrial relocation and localization of parts. An industrial cluster was thus established in consideration of sea transportation, industrial water supply, electricity and energy networks. The Promotion of Industrial Base Development Act 1973 provided the legal framework for this policy. Thereafter six zones of industrial clusters and individual industries were disposed to those zones, respectively. Thus, industrial clusters of petrochemicals and fertilizers, electronics, steel, shipbuilding, nonferrous metals, and machinery plants and factories were established in an appropriate zone according to the characteristics of individual industries.

As was discussed in Section 5.3, a host of policies were initiated to improve competitiveness of small and medium-sized enterprises (SMEs) to operate within the required value chain of manufacturing parts and intermediate goods of large corporations. It started with the earmarking of a timeline for parts localization and granting access to a host of incentive systems such as providing concessional loans and tax breaks for that purpose. Infrastructure construction and subsidies for utility prices were provided during its gestation period if it was necessary. The government required approval for the import of industrial and machinery products, through which the import of locally produced parts for HCI were not allowed. It also included provisions for the implementation of a reverse tariff system that surcharged higher rates on imported parts. Finished goods were thus relatively cheaper. Supported by such policies, engineers and entrepreneurs of SMEs devoted themselves to developing parts with the same quality as foreign ones by disassembling and assembling imported sample parts repeatedly, and sometimes by consulting with retired engineers from parts-producing companies in advanced countries. This policy worked to encourage localization of parts rather than preference for imports of the same.

In some cases, the price of final products had to be differentiated between the local market and the international market. Because Korean companies could ill afford to charge high prices in international markets, they offered lower prices on the international market, and higher ones on the local market to compensate for losses from the international market. This was a classic case of pursuing a deliberate policy of a state-led price compensating differential. Thankfully, it allowed for Korean companies to step into the residual market left by Japanese firms with the weapon of low prices and gradually expanded their market. For instance, Hyundai completed the design of the Pony car in February 1974 and the first Pony was built in January 1976. Export of the Pony began in June 1976, yet it was not until 1986 that the Pony could enter the lucrative US market, after years of dangling on the periphery of the international market, and with it bolster its brand reputation.[21]

The HCI policy therefore provided the momentum for a quantum leap in the country's industrialization drive toward the 1970s. In no time, these policies enabled local industries to sink roots into both the global and domestic value chain system, taking advantage of every opportunity to step up the plate. Using the Hoffmann coefficient as an indicator of industrialization as was discussed in Section 5.1, South Korea achieved less than 1.0 in 1977 and it finally broke through the 0.5 level in 1990, formally becoming an advanced industrial state. In the world market of steel, automobiles, shipbuilding, petrochemicals and electronics, Korean companies soared up, as will be discussed in the next section. It was on the back of these stellar achievements that culminated to what has become widely known in popular culture as the "Miracle on the Han River." Ultimately it reached the top stage of the pyramid-type industrial development model of Figure 5.1, establishing itself as a fully fledged industrial economy at the turn of the century.

Suffice it to take a closer look at a few important aspects of the industrialization process that took place. I think it is necessary to provide vital context for how the industrialization process was achieved at a record breathtaking speed, unprecedented in the annals of history. The Industrial Revolution started in England and spread out to all other parts of the Western world and to Japan. All in all, it took 200 years in Western Europe and 100 years in Japan for full industrialization to take root.[22] No other country born in the post–World War II era has since turned itself into an industrialized country until South Korea did so in 1990, as shown by the coefficient – a mere several decades after the revolution of May 16, 1961.[23] One possible explanation for the speed of industrialization is "the advantage of late starters." It simply means such economies that come into the game late can reduce the learning cost for industrial development. According to Alexander Gerschenkron's seminal 1962 work on economic backwardness, the greater the relative backwardness, the higher the rates of economic growth in the early stages of economic growth.[24] Whatever way you look at it, the industrial performance of South Korea is unique.

Moreover, full industrialization or what I have referred to as the HCI could still take place despite the country's relatively marginal population size. As general economic theory went, the size of a population matters, and a country with a population of 100 million or more was amenable to full industrialization. But the South Korean population was a mere 35 million in 1976, 3 years after the HCI policy was launched, and yet it was still able to pull this off. But beneath this achievement was a consistent travail of improvisational and experimental attempts at swimming against the tide. This is seen in the fact that very few people, including supposed experts and scholars, believed that there was even the remotest possibility of achieving any of the gains made in the HCI process.

If we look into the process of building HCI in Korea, we may find that it was really a thorny path. First, most people including leading scholars and intellectuals, domestic as well as international, thought that building steel mills and automobile and shipbuilding industries is infeasible in Korea when the projects were proposed by the government. When President Park claimed that Korea would export cars to the world and open up one-vehicle-for-one-household-age, even leading intellectuals and scholars of Korea accused that, in an attempt to prolong his political regime, he was cheating the people with unfeasible promises. International institutions or experts argued that most Korean HCI projects had no viability, as in the case of steel mills and automobile and shipbuilding projects. Second, the HCI plan provoked harsh criticism on account of market distortion. Scholars, professors and minority political party leaders argued that the government was distorting resource allocation in the market, and in doing so causing inefficiency and fueling inflation. As a consequence, they went on to say that large corporations were growing fast at the expense of SMEs.

Multilateral development banks and foreign financial experts who were skeptical about the drive for an HCI also maintained that most of the big-ticket HCI projects that the Korean government had launched or was planning to launch had no economic feasibility. Moreover, they argued that its unwarranted excess intervention in the market would result in government failure. The criticism made it difficult for the Korean government to secure financial support and technological help from advanced countries. Their skepticism and criticism, based on well-researched analyses, could not be simply brushed aside as unwarranted. Yet, their analyses were limited, as was later evidenced by the outcome of successful industrialization in Korea: so many of the HCI projects attained the intended goals of economic viability.

Two flaws were found in those otherwise flawless analyses. One was that they did not take the role of political leadership and the people's desire into account. If a political leader succeeded in harnessing the strong desire his people had for prosperity into a driving force, he could turn what appeared to be an unattainable goal into a reality. That was what President Park did in defiance of mounting pressure against his HCI plan. In the case of the Korean steel mill project, as was referred to in Section 7.4, Dr. John P. W. Jaffe, the World Bank's expert, who derided South Korea's proposal of a steel mill project, was years later compelled to eat humble pie. He was to gleefully admit that he underestimated the depth of the resolve and the strength of the leadership personified in Park Tae-jun in getting the steel mill project off the ground. On its surface, it may be excused as an escapist meander from a well-meaning individual speaking from an ivory tower, and would have to bear no responsibility whatsoever for the success or failure of the policies he recommends to begetting governments.

The other was that those analyses, based on Korea's dismal past performances alone, did not take its potentiality into account. The forecasts by multilateral development banks and foreign financial experts were rendered useless when demand for domestically manufactured HCI products surged beyond the liberal expectations of optimistic Korean government planners.

Of course, this is not to say that the pursuit of industrialization produced nothing but good results. Far from it. Citizens had to bear the brunt of these grand projects in the form of heavy tax burdens. You didn't have to subscribe to libertarianism to understand why this naturally triggered considerable tax resistance. For instance, the introduction of the value added tax (VAT) in 1977 for this very purpose was met with popular protests and disaffection to the government. As I stated earlier, the fear of domestic critics about the government's HCI policy being disproportionately skewed toward large corporations at the expense of SMEs also had its legitimate place in this rancorous debate.

True, the drive for HCI resulted in the concentration of economic power in the hands of a select few conglomerates (*chaebol*). Therefore, the nation had to pay the price for deepening economic bipolarization. I make these comments within the context of the importance of understanding the difference between intentions behind a given policy and the ultimate effects of that policy. The HCI policy did indeed leave some sectors of the economy behind. But then in terms of effect, it also holds true that in aggregate terms the country is far better off with the development of its own indigenous corporations, which for all the criticism have been important drivers of economic growth just as any foreign multinational could have conceivably done. We also see that attempts, albeit somewhat belatedly, were instituted to address this imbalance and give SMEs an opportunity to get a foot in the door.

The growth of South Korea as an industrial power contributed not only to a high level of income of the people but also to national security. The economic gap between the South and the North reversed in the early 1970s, and the latter steadily ceded its perceived geopolitical advantage. Diplomatically, the base of national security was consolidated, as will be discussed in Section 11.4. What we see is that a sustained economic growth had a spillover effect on the geopolitical contest for supremacy between the rival Koreas. A bolstered national security landscape is the palpable outcome of these industrialization policies. What would the country be like today if it had abandoned its pursuit of an HCI in the 1970s?

It takes no genius to imagine that it would not have as high levels of income and trade surplus as it current does.

Behind the great achievement that changes the fortune of a country or people lies incredible sacrifices and pains, as was discussed in the previous chapter. One more individual, former Deputy Prime Minister Kim, immortalizes this journey. Appointed to the position at the age of 46, his unwavering commitment to the president's vision of industrialization even at great cost to his health eventually led him to die of cancer at the age of 49. Upon hearing the news of his death in a meeting, President Park left for the restroom, where he wept bitterly, sobbing that "I drove him to overwork which led Kim to unexpected death."[25] President Park, for his part, before his own untimely death was the moral force behind the dedication of his staff and team.

4 The rise of national industries

Steel[26]

Steel is to industrialization what rainwater is to an oasis. Demand for steel surged as reconstruction and industrial development proceeded in the 1960s. However, in 1961, the domestic demand for steel was at most 116,000 metric tons. The majority was produced through a process of melting scrap iron in small-scale electric smelting furnaces. As in other areas, South Korea was lagging North Korea in steel production during this period too. North Korea for instance had the capacity to produce 1 million metric tons of pig iron at the time. South Korea meanwhile lacked the fundamental conditions favorable for developing an iron and steel industry, because of both challenges of economies of scale and the difficulties associated with using iron ore as a primary raw material. South Korea had few sizable iron ore deposits on its territory. It also did not have the requisite technology and capital for the construction and maintenance of an integrated iron and steel plant.

It wasn't just a question of limited domestic production, but also as alluded to earlier, the country had a very marginal domestic demand that made the construction of a steel mill an impossible proposition. If you think of the fact that the average international annual capacity standard required for a steel plant stood at 3 million metric tons, then it becomes clear why this was the case. These explain why it was mainly established industrial economies of the day such as the United States, Japan, Germany, Great Britain and a few others who had the capacity to produce industrial scale steel mills. Despite the unfavorable conditions, President Park wanted to build an integrated iron and steel works as he had an unwavering belief that it was an integral part of the industrialization he was in pursuit of. Moreover, it was one of the three pieces of advice given him by West German Chancellor Ludwig Erhard in 1964.

As part of the first steps toward the realization of this goal, Dr. Kim Jae-kwan, a Korean scientist resident in West Germany, commissioned a report entitled "Proposal for Development of Iron and Steel Industry in Korea," as the primary policy framework for steel.[27] Toward that end President Park asked Fred Foy, chairman of Koppers Co. of the United States, to organize a consortium for steel mill construction in Korea, which culminated in the Korea International Steel Associates (KISA) being formed in December 1966, bringing together steel mill builders and engineering companies from the United States, West Germany, Britain, France and Italy. Under a presidential decree, a long-term project to develop a domestic steel industry was incorporated into the second Five-Year Economic Development Plan starting in 1967. The KISA decided in October 1967 that the mill's annual production capacity would be 600,000 tons and that its construction would be financed with $100 million in loans from abroad and another $25 million from domestic sources.

For some reason, the government put the cart before the horse in 1968 when it went ahead to establish the Pohang Iron and Steel Co. (POSCO) and declared the launch of steel mill construction without procuring the required funding for the project. Unsurprisingly, the negotiation for procuring a foreign loan hit a snag along the way, seriously calling into question the entire project. President Park dismissed Chang Ki-young from the post of deputy prime minister, holding him responsible for the delay in securing the funding and appointed Minister of Trade and Industry Park Chung-hoon as his replacement. No immediate progress was forthcoming even with this personnel shift. The new deputy prime minister visited the United States and West Germany to persuade their export-import banks to commit themselves to the provision of loans to the country's steel mill project, but his efforts were to no avail.

Although no progress was being made in its negotiations with potential loan providers, the KISA urged the government to conclude a contract with a technical service provider on operating the plant for the first several years. Around this time, an official in charge of the Korea desk at the World Bank published a report claiming that the country's steel mill project had no economic viability. You could hardly quarrel with such a conclusion, in part, as the evidence on the ground seemed to precisely point to just that.

In fact, it is worth noting that there is a precedence of developing countries failing at steel mill ventures. A number of developing countries, including India, Turkey, Mexico and Brazil, ventured into similar grand projects in the early 1960s, with economic viability in mind. However, they ran into various difficulties concerning financing, technology, operation and diseconomies of scale. South Korea's conditions for integrated steel mills was even worse than those countries in terms of domestic market and resource endowment. It therefore came as no surprise that the project failed to attract the required funding, to which President Park was quoted as saying, "We will still have to build a steel mill no matter what."[28]

President Park was under pressure to abandon his steel mill plan. Newspapers came out and demanded in their editorials that the nation should choose to import steel products instead of pushing for domestic production. Rather than yielding to mounting pressure, he renewed his resolve, appointed Kim Hak-yeol to succeed Park Chung-hoon as new deputy prime minister and put him in charge of building POSCO. Entering his office for the first time as the new deputy prime minister, Kim Hak-yeol wrote "Construction of an Integrated Iron and Steel Plant" on the blackboard in his office.[29] Then he told his secretaries that it should only be erased when he leaves office or when the steel mill construction is completed. As the new man at the helm of the bid to secure funding for the project, he was practically burdened by the pressure to deliver results.

After nearly every effort had failed, the last resort was to go against the terms of the bilateral agreement with Tokyo over the reparation funds. The fund projects were already underway based on the formal agreement between both governments. Given that the funds were a compensation for Japan's colonial rule, few would have imagined they could justifiably be used for such an industrial project. It was generally believed that they should be used to improve the quality of life of all Korean people, because they were the victims of Japan's colonial occupation in one way or another. Yet, the negotiators proposed to spend them on a large industrial project.

On hearing the proposal, President Park ordered that the existing spending plan of the reparation be suspended and renegotiated.[30] His aim was to spend the remainder of the fund on the steel mill project. As was discussed in Section 6.2, it took a great deal of persuasion to get Tokyo to accede to the proposed changes to the originally agreed terms. Then a new agreement was signed on December 3, 1969, paving the way for POSCO to build an integrated iron and steel mill. In fact, South Korea was indebted to Yoshihiro Inayama, Nippon Steel chairman, for the successful renegotiations.[31] He endorsed the steel mill project in the face of opposition from China, which declared the four Zhou Enlai principles in May 1970, effectively banning Japanese companies doing business with Taiwan and South Korea from entering the Chinese market.

A task force on the steel mill project, established on orders of President Park, set the capacity for pig iron production at 1 million tons, much smaller than the international standard capacity mentioned earlier. To get the project up and running, an additional KRW 23 billion from state coffers had to be injected into the project in addition to investing $30.8 million from the reparation fund. The government also appropriated $42.9 million in soft loans from the Japanese government and another $50 million in commercial loans from the Export-Import Bank of Japan to help cover the remainder.[32] Another measure taken by the government to help POSCO attain sound financial management was to shoulder the burden of financing the construction of all required infrastructure. In addition, it also made it possible for POSCO to turn loans from public institutions and banks into equity shares to retain profits instead of paying them out in dividends to its shareholders – the Korean government, Korea Development Bank, commercial banks and the Korea Tungsten Mining Company.

If funding proved to be an extremely tall order, construction was not any easier. When construction started, none of the 30-odd POSCO founding members knew what a smelting furnace was really like. Those responsible for construction later compared the construction process to waging a war. Yet they accomplished the mission, comprising 22 huge plants, in record time and at the lowest possible cost.[33] POSCO had to reclaim 8.26 million square meters of coastal wetland by dredging sand, rocks and clay from the seabed for the construction site, occasionally fighting high tidal waves. Work had to be done around the clock if the deadline was to be met. Normal operation would not have required more than 300 square meters of concrete to be poured each day, but the tight work schedule raised the amount to 700 square meters per day.[34] Based on its business strategy of manufacturing final steel products with imported intermediate products during the period of construction works underway, POSCO built rolling mills ahead of smelting furnaces and other plants. By doing so, it could use profits from the final products to help defray the construction cost. POSCO's growth into a global steelmaking powerhouse cannot be talked about without mentioning the unwavering support President Park had as its patron and the unreserved devotion Park Tae-jun maintained as its founding leader.

President Park protected POSCO from undue influence of special interest individuals and groups. One case in point involved political contributions by corporations. It was a political custom that a part of foreign loans that Korean businesses procured to finance their projects found its way into the pockets of political parties and leaders. Aware of this canker, President Park ordered Tae-jun to never yield to any unjustifiable pressure from politicians and told him to report any such cases directly to his office.[35] Moreover, as chief of POSCO, Tae-jun was given a free hand in making procurement decisions. This made it possible for POSCO to avoid cumbersome procurement procedures that was the red tape that corporations had to grapple with. Freed from red tape and undue pressure from the outside, POSCO could purchase quality products and services any time it needed. It also selected its suppliers in consultation with a Japanese advisory group and entered private contracts with them, which the government would later endorse. When the construction of POSCO was underway, President Park paid a visit to its construction site 13 times. Park Tae-jun reportedly said to a newspaper reporter covering the presidential office, "I regained strength when I recall that the President said to me, 'I'm fully backing you. Push ahead as you please.' "[36]

Under the leadership of Park Tae-jun, POSCO steadfastly improved its production capacity to 1.03 million tons of pig iron in 1973. The steelmaker turned profitable in the first year of its operation, contrary to the World Bank's feasibility evaluation. Not paying out dividends until 1982, it reinvested its profits into expansion, making it a global steelmaking giant.[37] How POSCO would fare was a matter of concern to the international business community. Robert McNamara, former president of the World Bank, reportedly told POSCO executives that it was a mistake for the World Bank not to endorse South Korea's steel mill project. He was curious to know how the company could pull it off in contrast to a similar failed steel mill project in Brazil, which had been built with the World Bank's support.[38]

As the new kid on the block, POSCO was soon to attract interest from foreign investors. One such opportunity came when POSCO and US Steel Corp. announced a plan for a joint venture to build a cold rolling plant in Pittsburgh in

December 1985. USS-POSCO Industries (UPI), their joint venture, was incorporated on April 1, 1986. But UPI ran into difficulties not long after it was launched. Unionized workers in Pittsburgh opposed the joint venture from the very start because importing cheaper intermediate steel products would force its union members out of their jobs, so they staged a prolonged protests and industrial actions.[39] After 6 months of negotiations, UPI signed a labor contract with the union. The company began to develop corporate loyalty among its employees by providing them with various fringe benefits, including free overseas tours for selected model workers and their spouses. Improved labor relations helped turn the company around from $12 million in losses in 1985 to $3.4 million in profits in 1986 and another $15 million in profits the next year.[40]

With demand for steel soaring, POSCO decided to build a second integrated iron and steel plant on the coast of Kwangyang Bay. Here again, POSCO relied on the Japanese steelmaking industry for technical assistance. Japanese steelmakers, who were wary of POSCO making inroads into the Japanese market, were initially reluctant to provide technical assistance. Due credit should be given to Yoshihiro Inayama, Nippon Steel chairman, who reportedly persuaded wary Japanese steelmakers to provide technical assistance for POSCO's new construction project here too.[41] On meeting Lee Byung-chull, chairman of Samsung Group, in 1981, Inayama reportedly said that he would persuade Nippon Steel president Eihiro Saito, who declined to help POSCO, to change his mind. Following a lengthy discussion, Japanese steelmakers decide to provide POSCO with technical assistance, instead of engaging directly in construction. With the combined production capacity of the Pohang and Kwangyang steel plant reaching 41.43 million tons in 2014, South Korea became the fifth largest steel producer in the world after China, Japan, the United States and India. Moreover, the World Steel Dynamics (WSD) selected POSCO as the most competitive steelmaker in the world. The WSD selection clearly distinguished POSCO as being the world's number one steelmaker eight consecutive times over the past 6 years. As of June 2015, it evaluated 36 of the world's steelmakers on a set of 23 criteria including production capacity, profitability, technological innovation, pricing power, cost reduction, financial stability and acquisition of raw materials.[42]

As was pointed out in Section 6.2, Dr. John P. W. Jaffe, who authored the World Bank report that cast aspersions on the POSCO project, recalled later that "Korea virtually created something out of nothing when it built steelworks, despite a feasibility study that had concluded it would not be viable in any way. It was nothing short of a miracle." As its integrated iron and steel plants had very effective forward and backward linkages, POSCO was of great help to the country's industrial development. In retrospect, it clearly goes without saying that had the steel mill project not being carried out, then it clearly would have imperiled the country's HCI and thus placed the nation's economic development behind Taiwan and China.

Petrochemical industry[43]

The petrochemical industry consists of naphtha-cracking and 12 associated sectors. In the absence of an efficient petrochemical industry, a nation cannot keep its light industry independent of foreign suppliers and ensure that industrial products remain competitive. The country's first oil refinery, Korea Oil Refinery Corporation, was established in 1962 at Ulsan Industrial Complex as a 50–50 joint venture with the Gulf Corporation. Until the early 1960s, all the nation's petroleum had to be imported and rationed to control demand amid the limited supply. The optimal production capacity of a naphtha-cracking plant in terms of ethylene production was 300,000 tons per year or more in 1965. At the time, while Japan was scaling up their petrochemical plants to the international standard, South Korea had neither the capital nor the technology to start what was seen to be a petrochemical industry in name only.[44] No less serious a problem was a yawning gap between domestic demand and the capacity demanded by economies of scale. The maximum capacity of a petrochemical industry that could be built in the country was no more than 30,000 tons per year.[45]

A plant built to fit such a scale would have raised the prices of domestic feedstock much higher than imports. If domestic producers of final products had only relied on domestic petrochemical companies for the supply of their feedstock, there was no way they could survive competition from Japan. Waiting until domestic demand rose to 300,000 tons per year or more would not be a viable option, either. By then an advance in petrochemical technology would have changed the situation to Korea's disadvantage. Should petrochemical plants be built with old technology later, they would not survive foreign competition. A case in point was a methanol plant built in the Ulsan Petrochemical Complex. When it was unveiled, Japanese companies lowered their methanol prices from $70 per ton to $40 per ton. No wonder it was perceived that only advanced countries, such as the United States and Japan, could develop their own petrochemical industries.

During one of President Park's routine inspection tours of government agencies in the beginning of 1965, the MTI presented to him a plan to develop a petrochemical industry in its report. Apart from a few industries, you would be hard-pressed to find many people in the country who were familiar with the petrochemical industry. As far as its development was concerned, South Korea was 20 to 30 years behind the United States and Western European countries and 10 years behind Japan.[46] Unsure of what the president would make of the plan, the bureaucrats of the MTI conceived of the plan as a tentative one. Even in putting together this plan, they were certainly acutely aware of the fact that the president was already way too fixated on getting the nation's first integrated steel mill plant up and running, and could thus ill afford to launch another expensive, high-profile project. In fact, the MTI was not alone in reasoning this way; the EPB also felt the same way about the tentative plan.[47] That was a seemingly implausible task, but it did not take long for them to discover that they had misread the president's resolve, after he requested a detailed plan of their proposal.[48]

In February 1966, the MTI commissioned Arthur D. Little, a US-based consulting company, to conduct a feasibility study for a petrochemical industry in Korea. The MTI believed that a feasibility study by a renowned foreign consultant would be able to induce interest from foreign investors. But the outcome was disappointing to say the least. In a report submitted in September 1966, the consultant concluded that to guarantee viability, the country's annual production capacity should not exceed 30,000 tons, given that domestic demand was abysmally low. How could a plant with an annual production capacity of 30,000 tons compete against any of its foreign rivals with such a target?[49] The ministry decided a naphtha-cracking plant needed to have an annual ethylene production capacity of 66,000 tons at a minimum, and added its construction to the second Five-Year Economic Development Plan (1967–1971) as one of its core projects.[50]

To ensure a petrochemical industry with an annual ethylene production capacity of 66,000 tons would survive, the ministry took special measures, including the provision of tax credits and subsidies in utility prices. A state-funded corporation for the management of petrochemical industry complexes was accordingly established for this purpose. The following are key measures the government took to help keep the prices of domestic petrochemical products below those of imports:[51]

- The imported equipment and materials for petrochemical plants were exempted from tariffs.
- Newly incorporated petrochemical companies were exempted from corporate tax, business tax and other related taxes for 5 years.
- The Foreign Capital Inducement Act was revised to exempt foreign direct investments in the petrochemical industry from taxes.
- Those buying land for the construction of a petrochemical plant were allowed to make a payment equivalent to 20 percent of the price as down payment and pay the remainder in installments in 5 years after a 2-year grace period.
- Although cash loans were prohibited at that time, by setting the required equity capital rate at 30 percent, the government allowed international cash loans exceptionally for the extra funds to abide by the equity capital rate.
- To help keep the price of final products low, the government subsidized the prices of all utilities, including electricity and water.

The MTI created a consultative commission on the petrochemical industry, organized an office of planning and research for the commission's day-to-day work and staffed it with officials from relevant government agencies. A survey was conducted to determine which companies would be interested in building petrochemical plants at a proposed designated industrial complex, selected a plot of land in Ulsan as the site for the complex in 1967 and held a groundbreaking ceremony in March 1968. Even at this point the government was still dictating the pace of who gets in and who doesn't. That was understandable, given that only few local companies had expertise in petrochemical engineering and the requisite ability to make investments.

The Ministry of Construction, which oversaw building the petrochemical complex, purchased the land and thought of commissioning Bechtel of the United States to design the complex, but gave up the idea due to the high cost. Instead, it selected Korean engineers, sent them on a tour of Japanese petrochemical complexes and commissioned them to design the complex. It also employed Korean engineers to conduct a geological survey of the selected site, set up a construction plan and construct all needed infrastructure on their own before selling plant sites to petrochemical companies on a deferred-payment basis. One of the two critical plants to be built was a naphtha cracker, and the other producing benzene, toluene and xylene (BTX). Having concluded that no privately held company can build such plants with foreign assistance, the MTI turned to Korea Oil Corp., a state-invested company in which Gulf Oil Corp. had a 50 percent equity share, for the task of building naphtha-cracking and BTX plants. The government also selected business enterprises that would build downstream plants. It assigned a state-invested fertilizer maker to build five core plants and private companies selected under a strictly applied set of rules to build the rest. It fended off political pressure to keep unqualified companies from foraying into the newly emerging petrochemical industry.

The government was also out in the international market, trying to court foreign petrochemical companies for 50–50 joint ventures. Given that few foreign companies were willing to invest in Korea, citing political instability as a key reason, the government had to select potential partners to joint ventures and persuade them to make investments. Among them was Allied Chemical Co. of the United States, which declined to go into a joint venture to produce caprolactam. As such, the government decided that a company would be established with investments from domestic sources and that it would bring in the required technology in a licensing agreement with a foreign company. For those foreign companies willing to take the risk, they were granted firm guarantees of recouping their investments during the first 5 years of operation.

As construction continued, the production capacity was readjusted in response to increasing demand. Finally, a large petrochemical complex with a production capacity of 100,000 tons was dedicated in Ulsan in 1972. But the government's estimate went off the mark, as demand for petrochemical products grew explosively when the Ulsan complex went into operation due to accelerated economic growth and exports. A worsening demand–supply mismatch in petrochemical products was anticipated, as the economy was gearing up for $10 billion or more in annual exports in the 1980s.[52] Against this backdrop, the government had to expand the Ulsan complex and build a new complex in Yeocheon.

Buoyed by expectation of a rise in petrochemical demand, the government wanted to build two naphtha-cracking plants, each with the ethylene production capacity of 300,000 tons in a new petrochemical complex in Yinchuan. However, the plan had to be scaled down to one with a production capacity of 350,000 tons in the wake of the first global oil shock. Problems with funding and partnership forging further delayed the launch of construction to November 1975. The new complex was dedicated near the end of 1979, later than the original plan.[53] The annual ethylene production capacity rose to 505,000 tons with the dedication of the Yeocheon complex, making the nation the 15th largest petrochemical producer in the world in 1981. But the new complex did not fare well in the wake of the second oil shock.[54]

Demand for petrochemicals picked up as oil prices started to drop and the world economy began to recover in the mid-1980s, spurring a debate in Korea on building new petrochemical plants and expanding the existing ones.[55] In 1984, the government finalized its plan to build new downstream plants and expand the existing downstream plants to fully utilize the two existing naphtha-cracking plants, each with an annual 350,000-ton production capacity. In 1987, another naphtha-cracking plant was built in the Yeocheon complex with an annual production capacity of 350,000 tons.[56] As the petrochemical industry matured, the law on petrochemical industry development, enacted to regulate entry into the market, was scrapped in June 1986, thereby liberalizing investments in the industry.[57]

The two global oil shocks were truly testing moments of the resiliency of the country's petrochemical industry. Even within that same context, the government routinely came up for severe criticism as being reckless in its expansion of existing facilities and building new plants without due recourse to the realities of global market conditions. The petrochemical industry in Korea has grown into the fourth largest producer in the world as of 2014.[58] A country that not too long ago entirely depended on imports for all petrochemical needs as a non-oil-producing country is now self-sufficient and one of the major petrochemical exporters in the world.

Machinery and automobile industry[59]

At the time of liberation, South Korea had 7,386 vehicles – almost all of them being imported used trucks, buses and passenger cars. Automotive imports somehow started to rise as demand for transportation increased, pushing up gasoline consumption to extremely high levels.[60] An emergency presidential decree was issued to limit vehicle ownership to the number of vehicles registered as of May 8, 1957, as a way of preventing the upward trajectory of prices. New registrations were allowed when they replaced scrapped vehicles. Parts production was conducted in a form of cottage industry, in part because many small manufacturers had previously been all but wiped out during the Korean War.[61] In the mid-1960s, there were about 150 auto assembly shops in the nation, each of them with five to six employees doing manual work.[62]

Also notable was the paucity of shops producing auto-related parts, accessories, machines and other products in the 1950s to mid-1960s. The military junta decided that the machinery industry would start with the auto industry, then enacted a law on the protection of the automobile industry in 1962 – a law designed to prevent auto assembly plants from mushrooming. Convinced that too many auto assembly plants would do harm to the development of the industry, it decided that their number would ultimately be reduced to one.

As you would imagine, this new directive did not go down well with people in the small auto factories. On one occasion, a group of protesters numbering about 100, confronted government officials in protest of the directive. The government also contradicted itself by granting approval for the establishment of a new auto company called Saenara Motor, apparently in response to some backroom politi-cal deal.[63] Equipped with modern assembly facilities, Saenara assembled passen-ger cars with imported parts contained in semi-knock-down (SKD) kits and sold their cars at prices higher than those of equivalent Japanese-assembled imports.[64] No Korean-made parts were used in its SKD assembly. Benefiting from exemp-tions from customs duties and tax breaks, Saenara assembled 1,910 passenger cars in 1962 and another 1,063 before it collapsed when the government could no longer permit it to import SKD kits because of a shortage of foreign exchange.[65] What is equally true about the real reason for Saenara going bust was the fact that it was engulfed in a major influence-peddling political scandal, causing it to become the public bogeyman.

Convinced that parts production was the foundation for the promotion of an auto industry, the MTI set up a comprehensive auto industry promotion plan in 1964, encouraging domestic automakers to use more Korean-made parts in the vehicles they produced. But the ministry's plan was not entirely effective. Worse still, its one-automaker policy crumbled as Shinjin Automobile, Asia Motors and Hyundai Motors were established with the backing of political big shots in the next several years. Parts imports soared as they ignored the government's policy of raising the level of local components. For the carmakers, it was more profitable to import parts than to manufacture them.

President Park expressed discontent about delaying the localization of auto parts in October 1968, and the MTI prepared a Five-Year Automobile and Major Parts Localization Plan, which was officially announced in Novem-ber 1969.[66] It started with the setting up of yearly local content ratio targets for major automobile parts aiming for complete localization of parts of passenger cars by 1972, and of buses and trucks by 1974. Second, it separated assem-bling companies from parts manufacturers and concentrated on parts localiza-tion. Third, each part would be produced by an individual factory so that parts manufacturers could steadily develop their expertise in specific specializations. Fourth, it simplified the number of car models from 26 to fewer than 19. These policies are revolutionary. This policy decision enormously shocked major car and parts manufacturers. In the case of Hyundai, it aimed not just at the local production of parts and components but also at developing Korean passenger car models. The decision had a great impact on Hyundai, which was assembling a Ford model under an agreement with the US automaker. Ford insisted that, if a car contained any Korean-made parts, the use of Ford's Cortina brand would not be allowed.

For a Korean automaker, to develop its own model would be a risky business. It would have to build an assembly plant with economies of scale for the global market if it was to survive competition from foreign automakers such as Gen-eral Motors and Toyota. It was automakers in some advanced nations, such as the United States, West Germany and Japan, that had their own models. At the time, GM, Ford, Volkswagen and others wanted to build their assembly plants in Korea, apparently with an eye to using it as a launching pad to advance into the Chinese market.

Opinion was divided among different government agencies and policymakers. Claiming that it would be too risky for a Korean automaker to build an assembly plant to produce its own models, the EPB proposed to the nurturing of a local parts industry for exports. But the MTI insisted on a Korean automaker producing its own models. Its argument was that the domestic auto industry would otherwise run the risk of being hollowed out if foreign makers move to other countries for their strategic interests. It maintained that a foreign automaker mass-assembling its models in Korea, depending on changes in the market, could move its assembly lines elsewhere. Ultimately the ministry's position carried the day.

About the same time, Volkswagen and other multinational automakers were briskly making plans for the Korean market. To their surprise, the government turned down applications by foreign automakers to build their plants in the country. At the request of the then US Ambassador Richard Sneider, a meeting was convened with the chairman of Hyundai Motors, Chung Ju-yung, during which the envoy is said to have advised the Hyundai boss that Korean automakers would be better off assembling US models in partnership with an American automaker. He argued that it would not be viable for a Korean automaker to develop its own model. Chung told Sneider that he could not abandon the idea of developing Hyundai's own model, given the immense impact it would have on other Korean industries. Chung also told Sneider that Korea needed to build its own auto industry if it wished to join the ranks of industrialized countries, adding that he would not regret his decision if his auto crashed after he spent all the money he had earned in his life.[67]

As auto sales increased rapidly, growth in automobile parts production picked up speed. Restrictions on parts imports also helped boost local production. In addition, the MTI persuaded domestic automakers to go beyond the targeted local content ratio and substitute Korean-made parts for imported ones. About this time, the South Korean government started to draw up a plan to foster a machinery industry as a part of its industrial development plans. It was also aimed at laying the foundation for weapons production in the face of a security threat from North Korea. The plan had four core areas – foundries, shipyards, special steel factories and integrated heavy machinery factories, which was stymied when Japan refused financing to the project, as was discussed in Section 7.2.

Despite auto parts manufacturing being promoted as part of the machinery industry, it did not take root until the government announced plans to develop an indigenous defense industry in 1970 and a national drive for the development of HCI in January 1973, all this while the MTI had the last word on approval of auto parts imports and persuaded carmakers to use local parts as much as possible. To facilitate the machinery industry and auto parts manufacturing, the Changwon Integrated Machinery Industry Complex was constructed in 1973 at a site of 33 million square meters, which became home for 88 machinery plants in 1977.[68] The complex allowed Korea's automobile industry to grow to become the fifth largest in the global ranking in the automobile industry.

As a link to the aforementioned plan, the MTI announced the "Automobile Engine Construction Plan" in February 1970, initiated by O Won-chol, then serving as deputy minister in charge of the mining and manufacturing industry. It was designed to ensure that only one manufacturer of engine foundry is chosen among three carmakers. Naturally, this placed the three companies under immense pressure because if they were not selected, they would become subordinate to the engine producing company. Among the three of Shinjin, Hyundai and Asia, the former two submitted proposals: the Shinjin-Toyota and Hyundai-Ford consortiums submitted their plans to build engine plants. But it did not take long before the Shinjin-Toyota consortium collapsed when the Japanese company pulled itself out of its consortium agreement with the Korean automaker. With the looming threat of being blacklisted under the so-called Four Tzu principles – which was that foreign companies having business with either South Korea or Taiwan would not be allowed business in China – Toyota withdrew its investment plan with Shinjin. O Won-chol recalled how contemptuous and devastating Toyota's decision was. Ford also parted with Hyundai over a disagreement on their partnership scheme.[69]

While the two companies were squabbling with collaborators in engine production, Kia Motors broke ground in November 1970. Kia began to produce 2,000 cc engines in 1973 and assembled "Brisa" passenger cars in October 1974. Shinjin, after been hit by the unexpected setback, could forge a new partnership with GM, and built a large-scale plant with an annual capacity of 50,000 vehicles through a 50–50 venture. In the process, there was a rise and fall among the three carmakers. Shinjin-GM failed due to a collision of interests between the two partners and it was taken over by Daewoo. However, during the Asian financial crisis in 1997, it declared bankruptcy and was again taken over by GM. The relatively small-scaled Kia later merged with Hyundai. Hyundai pursued independence in engine development, and automobile manufacturing eventually could take root. The fall of Shinjin provides a lesson that missing the timing of developing a unique engine and model had a profound effect on the future of the company.

Meanwhile, Hyundai pursued car manufacturing independently with technical cooperation with Mitsubishi of Japan. Abandoning the joint venture with Ford, Hyundai Motor designed its original Pony model independently in 1973. It was well received at the International Automobile Exhibition in October 1974. When the Pony model was on the drawing board, a GM representative was quoted as saying, "If Pony is made, I'll eat my hat."[70] But Hyundai succeeded in developing the model in 1974, and began to export Ponies in 1976. Hyundai has since pulled off phenomenal growth to the point of selling eight million vehicles in 2014, and Korea became the fifth-largest auto-producing country after China, the United States, Japan and Germany.[71]

Many developing countries unsuccessfully attempted to build self-sustaining auto industries at around the time Korea did. For instance, Taiwan wanted to pursue a policy like that of Korea, but in the face of opposition from the National Assembly and the press, it opted for many companies assembling autos with parts imported in complete-knock-down kits.[72] When the Philippines started to develop an auto industry, it permitted as many as nine companies to build their assembly plants under pressure from public opinion. Its efforts ended in failure.

When the decision was made to build an auto industry as an engine of exports, there were no shortage of skeptics, ranging from economic experts and intellectuals of all stripes and shape. This was evidenced by the testimony of Kim Moonsoo, a former governor of Kyunggi Province, who was an economics major and anti-government activist in college. Recalling President Park's promise to make cars a major export item, Kim said, "All the professors and scholars I met at that time said it was impossible for Korea to manufacture cars for exports. They accused the President of duping people to tighten his grip on power and prolong his rule."[73] But President Park's visionary leadership, the entrepreneurship of Korean business leaders and the government's continued support worked together to make the Korean auto industry what it is today.

Shipbuilding industry[74]

As Figure 7.1 shows, since stepping stealthily into the shipbuilding industry in the 1970s, South Korea has grown to be the top shipbuilder of the world in just a few decades. In the 1960s, few would have thought the country's shipbuilding industry would grow to be a global leader. It was anything but insignificant when the government decided to develop it as one of the nation's core industries.

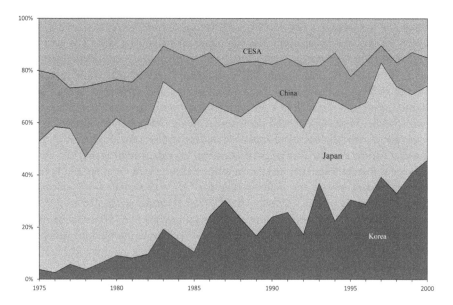

Figure 7.1 Global trend of shipbuilding market share

Note: CESA (Committee of European Shipbuilders' Association)

Source: HIS (Former Lloyd's Register) "World Shipbuilding Statistics" and www.koshipa.or.kr/

Developing a shipbuilding industry, like many other things, requires capital, technical manpower, managerial skills and a market. Moreover, it was an industry where economies of scale couldn't be ignored. Again, as has been discussed all through this book, the country back in the 1960s had nothing going its way. It did not avail itself of either sufficient capital or a steady supply of skilled manpower. Nor did it have easy access to global markets. With its domestic market too small, it had to aim for exports, which did not seem to augur well. To say the least, nurturing shipbuilding as a viable core industry appeared to be an impossible task for an underdeveloped country that emerged severely scathed from a devastating fratricidal war. Those gloomy prospects were shared not just by outsiders but industry insiders as well.

At its liberation, Korea inherited Daehan Shipbuilding Corporation (Daehan) from the retreating Japan. During the chaotic years that followed, the shipyard soon fell into disarray. No competent managers were left behind to run it. All corporate managers and technicians had been selected among Japanese people, with Korean employees given nothing to do but manual work. With management now left in the hands of incompetent and irresponsible people, it was not unusual to see hired workers steal tools, materials and other items from the moribund shipyard. Government subsidies were the shipyard's only lifeline. As the pernicious decline of the shipbuilding company continued, it reached a major crisis point when all it did was sell off some machinery to purchase rice for its employees.[75] During the 15 years and 10 months until the advent of the military junta, the company changed its chief executive officers as many as 12 times.[76]

With an uncanny ability to forecast a bright future for the shipbuilding industry, Shin Dong-shik, Chief Secretary for Economic Affairs II, was convinced that South Korea could become a leading shipbuilding nation if it strategically invests in the industry. Consequently, a related proposal was brought before the president in 1965, thus setting in motion what has become a historic turn around for the nation's shipbuilding industry. But behind this glossy success is yet another history of misgivings about the viability of the project. Many of the president's cabinet were not too amused about the proposal to construct a large dockyard for a country that produced neither nails nor iron plates. Rumors kept flowing that an out-of-touch president was drifting from reality because he largely surrounded himself with sycophants.[77]

An unyielding President Park continued to back Shin. To understand the president's confidence in Shin is to understand the story behind how he emerged from being an obscure and unassuming Korean expat to serving in the upper echelon of South Korean political power. Graduating with a major in shipbuilding soon after the Korean War, he decided to take his chances abroad after fruitless attempts to secure a job at home. By some stroke of luck, one of his many letters for employment was favorably received by KOCKUM in Sweden, who then gave him a job offer. After 4 years of working there, he had the opportunity to become an inspector at Lloyd's Register in London, which was a very prestigious position. By some twist of fate, the young Shin was to meet President Park for the first time in 1961, at which point he left a very good impression on the head of state. Then during another state visit to the United States, they met once again, and this time round the president impressed upon him to bring his expertise in the shipbuilding industry to help South Korea develop in this respect. Shin was appointed as deputy minister at the young age of 33, and 3 years later as Chief Secretary for Economic Affairs II at the age of 36.

He was thrust into political office at a time the government was keen on resuscitating its faltering shipbuilding industry. It chose a two-pronged strategy to get this done. One was an imminent task of helping Daehan stand on its own; the other plan was to build modern shipyards. To attract foreign investment, Shin addressed the diplomatic corps in Seoul, offering what would he considered to be an excellent sales pitch. The presentation did however elicit the opposite impact, as some of the very people he wanted to woo bluntly made him understand that his plan was utterly misguided. The UK ambassador was the least amused by the proposal, given the history of the UK's dominant position in the shipbuilding industry. The UK was by then being fiercely challenged by Japan for the apex of the industry. Some critics went as far as saying this whole amateurish plan was all down to the president appointing and listening to the counsel of such youngsters as Shin.[78] Upon hearing their responses from Shin, President Park was disappointed.

Daehan was to be turned into a private company, and as part of that Yeon Namgung, one of the few Korean businessmen with experience in the industry, at the behest of the government was compelled to take on half of the stakes in the company. The change of ownership provided a turning point for the shipyard that was on the verge of collapse. Daehan wanted to repair the dilapidated shipyard constructed in the 1930s and take orders from abroad. The first job Daehan did for its survival was to place a bid for 20 ships for 250 gross tons deep-sea tuna fishing vessels, ordered by the Taiwanese government with a World Bank loan in 1968. Daehan won the order when it made a lower bid than those by its rivals from West Germany and Japan. Dispelling negative sentiments about its shipbuilding capacity and a strike by the union with the abled leadership of Namgung Yeon, Daehan could deliver the orders to Taiwan in December 1969. This helped improve the international reputation of Daehan.

With Daehan on its way to recovery, the Ministry of Trade and Industry wanted to upgrade the shipbuilding capacity by government procurement. It started to work on a more ambitious plan to build 10,000-ton or larger seaworthy ships that would fly Korean flags. In consideration of no local demand for large ships, it sweetened the contract stipulations – a contract under which the buyer would be permitted to pay 10 percent of the cost in cash, 40 percent with government subsidies and the remainder with loans that would be offered at a concessional interest rate of 4 percent.[79] Daehan started construction of the ship for the buyer with the aforementioned financial contract with the MTI in 1971.[80]

A previous breakthrough had come a year earlier, when Daehan was informed that Gulf was in the market for "product carriers." Namgung Yeon had never heard of a product carrier until then, a technical term denoting "an oil tanker engaged in the trade of carrying oil other than crude oil."[81] However, Daehan decided to make a $7 million bid for each of the two 20,000-ton vessels. When its representatives submitted the bid, they were shown the door immediately. The reason was that Gulf received a $5 million bid from a Japanese shipbuilder. However, Namgung convinced Gulf that it would have a better deal with Daehan, saying that the ships would be virtually European-made. He promised that Daehan would use only high-quality European-made parts and components except for the hulls, which would be Korean-made.[82] The use of European-made parts would make the product carrier higher in quality than the Japanese-made vessels, which Namgung said would do more than compensate for the price gap.[83] Meanwhile, O Won-chol, then assistant minister of the MTI, was negotiating with Gulf on an amendment of crude oil transportation clauses. As a compensation for the amendment agreement, O demanded contracts to build several product carrier vessels for Gulf. Gulf responded, "Ship building is not a game of children. Korea has no capacity." O replied, "Do everything you need to ensure its quality from designing, procurement of materials to inspection. Korea will provide labor and the place. All we need is the record of shipbuilding." Gulf came around and signed a contract on the delivery of two 20,000-ton product carriers at the total cost of $14.1 million in November 1970. This contract helped make Korea the 11th largest shipbuilder in the world.[84]

With newly gained confidence from the construction of product carriers that demanded the use of state-of-the-art technology, Namgung decided to build even more technology-intensive ships. An opportunity came from a chemical tanker order from the Stolt Nielsen Company of Norway. A chemical tanker, transporting chemicals in a liquid state, had a high risk of corrosiveness. Obtaining a funding guarantee from the Korean government, Daehan signed a contract to build a chemical tanker for the Norwegian company. The agreement came with a condition that Namgung would hold the ship in his possession until a test conducted in navigation proved that the tanker would sustain no corrosion damage. The government decided to endorse the deal in the belief that a chemical tanker built by Daehan would be another monument for the Korean shipbuilding industry.[85]

President Park said, "Namgung knows about shipbuilding. Help him do it (build the ship)."[86] The tanker performed without a hitch during the navigational test. This success brought to both Daehan and the entire Korean shipbuilding industry a new recognition of their technological prowess by the international industry of shipbuilders and shippers. It also enabled both Daehan and the entire Korean shipbuilding industry to achieve new heights of respectability. The government for its part felt genuinely vindicated in its decision to invest in reviving the shipbuilding industry. It proved Daehan was no longer a money pit. Namgung's entrepreneurship, coupled with support from President Park, turned the money-losing shipbuilder around. Now world financial institutions were ready to give the green light to Daehan when it wanted to expand its shipyard.

As part of the program the government of Japan dispatched a team headed by a senior official from the Ministry of International Trade and Industry for a feasibility study. The team concluded that it would be neither appropriate nor possible for South Korea to build a large shipyard.[87] A report from the team said no previous shipbuilding experience was enough proof of the country's lack of capacity to build a new shipyard for 100,000-ton to 200,000-ton vessels. Instead, it proposed an alternative plan that called for starting with 10,000-ton to 20,000-ton vessels and move on to 50,000-ton to 100,000-ton vessels.[88] The association of Japanese shipbuilders, citing the report, turned down South Korea's request for assistance. Instead, it suggested the building of a shipyard for medium-sized ships. The most likely explanation for this decision was legitimate concerns about Korea eventually developing the expertise to compete against Japan in the global market. The Korean government, which did not want to turn Korean shipbuilders into clients to their Japanese counterparts, turned down the Japanese advice and went along with its original plan.

Deputy Prime Minister Kim Hak-yeol invited Chung Ju-yung of Hyundai to a meeting in which he was informed about the president's desire to get a shipyard business launched in the country. Most importantly, Chung was specifically charged with the responsibility of bringing that mission to fruition. As with everything else about grand projects, Chung immediately engaged in a globetrotting campaign in a bid to raise funds to get the project off the ground. After a long unsuccessful bid, a crestfallen Chung reported back to the deputy prime minister, lamenting his inability to convince creditors to fund the shipyard project. Because this was yet another one of those projects so dear to the president, the deputy prime minister felt it would be best to have Chung personally report to the president. Chung reportedly had this to say to President Park:

> My effort to promote the project is not materializing. I explained the difficulties (that I encountered), when I met President Park the next time. When I told him that I could not bring it to fruition, he fiercely stared back at me and said, "What did you mean to say? Did you mean to say you cannot do it even when I promised to help you?" I was so scared that I said, "Okay, I'll do it, Your Excellency." That was how I started to build the Hyundai shipyard.[89]

The shipyard construction was the largest project a Korean private business concern had ever launched by the scale of investment. Chung intended to fund the project with $40 million from domestic sources and another $43 million in foreign credits.[90] With the president having committed his support for the project, he was all but guaranteed of the domestic funds. The problem was how to secure foreign loans, which is the key to the success of business. Following a previous unsuccessful gambit in the United States, he flew to London. While in London, he set out to secure a loan amount that far exceeded the entire assets of the Hyundai Group. You don't have to be a seasoned investor to tell right away that there was hardly any way this request would fly. It is so striking that Chung could let his zeal blind him to the fact that the chances of a corporation from a developing country with no proven track record in the industry was seeking investment was going to sound convincing.

Undeterred, Chung contacted Mr. Charles Longbottom, chairman of A&P Appledore Company, and Scott Lithgow of the United Kingdom for seller's credit. Chung offered procurement of technical service and equipment from A&P Appledore for the Hyundai dockyard to be constructed, and Mr. Longbottom could successfully intervene to get Barclays Bank to approve Hyundai's application. To Hyundai's joy, the bank decided to approve the loan. Through the agency of Barclays, a consortium was formed for Hyundai's dockyard project, which consisted of Barclays as the managing company, the IndoSuez Bank from France, Cofay from Spain and Franz Kirfelt from West Germany.[91]

Another hurdle was obtaining approval for the loan from the Export Credit Guarantee Department of the United Kingdom, which questioned how an unknown shipbuilder from an underdeveloped country was going to be able to find suitable buyers for its products. Chung had to provide convincing proof for the British regulator to give the all clear. It was along this line that he stumbled into a meeting with Yorkos Livanos, a Greek ship owner, in October 1971. Livanos was in the market for a shipbuilder. Chung offered to build two oil tankers for him, but then Livanos suggested a payment of $30.95 million, 16 percent lower than the prevailing international price. Moreover, Hyundai would be required to deliver the tankers in two and a half years. Should Hyundai renege on this delivery term, Hyundai would be obligated to pay back the principal plus interest as compensation. By signing the contract on December 5, 1971, Hyundai could borrow $50.75 million from the consortium, far greater than the original proposal to Barclays. In a triumphant mode, Chung contacted Deputy Prime Minister Kim Hak-yeol and upon seeing him, Kim quipped, "is my neck safe or not?" Chung replied with a smile, "Don't worry about it." He duly reported to the president about the breakthrough who welcomed the news with a broad smile.

To his credit, Chung's Hyundai could pull this one off too and would years later describe how he felt as being "in a transport of joy."[92] This deal also paved the way for Hyundai to build large oil tankers from the beginning although it had no shipbuilding experience.[93] Hyundai had no time to waste in building the shipyard. It had to work on its site in Ulsan 24 hours a day under Chung's supervision. Recalling the days of construction, Chung said later:

> We launched the shipyard construction in March of 1972 and completed it in two years and three months. Most workers woke up at dawn and washed their faces with water in puddles. They worked until late at night and went to bed with their shoes on. This kind of daily life continued all year round. The days at the Ulsan Shipyard were the liveliest part of my life, of which I don't have the slightest doubt.[94]

Hyundai set two world records – in time spent on digging up the docks and building ships. It started digging in March 1972 and completed construction in 2 years and 3 months. During this time, it dredged the seabed off the Ulsan coast, built 462,809 square meters of plant floor space and dormitories for 5,000 workers, while simultaneously building the two oil tankers ordered by Mr. Livanos.

Now it had a shipyard with a 700,000-ton capacity on 1.983 million square meters of land with two dry docks.[95]

In the meantime, Daehan launched construction of a dockyard in Okpo in December 1973 on a site of 1.3 million square meters, thanks to a loan of $72 million from the US EXIM Bank. Then, Daehan was transferred to Daewoo Chairman Kim U-jung in 1978. In 1973 Samsung Chairman Lee Byung-chull, who initially was among those who doubted the country's ability to make forays into the shipbuilding industry, was soon to join the throng by taking over the dockyard at Jukdo initiated by Lee Hak-soo. The Jukdo dockyard built by Samsung was completed in 1979 with technical cooperation from Japan and Denmark. This was the beginning of Samsung Heavy Industry Co.[96]

It did not take long, however, for Chung to find himself discontent with the existing shipbuilding capacity. He found himself driven by a desire to build the largest shipyard in the world. Proceeding with the first construction work, Hyundai started expansion work, and the shipyard was to grow into a world-class one in 1975 with maximum shipbuilding capacity of 1 million tons on a site of 5 million square meters, with three dry docks having a 2.4 million ton annual ship-construction capacity.[97] During the past four decades, Hyundai Heavy Industries has maintained its status as the world's top shipbuilder, contributing to cementing the country's reputation as one of the big shots of the global shipbuilding industry in terms of orders received and output since 2000.[98]

Followed by the success of Hyundai and the completion of Samsung dockyard at Jukdo at a scale of 100,000 GT (gross tonnage) in 1979, the total shipbuilding capacity of South Korea increased to 2.8 million tons, with which Korea emerged as a top-ten shipbuilding country of the world. With the additional completion of Daewoo's Okpo dockyard the same year, Korea joined the top five. Entering the mid-1980s as the world economy recovered, ship orders began to increase, and in 2008 Korea ranked at the top in shipbuilding orders in the world, occupying more than 41 percent of market share. Among developing countries, South Korea stands out for successfully burrowing into the world's shipbuilding industry.[99] Considering that the shipbuilding industry started with practically nothing in the 1960s in Korea, its performance may rightly be referred to as the miracle of the century in the international shipbuilding industry.

Behind this glossy success is the fact that the company had to weather a series of storms before achieving this feat. The best example is how the 1973 global oil shock threatened to undermine its smooth takeoff. Two major events are credited for helping Hyundai keep its head above water during this crisis period. The MTI in its contract with Gulf included a clause that indicated that the government of Korea reserved the right to revert to Korean national carriers of crude oil. It specifically indicated that this would be the case, if at any point during the contract, the government deemed that local carriers had developed sufficient capacity to perform the same task as Gulf. It was based on this provision in the contractual terms that the MTI contracted Hyundai to transport the nation's crude oil. The second is the wind of fortune that came with the construction work of Jubail port in Saudi Arabia in 1976. At great risk, Chung decided that the huge steel structures for the work be constructed in Korea and then transported by large barges to Jubail, which led to huge demand for Hyundai barges. It is also worthwhile to take the case involving Taiwan into consideration. At the time of entering the shipbuilding industry, Taiwan was already ahead of South Korea in shipbuilding capacity. Yet, the Taiwanese shipbuilding industry did not attain global recognition five decades later as its Korean counterpart did. The main reason for this outcome was the Taiwanese government's decision to let Taiwanese shipbuilders serve giant Japanese shipbuilders as their subcontractors.

This comparison shows the Korean government played a key role in making the Korean shipbuilding industry what it is today.[100] Why was this the case? First, it would have been next to impossible without the role of leadership and the government, which helped make the moribund Daehan stand on its own, and prodded Hyundai to start a shipbuilding business. Again, the shipbuilding industry would not be what it is had it not been for the clear vision, unwavering aspiration and strong support President Park had maintained for its growth. Second, entrepreneurship deserves mention as an important a factor, as either the workers' attitude or the government's leadership role. Prominent among the competent businessmen was Namgung, who turned around his ailing shipbuilding company, and Chung, who obtained ship orders before he constructed his shipyard.[101]

Third, more fundamentally diligent and passionate workers provided the basis for the development of the shipbuilding industry, as is the case overall in industrial development. Leadership and entrepreneurship could be exerted on the grounds of diligent and passionate workers. They did their best for the ships they built to be well received in the world market.[102]

Electronics and IT industry[103, 104]

The electronics industry is defined as an industry producing products by using vacuum tubes or semiconductors.[105] It began with the production of vacuum tubes. Korea, which had never produced vacuum tubes for commercial purposes, virtually had no electronic industry in the era of vacuum tubes. Almost all electronic products used in Korea at the time were imports. Among the few electronic product producers was Goldstar (the antecedent of LG), which assembled radios with 200 parts imported for the first time near the end of 1959.[106] But it relied on imported vacuum tubes and other parts for simple assembly of electronic products.

In the 1960s, the government had little concern for the electronics industry. The Electrical Engineering Department of the MTI dealt with the electronics industry as a tiny part of its affairs. An anecdote about commotion over sample television imports explains where the electronics industry stood at the time:

> In 1966, some companies, which were considering television manufacture, wanted to import televisions as samples to enable them to understand how to guide their own local production process. On behalf of the companies, the Director of Electrical Engineering Division applied for permission to

import them. He believed the Trade Bureau of the ministry would approve the request despite the tight control it maintained on imports because of a chronic balance-of-payment deficit. The official in charge at the bureau reportedly said to the director: "Are you out of your mind? Or are you the stooge of the companies?" The director insisted that the companies needed sample televisions if they were to start local production, which he said would save on foreign exchange. After a fierce argument against sample imports, the official said, "The hell with local production," and slapped him in the face. The angered director appealed the case to the director-general of the Trade Bureau only to be told, "You are of no help to the nation. You'd better go to the Han River and drown yourself." The director-general apparently had no idea what the electronics industry would do for the nation when it matured.[107]

But it did not take long before senior government officials recognized what benefits a well-performing electronics industry would bring to the cash-strapped nation. It was evidenced by an address President Park delivered in January 1967. In his New Year's message, he said his government aimed at attaining the goal of $35 million in electronics exports in the year, and $1 billion before the 1970s was over. He vowed to develop an electronics industry as part of his export strategy.[108] O said later that he had the impression that President Park, rather than the Ministry of Trade and Industry, was pushing ahead with the electronics industry with a clear vision.[109] It seemed that the president gained in-depth understanding about the electronics industry from academics and international experts and was acting on their advice. Records show that among them were Dr. Kim Wan-hee of Columbia University, other Korean-American scientists and Japanese business leaders.[110]

In accordance with the presidential direction, relevant junior officials at the ministry drafted a plan to increase electronics exports to $100 million in the final year of the second Five-Year Economic Development Plan (1967–1971) and reported it to the director-general in charge only to have it turned down. He told them that it would be preposterous to expect that a nation that exported a mere $1.78 million worth of radios in 1965 would increase its electronics exports to $100 million in 6 years. The officials, still convinced that the goal could be attained, reported the draft plan directly to the minister and obtained his approval.

One year before it was gearing up to develop an electronics industry, the government established the KIST and appointed Dr. Choi Hyung-sup to head the institute, which will be detailed in the next chapter. Dr. Choi, who played a key role in making government policy on science and technology, recommended President Park meet Dr. Kim Wan-hee of Columbia University for advice. Dr. Kim submitted a report titled "Promotion of Electronics Industry in Korea" to President Park in September 1967. His proposal centered on three measures to be taken: legislating an electronics industry promotion act, establishing an electronics industry promotion fund and establishing an agency tasked with electronics industry promotion. President Park asked him for a more detailed study, for which $100,000 was set aside. Based on a report that came out in May 1968, the Electronics Industry Promotion Act was legislated in December 1968. The government, which launched the Electronics Industry Policy Committee, started to push for its policies on electronics industry promotion. It also sent its officials in charge to the United States, Japan and Taiwan, together with business leaders, on a study tour of the electronics industries. As a Chinese proverb goes, it was better to see once than to hear 100 times.

Under instructions from President Park in June 1969, the Ministry of Trade and Industry selected 95 electronic items to be developed for local production – 62 in 3 years and the rest in 5 years.[111] Then the ministry selected companies developing them for its subsidies. In addition to developing the items, the MTI set yearly targets for exports – $42 million ($8 million from finished products and $34 million from parts) in 1969 and $400 million ($160 million from finished products and $240 million from parts) in 1976.[112] To President Park, the deputy prime minister committed himself to providing government support without a hitch for the ambitious project to increase electronics exports almost tenfold in 8 years.

But the plan to develop electronics products did not proceed as planned. The selection of companies for the development of 29 items, all of them parts, was delayed a year and a half. In January 1970, taking in charge of assistant minister for mining, manufacturing and electricity, O took swift actions for designation of companies for electronics parts development in 1971 after one and a half years had passed. Benefited by the government's support, the export of electronics goods began to increase sharply. In 1976, electronics shipments went far beyond the target of $400 million and reached $1.1 billion.[113]

Another strategy the Korean government had for the development of an electronics industry was to build an industrial cluster producing electronic parts and finished products. For this purpose, the government built a large electronics complex in Gumi in 1971. But that was not enough for Korean electronics companies that urgently wanted to acquire technology for the manufacture of parts. A solution to this problem, the government concluded, lay in foreign direct investments by Japanese parts producers, many of them SMEs. At that time, Japan was the world's leader in manufacturing electronics goods. The problem was that Japanese firms were reluctant to invest to Korea. As an incentive for their investments in Korea, the government established an industrial complex in Guro, Seoul, exclusively for Japanese electronics parts producers. To manage the complex more effectively, the government named an influential person, Yoo Chang-soon, who would later be appointed prime minister, to supervise the complex. The government also encouraged ethnic Korean businessmen in Japan to invest in their mother country accompanying Japanese SMEs. All these measures the government took indicated how much it valued foreign direct investments as a means for Korean companies to learn advanced technology.

In an effort to draw public attention to the electronics industry and facilitate the exchange of information among electronics companies, the government sponsored annual Korea Electronics Exhibitions, the first of which lasted 8 days in October 1969. As a demonstration of his commitment to the promotion of the electronics industry, President Park attended all the exhibitions until he died in 1979. Among the few Korean companies that took an early business opportunity in the electronics industry was Goldstar, the predecessor of LG, which started to produce radios in November 1959 for the first time in Korea. The price of a vacuum tube radio was set at KRW 20,000, roughly three times the entry-level monthly pay for college graduates.[114] The next year, it put electronic fans on the market. It produced monochrome televisions in 1966. A television was sold at four times the entry-level monthly pay for college graduates. Supply could not meet demand, although the price was so high.[115]

Another company that was to lead the Korean electronics industry was Samsung Electronics, which started as a joint venture with Sanyo of Japan in March 1969. When Samsung and Sanyo of Japan agreed on a joint venture for television manufacturing in Korea, other Korean companies lobbied the government against their joint-venture plan. This opposition claimed that Samsung's dependence on Japanese technology for television manufacture would do harm to the entire Korean electronics industry. Under the circumstances, the government approved of its incorporation on the condition that all its products would be exported.[116] It also approved Samsung-NEC's incorporation under the same condition in 1970.

Korean companies that acquired technology through joint ventures with Japanese electronics giants and foreign direct investments by Japanese parts makers entered the niche market for low-end products left behind by Japanese home appliance makers. Then, they started to reduce the wide gap in technology with Japanese companies and produced higher-end products. It was Anam Electronics, a joint venture with Matsushita Electric of Japan, which produced color televisions in 1974 for the first time in Korea. Soon after, Samsung Electronics also began to produce color televisions. It was the first Korean company that produced color televisions with its own technology. However, none of the Korean companies could sell color televisions in the domestic market because color television broadcasting was not permitted in the nation.[117] President Park banned it on the grounds that it would fuel consumer spending and class conflicts. A new junta, which took power in a coup in December 1979, permitted the sale of color televisions in 1980 to support development of the electronics industry. Color television broadcasting started the next year.

Assisting the electronics industry about this time were the KIST and other government-funded research institutes. In a strategy to reduce Korea's gap in technology with advanced countries, the Korean government brought home many Korean scientists working at foreign research institutes and staffed domestic research institutes with them. Those scientists, rewarded with a high level of pay and other incentives, worked hard in coveted research environments to help Korean corporations acquire needed technologies. Frequently, they worked together with corporate engineers on technology-development projects.

A turning point in the development of electronic technology came when Lee Byung-chull, Chairman of Samsung Electronics, decided to make a massive investment in semiconductor manufacturing back in 1983. During a long period leading up to his "Tokyo Declaration" on an investment in chip-making plants in the year, executives of Samsung had voiced opposition to Lee's investment proposal, saying it would be impossible for Samsung to manufacture semiconductors similar in quality to or higher than those being manufactured by Japanese and other globally renowned chipmakers, given that it was now barely producing color televisions. People used to whisper that however foreseeable Chairman Lee was, the investment on semiconductor chip industry would be fatal for Samsung.[118]

But Lee was determined, and thanks to his decision, Samsung has emerged as the largest memory chip producer in the world. In addition, it has turned itself into a top-ranking manufacturer of smartphones, electronic home appliances and other technology-intensive products in the world. With a successful launch in the chip-making business, Samsung could lead the Korean electronics industry, surpassing its Korean rival LG. It is not Samsung alone that is doing well in global markets. LG and other Korean companies have substantial shares of world markets for electronic and information technology-intensive products.

The history of Samsung's semiconductor industry represents a good example of the entrepreneurship of Lee Byung-chull. Lee set 64K DRAM as the first product to develop, which was only produced in the United States at the time. Japanese firms hooted at Samsung that it would take 20 years for Samsung to develop it.[119] However, by the forced march of Lee, Samsung succeeded in its development in 6 months. With this success, Korea became the semiconductor chip producer by shoulder with the United States and Japan. It was followed by the first 256K DRAM development in 1984 the next year, the first 64K SDRAM in 1985, the first 1M DRAM in 1986, and the first 256K SDRAM in 1986. Hynix of Korea joined in the market by developing 64K DRAM in 1992. In the process, the talents fostered by KAIST, the elite education institute for science and technology, played a significant role. Lee reflects that one-fourth of KAIST graduates were recruited by Samsung.[120] In 2013, Korea became the second in the world semiconductor market, pushing out Japan. In retrospect, Samsung and Hynix had been held by the Japanese and US makers through dumping activities and anti-dumping lawsuits. According to Figure 7.2, Korea occupied 75 percent in D Ram and 33.6 percent in television sets in 2015 in the world market, ranking number one in these industries. The principal actor of this IT dynamics in Korea is Samsung Electronics. Having started in 1986 as a joint venture with a Japanese firm wholly depending on Japanese technology, Samsung surpassed Sony, the symbol of Japanese electronics technology, in market value and sales volume in 2002 and 2004 respectively.[121] Continuously, by pushing out Hewlett-Packard of the United States and Siemens of Germany, it finally ascended in 2009 to the top in sales volume of world IT business.[122] In the global smartphone market, from 2011 until recently, Samsung has ranked number one followed by Apple.[123] Looking at business performances in the second quarter of 2017, Samsung outran Apple, acceding to the throne at the top of the global manufacturing industry in sales volume, operating profit and profit rate.[124]

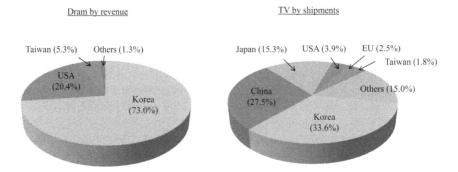

Figure 7.2 World market share in DRAM and TV sectors (2015)
Source: DRAMeXchange and IHS

Many developing countries, marveling at the outstanding performances of Korean companies in IT industries, may want to follow the footsteps Korea has taken in fostering those industries. The government officials from developing countries used to ask me about the secrets of its success in Korea's IT industry. As for me, it seems to take no spectacular policy skills or managerial know-how in Korea for developing the industries. The government had a vision of an IT industry and made a head start in investing in IT infrastructure. Then, it took care of business start-ups and enterprises as parents do for their children. It launched a national drive to fostering technicians and skilled workers. When nobody thought that Korea was ready for development in science and technology, the Korean government initiated research investments, providing exceptional treatment for scientists returning from advanced countries with higher salaries than that of the president. Under the circumstances, entrepreneurs exerted their full entrepreneurship to survive in the market and catch up with IT companies of advanced countries. In line with growth of private companies, the government disengaged itself in its engagement in the industrial development. There is no royal road to the development of IT industries and advanced technology. As children grow with the care of their parents, so enterprises and industries grew with the devotion of the government.

Notes

1 O Won-chol, *The Korea Story: President Park Jung-hee's Leadership and the Korean Industrial Revolution* (Seoul, Korea: Wisdom Tree, 2009), 156.
2 O Won-chol, *Hanguk-hyeong gyeongjegeonseol 7: Naega jeonjaengeul hajaneun getdo aniji anneunya* [Korean Type Economic Construction 7: An Engineering Approach] (Seoul, Korea: Korea Type Economic Policy Institute, 1999), 244–245.
3 *Ibid.*

4 They might also worry about that Korea would soon catch up Japan if they transfer technology.

5 The facts of this section were derived from Kim Chung-yum, *From Despair to Hope: Economic Policymaking in Korea 1945–1979* (Seoul, Korea: Korea Development Institute, 2011).

6 Hong Eun-ju and Lee Eun-hyeong, *Korian mirakeul 3: Sumeun gijeokdeul junghwahakgongeop, jichukeul heundeulda* [The Korean Miracle III: Heavy and Chemical Industry Shakes the Axis of the Earth] (Seoul, Korea: Nanam, 2015), 91.

7 *Ibid.*, 95.

8 *Ibid.*, 96–97.

9 Kim, *From Despair to Hope*, 408.

10 *Ibid.*, 408.

11 O Won-chol, *The Construction of Pyramid-Type Export-Oriented Industries* (Seoul, Korea: The Korea Type Economic Policy Institute, 2003), 410 [in Korean].

12 Hong and Lee, *Korean Miracle III*, 107–109.

13 Hong Eun-ju, Lee Eun-hyung and Yang Jae-chan, *Korian Mireokeul 1* [The Korean Miracle I] (Nanam, Seoul, Korea: Nanam, 2013), 103–105.

14 *Ibid.*

15 O, *The Korea Story*, 255–256.

16 Paul Akamatsu, *Meiji 1868: Revolution and Counter-Revolution in Japan* (New York: Harper & Row, 1972), 1247.

17 O, *Economic Construction 7*, 37.

18 Hong and Lee, *Korean Miracle III*, 156–157.

19 Hong, Lee and Yang, *The Korean Miracle I*, 103–105.

20 *Ibid.*, 105.

21 Hong and Lee, *Korean Miracle III*, 350–352.

22 In Japan, it took above 100 years to reach the Hoffmann coefficient 1, while Korea took a couple of decades, according to Toshio Watanabe, *The Analysis of Modern Korean Economy* (Tokyo, Japan: Keiso Shoboo, 1982). Quoted from O Won-chol, *Hangukhyeong gyeongje geonseol 2* [Korean Type Economic Construction 3: An Engineering Approach] (Seoul, Korea: Korea Type Economic Policy Institute, 1996), 200–201.

23 O, *The Korea Story*, 60.

24 Alexander Gerschenkron, *Economic Backwardness in Historical Perspective: A Book of Essays* (Cambridge, MA: Harvard University Press, 1962), 6–8.

25 Hong, Lee and Yang, *The Korean Miracle I*, 321–321.

26 Korea Engineering Club, *Joguk geundae juyeokdeul* [The Heroes of "Quantum Jump"] (Seoul, Korea: Quiparang Press, 2014), 127–150.

27 Korea Engineering Club, *Heroes*, 100–103.

28 Park Tae-jun, "The Memoir of Park Tae-jun," *JoongAng Ilbo*, August 31, 2004 [in Korean].

29 O, *Pyramid-Type Export-Oriented Industries*, 63.

30 Park Tae-jun, "The Memoir of Park Tae-jun," *JoongAng Ilbo*, August 31, 2004.

31 *Ibid.*, September 17, 2004.

32 O, *Economic Construction 7*, 139.

33 *Hwangmujieseo ilgun soetmul, pocheol sinhwa* [POSCO Myth]. Directed by Kim Dong-guk, (Seoul, Korea: KBS, 2013), accessed August 10, 2017, www.kbs.co.kr/1tv/sisa/docucinema/view/vod/2186813_66621.html

34 *Ibid.*

35 *Ibid.*

36 *Ibid.*

37 In 2010s, Korea ranked the fifth in steel production of the world. Refer to www.worldsteel.org/statistics/statistics-archive/yearbook-archive.html

38 O, *Economic Construction 7*, 141.
39 Park Tae-jun, "The Memoir of Park Tae-jun," *JoongAng Ilbo*, November 10, 2004.
40 "POSCO Named 'the World's Most Competitive Steelmaker' for 6 Consecutive Years," POSCO, accessed August 14, 2017, www.posco.co.kr/homepage/docs/eng5/jsp/prcenter/news/s91c1010035p.jsp?idx=2395.
41 Park Tae-jun, "The Memoir of Park Tae-jun," *JoongAng Ilbo*, September 10, 2004.
42 "POSCO named 'the world's most competitive steelmaker.'"
43 For details, please refer to O, *Economic Construction 3*, 13–155, and Hong and Lee, *Korean Miracle III*, 229–250.
44 O, *Economic Construction 3*, 13–155.
45 *Ibid.*, 13–155.
46 *Ibid.*, 46.
47 *Ibid.*, 13–155.
48 *Ibid.*, 22–24.
49 *Ibid.*, 46.
50 *Ibid.*, 46.
51 *Ibid.*, 63–64.
52 Park Hun, *Hankuk Sokyuhwahakgongup 30 Nyonui Hoigo* [Reflection of Korea's Petrochemical Industry 40 Years] (Seoul, Korea: Korea Petrochemical Industry Association, 2004), 3.
53 *Ibid.*
54 *Ibid.*
55 *Ibid.*, 4.
56 *Ibid.*, 3–4.
57 *Ibid.*, 4.
58 www.kpia.or.kr/index.php/pages/view/industry/phase [in Korean]
59 For details, please refer to O, *Economic Construction 3*, and Hong and Lee, *Korean Miracle III*, 315–355.
60 O, *Pyramid-Type Export-Oriented Industries*, 263.
61 *Ibid.*, 263–264.
62 *Ibid.*, 267.
63 *Ibid.*, 9.
64 SKD means that cars are in a state of semi-assembly, and CKD means completely dis-assembled.
65 O, *Pyramid-Type Export-Oriented Industries*, 271–273.
66 *Ibid.*, 279.
67 *Posco Myth*, KBS.
68 Hong and Lee, *Korean Miracle III*, 108.
69 O, *Pyramid-Type Export-Oriented Industries*, 290.
70 *Posco Myth*, KBS.
71 Hong and Lee, *Korean Miracle III*, 353–354.
72 Cars are imported in a form of completely disassembled parts.
73 Kim Seong-uk, "Bakjeonghuiui 'maika sidae' reul biutdeon hakjadeul" [The Academics Who Sniggered at Park Chung-hee's "My Car" Generation], *Cho Gab-je dot Com*, December 2, 2008, accessed August 10, 2017, www.chogabje.com/board/view.asp?C_IDX=25555&C_CC=AZ
74 O, *Pyramid-Type Export-Oriented Industries*, 315–380, and Hong and Lee, *Korean Miracle III*, 251–313.
75 Hong and Lee, *Korean Miracle III*, 263–264.
76 O, *Pyramid-Type Export-Oriented Industries*, 323.
77 Hong and Lee, *Korean Miracle III*, 277.

78 *Ibid.*, 278.
79 O, *Pyramid-Type Export-Oriented Industries*, 333–335.
80 *Ibid.*, 335–336.
81 O Won-chol, *Construction of the Shipbuilding Industry: A Model for Korean Industrialization* (Seoul, Korea: Korea Development Institute, 2002), 35–36.
82 *Ibid.*, 36–37.
83 O, *Pyramid-Type Export-Oriented Industries*, 339–340.
84 Hong and Lee, *Korean Miracle III*, 283.
85 O, *Pyramid-Type Export-Oriented Industries*, 355–356.
86 *Ibid.*
87 O, *The Construction of Pyramid-Type Export-Oriented Industries*, 358.
88 O, *Construction of the Shipbuilding Industry*, 80–81.
89 *Ibid.*, 87–88.
90 Hong and Lee, *Korean Miracle III*, 295.
91 *Ibid.*, 292.
92 *Ibid.*, 294–295.
93 O, *Economic Construction 7*, 182–184.
94 O, *Pyramid-Type Export-Oriented Industries*, 376–377.
95 O, *Construction of the Shipbuilding Industry*, 113.
96 Hong and Lee, *Korean Miracle III*, 301–302.
97 O, *Pyramid-Type Export-Oriented Industries*, 377.
98 Hong and Lee, *Korean Miracle III*, 310.
99 *Ibid.*
100 O, *Construction of the Shipbuilding Industry*, 93–94.
101 *Ibid.*, 123.
102 *Ibid.*, 122.
103 Hong and Lee, *Korean Miracle III*, 315–355.
104 For details, please refer to O, *Economic Construction 3*, 283–408.
105 O, *Economic Construction 3*, 284–285.
106 Hong and Lee, *Korean Miracle III*, 362.
107 O, *Economic Construction 3*, 304.
108 Hong and Lee, *Korean Miracle III*, 373.
109 O, *Economic Construction 3*, 309.
110 *Ibid.*, 309–326.
111 Among them are resistors, cathode ray tubes, speakers, microphones, rod antennae, condensers, batteries, connectors and integrated circuit boards.
112 Hong and Lee, *Korean Miracle III*, 378–383.
113 O, *Economic Construction 7*, 148–152.
114 Park Sun-chan, "Geumseong TV, Samseong hyudaepon, hyeondae poni . . . gananhan naraui gongjang, gijeokeul mandeulda" [Geumseong TV, Samsung Mobile Phones, Hyundai Pony . . . Miracles Made in a Poor Country's Factories], *Chosun Ilbo*, March 4, 2015, accessed August 10, 2017, http://news.chosun.com/site/data/html_dir/2015/03/04/2015030403250.html
115 *Ibid.*
116 O, *Economic Construction 3*, 344–347.
117 *Ibid.*, 385–387.
118 Hong and Lee, *Korean Miracle III*, 398–399.
119 Korea Engineering Club, *Heroes*, 469.
120 *Ibid.*, 473.
121 Lee Ji-hoon, "Yunjongyong gomuni teoleonoeun 'samseongjeonja CEO 12nyeon" [The Story of Jong-yong, Ex-Chairman of the Samsung Electronics], February 20, 2010, accessed August 10, 2017, http://news.chosun.com/site/data/html_dir/2010/02/19/2010021901202.html

122 Lee Chae-yun, *Samseong jeonja 3.0 iyagi* [*The Story of Samsung Electronics 3.0*] (Seoul, Korea: Book Ocean, 2011), 4.
123 strategyanalytics.com, August 4, 2017 report, www.strategyanalytics.com/access-services/devices/mobile-phones/handset-country-share/reports/report-detail/global-smartphone-vendor-marketshare-for-15-countries-q2–2017?slid=207468&spg=29#.WZVwqdgUmzk
124 Park Geon-hyeong, "Samseongjeonja, segyejeongsange seotta" [Samsung Stands on Top of the World], *Chosun Ilbo*, July 8, 2017, accessed August 10, 2017, http://biz.chosun.com/site/data/html_dir/2017/07/08/2017070800156.html

8   Development of human resources and technology

1 Human capital as a catalyst

Uganda's mercurial dictator, the late Idi Amin, went on an out-of-the-blue convulsive lustration tirade in 1972, during which he ordered the immediate expulsion of the country's entire Asian minority. Amin argued that the expellees who constituted the heart of the country's industrial magnates were fleecing the wealth of the majority black African population. He therefore believed that the problem of the country's poverty would be addressed by confiscating the assets of the expelled minority. By year's end his order had ensured that nearly 5,655 companies, farms, ranches, homes, automobiles and agricultural estates were redistributed to indigenous Amin loyalists.[1] It didn't take long for the result of Amin's jingoism to fall under the weight of its own contradiction.

Many of the expellees migrated to the United Kingdom, where they had to restart all over again, with nothing but the few personal belongings they were allowed to take along with them out of Uganda. As the expellees started to pull themselves by their bootstraps in the United Kingdom, the Ugandan economy began what became a pernicious degeneration and ultimate implosion. This example is not meant to justify any ethnic-based superiority or lack thereof, but more to underscore the basic premise of the fact that poverty is addressed by creating wealth rather than appropriating. How then is wealth created? Wealth, as we will see in this chapter, is the product of a competent stock of human capital. What Amin and many other populists of his caliber often fail to realize is that poverty is addressed by unleashing the entrepreneurial genius of a people rather than pandering to the galleries.

On a macro level, we see a similar trend in terms of the fate of nations across the world. Even though I don't personally entirely subscribe to the resource curse thesis, I am still inclined to believe that, irrespective of a nation's natural resource endowments, it will ultimately take a disciplined stock of competent human capital capabilities to make it a prosperous nation. Were it not so, countries such as South Korea would still be stuck in the limbo of dirt poverty. But it was this stock of human capital that was an indispensable part of the country's industrialization. I also believe that industrialization can scarcely take place without having the requisite funding to get it done. But unlike financial capital that can be acquired externally, human capital must be endogenously cultivated. With respect to human capital, in a state of absolute poverty, South Korea suffered serious problems although it had a large population.

First, it did not have any sizable pool of disciplined labor force to speak of. True, its outstanding economic performance can be attributed to the high aspiration Koreans had for education, which facilitated human capital accumulation along the way. But that was never the entire case throughout much of its modern history. Until the early 1960s, the level of human capital accumulation was low as was discussed in Chapter 1. Industrialization came to a critical head the scale of the dearth of technicians, skilled labor, engineers and scientists became all too apparent. As was discussed earlier, for all its sprawling population, there was nothing to show for in terms of human capital capacity. Korea traditionally had a senselessly low regard for labor on one hand. This worked together with the legacy of colonial rule, most notably a lack of self-reliance and a sense of inferiority that had been instilled in the populace. On the other hand, jobs were not easily available. Of course, it was only a natural that under these circumstances they could not easily acquire necessary skills.

Subsistence farming was among the few sources of work available during colonial rule, but it did not demand the kind of skill required of factory workers. All that was demanded of farm workers at the time was showing up and knowing how to use simple tools such as shovels and hoes, which do not require learning specific skills. Under colonial rule, except for manual labor, Koreans were denied jobs in large textile factories and small factories producing machines, almost all of which were owned and managed by Japanese settlers. The colonial regime denied Korean students the opportunities to study science and technology. Given that people learn how to work through experience, Koreans at the time could not acquire astute work habits like punctuality, devotion and accuracy in final touches required of factory workers. Ironically, at liberation, Koreans had a natural hatred for everything related to Japan and the Japanese and even joined in destroying industrial facilities. They did not even want to learn about the Japanese work ethic.

There was no substantial change under the US military government, which replaced the Japanese colonialists in South Korea when the Korean Peninsula was partitioned. The US military government did not pay much attention to the management of former Japanese industrial properties. Their operations were frequently interrupted or came to a complete halt when Japanese managers and engineers were withdrawn. Workers were frequently on strike. To make matters worse, North Korea cut off the electricity supply to South Korea, whose factories had relied on a power supply from the North. The government of this new republic was striving hard to manage nation building and reconstruction after the Korean War for a decade or so.

Second, the value system in Korean society was not in favor of industrial development. In Korea, social status was traditionally identified with occupation. Occupation was valued in the order of (1) scholars, (2) farmers, (3) technicians and (4) merchants. Because of the nature of the traditional social values that valued scholars and government officials over technicians and merchants, it was generally perceived that children from poor families in rural regions should go to technical high schools because the school fee was cheap.[2] Under this value system, the literati, traditionally the governing elite, were the highest social class; technicians and merchants were placed at the lowest rungs of social hierarchy. Consequently, talented people did not want to become technicians or merchants. This value system was so deeply rooted that the educational system itself favored the humanities at the expense of science and technology. Gifted people were encouraged to become government officials and scholars.

Third, the education system, which was in poor shape, could not effectively nurture industrial manpower. The limited technical schools failed to produce an adequate number of skilled workers demanded by the industry. There were 45 technical high schools and 17 general high schools with engineering departments, which accommodated 36,699 students as of 1963. However, the education and facilities were so poor that the graduates were not useful in their fields even though they were lucky to be employed. Worse still, few teachers at those schools were qualified to train students in skills and techniques for industrial use. No wonder, the technical schools were focused on classroom education suited for admissions to institutions of higher education instead of on-the-job training. Companies that hired unskilled workers could not produce high-quality products that could be sold in the market.

There is no doubt that Koreans were naturally endowed with intellectual abilities to pursue educational training in the natural sciences and technical education. As was referred to earlier, however, its tradition of holding the technician and merchant classes in a low regard and the denial of Koreans opportunities to study science by the colonial regime prevented education in science and engineering from taking root. Until the early 1960s, education had been concentrated in the studies of law and social sciences instead of the hard sciences.[3]

After its independence, only a few Koreans had completed advanced science or engineering programs in developed countries, most of them through aid programs provided by donor countries. However, most did not want to return to Korea – a country with social unrest and political instability that could not provide adequate facilities for research and development. Almost all of them chose to remain in the advanced countries; this was a typical case of "brain drain" in underdeveloped countries. Endowed with few resources other than labor, the country had to start fostering a skilled workforce one way or another as it wanted to develop its moribund economy. Back then few would have thought that South Korea would one day train its workers in a highly skilled labor force, proceed with industrial development successfully and even compete with Japan and Western countries in world markets.

Human capital can be accumulated in two ways. One is for individual economic units to put their time, financial and other resources into human capital accumulation on their own in anticipation of rewards for their investments within the social-rewarding system in the market. The other is for the government to invest directly in education or vocational training services for people and to give signals through economic policies to affect investment decisions of economic units. For instance, for the industrial development drive by the government, people may respond with higher investments in technical education, expecting higher returns from it.

Regarding the former issue of human capital accumulation by individual economic units, the market mechanism in the country worked in such a way that investment in education had a high yield. Investment in education was a vehicle for upward social mobility. Even poor farmers were ready to sell off cows and rice paddies to send their children to university. This was the reason why universities were often referred to as "cow-bone towers," instead of ivory towers.[4] The parody reflected the desperate desire poor families in rural areas had for upward social mobility. The fever of investment in education was fueled by the fact that few had a head start in a race for high positions when the Korean War ended. Koreans believed that almost everyone was placed at the same starting line. Indeed, the market for human capital was rewarding them based on their ability. Nonetheless, the effect of heavy investment in human capital through education had only a limited effect on the supply of skilled labor for industry.

In addition, social mobility was made easier by a series of historical events. The landlord class collapsed when land reform was undertaken before the 1950–1953 Korean War. Thanks to this reform, the population were rendered equal in poverty when the fratricidal war ended. Social mobility went through another phase when military officers hailing from poor rural areas were drawn into the ruling elite in the wake of the 1961 military coup. Positions of higher social status were up for grabs. In recruiting people for public service, which was a major source of employment at the time, the transparent meritocratic system was upheld at all levels. The Higher Civil Service Examination system provided a gateway to high-ranking government positions. Those who pass the examination start at the fifth grade in public service instead of at the bottom (ninth grade), and may reach the top level within the government bureaucracy. This kind of meritocracy, which started in ancient China, was adopted centuries ago by Korean monarchs.

As to the latter issue of the role of government in education, the capacity of the Korean government to invest in education was limited. As an elementary school student in a lower grade in the late 1950s, I had to take lessons in the open field rather than in a cozy classroom. However, the government delivered a strong impact to the education market by investing heavily in technical and science education and by giving strong signals of an economic development drive. The main turning point in industrialization was provided when President Park made two critical declarations in 1973: the first was development of the heavy and chemical industry (HCI); the other was the promotion of science and technology nationwide. In other words, it was promising to build a strong state by launching a costly project, building an HCI, and helping all people participate in a project to promote nationwide science and technology education. These were ambitious projects that many Koreans had previously associated with only developed countries.[5] Section 8.3 will provide a detailed explanation of how science and technology was promoted in the country, using the Korea Institute of Science and Technology (KIST) as an illustration.

The signals the government sent in pushing for economic development changed the behavior of individual economic units participating in the education market. With economic development opening job opportunities in the industrial sector, the value system based on the top-down order of scholars, farmers, technicians and merchants began to crumble. The popularity of law and social sciences waned as a growing number of talented students were choosing to study science and engineering at university. One good example was the changing status of the college of law at Seoul National University, which had been the most coveted by high school graduates as well as their parents. But the university ceded its premier position to engineering colleges and chemical engineering, machinery and electronics departments when the government was carrying out its Five-Year Economic Development Plan in the 1960s and 1970s.

Later, the government did not limit its role in sending out behavior-changing signals. Instead, in running education and training programs, it challenged to have the labor change their behavior or attitude toward work, and equipped workers with practical skills in industrial fields rather than theoretical knowledge at the desks. It was at this stage that the policy of Technical and Vocational Education and Training (TVET) program was beginning to take root, thanks to a technical collaboration scheme with the government of West Germany. President Park, who called skilled workers the "crown jewels of the nation," directly involved himself in running programs designed to train workers for skilled manpower. As the government launched plans for fostering a defense industry and HCI, it was not sure that Korea could manufacture and export technological products with its labor force. In this regard, the Korean government established a pilot technical high school. Convinced through this experiment that vocational training and technical education could catapult the country into the ranks of advanced nations, the Korean government expanded and upgraded technical high schools across the whole country, which will be discussed in the coming section.

Indeed, for industrialization to take root you cannot rely entirely on skilled manpower, as was used in South Korea for the labor-intensive production of exportable items. Another pillar for industrialization was a sizable pool of highly educated scientists and engineers capable of conducting research and development. Scientific research and technological development were required for sustainable industrialization. They were needed to cut the cost of producing sophisticated new products. At the early stage of economic development in the 1960s when development of its own technology was unthinkable in the business sector, South Korea established a special institute for the research of science and technology to help enterprises in developing technology. By doing so, it could build its research and development capabilities from scratch. Later, under the circumstance that the level of education in science and technology were very low nationwide and the country was not capable of upgrading its educational level, the government also established an elite education institute focusing on science and technology in line with its financial capacity. These two institutions laid the foundation for advanced research and development and education in science and technology.

The government's policy of making a heavy investment in human capital, which was highly rewarded, paved the way for an unhindered supply of highly trained manpower, a core ingredient for industrialization. On the one hand, under the circumstances that the rewards of human capital investment are high, the government's industrial development drive worked as a signal for creating a boom for the demand of technical training and study for science and technology nationwide. On the other hand, under the circumstances that the supply conditions were very poor, the government's investment in the international standard of technical training and scientific research and education in concentration-facilitated benchmarking by all other educational institutions, which provided momentum for upgrading the education supply capacity to the international standard in a moment. The decision to spend heavily on the accumulation of human capital set Korea apart from developing countries in Southeast Asia, where unjustifiable large tracts of land held in the hands of a select few landlords tended to hamper social flexibility. As such, tenant farmers in large numbers neither expected returns on investment in education to be high, nor could they afford to make such investments.

2 Korea's national treasure[6]

Key to industrialization was the supply of technicians and skilled workers. Then the question was how to turn farmers into technicians and skilled workers, the type of manpower demanded by industry. Korea had to make such a change in manpower as it was demanded for its own survival. In doing so, it had to surmount all the barriers and doubts about it. The most critical component for industrialization is the supply of technicians and a skilled labor force capable of operating machines and tools in factories – most of them requiring education in technical high schools and on-the-job training. The acquisition of industrial skills must start at a young age, similar to an artist or an athlete. In Germany, technical education starts after having finished 5 years of primary education.[7] Such training in Korea starts 4 years later, after graduation of junior high school. Although Korea needed to start industrial training at an earlier age, its educational history and tradition tied its hands and prevented it from training children matriculating from elementary school.

Fostering technical manpower proceeds in a two-pronged way; one is formal technical education by regular high schools, colleges and engineering universities; the other is vocational training institutions. Regarding the former, the Korean government made a great investment in the schools, reducing class sizes, improving facilities, and specializing schools and colleges in the fields of electronics, machinery, and so forth for effective education during the 1960s and 1970s. As to the latter, the government decided to set up a new vocational training system in 1961. However, six long years had passed before the Vocational Training Act was legislated. The culprit was the conflict of interest among the ministries concerned. The Ministry of Education held that vocational training be provided within the framework of a formal education, maintaining that no separate training institution was needed. The Ministry of Trade and Industry (MTI) voiced opposition to an additional financial burden being shouldered by business enterprises for the provision of vocational training. The Ministry of Labor claimed that separate institutions are established for vocational training and placed under its supervision if workers were to upgrade their skills required in the industrial fields. The law, enacted following coordination by the Economic Planning Board, made the Ministry of Labor responsible for vocational training.

Under the 1967 law, the government set up vocational institutes in every province in the nation. In total, 24 vocational training institutes were established from 1968 to 1982. First Lady Yuk Young-soo also chipped in on the project with the establishment of Chungsoo Vocational Training Institute. Originally, the vocational training institutes were at the junior high school level; however, as senior high school education become prevalent, the centers were renovated to the level of senior high school and their names were also changed to masters colleges, like the "Meister Schule" in West Germany. However, because the Korean government could not afford the financial investment, 22 of them were built with foreign aid. In the early days of vocational training in Korea, West Germany contributed much in terms of financial investment and technical transfer. West Germany made a great contribution for vocational training systems to take root in Korea. Germany had more than 100 years of experience in vocational training. During the period 1974–1996, the West German government provided mid- to long-term vocational training for more than 1,000 Korean vocational instructors, who played a key role in the development of vocational training in Korea.[8] Additionally, the German government, IBRD (International Bank for Reconstruction and Development) and ADB (Asian Development Bank) helped establish vocational training institutes, provided experiment equipment, and dispatched technical experts to the Korean government and vocational training institutions.

The government established a central vocational training institute for teachers with IBRD aid in 1968. In consideration of financial limits to the public investment on vocational training, it imposed a duty upon corporations to conduct vocational training by law; large corporations were obliged either to establish their own training centers or to make contributions to the vocational training fund to finance public training. In 1973, the government unified all qualifications recognized by each of its agencies concerned into a National Qualifications Standard and established the Korea Manpower Agency (now renamed Human Resources Development Service of Korea), which was authorized to issue national recognitions of skills acquired by trainees. By taking these measures, the government could standardize skills and technical expertise demanded on the job and to help match the demand and supply of technicians and skilled workers on the market. Entering the 1990s of the information technology (IT) revolution, vocational training systems also began to take new shape. Now most work should be done by a computerized control system and information technology. In line with the change, a 1-year training program following senior high school was renovated to a 2-year college-level program. In 1994, the government began to provide public employment service through provincial centers to match employers and employees. The supply of technical and skilled manpower was made easier by the introduction of the National Qualifications Standard, official recognitions to trainee skills and expertise, and a service of matching employers and employees.

As part of the official education system under the supervision of the Ministry of Education, the government established more technical high schools and increased its investment in improving training facilities at those high schools. The government also launched a public campaign to make donations to buy milling machines for the schools. It also encouraged its own enterprises and large companies in the private sector to establish technical high schools. Such efforts led to the creation of foundations running technical high schools. Some other business enterprises established vocational training institutes on their own to meet their demands for skilled workers.

In the early 1970s, it dawned on the government that Korea could not rely on a mature light industry alone to continue to expand its exports. The Korean government concluded that, as a solution to this problem, Korea had to move into machinery and other sectors of the HCI. As was discussed in the previous chapter, President Park pushed to develop a defense industry for national security considerations in 1970, and declared state building on HCI in 1973. The light industry is the realm of manual workers, like needleworkers. However, HCI is the realm of engineers and technicians who can work at a high level of accuracy. Japan was estimated to have 150,000 technicians and engineers for HCI. Korea was estimated to have that manpower in several hundred at a low level of accuracy. O Won-chol reported to President Park that Korea needed at least 50,000 skilled technicians to build the HCI for the export of $10 billion. However, the problem was that the MTI was not fully convinced that Koreans had the talents and characters to be highly qualified technicians to successfully support the HCI.

Moreover, it found many naysayers among the Japanese trade-and-industry officials working on relations with Korea, some of whom said that the Korean temperament might not be suitable for the kind of industrial work that demanded a high level of precision. Indeed, the Korean government acknowledged that the HCI demanded different types of work behavior, as Japanese officials suggested. Koreans were not disciplined enough for that kind of job. They were neither punctual nor careful in putting the final touches on the products they were producing, with the final touches being vital in determining the quality of finished products. If no action was taken to change work attitude, the proposed transition to the HCI was deemed impossible.

Highly noteworthy regarding the operation of technical high schools and an increasing need for highly skilled workers in the industry was an experiment the government conducted in the early 1970s. The MTI thought that it needed a new model technical high school to experiment whether Korean learners could develop the kind of talent demanded by companies producing precision machinery. Fortunately, the MTI could establish a technical high school to its own specifications using the technical assistance fund of Japan. President Park approved the project in 1970, demanding that the school be made one of the best in Asia.

With the presidential blessing under his belt, the Minister of Trade and Industry called training experts into session to determine what needed to be done for the school project. Some argued students should be encouraged foremost to have a strong will to become a master in a specific technical field. Many others argued that spiritual and attitudinal fortitude is more important than anything else in acquiring skills. Finally, it was agreed that an emphasis would be put on three characteristic traits for skilled workers: devotion, integrity and respect for precision, the words beginning with the phonetic representation of *jeong* in Korean – *jeongseong*, *jeongjik* and *jeongmil*. A student at the technical high school would be called on to devote himself to a product being produced as a mother did to her child, to pursue utmost precision in the process of production, and to keep himself from cutting corners and honestly follow the production procedure as specified in the blueprint. Students would be called to hold onto the three-*jeong* principle for 24 hours a day and 6 days a week during the 3 years of residence in the dormitory.

The model school opened in March 1973. Unlike the ill-equipped provincial schools, the new Kumoh Technical High School had many of the finest training facilities available in Asia. In addition, it had some faculty members recruited from Japan and had a curriculum modeled after those of its counterparts in Japan, a country reputed at the time to provide the highest quality of vocational education and training in the world. Despite overriding opposition from the Ministry of Education, the government handed the authority to supervise the school over to the MTI. The MTI officials thought that technical education at the technical high schools under the supervision of the Ministry of Education was failing to produce technicians with the qualifications demanded by industrial fields. The Ministry of Education claimed to no avail that education should be for the whole man rather than for providing simple skills or knowledge. However, the view prevailed that education at the school must be practical, not idealistic.

The admissions policy of Kumoh Technical High School, which put a special emphasis on work attitude, was different from that of other technical high schools. Instead of granting admission based on a written test, the model school selected candidates based on interviews with the top 10 percent of graduates from each junior high school, with a recommendation from the principal of the school and a regional police chief. Behind this admissions policy was the belief that a student's work attitude was no less import than the scores he gained in a test. One of the main criteria for admissions was the applicant's passion to become a master in a specific technical field. Unlike other schools, it did not charge tuition fees or any other expenses. Instead, it provided all students with a scholarship. Therefore, talented students applied for the model school all over the country.

The new school also set itself apart from others when it demanded discipline from its students. All students, housed in the dormitory, were constantly reminded of their commitment to the three-*jeong* principle mentioned earlier.

They were also required to rise at 6:30 a.m. and go to bed at 11:00 p.m. every day. Their rigorous life in the dormitory was little different from that in a military boot camp. For efficiency in education and training, the class size was reduced to a maximum of 20. The ratio of instructors to students increased as the years went by.[9]

As graduation neared for the first batch of students at the school, the government wanted to test their performance. That was the reason why the government sponsored a contest among students graduating from the Korean technical high schools and those from the Japanese technical high schools in 1976. To the surprise of ministry officials, the Korean students scored higher than their Japanese counterparts. In the eight vocational training items including manufacturing of precision machines, milling, turnery, molding and welding, Korean students obtained an average score of 88.4 and their Japanese counterparts an 80.9 out of 100, the Koreans surpassing the Japanese in every training item.[10] These results convinced the government that Koreans, given proper education and training, would work as well in the HCI as Japanese and Westerners did. No wonder, the government channeled huge sums of money into provincial technical high schools emulating Kumoh in education and training.

With all the assistance, they had from the government, many of the students at Kumoh could obtain precision engineer certificates after 2 years of education and training, 1 year ahead of graduation. When the school matriculated the second batch of students in 1977, four graduates participated in the 23rd World Skill Competition (WSC) and won two gold medals, a silver medal and a bronze medal. Since then, students and graduates of Kumoh Technical High School have swept the domestic and international skills contests. Gaining confidence, the government further established 11 more schools like Kumoh Technical High School. The graduates from the schools elevated Korea's underdeveloped machinery industry to the level of advanced countries.[11]

In this manner, the formal education and vocational training system ensured a steady flow of technicians and skilled workers into Korean industry. Armed with an immense sense of pride in their standing as pioneers of the modernization of the country, technicians and skilled laborers threw themselves wholeheartedly into the acquisition of precision processing techniques. After graduation, they went on to attain their qualification as precision technicians and played key roles in building HCI in Korea. Fostering technical manpower is a primary policy task of developing countries. Of all the steps taken to foster skilled industrial workers, the following three were noteworthy.

First, the government provided love to skilled manpower and devotion to fostering technical manpower. As children grow taking love and care from their parents, so was the technical manpower fostered with love and devotion by the country. TVET was a top concern for President Park, who realized industrialization cannot proceed when technicians and skilled workers are in short supply. He showed a keen interest in developing technology and fostering skilled manpower early on. He said in his 1968 New Year's address, "skilled workers are a driving force behind the nation's economic development. They are as the 'nation's crown jewels.'" He even believed that they played a key role in promoting national security. He went on to say in his address, "National security cannot be guaranteed in the absence of technological advancement. In this regard, engineers and skilled workers are the nation's weapons and shields."[12] During his tour of the provinces, he often visited technical high schools. He once said after such a tour, "When I visit Busan, I try to make time to visit Busan Mechanical High School. When I find the lights are on until late at the school, it fills me with a great sense of contentment."[13] Social recognition was also great. The medal winners of the WSC were greeted as national heroes upon arrival at Gimpo Airport and were given a parade from the airport to the Blue House amid a storm of applause. National medals were awarded by the president. They could take pride in their jobs.

Second, in fostering technicians and skilled workers, the government thought that establishing a work ethic and labor discipline was much more important than transferring techniques. That is why the model technical high school, Kumoh, introduced the three-*jeong* principle as its educational philosophy accommodating all the students in the dormitory house. As such, institutions of technical and vocational education and training demanded of them the same level of discipline as the military demanded recruits undergoing training at boot camp.

Third, technicians and skilled workers thus fostered were guaranteed by sufficient employment opportunities.[14] Due to a drive for the development of HCI, many industrial plants were appearing with great demand for technical manpower. Moreover, technical high school graduates were allowed to go on to college after several years of work and even enroll themselves in graduate and doctorate programs later. More to the point, universities were to reserve up to 10 percent of freshmen slots in their pertinent departments for skilled workers with a technical high school diploma. The government also hatched plans to turn some of the 2-year technical colleges into 4-year colleges and establish new 4-year technical colleges.[15]

The performance of this strategy for fostering technical manpower was represented in two ways. One is that Korean youth showed the excellence of their skills and technique in international society. The WSC, or the "Skills Olympics," had been held almost every other year since its inception in Spain in 1950 until 1971, before switching to the current biennial format. The competition invites technicians aged 21 and under from most of the vocational training fields including welding, auto-body repair, aircraft maintenance, plumbing and heating, carpentry, cooking, and showcases of a country's technological prowess. The top rankings of the competition were usually dominated by advanced countries such as Japan and West Germany. However, despite Korea's relatively short history of technical education and training, which started in 1973, Korea won the championship nine consecutive times from 1977 through 1991, whose trend continued until recently.[16] The other was their contribution to the industrial development of Korea. With a sense of immense pride and deep devotion they had as would-be pioneers of modernization in the nation, students and trainees were motivated to develop the kind of fine motor skills that were in high demand in the precision and other high-tech industries. After attaining certificates as technicians, they were to play a key role in the relevant industries.

3 The birth of Korea's science and technology[17]

A prevailing view of the 1960s Korea was that Koreans were not imbued with the intellectual capacity to conduct scientific research and technology development. Research and development was believed to be an area exclusively set aside for advanced nations. Moreover, science and technology were not high on the ladder of social values in Korea at the time. Gifted students who were inclined toward science and technology were under immense social pressure to major in law and other social sciences to become judges, prosecutors, government officials or scholars.

A case in point involved Dr. Choi Hyung-sup, who became the first president of the KIST and later Minister of Science and Technology. He said he faced fierce opposition from his family members when he decided to apply for admission to an engineering college. At the time, few Koreans were aware what engineering colleges were like. Many people thought that engineering colleges taught such trades as carpentry and plastering.

On the occasion of the formal decision of the first Five-Year Economic Development Plan, President Park asked, "What to do with the 'technology' issue to support economic development?" Being utterly taken aback, nobody answered the question. The vice minister broke the silence by saying, "the technology issue will be reported later." This anecdote reveals the perception of policymakers and economists of Korea. They simply thought that technology did not have anything to do with Korea, which is to be pursued only by the Western people and Japanese. In 3 weeks, the Five-Year Science and Technology Promotion Plan were prepared in haste. Followed by the plan, the Technology Management Bureau was established within the Economic Planning Board, and in 1967 the Technology Bureau was renovated to establish the Ministry of Science and Technology independent from the Economic Planning Board (EPB).

In the early 1960s, Korea had no decent institute capable of conducting research on science and developing technologies demanded by business enterprises. Nor were colleges capable of doing such work. It would not be too difficult to imagine in what shape the colleges were given that they could not afford to burn coal in stoves to heat their classrooms. Against this backdrop, Dr. Choi Hyung-sup and other scientists called on President Park to take action to help people get easier access to science and technology. In the 1950s and 1960s, advanced countries including the United States, West Germany, and the United Kingdom provided grants for fostering scientists and engineers in Korea. Among them, the US Minnesota project stood out, which provided opportunities for 220 Korean students of science and engineering to study at the University of Minnesota for a period of 7 years from 1955 with $10 million from the US aid fund.[18] Some scientists fostered by this aid program played key roles in developing science and technology in Korea. President Park took their advice seriously and took appropriate action when an opportunity to this end arose.

In 1964, the government, despite surmounting strong objections from the opposition party, decided to send combat troops to South Vietnam to help the United States in its war efforts. In return for the troop dispatch, the US president was willing to give a gift to Korea. Discussions were made over the gift of President Lyndon B. Johnson between the ruling party and the administration. The key members of the military coup dominating the ruling party and cabinet proposed "A bridge crossing over the Han River named after Johnson or Johnson Memorial Hall."[19] The young economic advisor Shin Dong-shik proposed a science institute, which faced enormous opposition from influential persons. They heavily criticized Shin, asking: "Have you lost your presence of mind? How much time does it take to build an institute, and recruit scientists and have them conduct research for economic development?" Because no conclusion was reached, the president decided to request a science institute.[20] At a summit with President Park in Washington, DC, President Johnson committed himself to helping Korea modernize its military equipment and establish an institute of science and technology. His pledge was contained in a joint statement issued following the summit.

As a follow-up to the Park–Johnson agreement, Korea and the United States equally co-financed the $20 million project to establish the KIST. The lion's share of the $10 million from the United States was earmarked for equipment imports and a consulting fee to the Battelle Memorial Institute.[21] President Park gave two standing orders to Dr. Choi, who was tapped to head KIST in February 1966. He told him not to beg the EPB for any funding, as the institute is required to devote itself entirely to research, and is not to yield to lobbying from the outside when recruiting people as staff members, with members of the National Assembly all out to put undue pressure on public offices for the employment of their relatives and constituents.

The first job that needed to be done to establish the proposed institute was to determine what legal status it would be given under a special law to be enacted. The draft bill on the KIST stipulated that the government subscribes funds of its coffers, and that the institute not be required to subject its books to auditing by the government and obtain approval of its annual management plan from the government. It drew strong opposition when it was being deliberated on at a cabinet meeting. If KIST was to be funded by the government, the critics said, its expenditures could not be exempted from a government audit. They went on to argue that the bill that would give the institute the status of an independent legal entity was against the National Property Law, as it prohibits the government from transferring any of its assets to an independent legal entity. But the president threw his weight behind the advocates, who silenced the vocal critics and sent the bill in its original form to the National Assembly for approval.[22]

During parliamentary deliberation, the relevant committee of the National Assembly rewrote the bill to subject the institute to the government's audit of its books and approval of its spending plans. Angered by the move, President Park told Deputy Prime Minister Chang Ki-young to take prompt action to restore the bill to its original form. Lawmakers affiliated with the ruling party foiled the opposition and passed the restored bill through the National Assembly with the backing of the president. The institute was given a free hand as far as research and development was concerned.

Second, another important issue concerning KIST was selecting a site for its home. President Park suggested the institute's building be constructed within the region of the Forestry Experiment Complex in downtown Seoul, a place that had easy access to public transportation and a cozy environment for research and living. In fact, according to the recollection of Shin Dong-shik, the president had already checked with the secretary accompanied by Shin, and decided the region should be the site of the KIST, and gave instruction to Choi.[23] But the Minister of Agriculture and Forestry voiced strong opposition, saying even a square foot of land the complex held in its possession could not be handed over because it was critical to its mission. When negotiations were deadlocked between the Ministry of Agriculture and Forestry and KIST, President Park toured the site with the minister and the mayor of Seoul in tow. He told the minister to hand over 1,256 hectares of land to the KIST, saying "The Forestry Experiment Complex is doing an important job, but what KIST is set to do will be more critical to the nation's economic development."[24] Later Dr. Choi made a compromise and agreed to take 500 hectares in what appeared to be an action designed to help the Minister of Agriculture and Forestry save face.

Third, research instruments were to be imported with aid from the United States. KIST made it a rule to buy parts and assemble them on its own where

Picture 8.1 Establishment of KIST in Hongreung. KIST was set up in Hongreung, an area near downtown Seoul in the grounds of the Forest Experiment Center, to ensure a convenient and cozy research environment

©Korea Institute of Science and Technology

possible. In this manner, KIST could save $1.35 million out of the $10 million grant, which the institute returned to the US Agency for International Development (USAID). The USAID was puzzled because it was the US president's project. To the director-general of the USAID visiting Korea on the news, KIST said it did not need the unspent money because it purchased all the instruments it wanted and that more purchases than needed would do more harm than good.[25]

Fourth, what was most critical to KIST was recruiting researchers of high caliber. As an incentive, the government assured they could conduct research and work in a comfortable environment under no undue pressure from the outside while using cutting-edge research instruments. Nonetheless, KIST had yet to solve a host of thorny problems concerning remuneration, residence and other issues.

Payment could not be taken lightly. But no less important was the prestige to be bestowed on the researchers for the missions they would carry out and stability in life they would be ensured. KIST decided that they would be provided with homes in the residential areas where their children could have access to quality education and medical insurance, which had yet to be introduced in Korea. It also decided that they would be paid three times the amount their counterparts were paid as faculty members of Korean national universities.

It was only natural for national universities to complain vociferously about what they regarded as discrimination against their faculty members. Some of them filed direct petitions with the presidential office.[26] It was not national universities alone that were disaffected. The Ministry of Science and Technology also submitted a formal report to President Park against the proposed pay levels for KIST researchers.

When the issue was brought to the fore, President Park summoned Dr. Choi to his office. In mock surprise, the president reportedly said to Dr. Choi, "As I am told, your researchers will be paid much more than I am." In reply to this remark, Dr. Choi was quoted as saying, "You may cut my salary if you regard my pay scale as unreasonable. But I cannot cut the pay for my researchers."[27] President Park approved KIST's remuneration plan.

Despite all these benefits in store, it was far from easy to recruit competent, knowledgeable persons as research fellows. The reason was that not many of the applicants were qualified for the KIST jobs and that the political situation in Korea was not so favorable. KIST was looking for people with engineering backgrounds, not basic science majors but applied ones in industrial technology. Among those who applied for research fellow positions, only ten held degrees in mechanical engineering while nearly 400 were people who had finished courses in physics.[28] The paucity of engineering majors had much to do with the preference of basic sciences in the United States at the time. Korean students were pressured to study basic sciences, theoretical and nuclear physics, when they went to the United States for advanced studies. It was easier for them to get scholarships from American universities if they chose to study such sciences because research in those fields was in vogue and better funded.

Another recruiting problem was posed by political instability in South Korea, which was under a constant threat of attack from North Korea. Many of the South Koreans who had obtained graduate or doctoral degrees from American universities were reluctant to come back because of the security threat. Instead, many them chose to stay in the United States. The difficulty in staffing was well described in the remarks of a South Korean scientist who had moved from the U.S. National Aeronautics and Space Administration (NASA) to KIST. Dr. Chun Gil-nam said,

> The political situation was very unstable [in South Korea]. People around me [when I was working for NASA] told me it would be insane of me to return to Korea. They were betting that, if I did, I would come back to the United States in a few months because I could not stand living here.

Yet the terms of employment were enticing to him. Later, recalling his early days of life as a KIST research fellow, he said:

> The conditions of my employment were beyond description. They were nothing short of overwhelming. As a man who had received a doctorate a few years back, I wondered if I deserved to be treated the way I was. I was told I was paid much more than the president himself. Moreover, I was chauffeur-driven and given a nice home. My goodness, can you believe that I was chauffeur-driven?[29]

Fifth, being equipped with modern facilities and staffed with research fellows, the remaining issue was how to conduct research. KIST thought that the research had to focus on what business circles needed, not on scholastic ones. Usually the learned people who had PhDs from overseas preferred academic research to practical research. At the time when KIST was established, there was no technology worthy to call it as such in Korea, and field guidance of techniques for companies was more urgent than academic research. In this consideration, upon the suggestion of the Bell Institute, a top-level institute in the world, as a sister institute with KIST by Dr. Horning, KIST chose the Battelle Memorial Institute, which was a business-oriented institute conducting research based on contracts with business firms. In this respect, KIST wanted to maintain close links with the private business sector when it was starting research and development projects.

Research and development conducted in developing countries mostly followed a typical pattern: (1) a research institute was established, (2) the institute formulated a research project on its own and (3) it sought a private business that wanted to apply the research outcome in the manufacture of its product.[30] But few were confident that new technology developed in this manner, when applied, would produce the desired effect. Businesses could not be blamed if they wondered aloud if it was too risky to put the new technology to use in the manufacture of their products. After all, it had never been put to the test in the factory.

But the company, which sponsored the research project, was forced to apply new technology regardless of its risk.[31]

KIST, however, set itself apart from other research institutes by changing the second and third stages of research and development mentioned earlier. Instead of formulating a research project alone, KIST involved a business in need of a new technology in the second and third stages. It signed a contract with the customer on the development of a new technology, selected a research item together with the client and carried out the research program with the participation of, and feedback from, the client. Although the terms of contracts were made more favorable to businesses, not many of them were enthusiastic about the idea of developing new technologies in a contract with a research institute. They wondered why they needed to sign a contract on developing a new technology with a research institute when it was easier and less costly to import such a technology from Japan.

But technology imports became more costly and difficult as time went by. A growing number of businesses turned to KIST for technological development as they learned of one or two research programs successfully conducted by the research institute. Researchers, freed from red tape and undue outside influence, worked hard as KIST gained fame as the leading research institute of the nation. KIST was seen as an institute at which the lights were never turned off. Its researchers took pride in being a driving force behind the nation's economic development. Their achievements also reawakened policymakers of the government to the importance of science and technology to the economic prosperity of the nation.

Lastly, all the aforementioned arrangements for KIST to rise to respectability in a short span of time would not have been possible without unreserved support from President Park. It might not have been his own brainchild, but President Park went the extra mile to foster it as a respectable institution tasked to advance science and technology for the nation. His care for the research institute was evidenced by his frequent visits to the KIST construction site during which he gave cash gifts as well as words of encouragement to construction workers. Despite his tight schedule, President Park visited the KIST headquarters twice a month, a practice that lasted for 3 years since its inauguration.

One researcher said of President Park:

> When he came to visit us, he would often mention a particular project we had undertaken. He would tell us that our nation would be in big trouble if we failed in our mission to carry out the project. Then all of us would start to work late into the night. We felt as if the fate of our nation were in our hands. Looking back over the years, I can say KIST had the cream of the crop devoted to research and development. Of course, we were amply rewarded for our work.[32]

When it conflicted with other government agencies, President Park rarely failed to come to its rescue. His unwavering support for KIST raised the morale of its researchers to an unparalleled height. President Park's role was critical in promoting science and technology, as Dr. Stevan Dedijer noted in his thesis titled *Underdeveloped Science in Underdeveloped Countries*, which concludes that it was impossible for a developing country to make a breakthrough in science and technological development unless its head of state played a leading role on the frontline.[33]

KIST presented itself as a model that could be emulated by developing countries that intended to build their industrial technology research institutes. As half the cost of its establishment was funded by the United States, some developing countries might be led to believe that it was created under the initiative of the United States and operated with US help. On the contrary, the US role was limited to funding a feasibility study and the purchase of research instruments for the institute covering half of the project cost. The feasibility study was just a formality and all the other costs of construction and operations were borne by Korea. Korea established the institute on its own initiative and managed its operations for itself.[34] It should be reiterated that KIST could not have proved to be a success without President Park's fullest support and the steadfast devotion of its research staff to the promotion of science and technology for the nation.[35]

In the 1970s, two models attracted attention for technological development in developing countries from international academia. One of the notable ones was the Nayudamma model of India,[36] and the other was Choi's KIST model of Korea. The former argues that every country should conduct research on its unique natural resources and raw materials for national development, while the latter claims to introduce advanced technology and develop it for industrial circle to absorb swiftly through the establishment of science and technology institutes initiated by government. Upon the request of the Indonesian government, in October 1972 the East-West Center of Hawaii University hosted an international seminar and the aforementioned two models were recommended to the Indonesian government to be chosen at the AID (Agency for International Development) seminar in November the same year. At the latter seminar, the KIST model was formally adopted by the Indonesian government as its technology institute model.[37]

As Korea's economic growth picked up the pace, so did its demand for technology. KIST could not meet the growing demand for technology alone, as the government was pushing ahead with its plan to develop an HCI. As such, the government started to inaugurate a variety of research institutes, each of which had a mission tailored to meet the needs of a specific industrial sector. They included the Korea Oceanic Research and Development Institute, the Korea Standards Research Institute, the Korea Research Institute of Chemical Technology, the Korea Atomic Energy Research Institute, the Korea Institute of Machinery and Materials, the Korea Electro-Technology Research Institute and the Electronics and Telecommunications Research Institute (ETRI).

In 1974, the government launched an ambitious plan to build a science park in Daedeok, Chungcheongnam-do, with a vision to create a research cluster that would bring both public and private research institutes into the one location. By doing so, the government intended to help them maximize the outcome of their investment in research and development, and to utilize their research and development resources to the greatest extent possible. It wanted them to share knowledge and resources and collaborate in certain projects. Daedeok Science Park, into which many private research organizations as well as public ones moved as was intended, played a pivotal role in the advancement of science and technology in the nation.[38]

As scientists and engineers, either educated in the nation or abroad, were doing outstanding jobs at KIST and other research organizations, it was necessary for the government to train college students as their assistants and then as the next generation of researchers. To meet such needs, KIST established an undergraduate course under its wing in 1968 and began to select some of the students enrolled in the course as research assistants. It was a first step taken under the government's unprecedented education plan to establish a science and technology graduate school in its pursuit of a brain pool much larger than the existing one.

Subsequently, a group of experts headed by Friedrich E. Terman, a former vice president of Stanford University, was commissioned to conduct a feasibility study. Based on the outcome of this feasibility study, the government decided to establish an independent graduate school and passed a Korea Advanced Institute of Science and Technology (KAIST) bill through the National Assembly. Under the law, the government created KAIST in 1971. KAIST has since established itself as a renowned institution of higher education in science and technology and evolved into a university with undergraduate studies as well.

KAIST, now located in Daedeok, had a set of founding principles: to introduce a new, modern concept of graduate school management; to break away from the rigid, bureaucratic educational system adopted by other Korean graduate schools; and to attain its goal of building a high-tech brain pool in a systematic way.[39] The government also intended other graduate schools of science and technology to emulate KAIST in reforming themselves. In other words, KAIST, which received huge institutional and financial support from the government, had an additional mission as a pilot project to reform graduate school education on science and technology.

One of KAIST's first tasks was to recruit renowned scientists as faculty members and admit gifted students by offering to provide all enrolled students with full scholarships. With full support from President Park, it could accomplish its mission without too much difficulty. President Park accepted almost all requests from KAIST. One exception was a request to exempt KAIST graduates from conscription. He turned it down, saying no able-bodied man could be exempted from military service because it was a duty equally borne by all male citizens of Korea.[40] It cannot be said that the process of founding KAIST was smooth and uneventful. Existing universities, feeling that they were being discriminated against, voiced strong opposition to what appeared to be a revolutionary idea of building a new institution of higher education of science and technology with all kinds of support from the government. Those universities had many influential politicians on their side when it was fighting the government's move.

A case in point was a demand that the government scrap its plan to fund its KAIST project with a loan from the United Sates. Under pressure from politicians and universities, the Minister of Culture and Education called on the deputy prime minister and the Minister of the EPB to withdraw a request for $6 million in a loan from the Development Loan Fund, the lending arm of USAID. Kim Hak-yeol, the deputy prime minister and planning minister who shared the same philosophy of science and technology education with President Park, would not even hear of the request. The conflict, however, did not end there. Opposition came from the United States this time. The Korean government received a cable saying that Dr. Edward E. David Jr., then science advisor to the US president, was coming to Seoul. Upon arrival, Dr. David raised a question about the planned educational institution, citing opposition from Korean professors on the ground of discrimination against their universities. He said that they called on the United States to turn down the loan request immediately.[41] But the Korean government did not yield to any of the demands from opponents.

Selecting many students for admission was not of much concern to KAIST, which believed one talented person well educated and trained to be a scientist would be better than a large group of mediocre ones. This elitism prevailed when it selected freshmen candidates from more than 500 applicants in 1973 – all of them from top-ranking universities in the nation. Of them, 450 made the preliminary cut. Pressure was mounting on KAIST to admit all of them, but only 106 made the list of finalists. No such practice in admissions could be found at any other Korean institution of higher education. No wonder foreign visiting professors reportedly said the academic performance of KAIST students was comparable to that of students at MIT (Massachusetts Institute of Technology) or Stanford University in the United States.[42]

The process of recruiting faculty members was no less rigorous at KAIST, which had sought advice from Stanford University. Unlike other Korean universities, KAIST ignored school, family and hometown connections in its efforts to select the best-qualified persons from among the applicants for faculty positions. Moreover, President Park permitted KAIST to disregard nationality in the selection of candidates. This measure went against the hitherto upheld policy of staffing state universities and other public organizations only with Korean nationals. KAIST was also permitted to invite faculty members from world-renowned institutions of higher education, such as MIT and Stanford University, to give lectures on its campus for 3 to 6 months.[43]

KAIST had encountered many difficulties and made many mistakes until it opened a new chapter in education on science and technology in Korea. Nepotism and easygoing manners were widespread in the academia of Korea. Strengthening the tenure examination provoked a backlash from faculty. Professors thought that evaluations of their classes by students were insolent. In recruiting faculty members, it was difficult to exempt personal consideration. Some students under stress for high grades committed suicide. KAIST had no other way than to learn by trial and error. But its achievement was beyond the expectations of the policymakers who had conceived the idea of building a new institution of higher education and, by doing so, helped to upgrade the nation's graduate school education on science and technology.

When looking back over the early days of research and development, few could deny that KIST and KAIST established themselves as the two main pillars for advancing science and technology in the nation. Their successful undertaking of this mission was made possible with firm support from President Park, who was at the forefront of the nationwide campaigns to promote science and technology, foster high-tech industries and create a research cluster in Daedeok Science Park.

Notes

1 Jan Jelmert Jørgensen, *Uganda: A Modern History* (Abingdon: Taylor & Francis, 1981).

2 In order to encourage technical or vocational education, the government provided greater subsidies to technical schools than traditional grammar schools.

3 Seol Bong-sik, *Bakjeonghuiwa hangukgyeongje* [Park Chung-hee and the Korean Economy], (Seoul: Chung-Ang University Press, 2006), 271–272.

4 O Won-chol, *Bakjeonghuineun edtteoke gyeongjegengguk mandeulleonna* [How Park Chung-hee Made Economic Power] (Seoul, Korea: Dongsuh Press, 2006), 717.

5 *Ibid.*, 181–182.

6 O Won-chol, *Hangukhyeong gyeongje geonseol 2* [Korean Type Economic Construction 2: An Engineering Approach] (Seoul, Korea: Korea Type Economic Policy Institute, 1995), 79–100, and Kim Chung-yum, *From Despair to Hope: Economic Policymaking in Korea 1945–1979* (Seoul, Korea: Korea Development Institute, 2011), 426–441.

7 Choi Hi-sun and Chung Mi-kyung, *dogil jigeop kyoyuk hullyeon jedoui gyeongje-tonghapeseoui yeokhal mit sisajeom* [The Role of German Vocational Training System in Economic Integration] (Korea Institute for Industrial Economics and Trade, October 2014), 35–36.

8 Lee Kyung-gu, *Hanguke daehan gaebalwonjowa heyopryeok* [Development Aid and Cooperation for Korea] (Korea International Cooperation Agency, 2004), 104–105.

9 O Won-chol, *The Construction of Pyramid-Type Export-Oriented Industries* (Seoul, Korea: Korea Type Economic Policy Institute, 2003), 218 [in Korean].

10 *Ibid.*, 219.

11 Kim Chung-yum, *From Despair to Hope: Economic Policymaking in Korea 1945–1979* (Seoul, Korea: Korea Development Institute, 2011), 431.

12 O, *Economic Construction 2*, 91–92.

13 O, *How Park Chung-hee Made Economic Power*, 515.

14 O, *Pyramid-Type Export-Oriented Industries*, 215–218.

15 Kim, *From Despair to Hope*, 437–440.

16 *Ibid.*, 433.

17 The facts about the establishment of the Korea Institute for Science and Technology was derived from Choi Hyung-sup, "Development of Science and Technology in Korea (1960–1980)," in *The Park Chung-hee Era: What Was It to Us* [in Korean], edited by Kim, Sung-jin (Seoul, Korea: Chosunilbosa, 1994), Hong, Lee and Yang, *The Korean Miracle I*, 521–539, and Hong and Lee, *The Korean Miracle III*, 179–191.

18 Kim Jun-kyung et al., *Modularization of Korea's Development Experience: Impact of Foreign Aid on Korea's Development* (Ministry of Strategy and Finance & KDI School), 2012, 52.

19 Hong and Lee, *Korean Miracle III*, 179–180.

20 *Ibid.*, 189–190.

21 Choi, *The Light Never Goes Off*, 65.

22 Choi, "Development of Science and Technology in Korea (1960–1980)," 276–277.

23 Hong and Lee, *Korean Miracle III*, 180.

24 Choi, *The Light Never Goes Off*, 59.

25 Choi, "Development of Science and Technology in Korea (1960–1980)," 278.

26 Choi, *The Light Never Goes Off*, 57.

27 *Ibid.*, 58.

28 *Ibid.*, 60.

29 Eom Bo-un, "Uriga mollattdeon daehanminguk inteonetui daebu" [The Korean Internet Godfather We Never Knew], *Chosun Ilbo*, March 21, 2014, accessed August 10, 2017, http://premium.chosun.com/site/data/html_dir/2014/03/21/2014032103085.html

30 Choi, "Development of Science and Technology in Korea (1960–1980)," 268–269.

31 *Ibid.*, 269.

32 Eom, "The Korean Internet Godfather We Never Knew".

33 Stevan Dedijer, *Underdeveloped Science in Underdeveloped Countries* (London: Minerva, 1963), 61–81.

34 Choi, "Development of Science and Technology in Korea (1960–1980)," 282–285.

35 Korea Engineering Club, *Joguk geundae juyeokdeul* [The Heroes of "Quantum Jump"] (Seoul, Korea: Quiparang Press, 2014), 73–79.

36 Proposed by Yalevarthy Nayudamma (1922–1985), Secretary-General of the Council of Scientific and Industrial Research (CSIR).

37 Lim Jae-yun and Choi Hyung-sup, "Choi Hyung-sup and the Origin of 'Korean Development Model,'" *History Critics* (Spring 2017), 176–178 [in Korean].

38 Kim, *From Despair to Hope*, 447–448.

39 Choi, *The Light Never Goes Off*, 102–104.

40 *Ibid.*, 106.

41 *Ibid.*, 105.

42 *Ibid.*, 109.

43 Choi, "Development of Science and Technology in Korea (1960–1980)," 301–302.

9 Attracting foreign capital to spark development

1 Foreign aid and development financing

Along the course of my work and interaction with officials of developing countries, I am routinely asked a range of questions about development in general. Without necessarily getting into all the specifics of the spectrum of questions, I am still able to broadly categorize them into two important subsets. The first tends to be about how South Korea, given its precolonial history, could remarkably transform the mind-set of its people from a lethargic bunch into a diligent development oriented polity. The second has to do with the issue of how we were able to mobilize the necessary financial resources required for the massive industrial development that ensued. The major resources for economic development are human capital and finance. In fact, the circumstances of development financing in Korea at her early stage of development were extremely poor. Financing sources are either domestic savings and/or foreign investment. As to the former, in a position of one of the poorest countries in the world making its subsistence on foreign aid, Korea could not expect anything at all for financial mobilization.

In fact, the circumstance of development financing in Korea at her early stage of development was extremely poor. Financing sources are either domestic saving, and or foreign ones. As to the former, in a position of one of the poorest countries in the world subsisting on foreign aid, Korea could not expect anything at all for financial mobilization.

With regard to the latter, aid and foreign direct investment (FDI) or loans can be sources. Aid is not provided for the recipients to become rich but to the extent to relieve immediate poverty. Moreover, for a coup d'état regime, no donor countries were willingly providing aid. In the case of FDI or loans, Korea was in a much more difficult position. As Figure 1.1 suggests, suffering from chronic deficit, Korea could barely manage an international balance of payments and public finance by foreign aid. Moreover, with the Korean War just over, Korea was in a state of armistice. Korea was classified as a war-risk country until the end of the 1950s, a situation that made the introduction of foreign capital next to impossible.[1]

Investment opportunities were scarce where no energy and natural resources were available and national income was the lowest in the world. If the international balance of payments is unstable, so are the exchange rates, which makes the value of money invested unstable. No country or investors would put their money into a country like this. You could hardly talk of FDI under such conditions – conditions back then could make many of the troubles of developing countries sound like a storm in a teacup. Under the circumstances of a seemingly insurmountable balance-of-payments deficit and dependence on foreign aid, Korea could not dare to prepare finances for development. To put this into context, the DSR (Domestic Saving Ratio) and IVR (Investment Ratio) remained at a low level of 10 percent until the early 1960s, according to Figure 9.1. In a poor country, public finances had to also be poor. Under the low tax burden ratio on a poor tax base, fiscal revenue also had to be very limited, and thus the government was incapable of coping with widespread poverty. For this reason, South Korea was deservedly considered as the classical basket case.

The military regime was bent on improving the international balance of payments and escaping default, and could scarcely entertain the thought of mobilizing financing for development. Like many reactionary populist revolutionaries of his cast, Park Chung-hee's junta immediately went on a misguided class witch hunt, believing that by going after the greedy rich business class, they could claw back some of the financial assets they had illegally accumulated. Parallels can be drawn with the stupor of the Bolsheviks' attempts to create an egalitarian utopia by wholesale confiscation and redistribution of assets of individuals

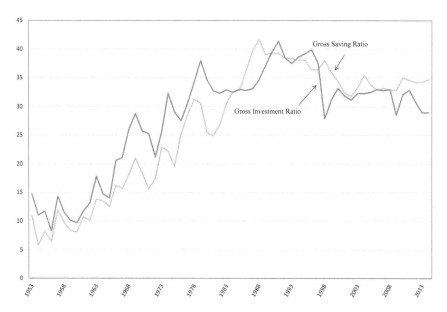

Figure 9.1 The trend of savings ratio and investment ratio in Korea

Source: Bank of Korea

and institutions perceived to be conspiring against the prosperity of the masses. Similar inklings, albeit to a lesser degree, were on show under Mao Zedong's populism. In both instances, we see that history has not particularly looked on these actions so kindly.

Long before the Soviet economy went into tailspin, it was all too obvious by the 1970s that such economic populism as was being touted by the ruling junta was a figment of a wholly bankrupt mind-set. Yet in Seoul, we had a government that was unveiling a very hasty monetary reform policy to redenominate the currency and compel those illicitly hoarding money to bring it into the open. The hope was that by clawing back this money, it would be used for public investment. Therefore, they set about a wild goose chase of income redistribution, which was soon to collapse on the weight of its own contradictions. All this while, Washington was growing uneasy with the radicalism of the junta, and quite rightly was concerned that it had set itself on a slippery slope of socialist revolutionary utopian idealism. To get the junta to reverse course, a routinely scheduled American aid consignment was temporarily withheld as a coercive measure against the junta. The military regime freed the businessmen and the monetary reform resulted in economic chaos.

The junta formally admitted the failure of its monetary reform. The economy became worse as time went on thanks to the same reasons. Moreover, the financial crisis accelerated as Washington became indifferent to the regime and left it in the cold. The military regime learned an important lesson from its flirtation with populist monetary reform. Unlike what the class theory espoused by Marxism would have us believe, reactionary egalitarianism is never the answer to the question of wrestling down poverty. What we rather see in both examples is the critical role of human capital in creating wealth. Physical assets don't constitute wealth but rather the intangible mental capacity is what creates wealth and prosperity. Then, the remaining task for the government was mobilizing financial resources to support investment and economic growth.

2 Belt tightening and attraction of foreign capital

For an economy to develop, it will require enormous amounts of both foreign and domestic investment. Even though there are no clearly defined sequences for determining at what stage foreign or domestic investment resources are required, in an ideal world it is always more rewarding to prioritize domestic revenue sources. An effective domestic revenue mobilization campaign can also be a good way to induce foreign capital investment. There are three ways to mobilize local finances for development: (1) encouraging voluntary thrift and saving, (2) compelling forced savings and (3) designating specialized banks for mobilization and distribution of funds.

Regarding the first issue, the government resorted to extreme efforts to maximize domestic savings through national thrift and savings drives and institutional arrangements. I still remember the experience of rhyming songs in elementary school with lyrics like "don't neglect homemade goods for foreign ones. This is a display of patriotism." Clearly, this is an example of precisely how seriously successive governments have tried to inculcate the spirit of patriotism from an early stage in childhood. Luxury goods and imported articles attracted high tax rates and tariffs were levied, such as a special excise tax at the rate of 7–20 percent by tax item and 10 or 20 percent by place of taxation, in addition to the value added tax (VAT) of 10 percent.[2]

President Park was an active proponent of the savings and thrift policy. The designated Annual Savings Day and Tax Day were the crowning glory of the individual efforts at ensuring its success. State awards were conferred on individuals and corporations who had achieved a distinctive savings record and tax payment during the year. The proscription of smuggling and the resulting punitive measures for offenders was a credible deterrent as the nation sought to achieve significant internal capital accumulation. Government regulations were actively deployed in thrift and food consumption as well. There was a massive call on the consumption of food to the extent that until the nation achieved its desired target of rice self-sufficiency, the use of rice to produce local snacks was severely frowned upon, and similarly the production of alcoholic beverages using rice as raw material was outlawed.[3] Lunch meals for students were encouraged to be prepared using mixed grains rather than pure rice.

President Park led this crusade from the front by his own practice of thriftiness. For instance, except on occasions when he hosted foreign guests, he kept his air conditioner off during the summer season.[4] Regarding his thrift and diligence, Kim Chung-yum, who served as his chief of staff for nearly a decade, recalls as follows:

> President Park was unassuming in every way. He lived a life of modesty and practiced diligence and frugality in every way. He had servings of rice with barley, and for lunch he took wheat flour noodles every day. He enjoyed drinking unrefined rice wine.[5] He always used local products, only resorting to imports when there was no alternative. Except for neckties, fountain pens, and electric shavers, the president's entire wardrobe – his suits, overcoats, shirts, underwear, socks and shoes – was homespun . . . President Park was not impressed by worldly desires nor did he seek wealth; a truth plainly revealed to the world after his death. . . . The president's wealth was in his country and his people.[6]

Owing to the government's positive policies for thrift and savings and the exemplary conduct of the leadership, South Korea became renowned for having the highest savings rate in the world in the 1970s.[7] As Figure 9.1 shows, domestic savings ratios were maintained higher than 30 percent during the period of 1970s to 2000s.

As to the second issue of forced savings, if inflation is high, people are more inclined to hold physical assets rather than liquid ones, converting liquid assets to properties like real estate to stimulate the general levels of savings overtime. As Figure 9.1 shows, during the development era of the 1960s and 1970s, South

Korea maintained a high investment ratio with high domestic savings and was also hit hard by the global oil shocks in the 1970s, which boosted inflation during those days. Wholesale prices and consumer prices for 3 years since 1973 following the oil shock were recorded at 100 percent and 72 percent, respectively.[8] The shift in the public mood toward investment in real physical assets also triggered speculation and a corresponding push on inflation.

In many ways, the trend of inflation was a double-edged sword. On the one hand, it contributed to capital accumulation through high savings rates. However, on the other, it deepened inequality between assets, income and labor earnings. Furthermore, high interest rates levied for borrowing took its toll on the international competitiveness of domestic enterprises. Given the situation of a weak domestic savings capacity, the active development policy of maintaining high investment rates through accumulation of foreign savings inevitably accompanied considerable levels of inflation, which thus contributed to the promotion of capital accumulation through forced savings. However, in the long run, it caused negative effects such as worsening inequality in income distribution and weakening international competitiveness of Korean industries and enterprises.

Regarding the third issue of financial management, the banking sector plays the role of intermediary between financial mobilization and distribution for investment. It is also an industry that requires autonomy in financial management according to the principles of a market economy. Because loans from banks were hardly available, corporations had to depend on the private loan market, which often charged very high interest rates. The money market in Korea in the early 1960s was totally abnormal. Although the savings capacity was poor, the money was not circulating through banks. People used to keep their money in cabinet drawers or the curb market, partly due to unrealistically low interest rates for savings. With poor deposits, banks had to also be poor in their lending capacity. Under the circumstances, the government thought that financing through banks and financial inflows into priority industrial sectors set by the government were more urgent than the autonomy of the banking industry at the initial stage of development. The government thought that prior industrial development was necessary for the sake of development of the banking industry in the long run. With this in mind, it pursued two important policies: (1) the policy of reverse interest rates and (2) subordination of the banking sector to state control.

Regarding the former, to channel savings to banks the government introduced higher interest rates for depositing and lower interest rates for loans, which is very unusual. Since the advent of the military regime, the economy was burdened by chronically high inflation, which resulted in high interest rates in the market. However, to support corporations, the official interest rates were set low throughout the period. As a desperate effort to encourage savings and increase money circulation through banks, Chang Ki-young, deputy prime minister and the Minister of the Economic Planning Board (EPB), introduced a reversed interest rate – higher interest rate for deposit than for lending – in 1965, in disregard of stern criticism and opposition. The interest rates of banks were set at 30 percent for deposits and 24–26 percent for lending. The deficits of banks had to be compensated by the central bank. The performance of the reverse interest rate policy was beyond expectations. The money hidden in cabinet drawers and curb market began to flow into banks. It provided momentum for the development of the banking industry.[9]

As to the latter, the government took the extraordinary measure of bringing all banks under state control. The object was to ensure that the government could direct financial supply to its target and strategic priority industries as stipulated in its development plans. In this regard, the central bank also came under the influence of the state. The government invested in commercial banks and established special banks such as the Korea Development Bank, Korea Small and Medium Enterprises (SME) Bank and Korea Exim Bank, which were mandated to specifically tailor their financing activities to reflect the government's development policy priorities. The appointment of heads of banking institutions had to be cleared by the government in those days. During its developmental phase, the banking sector was subordinate to the government. It was said that the Bank of Korea is a branch office in Sogong-dong of the Ministry of Finance (MOF). Even commercial banks were under regulations set by the MOF. The government thought that banks should be managed in such a way to ensure a smooth inflow of financial resources to the industrial sectors in accordance with government's development policy. Surely this policy is an intrusion of the sacrosanct concept of the autonomy ascribed to the central bank and other financial institutions, and the weak banking industry caused unbalanced development between industrial and banking sectors in a later stage in Korea. The circumstances of the banking industry in Korea in those days were different from that of many African countries, where most of the banks are operated in the form of FDI.

Beyond the complexities and theoretical arguments, the key takeaway from this experience ought to be viewed from the perspective of the ability of the government to galvanize a savings culture within the citizenry and its consequent impact on domestic capital accumulation and its allocation. Through those ways, the goal of mobilizing domestic funds and smoothly facilitating the flow of financial resources into strategic fields of economic development were effectively realized. Although, in the early stage of development, the quantitative effects on development financing were meager by the standards of a poor state, the psychological effects might nonetheless prove to be very significant. It is worth looking at this development from the psychological perspective and the historical baggage it evokes. As time goes on, when the opportunities were given to the people for employment and earning through the export of the labor force to West Germany, troop deployment to Vietnam, and the throngs of construction workers to the Middle East, domestic savings increased greatly due to the savings mind-set imbibed in them. Thus, the enormous foreign-exchange revenue from the remittances of laborers and companies abroad made great contribution to settle the shortage of investment funds for economic development.

The major source of development financing was foreign. During the early days of development, the entire South Korean state was sustained by foreign subventions. As was pointed out in Figure 1.4, during the late 1950s, the share of foreign aid reached almost one half of Korea's government revenue. However, the bulk of aid funding went into immediate relief purposes rather than for long-term investments in development. The experience of many of the aid-dependent countries provides definitive proof that foreign aid does not offer any real prospect of breaking the shackles of poverty. Aid dependence also raises real questions about national sovereignty in its truest sense. By the early 1960s, the Korean leadership had reached the stark realization that its reliance on foreign aid for development was untenable to say the least. In an ideal world, sovereign nations should be able to explore an independent path out of poverty, which explains my personal admiration for those that can achieve this. Experience and history has shown that the path to economic development must always traverse through primitive accumulation of capital, as was the case with Europe and other industrialized economies of our day. However, South Korea challenged the historical experience and conventional wisdom of the day. Under international competition, how can poor countries accumulate primitive capital, feed their poor people and construct industries? It would be like waiting for pigs to fly.

However, as was referred to in the preceding section, the circumstances of South Korea did not allow for the smooth inflow of foreign capital. The government expended a great deal of effort to attracting foreign capital. In 1960, it enacted a decent "Foreign Capital Inducement Act," which failed to attract the interests of foreign capital. Foreign institutions just did not find the prevailing environment during the period appealing in any way. Given the chronic deficits in international balance of payments and unstable exchange rates, a simple preparation of a legal system was not sufficient to attract foreign investment.

The government had to launch an exceptional measure, enacting the Act on Payment Guarantee of Foreign Borrowing in 1962. According to the Act, the government took on the role of guarantor of foreign loans raised by the private sector. As domestic firms at the time lacked the necessary credit in international markets to raise capital on their own, the government decided to allow state-owned banks to provide guarantees for foreign borrowings by private corporations. Absorbing risks for foreign creditors by the Korean government, the law paved the way for more confident channeling of foreign capital into the Korean market. It is extraordinary in the sense that loans are borrowed by businesses; however, its repayment is assumed by the government. Opposition parties strongly criticized the legislation, arguing that it would lead the country to national ruin. Indeed, the criticism of the bill was not without good reason.

In fact, the measure was so drastic that a bill of this sort had no precedent in Korea or elsewhere in the world in those days. Opposition leaders strongly criticized that the guarantee system will lead the state to default on its financial obligations. However, despite strong opposition and criticism, the Park regime pushed the bill forward. For President Park, the attraction of foreign capital and industrial development was couldn't be delayed by hypothetical arguments. Necessity had clearly compelled the government to sign up to this extreme regimen. Without foreign capital, economic development seemed to be almost impossible. In addition to payment guarantees for foreign capital, the government provided tax exemptions for imports by foreign capital, and tax incentives for companies of foreign investors.[10]

Notwithstanding these extreme policy prescriptions, the expected goals were never attained. Neither law made any significant difference to the nation's economic fortunes. Understandably so, there were legitimate questions about trust, or call it the credibility of the Korean government given all that was taking place in the region. The country did not appear to be a viable business destination. Even though the United States was its main backer, the Kennedy administration was hesitant to approve the military junta as a legitimate government of Korea and demanded Park return to the military. It also had serious reservations about the state-led development model the government was pursuing. Thus, Washington became reluctant to provide aid and US business sectors were acting with less deference to South Korea due to poor business opportunities and the reluctance of the US government to engage in economic cooperation. The rest of the Western world was in the same position as the United States. For foreign investors and multinational corporations (MNCs), they could not trust the poor government and did not perceive Korea to be a market offering profitable business opportunities.[11]

As a last resort, the government knocked on the door of West Germany for a public loan. West Germany was sympathetic to Korea with the same misfortune of division of its territory. In 1962, West Germany agreed to provide public and commercial loans worth DM 15 million, and in 1964 during a state visit by President Park it committed another DM 25 million public loan. Think of it as divine providence. As the loan was approved by the West German government, a host of German businesses started exporting their products to Korea; Siemens, Krupp, Mannesmann, Polysius, and GHH were among them. Until the mid-1960s, before formal resumption of diplomatic relations with Japan, foreign loans came only from the United States and West Germany.

Thankfully, the normalization of diplomatic relations with Japan in 1965 and the compensatory payments opened a new funding outlet to offer Seoul a badly needed reprieve. Through the agreement, Japan committed $800 million for economic cooperation funds (or reparations in the eyes of Koreans) in the form of grants ($300 million) and concessionary ($200 million) and commercial loans ($300 million).[12] For the Koreans, the compensation fund from Japan was blood money, reparations for 36 years of colonial rule – in other words, it was a fitting tribute to the sacrifices and blood of their forebears.[13] The government thought that even a penny of the fund should not be not be wasted.[14]

To prevent the misappropriation of funds for political purposes, a statute was enacted into law – the "Law of Operation and Management of Japanese Reparations," the most serious offense being punishable by death. The law proved effective in deterring corruption and misuse of the funds. The government barred individual claims, and instead opted to invest the funds for the collective public good. The remaining issue was what to use the fund for with respect to the best national interests. The Japanese side argued that because domestic industrial production was infeasible, Korea needed to use the fund to import finished goods.

The Korean side claimed that the use of the fund was up to Korea.[15] President Park said to Paik Young-hun,

> If the fund is entrusted to the government, it will be dissipating without trace. I'd like to use the fund in a way that will be of no regrets for later generations. Please study how to effectively use of the fund and report back.

Paik thought that it required consultation of scholars in advanced countries who knew well about Korea. Nakadan Seichi of Japan, former adviser to the governor-general of Korea, advised Paik that water management is vital for development, and to build Soyang River Dam and Paldang Dam. Upon hearing the report, President Park said, "that's it!," striking the table. President Park allocated $70 million for construction of two dams.[16] Thus, 26.5 percent of the compensation fund from Japan was used for importing raw materials, 4.4 percent for construction of dams, 1.4 percent for construction of the Kyungbu Highway, and later the remaining 23.9 percent of the fund concentrated on construction of POSCO. The Philippines and Indonesia also received a compensation fund from Japan, however they used the fund for buying luxurious articles for persons in power.[17]

Thanks to Tokyo's massive capital injection, the Korean economy could undergo a major turnaround especially in its balance of payments.[18] It thus

Picture 9.1 Soyang River Dam. Soyang River Dam was a multi-purpose dam with a height of 123 meters, length of 530 meters and water reserve capacity of 2.9 billion cubic meters, completed in 1973 taking six-and-a-half years. Its scale was the largest in Asia and the fourth-largest in the world at the time of construction

©ehistory.go.kr

www.ehistory.go.kr/page/view/photo.jsp?photo_PhotoSrcGBN=PT&photo_PhotoID=38761&detl_PhotoDTL=293174)

ushered the economy into an era of vibrancy. In cumulative terms, it laid the foundation for the eventual trickle of foreign capital into the economy. Benefiting from brisk introduction of foreign capital, investment for industrial development was drastically increasing.

Let us now take a closer look at the precarious foreign investment environment and the impact of the introduction of foreign capital on the economy the early stages of development. Many of the foreign capital investment projects were largely crafted on asymmetrical power relations. The process had the unintended consequence of perpetuating existing inequalities. In one such loan agreement that involved the construction of the fertilizer plant, there was a condition that until the principal and interest were fully recouped, the lender would retain all management rights. Furthermore, the Korean government also had to provide guarantees for sufficient profits within a very limited time.

Within this milieu, the government maintained a couple of principles. First, in introducing foreign investment, the government came up with its own shopping list. Having identified the target industries to be nurtured based on its resource endowments, it attracted foreign currency in this specific fields. The "positive list" was of one of the key instruments of Korea's FDI policy of restriction and control. The ability to control foreign firms' investment was very crucial and is one of the defining aspects of Korea's FDI procedures.

Second, the government and Korean businessmen preferred to keep ownership in their hands. Seeking to tap into foreign capital while limiting the influence of foreign multinationals was a sensitive issue for both the government and business. It was based on a legitimate fear that vesting control in the hands of foreign companies had the inherent risk of investments being withdrawn at the whim of the owners.[19] This was a particularly sticky political issue beyond its obvious economic implications. This is why most opted to seek foreign capital in the form of loans rather than FDI, because they could have more control over their business ventures with loans rather than direct investment. However, loans also have disadvantages in that the borrower must pay interest and if foreign investors suddenly withdraw their money, a financial crisis can be triggered, as happened in the 1997 Asian financial crisis.

The conditions were of such nature that no foreign investor was realistically interested in coming into the area. It was far more dismal in the technology sector, which was in urgent need by the Korean government. Faced with this uncanny reality, the government for the most part was resigned to accepting the unfair demands set by the few prospective investors willing to risk it. For that matter, the officials engaged in introducing foreign capital happened to be criticized as traitors.[20]

The desperate efforts by Korean government were taken with two reasons. Besides of the primary purpose of fostering industries for poverty reduction and economic development, it has secondary purpose of national security. If great power countries had their capital invested in Korea, they would provide help Korea when a war occurred, for the sake of protecting their capital and interests of their firms. Attraction of foreign capital was a way of national security as well as of fostering industries and economic development. The construction of fertilizer plants and the Guro Industrial Complex are good examples of attracting foreign capital of Korea in its early days.

Regarding the former of fertilizer plants, shortly after the end of the Korean War, the government set out to construct a fertilizer plant in 1955 with a United Nations Food and Agriculture Organization (FAO) grant of $23 million. Understandably, the goal was to boost the nation's food production capacity. Lacking the skills and competence to effectively negotiate favorable terms with foreign contractors, the government plunged into a flawed contract. Design of the plant, procurement, construction, test operation and performance guarantee were up to the contractor because the Korean government lacked the relevant expertise. There was no penalty levied for any delay in construction. The government was also responsible for paying for all the costs the contractor incurred, and the test for performance guarantees would be completed if the plant operated normally for 10 days within 180 days after the completion of its construction.[21] Thus, although the contract was revised five times, the construction cost increased from $19.55 million to $33.34 million – an increase of 70 percent – and the construction period increased from the planned 30 months to 51 months. Even with all these modifications, the plant never operated normally.

Having failed with the first project involving foreign aid, the government used its own funds for a second fertilizer construction plant and entrusted a West German company in 1958 to execute the project. However, the result was not very different from the first one. The third and fourth fertilizer plants were launched in 1964 with a US company. It took approximately one year to negotiate. Despite payment guarantees by the government, the company demanded additional approval by the National Assembly. It was a shame on the Korean government; however, the government could not help but accept the conditions and unfavorable contractual terms. Although it was a 50–50 investment by the government and the American company (excluding the foreign aid portion), the company would keep the right of management until 150 percent of its investment had been recouped. The Korean government had to ensure that the company's principal is recollected within 5 years, and for 15 years thereafter, a 20 percent annual rate of return on investment was to be applied. However, all the principal and interest was redeemed in 6 years, and the company became completely Korean owned. Thus, following successful implementation of contracts, introduction of commercial and public loans began to increase from nine projects in 1964 to 18 in 1965 and 23 in 1967. Public loans from the United States, which was initially hesitant, started to gradually increase.[22]

Regarding the latter of the Guro Industrial Complex, the government at that time was desperately seeking to attract foreign capital in critical technology fields. Although it required foreign capital in a large scale for construction of industrial plants, it was badly in need of technology investment in SME fields that produce parts and intermediate goods. Japan at that time was the world's leading manufacturing technology hub and they presented the most plausible source of foreign investment. Yet wooing Japanese SMEs to invest in Korea would prove to be a very hard sell. Undaunted, a specially designated industrial complex exclusive to Japan was established in downtown Seoul to woo Japanese SMEs through the Korean residents in Japan. Fully aware that the land price of Seoul would rise, they now began to come to Korea. The Korean government thought that the success of this single industrial complex was so valuable that it appointed a big figure, Yoo Chang-soon, as the first head of the industrial complex, who later became the prime minister. This shows a good example that how the Korean government was disparate in making a success story of attracting technology investments from abroad.[23]

As a momentum was provided through these efforts by the government, the inflow of foreign investments became brisk. Consequently, as can be seen in Figure 9.1, from the latter half of the 1960s to the early 1980s, led by foreign savings, higher investment rates were witnessed by far surpassing domestic savings rates. Promotion of economic growth through the increase in investment rates again contributed to the rise of the domestic savings rate itself. This trend remained steady into the mid-1980s and eventually the domestic savings ratio was higher than the investment ratio. This can be attributed to being able to wean off the dependence on foreign savings in investment. In the end, what we see is that the country had moved from to bolster its internal revenue mobilization capacity, in large part as a desperate response to the general difficulty to raise capital on the international money market.

3 Taxation and fiscal policies

The trend that almost half of the government's revenue came from foreign aid in the 1950s shown by Figure 1.4 persisted into the 1960s. The high dependence on foreign aid caused serious problems. First and foremost, being dependent on donors' help placed the state at the mercy of its foreign benefactors. Aid was contingent on the government's compliance with the terms set by the donors, which more often than not may reflect the interest of donors rather than the recipient country.[24] In the process, state sovereignty became but an abstract concept, yet the exigencies of the day limited its leverage.

Second, poor domestic revenue mobilization placed severe constraints on the capacity of the government to effectively function. Investment for the future was all but unconscionable, given that at this point the government could barely secure food self-sufficiency, much less addressing the basic human needs (BHN) of the populace. Under these conditions of poor public finance, the following tax and fiscal policies were implemented: (1) policies to maximize fiscal revenue, (2) broadening of the tax base by promoting investment and industrial development and (3) the realization of fairness and equity in taxation.

The pathetic state of the exchequer made it imperative to increase fiscal revenue. Because the state cannot afford the financial needs with tax revenue only under the meager tax base, it launched policy of business monopoly in specific sectors of the economy to boost state revenue. To this end, manufacturing and trading of tobacco and ginseng came under direct state monopoly. Under the oversight of the Office of Monopoly, revenue from these sources went directly to state treasury. Profits of the monopoly enterprise's share in the fiscal revenue accounted for above 7 percent on average during the 1970s and 1980s until the Office of Monopoly was closed in 1987.[25]

In most cases, tax revenue constitutes the major source of state revenue. However, until the early 1960s the increase of tax revenue fell short of rates of economic growth. The government's revenue shortfall was largely due to a weak tax base and the consequence of troubling leakages in the tax collection process. Tax dodging was taking place with the connivance of unscrupulous tax officials, who accepted bribes to look the other way. It bred a culture of corruption in the tax collection process, and a growing canker of tax officials living ostentatious lifestyles from their ill-gotten wealth started to irk society.[26] Tax administration had been performed by a bureau of the MOF since the launch of the Korean government in 1948 to 1966, which in part explains the corrupting influence. The Finance Minister had the authority to correct this misconduct, but he was too preoccupied with other pressing issues. This unprofessional organization had its limitations in raising sufficient tax revenue for development financing in a clean way.

The government had two options to address the revenue shortfall. The first would have been to radically increase tax rates or broaden the scope of taxable items, and the second would be to reform the tax administration system. With regard to the tax rates, the options could either be an introduction of new taxes or an increase in the existing tax rates whenever it found reason or occasion to do so.[27] Some of the typical areas that were touched included commodity taxation, the so-called education tax and the defense tax. Resolving this taxation dilemma required a great deal of tact, because it was liable to trigger opposition or tax resistance among taxpayers. A comprehensive tax reform was not enforced until 1976. According to the 1976 tax reform, 13 existing tax laws were revised and two tax laws were enacted for development financing. As a first step toward a gradual transition to a universal personal income tax system, it introduced a partial universalization of the existing scheduler system of personal income tax.

The large gap between the tax laws and tax collection in practice is certainly a serious problem confronting developing countries and South Korea as well.[28] This gap can undermine the public's belief in fair taxation, and cannot be resolved overnight. Taxpayers and tax officials generally exploit the "gray areas" in taxation, which results in significant tax leakage in tax administration, which also causes low tax compliance by taxpayers. It is said that a poor tax system well administered is better than a good tax system poorly administered. When President Park was eager to catch up with Japan in the mid-1970s, on meeting a Japanese business leader, Park asked for his opinion about what he thought differentiated Japan and Korea. After a brief pause, the Japanese business leader responded that in Japan nobody believed that tax officials took bribes. According to the Japanese business leader, clean tax administration is the most crucial index of social development in a country.[29]

Taking a cue from this, the National Tax Service (NTS) was established in 1966 and headed by a commissioner who had the rank and power of a deputy minister. The position of commissioner was of great importance, as the commissioner not only managed the major source of the state's revenue, but also exercised significant influence over corporations and taxpayers. Therefore, President Park had a keen interest in the position of the NTS commissioner. The NTS represented a separation from previous practices of taxation performed by a bureau within the MOF in two respects: (1) it commanded a nationwide organization, staffed with professional officials in tax administration; and (2) more significantly, the Tax Investigation Bureau was reinforced, as the government believed that tax auditing was crucial for the settling-down of the self-return and payment system. The key for fair and transparent taxation is in eliminating direct contact between tax officials and taxpayers. In other words, a system of self-return by taxpayers had to be settled. To help the tax self-return system take root, the state needed to establish a system to watch and oversee inaccurate reporting of income and financial transaction through tax audits. The director-general of the Tax Investigation Bureau was to face a lot of political pressure because the tax audit had a great influence over companies and individual taxpayers were prone to tax evasion practices. To ensure the independence of the tax audit, the director-general had a direct reporting channel to the president, who wanted to protect tax audit from any political influence. Lastly, to fight against corruption and modernize tax administration, the NTS introduced a qualification system for tax administrators, infused new blood into the agency from the successful candidates of the Higher Civil Service Examination and carried out administrative reforms to revamp its operations.

The first commissioner of the NTS in 1966 set the tax revenue goals for the year to KRW 70 billion, a 65.5 percent increase from KRW 41.8 billion in 1965. Designating the number plate of his official car 700, which is the target of tax revenue collection, the commissioner encouraged tax officials to collect more tax revenue in a transparent way. Thus, the record in tax revenue for the year exceeded its goals by KRW 70.5 billion.[30] At the same time, the government worked to promote public awareness of tax payments and savings. It designated the launch date of the NTS, March 3, as Taxpayers' Day, and awarded honest and exemplary taxpayers. It also gave annual savings awards to commemorate Savings Day. The tax law reform, together with tax administration reform, resulted in a great increase in doubling of the tax/GNP (gross national product) ratio from 9 percent level in 1961 to 15 percent level in 1970 as Figure 9.2 suggests.

Going back to the second issue of facilitating investment and industrial development for broadening the tax base, the government devoted itself to maximizing growth augmenting in fiscal expenditure. Taxpayers fulfill their obligation to pay taxes based on the benefits they will receive from the state. If the benefits are insufficient, tax compliance will drop, leading to tax resistance. Unreasonable tax increase under the existing poor tax base may cause difficulties in broadening the tax base by crowding out private business activities, thus triggering tax resistance.

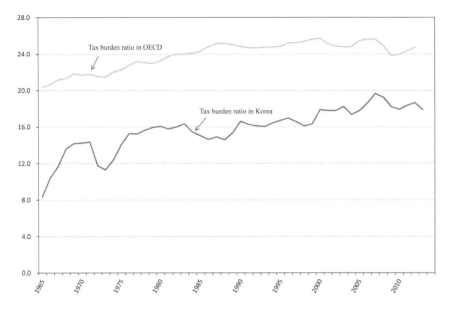

Figure 9.2 Tax burden ratio (2010 GDP)
Source: OECD, Korea Statistical Information Service

This restricts the capacity of governments in employing policies for poverty reduction and economic development. Under the circumstance that expenditure demand is enormously high and imminent, pursuing growth augmentation for tomorrow in fiscal allocation would be difficult to implement.

Based on this recognition, Korea's government exploited taxation and fiscal management by the following three points: The first was strong incentives for savings and investment through a tax system. In spite of a poor tax base, tax-exemption clauses and tax incentives were introduced in a variety of forms to encourage savings, research and development (R&D) and investment. These tax exemptions appeared to contradict the purpose of increasing tax revenue in the short run, but the government thought that the ultimate gains would outweigh the costs.

The second was all about squeezing consumption expenditure as much as possible and giving priority on infrastructure construction and job creation. A good example is that, as was discussed in Section 2.3, the first three Five-Year Development Plans were geared toward "growth," and the concept of social development policies such as public health and social security services were not formally incorporated into the plans until the fourth plan, 15 years after its first enforcement.

Although social development in many fields such as education, public health and welfare spending is urgent, it was thought that infrastructure to facilitate economic activities and job opportunities to generate more income are what people really need with more serious urgency. If people have income, they can take care of their education and health by themselves. The expenditure on such fields as education and medical care benefits a limited number of people concerned, and recouping the costs takes a long time. For an instance, education for men usually takes 16 years until their undergraduate education, and after that men make returns to society. Instead, infrastructure provides convenience to the public for a fluent flow of men and materials in a wide range. The Korean government put its limited money on infrastructure projects such as the Kyungbu Highway, Soyang River Dam and integrated steel mill. This kind of fiscal expenditure policy was premised on the philosophy that the best social welfare response to society was to create job opportunities and growth augmentation.

The third was the "selection and concentration" principle in fiscal allocation. Economic growth requires capital formation, but capital formation, in poor countries with limited resources, is hard to secure. Trying to satisfy all the demands for fiscal expenditures with limited financial resources and dispersing these limited resources widely or evenly would ultimately result in no significant outcome for capital formation. For this account, as mentioned earlier, investment expenditures were prioritized over consumption expenditures across the board, and investment decisions were made based on feasibility studies that identified areas that demonstrated higher rates of return with the alternative investment plans in the fiscal management of Korea.

By the 1970s the country's wretched tax system was further overhauled to make it more robust in terms of boosting revenue mobilization for long-term sustainable growth. Consequently, the existing system was broadened and strengthened to ensure greater fairness. As part of this overhaul, the MOF in 1971 formally proposed the concept of a VAT system. Since then, it took six and a half years to introduce the VAT in 1977. Prior to the official implementation of the VAT, the Ministry of Finance embarked on a comprehensive preparatory and consultative process. Tax experts from the International Monetary Fund (IMF) and European countries with experiences of VAT offered vital inputs to the ministry.[31] Local experts were also dispatched to England, West Germany, Belgium, Japan and Taiwan to study the tax systems in those jurisdictions and the possibility of replicating one of them in Korea. Their formal report was submitted to the government in 1974. The MOF announced in December 1976 that the proposed VAT bill was to be brought before Parliament for debate. Parliament was charged with the task of rigorously considering the pros and cons of the proposed bill in a way that best served the nation's interest. The core issues highlighted included (1) Korea's commercial practices were underdeveloped; (2) there was a significant impact on inflation; and (3) VAT was considered to be a regressive measure.[32]

The first issue, that the VAT was premature considering South Korea's trade practices, was the most critical one. The introduction of the VAT, considering that bookkeeping and exchanging tax invoices were rarely practiced, would cause serious problems in enforcing the exchange of invoices and the VAT, thereby imperiling its proper implementation. There was the genuine fear that failing this, it could trigger a massive tax resistance and thus defeat the purpose of the reform measures. On this ground, the critics argued,

> Currently the countries that introduced a VAT were limited to 12 European countries, 9 countries of the Caribbean and Latin American countries which are under the influence of Europe, one in the Middle East and Vietnam in Asia. Japan introduced the VAT law in 1950, but it was repealed before its formal execution, and finally adopted a consumption tax in a revised form in 1989. Taiwan is still under study.[33]

Second, it was argued that the enforcement of a VAT was expected to cause some degree of price increases. If a VAT is added, it will automatically not only have an effect of a price increase, but it also would stimulate general price levels. Third, an indirect tax is by its nature regressive. It should be complemented with comprehensive income taxation. On the grounds of the preceding three points, a serious appeal was raised from the price authority within the government and members of the National Assembly representing the interests of merchants and industrialists just before the due date for the VAT enforcement. However, having heard every argument from the persons concerned, President Park made a final decision supporting the original plan.

At last, in December 1976, the government carried out a large-scale tax reform and introduced the VAT and Special Excise Tax. Eighteen new tax laws were enacted or amended under the reform as well. The main VAT and a supplementary special excise tax replaced the traditional indirect tax system, which included a cascade-type business tax. A single and flexible rate of 10 percent was applied to all items subject to the VAT. For the VAT to take root, the NTS launched education programs in a wide range and had all establishments equipped with cash registers. Small business owners who did not have bookkeeping skills were classified as a special treatment of taxation and were excluded from eligibility for the VAT. With this measure, from the original potential VAT payers of 830,000, 670,000 were excluded in hopes of reducing any strong tax resistance.

However, there were accompanying side effects for a considerable period. The cash registers, which were ensured of no possibility of fabrication, turned out to be unreliable, as evidence emerged that a number of companies were involved in concocting their transactions records. General discontent about the tax programs spilled over into violent street protests. Kim Chung-yum, President Park's chief of staff, conceded the government had woefully underestimated the level of tax resistance within the populace. The new administration following the Park regime reviewed the possibility of repealing the VAT; however, it reached the conclusion that because the cost of the VAT was paid off already, it was unnecessary to reverse the situation.

Meanwhile, when it came to the issue of the composite income tax for fair taxation, major hurdles had to be overcome. Although it was legally required to maintain comprehensive taxation with respect to income, this policy turned out not to be that effective. People exploited a loophole in the system that made it easy to use borrowed names for their financial transactions to avoid taxes, which was a very widespread practice. Public outcry against the unwarranted exploitation of the loophole led to the reform of financial transaction regulations.

To stem the widespread financial fraud that came with that system, the National Assembly in 1982 passed the Real Name Financial Transaction Act. However, the enforcement of the Act was postponed to the date when the presidential order designated, after 1986. In 1986, again its enforcement was postponed to after 1992. In 1987, Roh Tae-woo was elected as president with his campaign pledge of implementing the act, but nullified his pledge in 1990. Finally, in August 1993, President Kim Young-sam enforced the Real Name Financial Transaction Act by presidential emergency decree. Now, the composite income taxation became effective with enforcing financial transactions by a person's real name.[34] A new dawn had finally emerged in the financial and tax regime of the country in a very transparent manner that also was instrumental in bringing the underground economy to the fore. Enhancing the system's transparency was by no means an easy task.

The reasons for the birth pangs of "financial transactions by real name" may be considered in two points. One is the influencing power of the "haves." By and large, the people who are under the influence of the aforementioned regulation are the rich and persons in power. They dislike that their process of accumulating wealth would be revealed. The other is bad effects on the national economy in the short run. The taxation on capital and property not declared might cause flight of capital to avoid taxation. In the process, the economy might be subject to contraction and disorder in the short run. The real name financial transaction might be harmful in maintaining the current economic situation in the short run, but it is a prerequisite to ensure the justice of taxation and social justification for wealth, which paves the way to sustainable and inclusive growth of a national economy.

Thus, starting in a state of extreme poverty and heavy dependence on foreign aid, the public finances of the country have witnessed a remarkable transformation. Benefiting from the active industrial development policy and growth-augmenting policy in public finance, the tax base and fiscal revenues were continuously increasing, which led to graduation from being an aid recipient nation in 1995.[35] Entering the late 1970s, with the great increase in fiscal revenue, the government could accommodate postponed comprehensive social development programs and an establishment of social safety nets. In the process, with the keynote composite income tax and the VAT, a modern tax system could be established. As was shown in Figure 9.2, although the tax burden ratio increased steadily over time, South Korea could maintain fiscal soundness managing the tax burden at a lower level than the average of the OECD (Organisation for Economic Co-operation and Development) member countries.

4 Consequences and destination

Under the circumstances of a seemingly insurmountable balance-of-payments deficit and dependence on foreign aid, Korea could not dare to prepare financing for development. Rampant poverty prevailed, and the DSR (Domestic Saving Ratio) and IVR (Investment Ratio) remained at a low level of 10 percent until the early 1960s, as Figure 9.1 shows. Because the nation was poor, public finances also had to be poor. Under the low tax-burden ratio on a poor tax base, fiscal revenue was also very limited, and thus the government was incapable of coping with widespread poverty. Therefore, the world said that Korea had no hope at all, as was discussed in Section 1.1.

Entering the early 1960s, the Korean government was convinced that the nation's long-term viability could not hinge on relying on aid. Even depending on loans, the government thought that it should seek to establish an industrial base. It considered that through primitive accumulation of capital waiting for gradual economic recovery, economic development and industrialization would be far off, and it had to depend upon foreign savings to accelerate industrial development. However, no sensible investors were willing to risk their investments in a state with the sort of precarious security, economic and political instability that defined the Korea of the past. Under the circumstances, Korea dared to launch industrialization programs for the sake of its survival.

Although it encouraged thriftiness and savings to the utmost degree and created a legal system to attract foreign capital, there were no countries or foreign investors willing to put their money in a poverty-stricken country with high risks and uncertainty. Under such conditions, the government devised an extraordinary measure, which was the provision of payment guarantees by the government for foreign commercial loans. However, with only that measure, it had no effects. To draw foreign investment, the government had to demonstrate its capability in supporting economic growth to international investors through sound public finance and stability in its international balance of payments. The Korean government tried to secure local financing and opened an irrigation gate of foreign capital from Japan by normalizing diplomatic relations between the two countries. Owing to these desperate efforts, foreign capital began to flow into Korea.

Forcibly attracting foreign capital accompanied inevitably unequal contracts. Foreign capital was desperately needed to finance the industrialization drive, which often placed Korea on its back foot in its negotiations with foreign investors. Loans were required to build factories, and most of the loans came with difficult terms that the government was resigned to accept in the face of limited options. But again, true to its mission, the risk and gamble did pay off effectively. It provided a momentum for growth.

Just as Figures 9.1 and 9.2 show, in the late 1960s and 1970s, there was a surge in foreign capital, which supports high investment rates. The meager domestic savings rate couldn't offset the demand for high investment. It was very ambitious but risky to drive high investment policy depending heavily on foreign debt. However, as Figure 9.2 suggests, as economic growth accelerated through high investment, the tax base became gradually broadened and the capacity of the tax burden could be also enhanced. Entering mid-1980s, sustained economic growth enabled DSR to surpass the foreign savings ratio (FSR), and a drastic decline in reliance on foreign aid was witnessed. In the late 1980s, Korea began to provide official development assistance (ODA) and the World Bank officially designated it as a graduate of aid handouts in 1995.[36]

Even though the inflow of foreign capital into the economy played a crucial role in spurring development at a critical stage of the development path, it provoked a great deal of backlash and brought with it significant adverse effects. About the former, based on the dependence theory, opposition forces strongly criticized that attraction of foreign capital would result in economic dependency on foreign investors and potentially undermine the viability of the state in the long run. Nowadays, the introduction of foreign capital may not be a critical issue; however, in the 1960s and 1970s it was a serious political issue that divided public opinion in Korea. Amid these criticisms, the Park administration remained resolute in its chosen path. In many ways, the resulting industrial growth was crucial in sustaining this momentum as domestic income levels rose along with state revenue, which has thankfully become the seedbed for ushering the country's break from aid dependence into a self-sufficient donor state.

With the introduction of foreign capital and the role of priming water by public finances, the Korean economy became robust. Business investment was increasing rapidly, and an investment boom was created by many enterprises. Disregarding economic feasibility or profitability, businessmen were blind in expanding investment with debt. With sustained economic growth, the savings ratio increased greatly and finally surpassed the investment ratio entering the 1990s, as Figure 9.1 shows. Economic growth moved at a pace that rapidly exceeded the accrued debt level.

In taxation and public finances, fundamental structural transformation occurred. Economic boom by high investment and the pump-priming role of public finance provided an opportunity for broadening the tax base and increasing fiscal revenue. Regarding the former, in line with an increase in the capacity of the tax burden, the tax burden ratio could be increased steadily, and the increase in tax revenue paved the way for a sound fiscal base. Regarding the tax system, the modern VAT system settled down as an indirect tax. Through the real name financial transaction system, composite income taxation for all sources of income covering labor, financial, real estate and other income could be feasible, and thus fairness and justice in taxation could be secured. Further, establishment of a modern tax administration system facilitated by information technology (IT) contributed to enhancing efficiency and transparency in tax administration.

In terms of the impact on fiscal soundness, the increased revenue base spurred the implementation of important state development policies. One such area that witnessed a massive boost was in social welfare policies. Fiscal constraints held back any real attempt at pursuing social welfare policies in the early phase of development during the period of the 1960s through the mid-1970s. A new wave of welfare policies now guaranteed the provision of state support and insurance programs to provide social safety nets such as a health insurance program, a national pension system for all the people, and subsidy for the vulnerable and the unemployed, at par with that of industrialized economies.[37] A major leap in the position of Korea in the international community came with its transition from an aid-dependent economy into a donor one in 2010 when it officially joined the Development Assistance Committee (DAC) of the OECD.

As to the latter issue of adverse effects, we cannot enjoy benefits without a cost. Under the aforementioned circumstances in a state of poverty, procurement of development funds and its allocation in a concentrated way accompanied a considerable strain and aftermath. Maintaining high investment rates through foreign savings and selective allocation of resources became pregnant of aftereffects from the beginning.

- First, the policy of high economic growth supported by high investment rates and thus the increase in the money supply inevitably accompanied inflation. During the 1970s, an annual rate of increase of the CPI (Consumer Price Index) on average was recorded as 16.5 percent.[38]
- Second, selective financial allocation to support industrial development plans by the government also followed by impeding development of the banking industry.

Regarding the first issue of inflation, high inflation works negatively against a national economy in two ways: on the one hand, through high interest rates, it deteriorates competitiveness of corporations; on the other, it discourages the will to labor and leads to an unequal distribution of income. High growth policy through high investment in a poor savings capacity inevitably accompanies high aggregate demand and inflation, which in turn hinders growth in the long run due to these reasons. Above all, sustained inflation discourages labor rather than speculation due to the income gap between property and labor in favor of the former, and promotes wage increase in compensation for the high cost of living through inflation, which results in the weakening of industrial competitiveness. The Korean government pursued a paradox, that while attempting high growth it tried to control inflation.

The market mechanism could not provide the desired price stability under the basic economic condition of high investment and high growth and limited supply due to restriction on imports to protect local industry. The government prompted to intervene in the market to control the surging inflation. The legislative price stability installment to enable the government's intervention in the market was the Act on Temporary Measure for Price Regulation in 1961, followed by the Act on Price Stability in 1973, then the 1975 Price Stability and Fair-Trade Act was to follow suit. These laws made it possible for the government to regulate prices of public utilities, some daily necessities and other monopoly goods and services.

To enhance its enforcement, the Price Measure Committee (chaired by the vice minister of the EPB) was established within the EPB, which consisted of vice ministers overseeing goods and services included in the CPI, related officials from the two institutions of the Bank of Korea (BOK) and National Bureau of Statistics (NBOS), and the National Tax Service (NTS). The committee monitored the movement of individual prices, and if the price increase seemed to be unreasonable, the government agencies or the NTS provided administrative guidance. In enforcing the anti-inflationary measures, it soon became apparent to policymakers that their measures were inadvertently creating price distortions and price regulation itself might not be effective in the long run. However, because the government prioritized poverty reduction and economic development above anything else, it attempted curbing inflation to some extent as a measure of last resort. Therefore, the reliability of the consumer price index during these days was raised by academia.

In the meantime, several attempts were made by the government to disengage itself from price controls and to entrust prices to the market since the late 1960s. In recognition of the side effects of direct price controls, letting prices be determined on the market, it was argued that the government should pursue price stability by affecting aggregate demand and promoting a competitive environment in the market. As for the latter, the Fair-Trade Act of 1966 and Monopoly Regulation Act of 1969 were submitted to the National Assembly, but they were repealed due to the end of the session. In 1971, a Fair-Trade Act bill was again repealed in the National Assembly, and in 1975 as a form of hybrid of price regulation and fair trade, the Price Stability and Fair-Trade Act was legalized. In the end, the Monopoly Regulation and Fair-Trade Act were enacted when the function of the National Assembly was suspended under martial law. Entering the 1980s, the Korean government delegated direct intervention in the market for price regulation and transformed its policy toward preparing competitive condition in the market. At the same time, the government moved toward regulation of aggregate demand through monetary and fiscal policy. Now, a market economy became normalized in Korea.

As to the second issue of side effects on the banking industry, the aftermath to the national economy came in the long run. The selective financial allocation on priority sectors by the government had contributed greatly to industrial and economic development; however, in the process, the banking sector could not develop itself with the lack of autonomy. The backwardness of the banking industry as subordinated by the government was one of the main triggers of the financial crisis that devastated the economy in 1997. Ironically, it took the painful pills of the Structural Adjustment Programs (SAP) to enable the economy to recover but also to build the critical foundational elements that have consolidated the economy this long. These structured policies for development financing to overcome poverty and the dramatic effects of increasing income levels had its obvious costs and challenges, as demonstrated in this chapter.

Notes

1 O Won-chol, *The Korea Story: President Park Jung-hee's Leadership and the Korean Industrial Revolution* (Seoul, Korea: Wisdom Tree, 2009), 76.
2 Choi Kwang, *Tax Policy and Tax System in Korea* (Seoul, Korea: Korea Institute of Public Finance, 2004), 45–51.
3 This policy continued for 14 years until 1977, when Korea reached self-sustenance in rice as a result of the green revolution drive as discussed in Section 3.2.
4 Kim Sung-jin, *Bakjeonghuireul malhada* [Speak of Park Chung-hee] (Seoul, Korea: Life and Dream, 2006), 303.
5 It is called Makgeolli which is very popular among the grassroots, and enjoyed by farmers when they are working.
6 Kim Chung-yum, *From Despair to Hope: Economic Policymaking in Korea 1945–1979* (Seoul, Korea: Korea Development Institute, 2011), 565–566.
7 The 1987 World Development Report (World Bank 1987) noted that gross domestic savings, as a share of income, ranged from 31 percent to 33 percent in Korea. In contrast, the highest savings rate for a Latin American developing country was 26 percent, for the United States 16 percent and Japan 32 percent.
8 During the same period, that of seven OECD countries' average was 49.3 percent and of Southeast Asian countries average 80.6 percent. O Won-chol, *The Construction of Pyramid-Type Export-Oriented Industries* (Seoul, Korea: Korea Type Economic Policy Institute, 2003), 610–612. [in Korean]
9 Hong Eun-ju, Lee Eun-hyung and Yang Jae-chan, *Korian Mireokeul 1* [The Korean Miracle I] (Seoul, Korea: Nanam, 2013), 209–213.
10 Seol Bong-sik, *Bakjeonghuiwa hangukgyeongje* [Park Chung-hee and the Korean Economy], (Seoul: Chung-Ang University Press, 2006), 117–118.
11 Paik Young-hun, *Joguk geundaehwa-ui eondeokeseo* [On the Hill of Modernization of My Fatherland] (Seoul: Mind and Thinking, 2014), 60–62.
12 To the Japanese, it is an economic cooperation fund, since they deny the responsibility of reparations for their colonial rule on Korea.
13 This was mentioned by Park Tae-jun in Section 6.2.
14 Paik, *Modernization of My Fatherland*, 133; and Hong, Lee and Yang, *The Korean Miracle I*, 134–135.
15 Hong, Lee and Yang, *The Korean Miracle I*, 134–135.
16 Paik, *Modernization of My Fatherland*, 133–135.
17 Hong, Lee and Yang, *The Korean Miracle I*, 134.
18 Kim Yong-suh et al., *Bakjeonghui Sidaeui Jaejomyung* [The Reflection of Park Chung-hee], (Seoul, Korea: Tradition and Modern Days, 2006), 90–96.
19 O, *Pyramid-Type Export-Oriented Industries*, 291.
20 Hwang Byung-tae recalled that he was criticized as a traitor, even from his professor, when was engaged in the introduction of foreign loans in the 1960s. See Publication Committee for Narratives of the Korean Economic Miracle, *Korian Mireokeul: Yukseongeuro deudneun gyeongjegijeok 1* [The Korean Miracle: Narratives of the Korean Economic Miracle 1] (Seoul, Korea: Nanam 2013), 147–148.
21 This refers to the Chungju fertilizer plant contract with McGraw hydrocarbon of the United States in May 1955. O Won-chol, *Hanguk-hyeong gyeongje geonseol 1: Enjinioring eopeuroch* [Korea Type Economic Construction 1: An Engineering Approach] (Seoul, Korea: Korea Type Economic Policy Institute, 1995), 138–141.
22 Hong, Lee and Yang, *The Korean Miracle I*, 149.
23 *Ibid.*, 140–142.
24 Apart from budget support, most aid projects are selected and designed with the engagement of donors, the interests of donors cannot be completely removed in foreign aid.

25 Chun Seung-hun et al., *Tax Administration and System Reforms in the Democratic Republic of the Congo* (Korea Development Institute and Ministry of Strategy and Finance, 2014), 202.
26 One of main reasons that Korean government established the NTS in 1966 was to prevent widespread corruption of tax officials at the time. Lee Hyung-koo and Chun Seung-hun, *The Evaluation of 50 Year Tax and Fiscal Policy of Korea* (Korea Institute for Public Finance, 2003), 192–196.
27 Lee and Chun, *The Evaluation of 50 Year Tax and Fiscal Policy of Korea*, 381–389.
28 The size of the shadow economy which is not revealed to tax system was larger in developing countries than in developed ones. See Munawer Sultan Khwaja and Indira Iyer, *Revenue Potential, Tax Space, and Tax Gap*, Policy Research Working Paper 6868, May 2014, World Bank, p. 12.
29 Lee Kye-min, Lee Hyun-rak, Kim Kang-jung and Hong Eun-ju, *Korian mireokeul 2: Dojeonkwa bisang* [Korean Miracle II: Challenge and Flight] (Seoul, Korea: Nanam, 2014), 381–385.
30 Lee and Chun, *The Evaluation of 50 Year Tax and Fiscal Policy*, 193–196.
31 Kim, *From Despair to Hope*, 364–365.
32 For details, please refer to Kim Chung-yum, *From Poverty to the Threshold of Advanced Countries: The 30 Year History of Korea's Economic Policies* (Seoul, Korea: Random House, 2006), 293–306 [in Korean].
33 Lee at al., *The Korean Miracle II*, 426.
34 The constitution stipulated that the president may decree an emergency order as effective as the law.
35 "Hangukui gaebal hyeopnyeok yeoksa" [History of Korea's ODA], Ministry of Foreign Affairs, accessed August 10, 2017, www.odakorea.go.kr/ODAPage_2012/T01/L03_S02_01.jsp
36 *Ibid.*
37 Kang Kwang-ha, *Gyeongjegaebal 5nyeon gyehoek* [Five-Year Economic Development Plan: Evaluation of Goals and Implementation] (Seoul: Seoul National University Press, 2000), 74–78.
38 *Korean Statistics*, http://kosis.kr/index/index.jsp

10 *Saemaul Undong*

Korea's new deal for rural modernization

1 A tale of two wages

Rural communities in Korea, like in most countries around the world, are associated with high rates of poverty. Until the industrialization putsch of the 1960s, it was also home to approximately 58 percent of the country's population.[1] Despite being overrun by extreme levels of poverty, there was little the government could do in terms of effectively intervening. Bear in mind that as the government was consumed with its industrialization programs in the urban heartland, it had precious little time and resources to attend to rural poverty.

The nature of the strategic industrial development policy also left the rural areas behind because of the selective and concentrated investments that were at the core of the policy measure. A steady gulf started to emerge between sectors and regions of the country as a direct consequence of these policies. The industrial sector grew astronomically at the expense of the non-industrial sector in very real terms, the manifestation of which was felt in four distinct areas. Asymmetric regional development started to become very conspicuous as the policy gained ground. Parts of the country that were suitable for manufacturing industries and thus hosted such plants had it all going for them. Alas, those regions without such endowments were left on the margins.

The obvious first point was the gap between the industrial sector and the agricultural sector. While the urban heartland, home to the manufacturing industries, was bustling, rural areas remained stuck in time. The second point of the gap is among regions. All the territory of the country is not equally suitable for development, which resulted in regional development gaps. The third point was increasing levels of disparities between groups in society. The entrepreneurial class, incidentally a minority, could disproportionately cash in on the gains of the strategic development policy. Call it the early signs of the imbalances of capitalism, and you would not be entirely wrong. Finally, the overemphasis of economic and financial value stifled equally crucial non-market values such as culture and spirituality.

All this underscores the underlying fact that the strategic development policy had its rough edges despite all the good it did. This is why the terms of sustainable development goals call for a system of harmonization that will ensure that the gains are consolidated while revising areas that have palpable shortcomings. In an ideal world, such a policy aims to bolster dormant sectors of the economy in ways that can ensure they spill over to other sectors. But when policymakers are confronted with a situation of pervasive poverty across the board, then trade-offs become an inevitable policy consequence. The issue is how to make use of limited resources more efficiently and effectively for substantial outcome of economic development. It was argued that Poverty Reduction Strategy Papers (PRSP) in developing countries pursuing harmonized, balanced development may result in failure in achieving targeted goals because they ignore the effectiveness of spreading limited investment resources too thin. In this respect, the Korean government concentrated the reparation fund from Japan on mega-projects with high forward and backward linkage effects, such as the construction of POSCO and the Soyang River Dam, rather than disperse the fund to the millions of people sacrificed during the Japanese colonial regime.

If we compare such practice with the strategic development paradigm, then it becomes all too obvious why balanced growth has never made for a wise policy. Yes, the gaps triggered by the strategic development policy are inherently costly. Prime examples can be in social unrest because of the perceived unjustified discrimination by sides that feel left out. It is also true that this policy is not sustainable in the long term; that is why it ought to be used as a short term means to a goal of multi-sectoral development.

Now, turning attention to the substantive issue of the impact of imbalances, I am reminded of a Korean proverb that says that one gets a stomachache when one's cousin purchases a rice paddy. Believe it or not, it underscores the place of envy as an intrinsic human nature that drives our actions on many levels. It is also true about the reaction engendered by the gaps created by the government's policies. But that was still not enough to break the lethargic inertia in most parts of rural South Korea, especially at a time when the urban sector was just bolting ahead. No responsible government could ignore this trend, especially not when much of the population lived in rural areas.

In 1960, 58 percent of the country's population was engaged in the agricultural sector their collective contribution was 36 percent of the total gross domestic product (GDP) and each household cultivated 1 hectare of land on average.[2] Poor access to amenities such as electricity, water and infrastructure severely constrained productivity. Put that together with poor post-harvest skills, and then you have all the hallmarks of mediocrity. That the country still could not sufficiently meet its food sufficiency needs highlights the inefficiency of the agricultural sector. It is worth remembering that up until now, there was nothing out of the ordinary in this lifestyle given that this had been the way of life of most Korean folks throughout their 5,000-year history.

Farmers who experienced this squalor described their living conditions as follows.[3] Their records witness that rural Korea at that time was the same as that of a currently poor country:

- It was typical to have between five and six family members share a small room of 3–5 square meters.

- We had children swarming in a house that all but resembled a dugout. There was barely any semblance of privacy that could allow for parents to procreate. It was all but a quiet mystery.
- Gambling was an endemic problem in the villages. There were times I had to hide my father's sandals when I was young, just to prevent him from going to the gambling house.
- Because there were no paved roads, you had men carrying farm produce on their shoulders and women carrying theirs on their heads en route to the market. It was subsistence in all its crudest form.
- It is pure joy to now have a road access in our communities!

As discussed earlier, the real pathway out of this chronic state of poverty was breaking the cycle of the unproductive obsolete mind-set that has shaped the nation's history for thousands of years. The drinking and gambling habits were the underbelly of the pervasive atmosphere of despondency that was part of the sociocultural mind-set seeping from the history of exploitation and exclusion. As a village boy himself, President Park had a particularly soft spot for his kin and kindred. He had also come to intimate terms with the suffering of the rural folks, which shaped his belief that like most aspects of life, an external financial intervention can go a long way in turning their fortunes around.

Up until then, succeeding governments had launched a series of plans to rebuild the agricultural sector, and President Park initially flirted with the idea of providing financial assistance to a few select rural communities.[4] That turned out to be ineffective, due largely to the government's inability to shoulder financial burdens but also because the folks on the ground could not easily buy into the goals of a top-down policy approach. A sort of dependency syndrome was being promoted in the village folks without making any real difference to their mind-set in ways that can empower them for self-development.[5] The program had to be abandoned.

Donor countries and multilateral development agencies advised the government to promote agricultural development in a harmonious way in pursuing economic development. Conversely the government was of a different opinion. It was convinced that poverty reduction was far off by tackling agricultural development, and finally pursued prior industrial development. Nevertheless, it did not mean that the government abandoned agriculture and the rural sector. At the beginning stage, it had launched community development programs, aiming to improve living standards in rural regions for some selected villages with financial investments, which turned out to be ineffective due to limited fiscal capacity and low effectiveness of financial assistance in pre-modern rural societies. It was like shoveling sand against the tide. Furthermore, if external assistance was disconnected, the villages immediately returned to the original feature. Without a change of the mind-set of farmers, limited financial assistance would not work as expected. No sustainability is to be secured by financial assistance programs for rural development.

Meanwhile, village folks were not abandoned. A new intervention under the auspices of the green revolution through the Rural Development Administration

(RDA) was unveiled to meet the food sufficiency needs of the country. Rural electrification programs were vigorously expanded with the aim of making it the first step of opening rural areas up to the rest of the country. The invisibility that once kept them out, it was reasoned, would give way to new interest in engaging with the opportunities of urban development. Beneath that was the possibility of extending agricultural mechanization processes with the electrification programs.

President Park had a personal interest in the electrification program, which took 15 years to complete at a cost of KRW 92.6 billion.[6] It cost twice the amount of constructing the famous Kyungbu Highway, whose cost was KRW 42.9 billion. Prior to the program's launch, only one in eight households was connected to the electrical grid.[7] Only a handful of households could afford the $80 cost of installing home terminal units. Access to electricity was an important step in improving the living conditions of rural communities, a view reinforced by the experience he had visiting farming communities in West Germany in late 1964.[8]

The legal framework for the electrification program was passed in 1965. Rural households were granted government-issued soft loans to enable them to cover the relevant costs. It required installment payment over a 19-year period and a 1-year grace period. That still proved to be prohibitively expensive for the clear majority, prompting a revision of the law in 1967 to increase the payment period to 30 years backed by a 5-year grace period. Financing of the project came from levying a 30 percent petroleum tax for its execution. Thankfully the program started to pick up speed, with an initial 12 percent sign up in 1964 to 97.8 percent in 1977.[9] Preparing a foundation for rural development with these two programs, the president was mapping out a scheme of driving for rural development in full scale.

2 *Saemaul Undong* for rural development

Entering the early 1970s, the initial industrial development policy created a new environment for further development in Korea. There was a yearning of change from rural folks who were becoming increasingly uneasy with the status quo. Similarly, President Park Chung-hee was becoming the target of simmering unrest from his most loyal constituency, the rural population, about the development gaps. Sensing an opportunity for decisive action to placate his constituency, President Park launched a rural development campaign. Gleaning from its previous unsuccessful experiment of granting financial aid to those same communities, he was keen to do things differently this time without sacrificing the goal of bettering their lot.

There had to be a way of endogenously triggering some degree of motivation within the communities to lead the charge. For that to happen, the folks had to be encouraged to imbibe the virtues of diligence, a spirit of self-reliance and understanding the power of communal cooperation. These thus became the cardinal cornerstones of the country's reinvigorated rural development campaign. Getting these principles out looks good in theory, but the practical dimension is an entirely different world altogether. Breaking the generational cycle of dependence was by no means going to be a walk in the park. President Park was certainly under no illusions about this critical fact of life.

The start of the *Saemaul Undong* (SMU) was humble. President Park proposed to village community leaders to nurture or, if you like, revitalize village communities. That became known as the new village movement (*Saemaul*). Beginning in the winter of 1970, the nation's 33,267 villages were each offered 335 boxes of cement worth KRW 123,000 ($424) with no conditions attached.[10] It somehow coincided with a brewing crisis in the local cement production industry, as many producers had an accumulation of inventory due to the slowdown in the construction sector. The government came to the aid of the cement industry by allocating 1 percent of the national budget (general account), worth KRW 4.1 billion ($14 million), for bulk purchase of cement.

It was this tranche of cement purchase that was gifted to the rural communities to use for community-generated revitalization programs. Each beneficiary community was expected to account for its share of the consignment. The cement was telling of just how much the communities perceived of themselves. Out of passiveness, some communities couldn't seem to come up with what to do with the packages, so they left them at the point of discharge. Because they were left to the elements, the cement soon became worthless. Another group of villages somehow decided that it was such a wise idea to distribute the cement to each individual household, so they could then use it for their domestic needs. Yet another subset of communities opted to invest the cement into communal projects like reconstructing their water supply systems and improving their narrow roads.

After the first round of disbursements, an evaluation was carried out to ascertain the effectiveness or lack thereof of the decision by the government. It soon became apparent that the decision had triggered a threefold increase in the value added from the KRW 12.2 billion ($46.2 million) cost of investment in the project. It also brought to the fore critical differences in the mind-set of the beneficiaries. Those whose account was a positive reflection of the goals of the project were generally seen to be within the cohort of communities keenly interested in the betterment of their socioeconomic conditions. Such communities also had the distinction of good community leadership.[11]

Based on this pioneering experience, the government tweaked the second phase of the project in 1972. Based on evaluation of performances, villages were classified into subcategories of achievers and non-achievers. The achievers constituting 16,600 villages were offered 500 bags of cement and a ton of iron rods equivalent to $497 to each village again at a total cost of KRW 3.3 billion ($8.25 million).[12] The non-achievers were simply excluded from the incentive scheme. The project was set to proceed with only the half that gave a good account of themselves and disregarded the other half. Many deputies of the ruling party saw the decision as a reckless political gamble, warning the president that such a perceived sense of discrimination would certainly blow up in their faces in the ballot box. Park Jin-hwan, then special adviser for rural affairs to the president, recalls how President Park offered a quipping response to his critics, asking "How can we break the five-thousand-year-long state of poverty without such a stimulating drive?" After hearing this, Park Jin-hwan said to himself, "this man is unlikely to get votes in elections. However, that was the lighting rod!"[13] It was clearly an unpopular decision, especially after those left out in the second phase felt they were being unjustly marginalized.

Somehow, a number of villages aggrieved by the decision to exclude them from the second phase petitioned the government to sign them up into the program and they waived their right to demand any material support for a reconsideration. To this, the government obliged. Like the first phase, the total value added from the project had surged nearly tenfold. From an estimated initial rate of KRW 3.3 billion it had thus grown to KRW 31.6 billion.[14] Obviously, what was construed as a misguided system of "discrimination" by separating achievers from non-achievers turned out to be an incentive after all.[15] Call it fate or coincidence, it was at this critical juncture that the positive outcome of this experimental process gave impetus to a structured mobilization campaign for transforming Korea's rural communities. It was formally named Saemaul Undong, meaning the "New Village Movement." Saemaul divisions were established under local administration at the grassroots level.

The government prepared a long-term Saemaul Undong plan from 1971 to 1981. In the first phase, from 1971 to 1973, it aimed to build a foundation for Saemaul Undong. In the second phase, from 1974 to 1976, it aimed to build a self-help base. In the third phase, from 1977 to 1981, it aimed to transform all village communities to be self-sufficient. The average farm household income increased from KRW 418,000 ($1,045) in 1972 to KRW 1.4 million ($3,500) in 1981. The ratio of household income between farm income and non-farm income changed from 79.9:20.1 in 1972 to 50.1:49.9 in the target year.[16]

One of the core tenets of the campaign was also to structurally group the villages into three categories: (1) basic villages, (2) self-help villages and (3) self-reliant villages. This categorization was derived based on criteria such as level of communal participation and the rate of transformation.[17] Basic villages did not have a full grasp of the virtue of cooperation. Self-reliant villages were deemed to be good candidates to receive technical advice to enable them to develop their capacity for income generation activities. Self-help villages were in between the two. Then, the government introduced community assistance programs tailored to each community's level of development. For the basic villages group, to stimulate a self-help spirit, government incentives were not provided, but training for village leaders was offered. For the self-help village group, it encouraged improvement in the environment and construction of infrastructure led by respective village leaders. For the self-reliant village group, it offered new farming know-how and technology to enable them to improve their crop yield.

An unintended consequence of the classification happened when the competition escalated into squabbles between the villages. Especially those placed within the basic group felt unjustly humiliated by the decision. Many of the villages were determined not to be counted out just yet. Appeals were sent to the government to reconsider enlisting them in the program in an apparent response to the aura of competitiveness that had been unleashed. To keep their pride, competition was accelerated among village groups, and among villages within the village group.

Therefore, the guiding principles of Saemaul Undong was thus two-pronged. One prong was the promotion of competition and discriminative incentives, and the other was devotion of community leaders. The initial non-performing villages who felt humiliated by their exclusion somehow could galvanize them to stronger action in an apparent bid to catch up. Incentives would be able to elicit desirable behavior within the community, and if properly reinforced, then it could grow into a natural way of life.

The devotion of community leaders turned out to be a critical driving force. Wherever villages were successful in community development, there were certainly devoted village leaders. The Saemaul program made it a point to steer off imposing bureaucratic hierarchies and structures on the communities. At the behest of the president, a decision was made to elect leaders to offer their services voluntarily for the good of the community. These leaders were to be different from traditional village leaders whose services were paid. It was intended to engender a spirit of selfless devotion within the community. Villagers were at liberty to convene development committees and structure it as they so desired. Instead of having rigid structures, villagers were encouraged to be as dynamic as they possibly could, so long as it served their needs effectively. In most cases, the committee's members were composed of individuals from the community who were genuinely committed to its advancement. Each committee was composed of five to ten members who deliberated on the decision-making process. Committees were also encouraged to have a gender balance by including women. Contrary to the common expectation, some of the committees had members who were viscerally opposed to the entire program itself, which aimed to have a consensus for all village folks.

There is an old Korean adage that says, "If the hen clucks, the house will be ruined." The bigotry of centuries of low expectations was in many ways confounded by the Saemaul Undong campaign. For instance, thanks to this campaign, women for the first time in Korean history could participate in community development initiatives. Bars were an all too common sight in many poor villages and offered a sad attraction for idle youth to binge away their otherwise productive days. Brawls often erupted during the drinking sessions. Adult men were all too prone to wager their assets in gambling activities at the expense of their families. With expatriation of social vices in the villages, folks devoted themselves to projects for increasing farmers' income. In line with development stages of villages, the government encouraged commercial farming of cash crops and vinyl house farming, and folks actively participated in commercial farming in full consultation with the government's extension service. Later, small scale industrial complexes were extended to such communities. It was reported that some women went out of their way to save a spoonful of rice from every meal, and this was collected to raise money for meager local community development chests. Many were also actively involved in community efforts to rid communities of vices like gambling and alcoholism.[18]

President Park contended that an effective rural development campaign required having young and ambitious farmers trained to lead the village movement. This is the brainchild behind the creation of the Saemaul Leader's Training Institute (SLTI) to serve this very purpose. The SLTI was established at the College of Agricultural Cooperatives in 1972, then in 1973 at the Suwon Farmers Hall, which became the cradle of Saemaul education throughout the 1970s. President Park moved the post of managing the Saemaul Training Program from the Ministry of Agriculture and Fishery to the Secretariat for State Affairs of the Blue House to ensure that he is able to personally be able to keep a tab on the pulse of the effectiveness of the training programs and prevent bureaucratic holdups.[19] Participating communities sent delegates for the SLTI's regular training sessions. They were joined by senior government officials and businessmen in a cooperative atmosphere of networking and learning together. While they lived together communally, the trainees were trained in five subjects: (1) presentation of individual community cases, (2) group discussions, (3) national security and economic development, (4) production technologies of farm products and (5) basic construction skills. It provided an atmosphere for learning from the experiences of each other and receiving inspiration for further development.[20]

According to the "Ten-Year History of the *Saemaul Undong*," the number of trainees reached 267,000 Saemaul leaders, 274,000 ministers and vice ministers, Parliament members, judges and prosecutors, university professors and business leaders, and 268,000 civil servants.[21] Besides that, technical training for farmers was counted at 3,000 man-days per annum. About 170,000–200,000 Saemaul leaders were active during the 1970s.[22] I have fond memories of participating in the training courses. We had very typical communal living quarters and all were smartly dressed in precision-grade uniforms, with a lively sense of camaraderie permeating the air. It was simply refreshing to be part of such a wave of enthusiastic community leaders whose selfless devotion to transforming their communities was simply very inspirational.

A Saemaul leader who participated in the training reported:

> At that time, the SLTI was called a smelting furnace. It is because the village leaders once spent several days there, they were completely melted and became newly born men. I've never had any experiences more heartfelt and emotional than the *Saemaul* training. The reason I devoted myself to the SMU is the education of the SLTI. Sometime when I made a presentation I found that the president was standing in the class. I was embarrassed but could not stop my presentation. President Park was listening to my presentation to the last minute. After the presentation, I was ushered to the restaurant and the president was there. I strongly remember the scene that taking noodles together. President Park encouraged me, patting me on my

shoulder. Except for this occasion, President Park secretly came into the class and listened to the lectures in the back.[23]

President Park took a personal interest in encouraging the Saemaul leaders. Many of the leaders were invited to present their achievements before him and his senior cabinet officials at such events like the meeting of the Economic Planning Board (EPB) and the Monthly Economic Monitoring Meeting, where medals were conferred upon them. For the first time in the country's history, the spotlight was beginning to shine on the achievements of the rural folks. For 9 years from 1971 to 1979 following his demise, about 150 village leaders were invited to make presentations before the president. An official in charge of the meeting recalls that the Economic Monitoring Meeting seemed to be held for the sake of presentation of the Saemaul success stories.[24] The result was a visible increase in enthusiasm in the program across all 36,000 villages nationwide; a massive turnaround in the consciousness of these hitherto lethargic communities into centers of boisterous industriousness.

For many of the village community leaders, who were used to being scorned because of their low educational attainment levels, the chance to convene at the training sessions and be taking that seriously was simply breathtaking. Many a community leader thus left these sessions feeling very rejuvenated for their cause. A community leader once muttered, "We have been discriminated historically; oh, this man understands our situation, and indeed wants to save our farming villages!"[25] A Saemaul leader, Lee Chung-ung, recalled

> If the King of Hell asked what I did in the world, I will say, "Fighting and arguing many times with my village inhabitants, that we can build structures to bequeath to the coming generations of our village, and the village inhabitants appreciated it." I am thankful to the village residents, and it was something to live for.

3 Unsung heroes of Korea's New Deal[26]

Activities of Saemaul leaders at that time still touch the heartstrings of the public. Three examples are selected to further elucidate this assertion. Let's begin with the story of Ha Sa-yong. In November 1970, the "National Competition Conference of Special Program for the Increase in Income of Farmers and Fishermen" was held in Seoul. At the event, Ha Sa-yong made a presentation of his farming experience before an audience of 3,000, including the president and other high-ranking officials.

Ha Sa-yong left elementary school after second grade. After marriage, he and his bride had to live apart for 7 years to work as a farm servant and a maidservant, respectively. Through these services, the couple saved money and bought 891 square meters of farmland. Later, the couple's hardship and thriftiness led

Picture 10.1 Village Leader Ha Sa-yong and his wife (1957) stand in front of their dugout, their residence, with A-frames on their backs which was the main means for transporting farming supplies at that time

©Anonymous

them to become commercial farmers of vegetables, owning 16 vinyl houses. With the money earned from vegetable farming, they increased their estate to 33,000 square meters (10,000 *pyung*) of land. Ha's phenomenal story attracted raving applause from the 3,000-strong audience at the event.[27] President Park was personally moved and couldn't help but descend from the stage to personally applaud his accomplishment, saying

> Indeed, you did a great job! Under the circumstances of being uneducated and having no one to provide help . . . You are a living embodiment of the few people who make something from nothing through the sweat of their brows.

President Park repeatedly thanked him as he conferred on him the medal of achievement. At that point both men were over-flooded with their emotions.

Thereafter, President Park gave an impromptu speech, saying "A man like Mr. Ha Sa-yong is a lamplight of our farm villages and an inspiration to our entire nation. The poverty of our rural villages can be eliminated if the spirit of Ha Sa-yong is replicated."[28] The couple was invited to the Blue House the next day, during which the president implored him to make a request for anything he genuinely desired. To this, Ha replied, "Poverty is my only enemy. I'll definitely overcome it by myself." Yet at year's end, Ha was offered an incentive cash package of KRW 10 million, equivalent of the value of 67,000 square meters (20,000 pyung) farmland. However, Ha politely declined to accept the royal grant, insisting on fighting poverty on his own terms. He further explained thus:

> on my wedding night, my wife and I vowed to work hard to overcome our poverty by ourselves. I've taken a stand against poverty for the sake of that pride. If I accept this Presidential grant, I will lose my pride.[29]

From working as a farm servant for 7 years, Ha bought 891 square meters of farmland, which was increased to 10,000 square meters through 13 years of diligent toil on the farm. The success story of Ha Sa-yong became a textbook case of the rural development movement, for which he became a tireless champion, traversing the entire country and abroad delivering a series of lectures. As of 2016, even at 86, he is still clinging steadfastly to his commitment to the campaign, delivering nearly 3,500 lectures from 1971 until 2016. He has lectured in Mongolia and China at the invitation of local leaders there. In 2007 his experience and journey with the movement was chronicled and published for inspiring peasants in China, as China rolled out the same campaign.[30]

The second story is about a young farmer called Yang Il-sun who lived in Keumok village of Naju country, Chollanam-do.[31] Keumok village was a late mover in the Saemaul wave. However, the seeds of change were sown by the then governor of the province, Ko Keon, who encouraged the inhabitants to emulate their neighbors by actively enlisting in the campaign. Yang took the governor's admonishment as a personal indictment of their collective failure to catch the wind of change blowing across the other villages. Thus, 36 young farmers ranging from 25 to 40 years old organized the village youth club and decided to launch their own village transformation program. Among the 36 members, only two were junior high school graduates and the others were either elementary school graduates or elementary school dropouts and uneducated. Yang became their leader. The farmers' main crop was rice, and each of them owned land of less than 0.6 hectares per household.[32] Chronic food shortage was the natural consequence, but the most worrying aspect was that these peasants routinely spent most of their free time idling, gambling and binge drinking.

The first thing they did was to prepare a fund for village development. For this sake, the young farmers went through fire and water. Sometimes they went on an expedition to their neighboring villages to earn money. As the fund accumulated, they started work to improve the environment of their village. They renovated the road leading into their village. As change occurred, farmers became more cooperative. After witnessing the changes and cooperative work among the peasants, the county provided the village with a KRW 10 million grant to support their development fund. They raised an additional KRW 20 million and launched environmental-improvement projects and other income-generation projects.[33]

Motivated by this budding success, the group took up the challenge of transforming the mind-set of their peasant kindred as the next order of business. In collaboration with the village women's club, they set about a campaign to take on vices like alcoholism and public indiscipline. Activities of bar operators were curtailed, banning the indiscriminate disposal of trash like cigarette butts, vinyl, papers and what have you. The womenfolk club saved a spoonful of rice from every meal to be sold to generate revenue for the village development fund. About the same time, they came up with the idea of increasing their income from agriculture by extending into commercial livestock rearing. But in this they were constrained, because they lacked any experience and the relevant financial ability to bring that about. Convinced that the idea was still worth pursuing despite the obvious constraints, Yang contacted an old acquaintance in a neighboring village 12 kilometers away who had run a successful livestock farm. He resolved to convince the farmer to migrate to Keumok village, but the good old farmer was having none of it. Yang embarked on seven rounds of bicycle trips altogether with this singular purpose. Moved by Yang's earnest persuasion, the man migrated to the village in 1978.

The goal of getting this successful farmer to migrate to Yang's village was to ensure that his peasant kindred could learn a thing or two from this experienced farmer. The peasants did indeed make the most of the proximity of their new resident's experience. In 1978, three farmhouses raised six head of cattle, which increased to 134 head of bullocks and 15 head of milk cows in 1983. Accordingly farming income raised greatly.[34]

In 1977, they decided to widen a 12-kilometer in-village road from 2 meters to 6 meters to accommodate cultivators. However, the landlords vehemently resisted the move. Yang and one more farmer donated 660 square meters (200 *pyung*) of land and visited every landlord to persuade them; it did eventually work out, allowing the project to take off. To build a village hall, a farmer donated KRW 1 million, with which the village bought 990 square meters (300 *pyung*) of land and built a modern village hall, which was used as a cradle for village development. There were instances when farmers violently resisted encroachment of their parcels of land for planned community development projects. In the summer of 1977, when they launched a program to improve the roofs of farm houses, at midnight, about ten farmers gathered outside of Yang's house shouting death threats against him with sickles in their hands. Frightened out of his wits, Yang, the third generation of only sons, fled in his undergarments, jumping over the back wall and walking 10 kilometers to take refuge in his wife's hometown. He spent 10 days hiding there before returning to his village. Yang kept a record of every detail of the process of their community development activities, including accounting books and records of village meetings and minutes, which amounted to one small truckload of notes. The records were registered with UNESCO World Cultural Heritage. In recognition of his contribution to the development of Saemaul Undong, he was conferred a host medal including a Saemaul Medal (president), Distinguished Service Medal (Minister of Interior) and various other prizes.[35]

The third story is about Ms. Chung Mun-ja, who was a pioneer of leading young women to participate in the Saemaul Undong.[36] She graduated from high school and was ignorant of all things farming before her marriage. She married with a deposit bankbook equivalent to 20 bags of rice (1,440 kg), persuading her mother to save marriage expenses. Her honeymoon started in a solitary house in the mountains 4 kilometers away from the neighboring village. Breaking up the soil and farming was her job. After an unsuccessful 3-year livestock business, the couple moved down to Oryu village, leaving behind the mountain life. Her first job upon arrival in her new village was raising young chestnut trees with the womenfolk club of the village. Because they did not own any land, the club rented farmland to plant the chestnut trees, of which 30 percent of the harvest went to the landlords and 70 percent was returned to the club. It was at this point that she had some semblance of stability in life, and a growing interest in the development of the village ensued.

You would have to remember that life as a woman was incredibly difficult. Most men routinely wasted away their times bingeing, only to return and subject their wives to physical and other forms of abuse. The patriarchal social system also made women entirely subservient to their husbands in every way. It was under these conditions that Chung was determined to challenge the existing order of things. She became president of the Family Planning Mothers' Club of the village, consisting of about ten women. She persuaded the women to take measures to improve their living standards. She was once quoted as saying,

> The reason we are living poor and being whipped by our husbands and are unable to provide adequate education for our children is that our village has no economic power. Why don't we renovate the existing Mothers' Club to earn money and enable women to lead decent lives.[37]

Such was her will and charisma that several women bought into her revolutionizing mind-set. The net result was an increase of their club to nearly 100 members after a relatively short period.

After a series of consultations with nearly 40 members of a village cooperation, they came up with a so-called plan dubbed the "Ideal Village Building Goals of Oryu." The plan had prioritized five items: (1) eradication of poverty, (2) village learning and teaching, (3) a convenient village to live in through family planning and improvement of the living environment, (4) becoming a patriotic village and (5) a village loving our neighbors. The goals were written on a placard and placed at the entrance to the village. Of course, many were those on the apex of the social structure who saw these campaigns with increasing hostility. An exasperated local once yelled that "If the hen clucks, the house will be ruined. . . . A bad urban woman came to the village, and corrupting naïve village women." However, united closely, the women did not buckle under their criticism.[38]

As mentioned earlier, one of Chung's group's contribution to the village fund was the store of rice grains for sale. But the revenue stream for that campaign was barely enough to make a difference. So, they took up other enterprising ventures, including taking contract orders to sew sportswear for a local elementary school and tree planting activities. A small cooperative savings scheme was also set up to encourage financial propriety among village women. Each member was given a bankbook for their savings. As the fund increased, the cooperative provided loans at a 2 percent interest rate per month for members and at 3 percent for non-members. Up until then, the standard interest rate in most villages was set at 6 percent per month, which was why the women's cooperative scheme attracted more interest, boosting their net worth in the process.

The Oryu Credit Cooperative was selected as a model cooperative and awarded an incentive bonus. When the Saemaul Undong campaign officially kicked off in 1971, so did it open opportunities for the women's collective to engage in many more activities. It was standard for them to rise at dusk and join in co-op activities for most parts of the day. Such was their commitment that many husbands were beginning to complain of their wives neglecting household chores to participate in community improvement projects. One of their notable projects was a campaign to plant 20,000 chestnut trees, digging 20,000 holes in the process. The venture was so profitable that it increased the group's revenue stream. Supplemented by the profits from their credit co-ops, they mainly used the resources to finance the education of their wards.

Traditionally, families used to conduct rituals one or two times every month for their deceased kinsmen. The majority of the burden of preparing these rituals fell to women, who had to single-handedly manage all aspects of the preparation of the ritual meals. In its stead, the women's club launched a campaign of holding memorial services for living elders twice monthly rather than wait till their passing away. The campaign, true to its goal, was roundly welcomed by the elders, who then agreed to an annual ancestral ritual to be held once instead of twice monthly.

In the mid-1970s, as industrial development proceeded, youngsters joined the rural–urban migratory flow. To introduce household industry, Chung contacted companies that could provide processing work for village folks. Finally, a company provided work and 50 machines. The women's club constructed a factory with a floor space of 99 square meters (30 *pyung*) built on 660 square meters (200 *pyung*) of land. In recognition of the great performance in managing a credit cooperative, savings campaign, improvement in the living environment, the attraction of a factory and education for children, Chung was awarded with a medal by the president with a KRW 2 million incentive bonus. Chung decided to use the bonus for construction of a bridge, which was a long-cherished project. Up until then, children could not go to school when the river flooded. However, the construction costs far exceeded the bonus. This story was presented as a case study in the SLTI. Moved by their endeavor, a businessman gladly committed to cover the extra costs, and thus KRW 10 million was secured and the bridge was completed for the convenience of the school children and village people.[39]

4 Evaluation of the Saemaul Undong (SMU)

For millennia, Koreans have lived and died in endemic poverty. There is hardly any doubt that many a Korean would have viewed their history of long association with poverty as indicative of a divine construction, for which nothing could be done. This degradable yoke of poverty was eventually broken down in the 1970s Korea by the full ownership of the people. The remarkable performance of the Saemaul Undong (SMU) is witnessed clearly by the shape and statistics of the living environment, great increase in farm household income and the standard of living of the people. Its most significant gains came in the form of the changes in mind-set and attitude of the people, and it happened to the whole rural community by participation of everyone and was not limited to a specific group. In recognition of performance of the SMU, *Newsweek* reported as follows in 1975:

> The first was in the improvement of the infrastructure of rural communities during the heydays of the program. Between 1971–1978, nearly a total of 85,000 kilometers of roads across 33,000 villages were paved, mostly at the initiation of the village folks themselves.[40] Communities that were hitherto cut off and invisible from most parts of the country now had accessible roads that also triggered a steady move towards agricultural mechanization. Food production was boosted along that same trajectory. At the micro level, there was a sudden thirst for improvements in the dwelling conditions of the peasants. Most houses back then were made of thatched roofs and mud bricks with very poor-quality features. These had to give way to a new trend in the construction of concrete houses and the installation of indoor running water facilities and other domestic sanitary amenities. Add that to the government's successful rural electrification project then you had all the trappings of an overnight transformation of the 5-thousand-year antiquated housing conditions.

Second, rural income levels started to move on an upward trend within the same period. Take the fact that from 1965–1969, while urban income levels increased at a rate of 14.6 percent, the income level of rural households rose at a paltry rate of 3.5 percent.[41] Then from 1970–1976 changes started to occur, with rural households growing by 9.5 percent and their urban counterparts growing at 4.6 percent. During the previous period, rural household income was 60–70 percent of that of urban households, which reversed entering 1974 in favor of rural households. As a direct consequence of the growing income levels, rural households started to enthusiastically embrace a healthy savings culture. In 1960, they had a savings rate of 10 percent, which doubled to 20 percent in 1970. Similarly, the proportion of deposits by farmers in the Bank of Agriculture Cooperative rose from 20.6 percent in 1963 to 50.5 percent in 1980. It was in fact attributable to the impact of the agricultural mechanization process that complemented the spirit of the Saemaul Movement.[42]

Another remarkable dimension is that save for the initial spark of the government material initiative, the chunk of the program's success is credited to the industriousness and sacrifice that was unleashed by village folks. It was a question of being galvanized to take advantage of the prevailing opportunities around them and a genuine desire to improve the quality of their lives; opportunities that came in the form of understanding the strength of their cooperative labor and the promise of its creative commons. To illustrate this point, in 1973 village folks had cumulatively voluntarily labored for 3.6 million days in Saemaul-related projects. Winter and off-season months especially saw a surge in voluntary activities from farmers.[43] They also contributed three times the value of the financial resources the government injected into the program.

Readers would also find it worth noting that there have been similar attempts at implementing effective rural development programs in a number of countries across the world such as Tanzania and North Korea. Some developing countries are currently receiving funds to implement such projects from a host of Multilateral Development Banks (MDBs) including the UN Millennium Village Project. However, many of these projects are bedeviled by the common problem of long-term effective implementation. Most get off to a very promising start only to falter once the donors begin weaning off the funding. Clearly, the distinguishing feature of the Korean case was the level of commitment by village leaders and folks that was elicited by the initial government support. It goes to speak of the importance of getting the beneficiaries of the project to take ownership of the project for rural development.

In fairness, it is worth acknowledging that the Korean case had two inherently distinctive features to which its success is owed. The prevailing land tenure system at the time was far more conducive for the project's successful implementation. This is what I alluded to earlier as the opportunities that the rural folks took advantage of. As stated in Section 1.2, the post-liberation land reform policies made this even more possible in contrast to societies that are still hostage to the feudal system. All it took was to get the farmers sufficiently motivated enough to till the land as their land, with the full knowledge that any resulting benefits is theirs to keep. This cannot be said of tenant farmers and other forms of share-cropping, with a few caveats of course, where tenant farmers are not allowed to have ownership, as is the case in Thailand and the Philippines with landlords occupying most land.

I say so in recognition of the differences in local conditions and how that ultimately determines potential outcomes. In the same spirit, I am not definitively saying that the success of rural development is predicated on private land ownership, just as the prior industrial development facilitated the process, credit cannot be definitively placed there as well. The Korean project also differs markedly in its expressed goals. While the initial material inducements sought to achieve long-term sustainable rural development, its immediate goal was to engender a change in the mind-set and attitude that allows poverty to flourish. Many of today's programs make the alleviation of poverty their goals without addressing the underlying factors that perpetuate the conditions of poverty. The spark created by the material inducements could only be sustained this way. Nothing can hold back a changed mind. Furthermore, unlike having projects designed and directed by so-called external experts, individual rural communities were given the free hand to make these pertinent decisions about their communities. These different perspectives have serious ramifications for outcomes.

There is something to be said about the soundness of the strategy employed by the government because the preceding factors were not altogether a given at any point of the program's span. Within its limited means, the government could only provide tokens that in many ways did the trick of stocking the creative and collaborative instincts of the population. That it also unleashed a can-do spirit in the target communities was a critical factor in creating the platform for the resulting competition between the rural population to improve its quality of life. In today's context, a policy of such kind that may be perceived to be discriminatory against some sort of groups would certainly be politically toxic for any well-meaning government.

Leadership on the ground played a complementary role in galvanizing wide participation across the board. Building on the central role of traditional leadership in the affairs of communities, the government tapped into this influence by placing them at the heart of the program's implementation. A natural alliance was thus created between the program's goals and the legitimate drive of the participating communities' interests. Community engagement, but even most importantly, community ownership, explains why the folks eagerly made out-of-pocket contributions to village improvement projects that were neither initiated nor funded by the government. That was the core of the domino effect.

And finally, none of this could have happened were it not for committed political leadership at the top. The decision to induce a behavioral change in the rural communities and the timeliness of that decision are strictly factors of political shrewdness coming from President Park personally. In fact, he staked his political capital on this program, especially coming from his most loyal constituency, the so-called outback. Not least of all, he was deeply engaged at every level of the program's implementation – from personally meeting community leaders to overseeing the smooth running of the program's affiliate organizations, his long shadow was cast over every aspect of the rural development program. A rare moment of political opportunism arose when members of President Park's party in Parliament proposed the idea of using the Saemaul grassroots network to consolidate the ruling party's networks on the ground. President Park is reported to have flatly objected to a comment to keep the sanctity of the program from political machinations, adding that if its purity became contaminated then it would undermine the whole essence of the community development movement.

His counterargument was to keep the sanctity of the program from political machinations because if "its purity becomes contaminated then it will undermine the whole essence of the community development movement."[44] Encouraged by the success of SMU in rural sectors, President Park wanted to expand it to workshops and urban sectors. In 1977, it started to establish organizations for the Saemaul movement at each workshop in urban sectors under the umbrella of the Headquarters of Saemaul Undong in Workshop. In workshops, labors and employers came face-to-face to put into practice diligence, self-help and cooperation, and its movement gradually expanded to its neighboring workshops and regions. However, as the leader stepped away from the scene, this movement could not be continued.

Indeed, the Saemaul movement laid the foundations of sustainable development through inclusive growth from the unequal-growth-by-strategic-development policy. With people now wedded to the belief that hard work and self-help are levers of economic growth, they grew by leaps and bounds, which reconfigured the social structure. Rather gratifyingly, the SMU already had inclusive growth at its core in the early days of its inception. Thanks to the initial successes chalked up by the SMU at the grassroots level, President Park set about to propagate its abiding tenets to the urban areas. Factories in urban areas were encouraged to embrace its normative basis of self-help to propel their development. It was to ensure that the urban areas should not be left out of the modernization experience in rural areas. Clearly, the national leadership deserves credit for its foresight in steering the country along this line.

In typical fashion, the Saemaul movement's moment waned with the demise of President Park. Based on the success of SMU in rural sectors, President Park began to expand the SMU to industrial and urban sectors, which had to be terminated at its beginning stage. The succeeding president showed no passion in SMU as his predecessor. It underscores an important fact that for all its gains, rural development programs require a strong driving force by political leadership. The SMU completed its mission for economic development in Korea. Critics associated the movement with the personality cult created by President Park, which succeeding governments were eager to purge. The political obfuscations aside, the compelling truth is that the country's rural communities were materially transformed under this leadership, irrespective of whether one agrees or loathes the regime under whose watch it occurred.

The significance of the Saemaul process, despite the impressive transformation it orchestrated in the country's rural development, continues to divide opinions in some quarters. Domestically there is quite an appreciable level of acknowledgement of its gains, especially in terms of it being a unique ability to trigger a radical transformation in the mind-set and attitude of previously ignored peasants. The political tainting of domestic politicians and dissident groups questioned whether it was a bottom-up autonomous movement or one led by bureaucrats. Yet others have charged that the campaign was used as ruse to prolong the political power of Park's regime. The political obfuscations aside, the compelling truth is that the country's rural communities were materially transformed through SMU, irrespective of whether one agrees or loathes the regime under whose watch it occurred.

Rather remarkably, the Saemaul model has attracted raving reviews internationally. In developing countries, rural sectors are hotbeds of poverty, and rural development has become a key national agenda beyond history and regions. Reporting the performance of SMU in increasing the incomes of farmers and improving the living environment, *Newsweek* (November 9, 1975) commented that in 4 to 5 years of Saemaul Undong, the mind-set, way of thinking, living environment and attitude of the Korean people were changed drastically.[45] It suggests the moment when Deng Xiaoping, after comparing China to its neighbors, was quoted as asking "Why do countries neighboring China live better than us?

Then we can possibly learn from them."[46] Thus, China formally launched a new village movement, benchmarking Korea's SMU, and sent hundreds of delegates to Korea for observation in the 1990s and 2000s.[47]

Foreign observers are impressed by the extraordinary performance in rural development through SMU in Korea as was discussed earlier. It is a benchmark for many developing countries working their own ways in rural development programs, as was witnessed in Uganda and Myanmar, which also established Saemaul Training Institutes. Many rural development projects apply the Saemaul modality of discriminative incentives and competition being conducted in such countries as Vietnam, Laos, Rwanda and Colombia under the auspices of Korea's ODA programs.[48] Civil servants and community leaders from 150 developing countries including China, Vietnam, Laos, Myanmar, Mongolia and Ethiopia have so far visited Korea to learn about the SMU.[49] Jeffery Sachs, director of Columbia University's Earth Institute, credits Korea's Saemaul Undong with broadening his insight into the potential of rural development programs to transform societies.[50]

Notes

1 The share of agricultural households among the total population was 58.3 percent in 1960, according to the Statistical Yearbook of 1975 by Statistics Korea, http://kosis.kr/index/index.jsp
2 *Statistics Korea*, http://kosis.kr/index/index.jsp
3 *Jal salabose, saemaeul undong* [Let's Live Better: Saemaul Undong] (Seoul, Korea: KBS, August 17, 2013), accessed August 10, 2017, www.kbs.co.kr/1tv/sisa/docucinema/view/vod/2181308_66621.html
4 Kim Chung-yum, *From Despair to Hope: Economic Policymaking in Korea 1945–1979* (Seoul, Korea: Korea Development Institute, 2011), 186–188.
5 Kwon Sun-jik, *Korian mireokeul 3: Nongchongeundaehwaundong peurojekteu, saemaeul undong* [The Korean Miracle III: Rural Modernization Project, Saemaul Undong] (Seoul, Korea: Nanam, 2015).
6 O Won-chol, *Hangukhyeonggyeongjegeonseol 6: Eneojijeongchaekgwa jungdongjinchul* [Korean Type Economic Construction 6: An Engineering Approach] (Seoul, Korea: Korea Type Economic Policy Institute, 1997), 137–160.
7 *Ibid.*, 136.
8 O Won-chol, *The Korea Story: President Park Jung-hee's Leadership and the Korean Industrial Revolution* (Seoul, Korea: Wisdom Tree, 2009), 40–43.
9 *Ibid.*, 40–43.
10 Chung Gap-jin, *Hankuk Saemaulundongui Seonggongyoin Bunseok* [Analysis of the Success Factors of the Saemaul Undong] (Seoul, Korea: Korea Rural Development Corporation, 2015), 12–13.
11 *Ibid.*
12 *Ibid.*
13 *Let's Live Better: Saemaul Undong*, KBS.
14 Chung, *Saemaul Undong*, 13–14.
15 *Ibid.*
16 *Ibid.*, 13–23.
17 The classification of villages was based on surveys of villagers about their opinion of the government's support program. Such responses included providing their own financial resources and labor, cooperating with each other, increasing productivity, and developing industrial products. See Kim Chung-yum, *From Despair*

to Hope: Economic Policymaking in Korea 1945–1979 (Seoul, Korea: Korea Development Institute, 2011), 223.

18 Kwon, *Rural Modernization Project, Saemaul Undong*, 132.
19 *Ibid.*, 128–131.
20 Park Jin-hwan, *The Saemaul Movement: Korea's Approach to Rural Modernization in 1970s* (Seoul, Korea: Korea Rural Economic Institute, 1998), 146–156.
21 Kwon, *Rural Modernization Project, Saemaul Undong*, 129.
22 *Ibid.*, 128–131.
23 *Ibid.*, 172–173.
24 *Ibid.*, 70.
25 *Let's Live Better: Saemaul Undong*, KBS.
26 Kwon Sun-jik, *Rural Modernization Project, Saemaul Undong*, 136–170.
27 *Ibid.*, 140.
28 *Ibid.*, 139.
29 *Ibid.*, 139–140.
30 *Monthly Chosun*, August 2016 (Chosunilbosa), 394 [in Korean].
31 For more details about Yang Il-sun, see Kwon, *Rural Modernization Project, Saemaul Undong*, 153–158.
32 Kwon, *Rural Modernization Project, Saemaul Undong*, 155.
33 *Ibid.*, 156.
34 *Ibid.*, 158–160.
35 *Ibid.*, 169.
36 *Ibid.*, 170–187.
37 *Ibid.*, 178.
38 *Ibid.*, 179.
39 *Ibid.*, 185–86.
40 Park Jin-hwan, *The Saemaul Movement*, 69–76.
41 *Statistics Korea*, http://kosis.kr/index/index.jsp
42 Cho Lee-jay et al., *Hanguk geundaehwa, gijeokui gwajeong* [Modernization of the Republic of Korea; a Miraculous Achievement] (Seoul, Korea: Chosun News Press, 2005), 463–465.
43 Park Jin-hwan, *The Saemaul Movement*, 82–85.
44 *Let's Live Better: Saemaul Undong*, KBS.
45 Seol, *Park Chung-hee and Korean Economy*, 92.
46 *Let's Live Better: Saemaul Undong*, KBS.
47 *Ibid.*
48 Prime Minister's Office, "International Expansion of the *Saemaul Undong*," April 2016, Korea, 7–10 [in Korean].
49 According to the preceding document (p. 7), during the period of 2011–2015, 5,009 people from 104 countries were invited to the *Saemaul* training programs of Korea, which covers most of the developing countries.
50 Seo Hwa-dong, "Jepeuri saks yuensamuchongjang 'saemaeulundongseo goyong-changchul, bingontoechi yeonggam eodeo" [Jeffrey Sachs, "I Got Inspiration of Employment Creation and Poverty Elimination From the Saemaul Undong"], *Korea Economic Daily*, October 10, 2011, accessed August 10, 2017, www.hankyung.com/news/app/newsview.php?aid=2011101087751

11 The people and state-community on a track of economic development

1 The people as the core of economic development

So far, we have discussed the great economic transformation of the country from a fragile, poverty-stricken state to a modern industrial one. In economic development, people are at its core. Mainstream economic thought has crystallized around the centrality of human resources as a vital ingredient of a nation's economic development as economist Paul Romer's endogenous economic growth theory in the late 1980s. In other words, a country's surest resource above everything else is embedded in the core of its people – be they skilled or otherwise. People's values and behavior may determine the future course of a country, even its rise and fall.

The dynamics of economic development is not always necessarily limited to the rise of income of the people. Economic development is affected by the people, and in reverse, it gives effects not only on the individual person but also on the state community to which the people belong. Having reviewed major factors of economic development in Korea, now is the time to shed light on the relations between economic development and people, and on its consequences on state community. This issue will be viewed in three respects: (1) how people can work for or against economic development; (2) in reverse, how economic development affects people and their mind-set or attitude; and (3) the consequences of economic development on a state community.

Regarding the first issue, folks in a state of poverty are helplessly exposed to poverty. The victims of poverty are seemingly helpless folks who are locked in the shackles without any prospect of reprieve. They usually lack the will and means to overcome poverty. People seem to be lazy, not punctual, discouraged and dishonest. These are factors that make overcoming poverty difficult. If so, are they poor because of innate consciousness, or is it just caused by poverty? Is it possible to change this during the development process? Failure to properly leverage this core can constitute an obstacle to development.

To attain economic development more smoothly and effectively, a traditional mind-set or attitude under poverty might be inappropriate. People take efforts instinctively to overcome poverty; however, people accustomed to poverty sometimes do not show the will to improve their living standard and exert positive efforts, and accept their poverty as their fortune, which might be a major obstacle to economic development. In this regard, the author remembers the question raised by Rwandan President Paul Kagame on a dinner dialogue on his state visit to Korea in 2009: "How could Korea reorient citizens' mind-set towards development oriented?" As the national leader for state building and economic development, it seemed that encouraging the people to have the will and to be self-confident must be his major concern. This chapter may provide my own answer to the question.

Not too long ago, my country traveled down this same path and along this course. It was often the target of the same kind of suggestive innuendos and sometimes exaggerated stereotypical labels that are all too commonly associated with underdeveloped countries. In fact, there were well-meaning people who argued that you only had to look at Korea's historical dependence on other states to realize that it inherently lacked the penchant for development. We were told that you had a better chance of finding a needle in a haystack than you would have building credible democratic governance in Korea. Then there were issues with the long list of vices that were attributed to the Korean people as a lazy bunch, fickle, incongruous and just content to be stuck in a cycle of mediocrity.

In truth, for several reasons, Koreans also internalized this deeply disparaging image of themselves. Yet within a couple of generations there has been a fundamental turnaround in not just the attitude of individual Koreans but also the image of the entire nation. We now talk of Korea in highly celebratory tones as having the most dynamic workforce anywhere in the world, noted for having the longest working hours in the OECD (Organisation for Economic Co-operation and Development) member countries up until 2007. From its wobbly and unpromising start, Korea's democracy is maturing and respected accordingly. It has a seat at the table of the world's premier elite organizations such as the OECD and the G20, the latter of which it proudly hosted in 2010. From a paltry, lazy bunch its fortunes have significantly turned, as it counts among the global powerhouses of semiconductor production, automobiles, smartphones, shipbuilding and major high-tech electronic industries.

This is why President Kagame's question had a resonant effect on me. Korea's economic development was in large part predicated on this reorientation of the mind-set and spirit of its citizens as aptly reflected in its wild development experiment. A more forceful form of this thesis can be juxtaposed by weighing into arguably the most definitive social experiment of recent times – the state of the two Koreas. We could also stretch this assertion further by asking whether the transformation is the consequence of economic development or the other way around. Both views have their passionate defenders.

A major challenge the government of Korea had to contend with in its early development was how to inspire this reorientation of the mind-set of its citizens. Retrospectively, there was scarcely anyone within the government that could have confidently conceived of the transformation as it currently is. Education, according to conventional thinking, offers the surest path toward building this momentum. Be that as it may, education in and of itself tends to be tilted toward long-term transformation but comes against conditions where immediate urgent needs beckon for attention, especially those that concern the bread-and-butter questions of now.

As to the second issue of possible effects of economic development on the people, the behavior or attitude of the people may change in the course of sustained rise in income. An Eastern proverb has it that knowledge of manners will only come after a person is well-fed and clothed. This proverb goes to highlight the link between a people's economic state and the state of their mind-set. In a pervasive state of poverty, the exigencies of life may compel otherwise decent folks to cut corners just to make ends meet. However, if basic human needs are satisfied, folks may not work as hard as before and may pursue other desires. This may be related to the phenomenon of the middle-income trap that prevailed in the international development arena. The possible effects of speedy economic development on the people also draw our interests.

The third issue is related to also fundamental value of security and human rights. During the development era, the Korean government was consistently criticized over the issue of democratic procedures and human rights. The Korean government argued that poverty elimination and solidarity of national security are more urgent than the value of democratic procedures. Freedom from want or poverty may not be more important than the values of security and democracy. The issue that in the course of development priority policy of the Korean government, how national security and democracy could be attained in Korea, will be our last interest in this chapter.

2 People for economic development

Regarding the first issue of the mind-set of people for development, we need to see what were the consciousness and attitude of Koreans at the base line. As was pointed out in Section 1.2, Koreans exhibited the classic syndrome of laziness – generally lethargic in their approach to work, rampant public-sector corruption and pervasive disorientation. To confirm this, it is necessary to consider the historical environment in which the way of thinking and behavior were formed. Did they live either having been exploited or rewarded sufficiently for their behavior or choices through their history? If the former was true, people should be tamed to be lazy and dishonest rather than diligent and honest. If the latter was true, vice versa. According to Acemoglu and Robinson (2012), nations fail when they have extractive economic institutions supported by extractive political institutions that impede and even block economic growth.[1]

As aptly stated by the Irish literary ace James Joyce, "history is a nightmare from which I am trying to awake." This provides an instructive context for explaining the vices to which the nation was hostage for a good part of its existence. Up until Imperial Japan's formal annexation of the Korean Peninsula in 1910, these were a people living under a system of unbridled feudalism and its cousin aristocratic control for several thousand years. A perfect environment of self-deprecation had been created by these conditions, which was accentuated by colonialism and its legacy, a classic case of a history laced in exploitation in all its manifestation – from feudal control, indentured servitude, colonialism and oligarchy. At no point in history is the human spirit ever predisposed to be motivated if the instincts of freedom are stifled. After all, motivation is predicated on being able to analyze the links between how gain and effort is countervailed. If the gain is disproportionately dwarfed by the effort, then motivation plummets. But where industry is legitimately rewarded in fair proportion to effort, then motivation becomes a natural given.

However, through the ordeal of recent history of nation building amid war during the late 1940s to the early 1960s, Korea was given a unique environment for economic development. First, there was a conscientious attempt to build the post-independent state on democratic and market economic tenets. Private property ownership was guaranteed, alongside the freedom of individuals to engage in free economic activities and accrue any resulting profits. Private property laws were enshrined in statutes and enforced by public institutions at all levels. This initial posture of openness to the market economy provided a foundation for the subsequent economic development to follow.[2] In contrast, many post-colonial states of the 1960s fell for the seduction of state socialism, and one can see a plethora of such examples of failed socialist policies right from North Korea down to many African and Eastern European countries.

Second, to some extent, the presence of a competitive environment in Korean society played an important part in facilitating a great degree of social mobility. Colonial rule worked to recalibrate the social structure of Korea to the extent that it diminished some of the traditional monopolistic role of the ruling class in society. The social structure was further upturned following the impact of mass migration after independence and the ensuing Korean War that followed. Approximately four million people migrated to the South from Japan and North Korea along the way.

That was also complemented by the massive land reform policies initiated by the independence government, which broke the back of feudalism on the nation. Unlike the South, land reform in North Korea reflected socialist populist positions that took control of land from the feudal class by the state. This system of unbridled state control has proven time and again to be counterproductive. In South Korea, through land reform, the landlords were requested to sell their land of more than 3 hectares on the market, and the government provided tenants financial assistance to buy the land. Therefore, most tenants became landowners.

However, the devastation of the 3-year-long Korean War became an equalizer of sorts as the nation reeled from the collective burden of poverty. In a way, it marked a critical point in the modern history of Korea when the entire nation, irrespective of classes, had to pick up the pieces and begin again together from the same starting point. The 1961 coup d'état that ushered in the military regime was yet another occasion for massive egalitarian reforms that socially uplifted military officials largely from poor farm families. The leveling of the playing field opened the door for unprecedented social mobility and fair competition. Compared to similar conditions in Southeast Asia, feudalism remains entrenched in many countries as tenant farmers remain stuck at the lowest rungs without any real prospects of social mobility. Thus, to the hungry people with a traditional mind-set a flat playing ground was given. Their poverty was maintained for several thousand years. A distinctive feature is that the ground becomes flat. However, the poor people have neither energy to work for themselves nor any means to improve their poverty. Under the situation, the people were running pell-mell to survive.

From its wobbly start as a nation, South Korea teetered on the brink of becoming a failed state until the advent of the Park military junta to put the nation on a national development orientation. He was under no illusions about the scale of the tasks that were before him and his cohorts. Because Korea was endowed only with an excess population on a small amount of land, the clue for economic development naturally had to be found in human resources. Therefore, the strategy for poverty elimination was focused on how to motivate the people to work for themselves, and when they work, to work harder. What policies did the Korean government adopt for this purpose, and what were the consequences of those policies? To the policies of development focused on the people, what did the Korean people assume as their role in national development, and how are they changed?

The first and the most urgent task was providing sufficient food for the people. Hungry soldiers cannot fight. The vital responsibility of the regime was in providing food and security for the people. How did the impoverished government deal with this problem? As mentioned earlier, the most imminent and urgent measure for enhancing agricultural productivity on the limited land ownership was to increase the input of fertilizer and launch a green revolution, as was discussed in Section 3.2.

Resorting to foreign capital was the only next viable option in the absence of capital and technology for the construction of fertilizer plants. Risk-averse international investors were hesitant to consider Korea as a destination, given the insecurity and political instability in the peninsula. To secure foreign capital for construction of fertilizer plants, the government had to provide solid guarantees to repay the principal and interest of the accrued loans within a short-term period. Therefore, the fertilizer had to be sold at extremely exorbitant prices beyond what the local farmers could afford. The government had to step in to provide huge subsidies that swelled the Bank of Korea's accumulated deficits. There was the added risk of inflation going over the roof, yet the government was willing to take its chances. This was followed by the establishment of the Rural Development Administration (RDA) to provide a nationwide extension service and distribute high-yield crop varieties it had developed under the auspices of the so-called march to realizing the green revolution realize.

The second task was providing job opportunities for the people. Because domestic opportunities were very limited due to a poor industrial base, the government opened the way abroad, as was discussed in Section 4.3. The Korea Overseas Development Corporation (1965) was established to facilitate the export of the labor force abroad. Most notable was that 7,936 mine workers and 11,057 nurses were sent to West Germany during the period 1966–1977, and 400,000 soldiers were dispatched during the Vietnam War in the late 1960s. From 1973 to 1978, many people went to the Middle East for construction projects. Only one Korean company was working in the Middle East in 1973, but by 1976 this number had increased to 60. The contracts from the Middle East construction projects amounted to $24 million for 1965–1973, which increased to $41.807 billion for 1974–1981. As job opportunities were given from abroad, the hungry Koreans dared to do hard and difficult work in mines, on battlefields and in deserts around the world to earn money with a dream of escaping poverty, as was illustrated in Section 6.3 for industrial warriors.

The third task was to facilitate business activities of the people and develop industries to provide jobs domestically, which was fully discussed in Chapters 5 and 7. In considering that laboring abroad has to be temporal at low wage rates, the government moved to support business activity and industrial development so that it could provide permanent job opportunities. Having enforced the two tasks listed earlier, it now became feasible to initiate industrial development based on the increased domestic savings and fiscal capacity. Four factors are prerequisite for promoting start-up and industrial development: financing, infrastructure, manpower and technology. In an industrial barren country, the government concentrated its full capacity and resources on industrial development, which has come to be known as the Miracle on the Han River. For Korea to accelerate industrialization effectively, the government took the initiative for upgrading and securing two major factors of human and financial resources.

The fourth task was upgrading labor skills and research and development (R&D) capacity, as was discussed in Chapter 8. Targeted vocational training skills became part of this grand goal of creating ideal employment opportunities at home. Trainees were rigorously trained under a regimen like a military boot camp to equip them for the job market. The trainers also imbued in them a sense of moral education to complement the skill acquisition process. A similar initiative was unveiled to attract and retain highly qualified personnel for scientific research. For instance, many of the scientists recruited from abroad were offered very competitive salaries, some of which often exceeded the president's, as part of the goal to keep them sufficiently motivated enough to serve the country's development needs. The Korean government challenged changes in mindset and attitude of people from traditional to modern ones through a national drive for rural development called Saemaul Undong (SMU), as was discussed in Chapter 10. The SMU aimed to encourage diligence, self-help and cooperation through incentive schemes, competition and active roles of village leaders. Rebalancing the gap between the industrial sector and the rural one could provide the basis for inclusive growth in Korea.

Regarding securing development financing, the government took extraordinary measures to attract foreign capital for investment into its priority areas, as was covered in Chapter 9. Private companies were given lofty government guarantees to enable them to borrow on the international capital market alongside the establishment of specialized financial institutions to cater to specific industries and the then-burgeoning small and medium enterprises (SME) sector. As the country's industrialization drive started to gather steam, employment opportunities at home could be created enormously, through which Korea was no longer required to export its labor force abroad.

Lastly, in managing a level playing field, the government tried to strictly enforce the principles of a market economy. That is equal opportunity to everyone, and rewarding according to one's contribution. There should be no free lunch. A good example is the distribution of aid food. Folks would be assigned to render community service in exchange for food rather than just doling out handouts.

The collapse of the landlord class and enhanced social mobility discussed earlier provide a good condition for equity in every opportunity. The system of recruitment of public officials hinged on a transparent competitive selection that offered equal chances to all qualified prospective applicants. Ambitious youngsters were confident in climbing the professional civil-service ladder through this open system and benefiting from its competitive conditions of service. In a sense, it was an assurance of social mobility on the sheer basis of an individual's merit.

The "no free lunch" principle was enforced even in the public health service and social welfare system. The government thought that a social welfare scheme even at minimal extent was beyond the capacity at its poverty stage, and it was more urgent to increase the economic pie above anything else. It was argued that the surest social security is to create employment opportunities for those willing and able to work. That is why issues of social welfare and security were conspicuous in their absence in any of the government's initial Five-Year Development Plans save for the fourth one. The same economic principle was applied even to the government's rural development program. Only high performing villages were allocated extra material aid; poor-performing villages were incentivized to up their game.

By all indications, running a country on such economic principles and transparent governance is a tall order. It partly explains why in many countries, those with access to resources tend to engage in rent-seeking machinations and sometimes resort to overtly populist policies within the democratic process to curry favor with the citizens. Indeed, these policies are often oblivious or even disregard the implications of long-term sustainability. It is easy to get used to free things if you are getting support for a long time. A good example is the experience of engagement in rural development projects in poverty-stricken countries by the Korea Institute for Development Strategy (KDS), for which I currently work.

To draw village development plans, our consultants asked village residents to fill out a household survey sheet. Residents responded, in some cases expecting something in compensation for their cooperation. It seems reasonable for them in their own right who are accustomed to receiving gifts in foreign aid projects. However, our consultants thought that from the beginning their attitude should be corrected, and explained by saying, "This is to draw a plan to make you and your children live better, rather than for us. Such being the case, why should we give something in compensation for doing this?" Finally, the folks agreed, and became very active in helping with the project. Worrying about the mental dependence of the people on aid, India's Prime Minister Jawaharlal Nehru set a policy not to accept ODA from abroad. Poverty elimination or economic development seems to start with the removal of the mind-set of expecting a free lunch or depending on others.

How did the poor and frustrated Korean population react to the conditions provided by the government? Having been relieved from famine to some extent at the first stage, people started to be relieved from desperation and lethargy, and to have some energy and the will to do something. Being given chances for work at the second stage, the people became the fish that met water. The people who had experienced the torment of famine did any work regardless of its hardship or danger without further hesitation. Once they started earning money and began to be able to obtain enough food, get treated for their illnesses, and being able to educate their offspring, they became more active in searching for work opportunities and sought to work even more diligently. To the widely opened business and job opportunities, entrepreneurs were born and the people became industrial warriors, manufacturing goods for export and threaded the ocean to sell those products. They were ready to absorb labor-skill upgrading programs at the fourth stage and transformed themselves to high-level technicians and skilled labor fitted for minute machine industry. As was pointed out by *Newsweek* in Section 5.4, the international community sees that the Koreans are the only people in the world to outpace the diligence of the Japanese.

In those three processes, education fever was set alight. As the race started at the same line, everybody was doing their best to get ahead. Human capital accumulation was a key factor in the race. In a family-oriented society, higher education for children means higher status for the family. Parents put together their nickels and dimes to educate their children. For the rural folks, that often required the selling of their cattle to educate their children – this must be viewed from the backdrop of cattle symbolizing the highest store of value for farmers. University campuses were thus colloquially called *Ugoltap* or "tower of cow bones," signifying the sacrifices Korean parents made for their children.

All these changes happened in two decades. It did not take long for the people who were discouraged and traditional-minded to become entrepreneurs in the global market and industrial warriors to manufacture sophisticated products. The world was soon to notice the transformation taken place when *Newsweek* magazine dedicated its June 1977 edition to discussing the Korean story, putting in the article, "The Koreans are the only people who view the Japanese as lazy," as was quoted in Section 5.4. Indeed, the primary force of Korea's economic miracle might be the diligence and hardworking of the Korean people. What a difference one or two decades made in the life of a nation. This glowing tribute stands in the face of how they were portrayed in very unflattering terms not too long ago. Quite often, the traditional mind-set of people in developing countries is painted as the major obstacle to economic development whose change seems to be difficult and take a long time. Going back to the question of the Rwandan president as to the Korean experience of reorientation of the people toward development, my own answer is that it will not take long. Once people begin to understand the value of money through job opportunities, they will soon be changed.

3 People under sustained economic growth

As people propel economic development, so does economic development affect the mind-set and attitude of the people in reverse. An Eastern proverb has it that knowledge of manners will only come after a person is well-fed and clothed. This proverb goes to highlight the link between a people's economic status and their mind-set or attitude. In a pervasive state of poverty, there is a general dearth of trust and integrity, given that the exigencies of life can compel otherwise decent folks to cut corners just to make ends meet. In the previous section, we discussed how the people affected economic development in Korea. What follows is the flip side of the same thesis.

When it comes to the question of modern economic growth, recent evidence indicates that countries that once exhibited high and fast growth are not necessarily able to maintain sustainability of economic growth in the long run.[3] As Figure 1.2 depicts the trend of gross domestic product (GDP) per capita in selected countries, some countries like Argentina and Brazil had a stellar start much earlier than Korea, only to lose steam along the way and slide backwards relative to other developing countries. Among the countries that started late, most countries did not show a conspicuous growth trend except for Korea. The reason might be that as the level of income increases, the attitude or behavior of the people can change from the early stage of development so that it may weaken the driving force of growth. The phenomenon of rapidly growing economies stagnating at middle-income levels and failing to graduate into the ranks of high-income countries is called the "middle-income trap."[4]

With respect to changes in the behavior of the people in the process of sustained economic growth, Itokawa Hideo at Tokyo University suggested the following hypothesis.[5] According to him, human aspiration may be classified into four distinct stages: (1) mouth, (2) arms and legs, (3) eyes and (4) brain. As economic growth proceeds, human behavior is changed following these four stages.

People at the poverty line are in the stage of the mouth, which is characterized by the quest for survival – when a people are more inclined to be driven to work to be exempted from hunger and to meet their basic needs. This is also the stage where the pressure of survival makes the individual willing to endure hardships as long as they are convinced that their labor can change their fortunes. Because folks at this stage are used to working hard regardless of working conditions as far as famine can be resolved, it may easy for the government to rule the people. South Korea in the early 1960s was certainly within this category.

Then it comes to the stage of the arms and legs, as a people's economic status grows from the subsistence level. Beyond the subsistence level, people begin to pursue some of the rudimentary elements of convenience of arms and legs. This stage is fostered by a consumption instinct that aspires to acquire things like cars, refrigerators, TVs, washing machines, computers and so forth. To have purchasing power of those items, people still work hard at this stage. In this regard, the Korean economy during the 1970s can be regarded as a salient example.

The stage of the eyes is characterized by the pursuit of the kind of satisfaction of the eyes rather than material needs. This is when fashion takes root and extravagant spending becomes socially acceptable. Despite the increase in standard of living, folks still have a desire for more because of differences in relative income in society.

This is when a person is no longer content with just owning a car, but desires a luxurious car because their neighbor has one. It is at this third stage that folks begin to engage with issues of social justice and political questions, which would have been hitherto considered a remote issue. Brewing discontent and agitation

Picture 11.1 Industrial dispute between business and labor. We should not let industrial disputes result in breaking the gourd and falling into a middle-income trap

©Na young Ahn

take root, which increases the probability of economic and social chaos, which in turn raises the specter of a national crisis. There are examples of countries in this stage that have been on the verge of becoming advanced countries, finding themselves falling back, as witnessed in Brazil, Mexico and Peru.[6] At this stage, labor disputes and internal discord become serious, and political stability is jeopardized. Unions and employers struggle over the economic pie, and sometimes the struggle becomes so serious that it may paralyze the industry that gives rise to the economic pie. In this situation, governments face a dilemma. If they raise the hand of employers for sustained economic growth, they will face difficulty in elections. In reverse, if they raise the hand of unions, the economy will be set back, which will make them again unpopular in elections.

The last stage of human aspiration, or the era of the "brain," revolves around the pursuit of spiritual satisfaction because the material desires have already been satisfied. People avoid hard labor coming to this stage, so that this stage might not be helpful for sustained industrial growth. This stage may lead the country either to a good direction of advancements in religion, art and culture, and philosophy, or to usher in less positive outcomes such as the emergence of hippies, nihilism and suicide.[7]

According to this hypothesis, the reason that many countries on their way to sustained economic growth fall behind is in their failure to respond properly to the third stage of the eyes. This is the stage when the government faces difficulties in executing policies. People may become extravagant and not devoted to work. Mutual discord may lead the society to serious social conflict. To overcome this stage with sustained economic development, it may require two conditions. On the one hand, the people should be able to practice thrift and frugality even at a high level of their income. Establishment of a sound value system among the middle class is important. On the other, transparency and fairness in income distribution in society could be secured, so that the people have no questions of justice or wealth.

Korea's experience traveling this growth path toward poverty elimination and economic development has been a difficult struggle to sustain the momentum. Figure 11.1 shows the trend of GDP per capita and the number of industrial disputes over the period of its economic development.

Driven by the extreme state of poverty of the 1960s, Korean workers could scarcely care about their working conditions and anything to do with low wages. It was the age of the mouth, so to speak. They continued to engage in strenuous labor even in the 1970s, which could also be said to be the age of arms and legs. You cannot deny that the greatest motivation for Korean laborers of that era was the prospect of making a living, and that remained a central driving force. The once lethargic and inferior complex-centered Korean, coming out of an era of debasing colonialism and extreme poverty, transformed into a diligent workaholic overnight. Unions were not that active in the 1960s during the age of the mouth, under the hard-line of the Park administration against illegal industrial disputes.

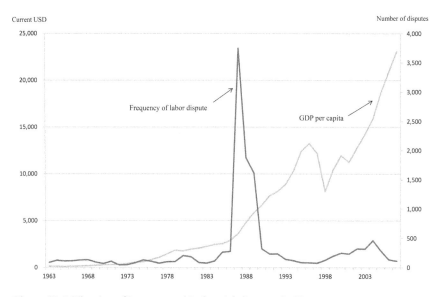

Figure 11.1 The rise of income and industrial disputes in Korea
Source: Ministry of Employment and Labor, http://laborstat.moel.go.kr/

People may not simply work passively abiding their doom in any working conditions. As human beings, they demand basic rights of labor. As industrial development proceeds, there arose a labor movement to demand its own rights, which led to the formation of labor unions. Unions, according to International Labour Organization (ILO) standards, are entitled to freely determine how they run and engage in political activities to some extent. In many cases, they have morphed into institutions of power ostensibly established to be countervailing forces against the peremptory powers of employers. Powerful labor unions have on occasions extended their overbearing power beyond the fine line between the art of compromise in collective bargaining and become self-righteous guard dogs.

However, at a stage where industry was not budding yet, a too-radical or violent labor movement may result in trampling the seeds of industrial development before they germinate. In South Korea, the forces of labor movement armed with the Socialist class theory backed up by the Socialist bloc of the continent and North Korea had posed big threats to the government's efforts in its early days. Many underdeveloped countries have a hard time in reconciling this straight-jacket posturing with the exigencies of their economic needs, which if not properly addressed becomes the seedbed for labor militancy.

The rapid economic growth, thus speed in the rise of the level of income, ensured a fast move from the stage of mouth and legs and arms, to the age of eyes within a heartbeat in Korea. As much as the virtue of hard work propelled them to that stage overnight, it also thrust them into a radical state that many were not yet quite frankly fully adjusted to living with. Moving from a dispensation where everyone is equally poor and witnessing a different level of changes certainly caught the eyes. Understandably so, a sudden departure from the old ways to the new ones can be unnerving. People are working hard to earn money, but they come to realize that others are having it easy. They witness that their neighbors are clad in all the novelties and luxuries of life, when the wealthy acquire lofty assets and accumulate power, then transfer such assets to their children who may not necessarily have worked to earn such a privilege of easy living. Without the opportunity for a favorable head start, those at the bottom will begin to question the system that allows for such inequality. The chasm between those that really have to tie their aspirations to work and those who step into privilege by dint of the system has ramifications for the motivation for entrepreneurship. It is precisely at this point that industrial dispute becomes serious and growth stagnated, which may lead the country to fall into the middle-income trap.

Figure 11.1 shows an explosive rise in the frequency of labor disputes to the extent that it may jeopardize national security and result in stagnation of economic growth. In the late 1980s and 1990s, the per capita GDP current price witnessed declines. Explosion of industrial disputes exacerbated social chaos in a way that spoke to the cost of the inability to match the economic development with public sentiments.

With this reason, the government rescinded its initial commitment to allow the unions a free pass in their activities, be it political or otherwise. Despite coming under immense criticism, the government refused to allow the political militancy of the unions couched in labor activism to impede the country's economic progress. A massive crackdown of illegal labor activities was carried out by the government thus. As shown in Figure 11.1, during the decades of the 1960s and 1970s, when there were few industrial disputes, economic development went ahead smoothly under the iron grips of the military junta. In 1970, a needle-worker named Chun Tae-il protested poor working conditions and violations of labor rights in the sewing factories of Korea at the time. At last, he burnt himself to death at the age of 22, claiming that laborers were not machines. This provided momentum to look back at the gray area of laborers and to spur the labor movement. However, the Park–Chung-hee administration kept the labor movement under its control, and during the period a foundation for economic development was prepared in Korea.

The demise of President Park Chung-hee and the end of his regime galvanized a new yearning for greater liberalism. It was also an era that brought renewed eruptions in labor disputes in the 1980s, as was shown in Figure 11.1. In some cases, industrial disputes were so violent that it was hardly believable the workers on strike were the same Koreans who dared to work in the German mines with no complaints but risking their lives. The dispute was so serious as to pose a threat to national security.

No longer able to forcefully restrain the unions, the government resorted to two pillar measures in the face of the crisis. One was compromising with unions to establish more advanced labor institutions, and the other was ensuring to make

Picture 11.2 Labor dispute in 1980s Korea. In 1980s Korea, labor disputes and strikes
        were common, seriously holding back industrial production

©Yonhap News Agency

a more equitable and transparent society, up to the expectation of the people in
the age of the eyes. Regarding the former, as a precursor to laying the foundations for harmonious industrial relations, it incorporated the more advanced ILO
standards of industrial relations. However, overall, the government of Korea was
discreet in managing industrial relations policy to minimize its impact on the
economy. It was only in 1988 when the country enacted minimum-wage legislation. Of course, the government tried to prohibit illegal union activity and strictly
punish illegal activities, but putting punitive measures in place was not easy.

Regarding the latter of making equitable and transparent society in the age of
the eyes, so far, the government was generous for those issues giving priority on
capital accumulation and enlarging the economic pie. The government found an
opportunity in the crisis to build a more transparent and a more equitable society,
however that was not going to be a mere walk in the park considering the sticky
and entrenched grievances that drive these divisions. In many ways, these social
agitations were fueled by income inequality and to some extent the question of
legitimacy of the wealth in society. In an ideal world, there should be no agitation
and apprehension granted there are no systemic loopholes that allow for illicit
enrichment by a few, who also grease their way out of the gleeful eyes of the tax-
man at the expense of public interest. In most developed jurisdictions, effective
public administration systems ensure enhanced transparency in private financial
transactions and taxation policies serve to inspire public trust and confidence.
A case in point is the United States, where cash transactions, except petty ones,
are to be done by personal checks or cards to be recorded by banks, and banks are
obliged to notify the Internal Revenue Service (IRS) of transactions of more than
$10,000 and suspicious transactions of more than $5,000. Korea has continued

to promote a series of reforms to ensure the legitimacy and transparency of the distribution of wealth as listed below:

- Tax administration reform launched with the establishment of the National Tax Service (1966)
- Public Offering Promotion Act (1973)
- Fair Trade and Anti-Monopoly Act (1980)
- Business accounting external audit system was introduced (1980)
- Public Officials Ethics Act (1981)
- Real Name Financial Transaction Act (1993)
- Basic Act on Administration Regulations, Regulation Reform Committee (1997)
- Money Laundry Prevention Act, Financial Information Analysis Center (2001).

In the process of economic growth and sustained rise in income, the obedient folks may become radical and violent on the one hand. On the other hand, enterprisers and the rich in a small number may become extravagant and greedy, leading the society to slavish capitalism. The process of legislation of the aforementioned systems struggled for survival and sustainable economic development by the Korean government and the people. On the one hand, the militant labor movement and opposition forces criticized employers and the rich, demanding fundamental reform of the economic system and government. On the other, the rich and rent seekers were reluctant to any changes that may jeopardize their rent, and critical that a violent and illegal labor movement by the unions posed major threats to sustainable economic development. In a sense, the last five to six decades of economic development of Korea was the history of struggle and mediation among unions, employers and stakeholders by the government with many trials and errors.

Fortunately, Korea could succeed in building a fully democratic political system by the late 1980s. The laws related to employment and industrial relations were revised and updated to become consistent with the ILO's standards. At the same time, the reform process had also seeped into the financial and tax systems and thus consolidated the earlier attempts to enhance transparency and fairness in financial trade and public services, which culminated in enforcement of the Real Name Financial Transaction Act in 1993. The steady march toward normalization of industrial relations had laid the groundwork for enhancing the next phase of the country's international competitive edge so that the economy could cruise safely to the status of an advanced, high-income country. The fact that many countries are falling behind in the course of economic growth may be attributable to two main reasons: (1) the nation failed in establishing credible and transparent institutions and managing industrial peace or (2) the way of thinking of the folks may not be sufficiently matured enough to maintain thriftiness and diligence to enjoy a high level of income and prosperity. In the course of economic development, governments should be able to hold the bridle strongly.

4 Economic development to the state-community

The liberating effect of economic development triggers an improvement in standards of living whose impact reverberates beyond the individual. Along the development sojourn, we also should contend with the issues of national security and entrenching democratic norms that safeguards human dignity. As a poor aid-dependent country, South Korea's existence as a state was severely questioned considering its own incapacity for self-sustenance, and international society claimed human rights violations against the Korean government in its early days of development. However, enormous economic development in Korea accompanied an equivalent impact on the state community in three aspects of the way of thinking of individual people, industrial or technological power and solidarity of the state community.

First, accumulation of human capital and great changes in human attitude were witnessed. By the rise of income level, the people could enjoy high level of education. The percentage of students advanced to college and more from senior high school increased from 27.1 percent in 1990 to 75.4 percent in 2010.[8] Furthermore, as the major portion of income being originated from international trade, the way of thinking of the people became internationalized. Out of per capita gross national income (GNI) increased from 15.4 percent in 1960 to 35.5 percent in 1970, 71.7 percent in 2000 and 99.8 percent in 2010.[9] The people are no longer the people engrossed only in daily subsistence depending on foreign aid under poverty, but are equipped with high education and knowledge, high life expectancy in better health, judging and behaving rationally and intelligently in line with international norms.

Second, industrial and technological power has grown enormously in Korea. In an industrial infertile land blossomed high-tech industries such as automobiles, shipbuilding, semiconductors, and information technology (IT) products. This enabled Korea to become one of the top manufacturing hubs in the world in those heavy, chemical and IT industries with advanced technology. The strong economic power enables Korea to have an equivalent voice in the international community.

Third, the state community becomes more harmonized and matured. In the process of rising income, middle class in social strata has grown to be the major in the social strata, which played a crucial role in the social stability of the national community. Political power had to face rising civil society, powerful business sectors and influential labor unions. Society became much more diversified with many countervailing powers to the political regime, through which the country could be led in a stable way.

The great changes in the three areas previously stated, triggered by economic development, were to give significant impacts on national security and the political system. National security is the primary focus of states on the external front, and then evolves into having profound impacts on the structures for establishing democratic institutions.

Regarding the former issue of national security, South Korea was viewed as a high-risk country until the 1970s in a state of armistice with North Korea. The latter was fully supported by Russia and China, and the former faced only the sea. Close fire cannot be extinguished with water from far away. Defensive power may consist of three powers: economic, diplomatic and military. The defensive power of Korea was greatly strengthened due to these three respects triggered by economic development. Due to the second consequence of economic development, the growth of industrial and technological power contributed greatly to the defense capacity of Korea.

Having a vibrant industrial base is in and of itself a source of national defense capability. Industrial technological development provides a solid basis to deploy similar technologies for military use, as has proven to be the case in the art of contemporary conventional warfare. Maintaining a strong national defense posture requires enormous financial investments. That explains why in many instances, economic strength always translates into military capacity, if required. The first and third consequences of economic development, which are upgraded human capital and solidarity of a state community combined with industrial and technological power, made great contributions to strengthening economic and military power for national security and sovereignty.

The superiority of South Korea over North Korea in economic power provided a strong barrier to military threats from its counterpart in military confrontation. North Korea has steadily fallen behind the South in terms of political and military capacity thanks to the South's obvious economic superiority. Up until the 1970s, North Korea maintained economic and technological superiority, a fate that has been materially redefined in recent years. Seoul has on several occasions had to offer humanitarian aid to Pyongyang. It is inconceivable that the ailing North Korean economy will be able to afford the cost of a military showdown in the foreseeable future, not when its ailing economy has reduced its population to virtual servitude. Facing an awkward dilemma, North Korean authorities started playing a very dangerous game for its survival through the development of nuclear weapons as a last resort.

The South Korean economy began to overwhelm North Korea's in every regard, from the light industry to heavy and chemical industries (HCI) such as steel, petrochemicals, machinery, shipbuilding, electronics, defense industries, energy (electricity, gas and atomic) and transportation (in terms of highways, harbors, or maritime travel). Living standards in North Korea began to decline rapidly in the 1970s. The average height of a man in the South has grown from 162.3 centimeters in 1940 to 174.2 centimeters in 2010, while in the North from 163.4 centimeters to 165.4 centimeters during the same period.[10] This means that the average height of the people in the North was higher by 1.1 centimeters in 1940, however, they became smaller by 8.8 centimeters in 2010. In life expectancy, the Northern residents are behind the South by 10 to 13 years.[11] All of this is the result of the sound economic competition that President Park launched in 1970. Taking cognizance of the primacy of the economic relations, China and Russia, which had strong ties with North Korea, came to form very close relations with South Korea due to their economic interests. The consequence of this economic and technological superiority is that Seoul has become the de facto hegemon on the debate of the terms of future unification of the two Koreas. Pyongyang's economic fragility has made its positions increasingly untenable, to say the least. The evidence of this comes from the badly needed aid Seoul offers to keep it afloat, as the regime fell on hard times in the 1990s.

Strengthened diplomatic power caused by economic development made great contributions to the national security of Korea. Take the case of the history of the geopolitical contestations on the Korean Peninsula as an example. The alliance of the socialist states including the Soviet Union, China and North Korea proved that beyond their overt ideological camaraderie, China and Russia have been consigned to accepting the reality of the economic imbalances on the Korean Peninsula toward the last decade of the last century. Putting aside the history of Cold War hostility, China established diplomatic relations with South Korea in 1992, which was preceded by Russia in 1991 following the implosion of the Soviet Union. Nothing best describes this diplomatic turnaround than the pursuit of sheer economic interests. Indeed, with the moribund North Korean economy, Pyongyang has little to no leverage whatsoever in its diplomatic relations. Without national security, economic development will burst like a bubble. It became of primary importance to create a solid base for the weak Korean national security.

Regarding the latter issue of democracy and political freedom, Korea has shown a rare example of success in both democratic institution and economic development. As was referred to in the preface, Singapore and China, which are good examples of economic resilience and high levels of income in East Asia, have been under the rule of one party. However, Korea showed uniqueness in that it attained a full democracy as well as economic development differently from its Asian peers.

First, Korea was given a democratic constitution and multi-party system at the birth of the republic by the influence of external forces. Having experienced trials and errors, Korea could prepare a foundation for economic development under the authoritative government. During the process, incessant struggles occurred between industrialization forces and democratic forces. Once economic desires were fulfilled, the pendulum moved toward the latter so that Korea could attain a full democracy and smooth turnover of political power among parties. Economic development accompanied the accumulation of human capital. During the period of late 2016 to early 2017, South Korea faced a constitutional crisis that arose after massive for and against rallies over the impeachment issue of President Park Geun-hye, which finally resulted in her impeachment and indictment. This was followed by the inauguration of the Moon administration after a presidential election in May 2017. About this, the *Washington Post* commented:

> South Korea still has many problems. But its people, buoyed up by an extraordinary wave of civic activism, are showing that they aren't prepared to accept the established way of doing things . . . South Korea just showed the world how to do democracy.[12]

The growth of a middle-income class strengthened social stability. Countervailing power correspondingly grew. Civil society extended its role in checking political power and government. Business sectors have grown to have their own voices. A well-educated and trained citizenry combined with the growth of countervailing powers in national community provided an environment in which a healthy civil society could be secured, and no longer was a non-democratic regime allowed. This naturally settled the lingering question about the place of democracy in the national development process. It paved the way for the country's capacity to join and take greater international responsibilities. By 1999, it had joined the OECD and then eventually the OECD/DAC (Development Assistance Committee) in 2009 – an unprecedented move in terms of a former aid recipient state graduating into a donor state. Then, it was followed by the hosting of the 2010 G20 Summit in Seoul.

South Korea's phenomenal and unorthodox ascent of the economic development ladder has ignited debate about conventions and its place in national development. It is of importance to contemporary developing countries as they wend their way through the mesh of economic development. Critics denounce the prioritization of economic growth over democratic norms in the loop of national development, as it happened in South Korea. Amid this hazy debate, one thing is certain. The South Korean case has proven that economic growth can precede and indeed, serve as the precursor to the growth of a democratic culture. For those locked in this whimsical cycle, this marks an important departure from the resonant narrative of national development.

Suffice it to cite an important caveat to this odyssey. Despite being established on the cradle of democratic aspirations, the brutality of poverty and the decrepit social conditions of the immediate post-war environment was of such nature that the tenets of liberal democracy in its truest sense couldn't have been followed through. Surely, a whole litany of factors account for this inevitable democratic detour. The post-war attempts at revival were also truncated by the military junta's intervention in 1961. Intermittent resistance to authoritarianism emerged again in the late 1980s in keeping with the yearning for open and participatory governance. Essentially, a genuine groundswell of democratic sentiments could never be entirely aborted.

It took Britain over 400 years after the passage of the Magna Carta in 1215 to fully evolve into a spirited democracy. As of 1754, voting rights were still the exclusive preserve of the nobility, then extended to cover only taxpaying males in 1884, and then to all women in 1928. Similarly, France, for all its rich democratic traditions going back to the February Revolution of 1848, could only grant voting rights to women in 1946. It took the 1965 Civil Rights Act to extend voting rights to black Americans in the United States. However, universal adult suffrage was at the very beginning of South Korea's democratic experiment in 1948, an obvious signpost against making universal generalizations.

For all the talk of the virtues of democratic governance, one would wonder why there are so few exemplary models of achieving economic development and democratization at the same time. The Korean development experience may give some implications to the issue. It was the case that South Korea prioritized in resource allocation, given the developmental exigencies it had to contend with. Resources had to be selectively and consistently focused on limited strategic sectors of the economy to turn its fortunes around. Such a policy measure runs counter to democratic tenets in the sense that under a democratic dispensation it behooves the government to evenly allocate resources to all state sectors. Electoral cycles further reduce government administration to a revolving door of administrations with diverse policy priorities. The cycles also make governments susceptible to short-term political calculations as opposed to strategic long-term planning.

Often painful and tough policies tend to be sacrificed on the altar of political expediency, and history shows that development becomes the unfortunate casualty of such short-sightedness. A look at South Korea's experience shows that its development is owed to this singular truth of political stability. Indeed, almost every facet of the development path was criticized by diverse political and social groups. In fact, the government came in for a serious tongue-lashing for its policy of concentrating resources in specific sectors, which critics charged amounted to a gross misallocation of resources. So were the widespread protests that greeted the process of normalizing diplomatic relations with Japan. The labor export period was also called an era of state-sponsored exploitation. So, vigorous was the opposition mounted against the construction of the Kyungbu Highway that opposition leaders threatened self-immolation in protest, as discussed in Chapter 5. The drive for industrialization provoked criticism that farmers were being neglected, and establishment of industrial clusters according to locational conditions was criticized as regional discrimination.

The plan to procure a loan facility to finance the construction of a steel mill was greeted with the same chorus of scorn. Taking aim at President Park personally, critics cast the plan in the same light as the typical obsession of dictators of underdeveloped countries. For all its worth, it was said of President Park as being in the second stage of the typical grandiose vanity projects dictators liked: first construct a highway; then construct a steel mill and crown it with giant statues of themselves. Then there was an unsuccessful assassination attempt on President Park at the behest of the apprehensive regime in Pyongyang. Progress on the economic front left Pyongyang panicking that it could be undercut by Seoul in the quest for claiming the highest pitch of the unification narrative. It certainly begs the question whether these achievements could have been achieved on a purely liberal democratic platform or mandate. From the Korean experience, it can be surmised that development is not just a thorny path, but one that is fraught with risks of drifting away from desired objectives. Could these tasks and challenges be overcome by consent through democratic procedure? Had the government not been an authoritarian one, many of the successes outlined earlier would have been simply inconceivable.

Traveling this path would have required meeting three fundamental points: (1) making the right decision, (2) the timeliness of the decision and (3) persistence in traveling. Regarding making the right decision, carrying out full consultation with all stakeholders or the public does not guarantee that the right decision will be made. By their nature, people usually pursue convenience and individual safety rather than hardship and public interest, as is usually observed in a sinking boat.

As the people in a sinking boat throng to the deck to save their own lives, which accelerates the sinking of the boat, so does desperation drive the actions of people living in poverty. Under the circumstances, it will be difficult to make the right choice to pursue the path for development, which often requires delayed gratification. The Korean experiences tell us that most innovative policy decisions were made not through democratic consultation procedures in Parliament but through authoritative decision-making by leaders and leading groups for development.

As to the second issue of timeliness, broad-based consultations are often very time-consuming. The story of South Korea for 12 years before the 1961 military coup witnessed that democratic procedure in a poverty state hindered timely decision-making, as was discussed in Section 1.3. The same argument may be made regarding the third issue of persistency or policy consistency.

It is customary for newly elected governments to rip up their predecessor's programs or policies only to engage in a needless cycle of reinventing the wheel, as was argued in Section 2.2. There is a similar trend in the current five-year single term cycle mandated by the current Constitution of Korea. What this has demonstrated is the needless recycling of the same policies under different slogans. For instance, the Kim Dae-jung administration (1998–2002) was voted into office sloganizing the "Venture startup" mantra as the best growth strategy to revive the country's economy after the devastation of the Asian financial crisis. Then came Roh Moo-hyun (2003–2007), who was touting his own brand of political campaign rhetoric dubbed "Strategy for financial hub in North-East Asia." Like his predecessor, nothing became of it by the time his tenure elapsed. You would think that would trigger a change of heart, but again, the conservative-leaning Lee Myung-bak (2008–2012) also sloganized his way to the presidency brandishing a "Green growth strategy" aimed at making the country's development premised on innovative sustainable premises. Then came President Park Geun-hye (2013–2017), who despite the premature end of her tenure was also trying to use a policy called "Creative economy" to differentiate her economic agenda from her predecessors. The progressive-leaning Moon Jae-in (2017–2022) succeeded Park and declared "Cleaning-up deep-rooted evils" and an "Income-driven growth strategy" – a sharp policy switch from the previous president. Similarly, up and down many developing countries, an environment is created in which even the most promising of policies gets tossed out of the window before its maturation and implementation.

In a democratic dispensation, there is also the risk of misplacing development priorities in ways that are often dictated by short-term political expediencies as opposed to real, long-term commitments to break the cycle of poverty. This should not be misconstrued for a universal endorsement of authoritarianism as the panacea to economic development. Dictators typically don't have the capacity to work toward achieving economic development and guaranteeing poverty reduction. They also may not have all the technical know-how to achieve this goal. There exists no guarantee for dictators to devote themselves to poverty reduction and welfare of the people with good will, and there is no countervailing power to contain the dictator to work for the people under a widespread poverty state. Korea's path to development through the mobilization of resources for strategic development points, and thus could achieve economic development, to steer toward national security, became a good model for international development. It seems difficult for economic development and national security with full democracy to proceed together smoothly, in the sense that economic development is a thorny path demanding hardships, resolutions and sacrifices of today for tomorrow, which may not be easily materialized by the voluntary of hungry leaders and people. The Korean experience shows one example that on the bases of economic development, national security and democracy could be consolidated. For a butterfly to fly as a butterfly, it should undergo the pain of breaking out of its chrysalis. Only the people who stand up to the pain of being reborn may enjoy sustainable and equitable growth in the long run.

Notes

1 Daron Acemoglu and James A. Robinson, *Why Nations Fail* (New York: Crown Business, 2012), 83–84.
2 Hernando de Soto, *The Mystery of Capital* (New York: Basic Books, 2000), 2.
3 Modern economic growth may be defined as a long-term rise in capacity to supply increasingly diverse economic goods to the population, this growing capacity based on advancing technology and the institutional and ideological adjustment that it demands, is based on Simon Kuznets's 1971 lecture to the memory of Alfred Nobel.
4 Shekhar Aiyar, Romain Duval, Damien Puy, Yiqun Wu and Longmei Zhang, *Growth Slowdown and the Middle-Income Trap*, IMF Working Paper, March 2013, 3.
5 O Won-chol, *The Korea Story: President Park Jung-hee's Leadership and the Korean Industrial Revolution* (Seoul, Korea: Wisdom Tree, 2009), 606–609. Itokawa Hideo was at the forefront of the development of rocketry in Japan and one of the pioneers of the new industrial field known as the human organization engineering.
6 Shekhar et al., *Growth Slowdown and the Middle-Income Trap*, 4.
7 Focusing on the industrial era, this hypothesis seems not to take full account of the coming of the IT era.
8 *Statistics Korea*, http://kosis.kr/index/index.jsp
9 *Ibid.*
10 Kim Myeong-seong, "70nyeon bundani mandeun ttansesang. . . 'oemo munhwa useumkodeu deung modeun ge dallajeo" [Another World Created by the Territorial Division of 70 Years], *Chosun Ilbo*, July 3, 2015, accessed August 10, 2017, http://news.chosun.com/site/data/html_dir/2015/07/03/2015070300136.html
11 *Ibid.*
12 Ishaan Tharoor, "South Korea Just Showed the World How to Do Democracy," *Washington Post*, May 10, 2017, accessed August 10, 2017, www.washingtonpost.com/news/worldviews/wp/2017/05/10/south-korea-just-showed-the-world-how-to-do-democracy/

Epilogue
Path to development under globalization

There is no precedence to the transformation of South Korea's modern history from a desolate wasteland to a modern industrial state. Its economy grew at a breathtaking speed and thus catapulted it from the fragile state of poverty in the post-war years to an upper-income country by the turn of the century, as was discussed in Chapter 1. The Korean case shows that several fundamental hypotheses in development economics that were raised in the preface could be overcome: Korea could successfully build its own institutions leading to democracy and market economy, as was discussed in Chapters 2 and 11; build heavy and chemical industries (HCI) leading to a full industrialization in spite of the limited domestic market, as was examined from Chapters 4–7; and realize inclusive growth to a certain extent despite its unbalanced growth strategy in the beginning stages. In the process, it graduated from being an aid-recipient country in 1995, and in 2010 became a member of the elite OECD DAC (Organisation for Economic Co-operation and Development/Development Assistance Committee). This phenomenal socioeconomic transformation also rubbed off its nascent fragility of the state. As was discussed in Chapter 11, these gains ushered in an era of social stability, it gained military superiority over North Korea, the socialization of human rights has become institutionalized and the conscious commitment to liberal democratic norms has been firmly consolidated. If for nothing else, these trends distinguish South Korea from the likes of Singapore, China and a good number of the Asian economic high-flyers discussed in the preface of this book.

We now talk of the country as a model for countries in the doldrums of poverty and struggling to find their feet in the sticky path of economic development. In this light, the obvious question that begs answering is the extent to which Korea's experience has implications for contemporary developing countries. It is especially so, given the specific contexts and complexities that have shaped the outcomes of her experimental quest in wrestling down poverty. There is no denying the critical dimension of exclusivity in this process that may not necessarily be universally applicable; yet there is something to be said about some of the universal principles of development that has a place for every determined contender for development.

To examine usefulness of the Korean development experience to currently developing economies, it requires analyzing similarities and dissimilarities of initial conditions of development, and environment of the times between the two cases. About the former of initial conditions for development, we found that Korea's post-war conditions of extreme poverty and underdevelopment have striking parallels with many of today's developing countries in Section 1.2. We particularly took aim at people's mind-set, attitude toward work, skill set, and the prevailing inimical business environment. However, we also argued in the same section that Korea had some positive endowments before launching modern economic development that are not found in every developing economy today.

The first was land reform policies initiated in the early post-war years. Peasants were given a fair shot at achieving economic sustenance through the land reform program. The fact that most farmers became landowners was really encouraging farmers in their efforts for overcoming their poverty. Second, Korea's modern history is an odyssey of progressive social mobility under conditions where people were predisposed to pulling themselves up by their own bootstraps. The traditional institutional hierarchical vested interests and inherited privileges that preceded this era were literally wiped out through these turbulent historical episodes of colonial exploitation, partisan of the land and followed great migration and war, in particular collapse of landlord class through land reform. The post-colonial history was thus that of a socioeconomic ground zero where all had to start from the same point of nothingness and crawl their way out of the doldrums. An externally imposed and unbridled egalitarian structure incentivized thrift and entrepreneurship across the board. It gives credence to the assertion that economic development can be conceived as an incremental process of improvisation and experimentation. Then the third point is the impact of the geopolitical undercurrents. South Korea was lucky in that it had Japan in its neighborhood, which had a successful experience of industrialization by benchmarking the West's development experience to incorporate into its indigenous program. Japan served as a good model.

Notwithstanding the importance of the factors outlined earlier in facilitating economic development, it will be rather too simplistic to overstate their place in the grand scheme of the development sojourn.

First, let me return to the land redistribution example to help explain this point further. It is worth acknowledging that while Korea was hardly unique among nations to implement land reform, the outcome of this policy had both positive and negative impacts. Small-scale land ownership through land reform may come with inherent risks of undermining capital accumulation and agricultural productivity if not properly managed. I can think of how Africa's publicly owned 202 million hectares of uncultivated land can be a source of boosting development. Public land in many African jurisdictions tends to be administered under a regime of public laws that essentially are set up to ensure that such lands are primarily allocated mostly for public use. Yet the underbelly of these regulatory regimes is that most of them are still relics of the colonial land administration systems. This is why thus far, the history of the administration of public lands in Africa tells a tale of how the promise of proper governance has not been fully leveraged to unleash the development potential inherent in land assets. Only

10 percent of the 202 million hectares of land in the rural areas have been properly registered, meaning nearly 90 percent remains informally administered and thus poorly governed.[1]

On the flip side, a number of countries were carried away by the Marxist-inspired egalitarian idealism in carrying out their land reforms. Just like nearly all aspects of Marxist extremism, the frenzy of such reforms often was so ideologically tainted that it was entirely devoid of pragmatism. In fairness, we can also see recent examples of unsuccessful land reform programs in Zimbabwe and South Africa. President Robert Mugabe's ZANU PF-led land appropriation policy, widely seen as recompense to the black majority for centuries of white-settler colonial injustices, is instructive in this case. For all its high-mindedness, Zimbabwe's land reform had deep-seated jingoistic motives as its chief driving force. Once dubbed the breadbasket of Africa because the land appropriation took off like a whirlwind, Zimbabwe's agricultural production capacity has severely plummeted, and the country now depends on international food aid to sustain nearly 25 percent of its population. Total revenue from agricultural production fell by $12 billion in the first decade of the implementation of the policy.[2] With the resignation of Robert Mugabe from the presidency, the task of restoration of agricultural production will be inherited by the incoming regime.

A similar situation is being played out in South Africa, albeit at a relatively slower pace than Zimbabwe. Unlike the radical appropriation in Zimbabwe, the African National Congress (ANC) has been pursuing its land reform programs with a degree of caution or pragmatism. The government has had to reckon with the fact that nearly 90 percent of all the land redistributed to black farmers is unproductive and many are woefully failing. Again, capacity and institutional factors cannot be entirely ruled out for this outcome. While social justice in its putative sense as inscribed in the land reform agenda is a worthy cause, it must always be tempered with a reasonable dose of pragmatism. In truth, the abhorrent relics of racial subordination manifested in the disproportionate land ownership regimes in the former settler colonies are simply indefensible. But we must also concede that it should by no means ever be deployed as a means for carrying populist political favors, as did Robert Mugabe in blatant oblivion to the greater economic good to the nation.

Second, in relation to dismantling vested interest classes, however, such conditions were prepared also in other countries through socialist revolution and political upheaval, the dissolve of rented group was not linked to successful economic development. Further, the social disintegration might involve cost of starting from scratch as well.

Third, there was the geopolitical advantage that Korea benefited from Japan in her industrial development efforts. However, Korea may not be the only country that had an example to benchmark. Many countries may have examples to follow in their own rights, and due to communications and transportation revolution, the convenience of benchmarking others and securing knowledge and information were enhanced greatly.

Then, given that the situational conditions of Korea in the past are not prereq-uisite or sufficient conditions for economic development unique to Korea, it can be said that currently developing countries may attain economic development if political leadership and relevant development policies be secured. We thus see from the foregoing that there needs to be a good mix of effective political and economic judgment in shaping development-oriented public policies as it relates to contemporary developing countries.

However, as to the latter of environment of the times, there is a material differ-ence in the conditions of the mid-twentieth century and the economic dynamism of the twenty-first century, if we have to objectively critique the history of South Korea's economic growth. For example, the shape of the global economic order of the 1960s and 1970s is palpably different from the one at work today. Good-ness knows, at this rate of innovation, there is no telling what the global economy will look like two decades from now. The 1960s was a time of rapid investment inflows from the Global North to the Global South. Free trade was the order of the day, but if you follow the political discourse of the day, you will soon come to understand why free trade has become a cursed word. Countries could even get away with a limited degree of protectionism, but not anymore, with the force of globalization lurking around.

Innovation in information technology, the bedrock of globalization, has revo-lutionized the world of work as we know it. Primitive societies conceived of work as the drudgery of rudimentary implements for subsistence. Then the advent of the Industrial Revolution unleashed an unlimited scope of productivity thanks to mass generation of electric energy. Fast-forward to the IT revolution, which brings a whole new world of work as we now should scratch our heads about things like artificial intelligence (AI). As unsettling as that may be, what was to be within the realm of science fiction is dawning on humankind. Think about the buzz created by Google's AI AlphaGo, which, having beaten top human go players, retired in May 2017 because it can no longer find a contender. IBM's AI Watson had earlier won the American *Jeopardy* quiz show, beating Ken Jennings, the show's all-time champion. Now the consensus is that AI has achieved a break-through in gaining some degree of mastery of the traditional human cognitive competencies.

The changes in the mode of work and communication have resulted in another revolution in the manufacturing and economic life of the human beings. The transformations have given rise to fundamental reforms in manufacturing, con-sumption modes and markets. The manufacturing revolution is being played out in how the role of labor is greatly diminished, and marginal cost approaches zero. Consequently, the supply capacity is greatly enhanced. It has impact in consumption patterns with people moving from goods to services and from stuff to fluff.[3] For instance, much of the value of a smartphone is derived from the original design and engineering of the product rather than from its hardware components. Markets are now in a global scope rather than a local one. Thus, the mega-competition in the whole world in the open market system is rugged on many levels.

This transformative upheaval has significant impacts in both developed and developing countries. On every level, competition becomes asymmetric, given that the developed countries come into it with an oversized advantage in terms of skills and general competitiveness. Thereby, it constricts the opportunities and space for the developing world's capacity to compete on anything close to equal terms. Despite these seemingly clear advantages, even developed countries should still contend with two problems. First and foremost, the transformation in the manufacturing sector has caused a significant decrease in the demand for employment. Futurologists are predicting the coming of a 20–80 society, in which only 20 percent of the population has access to jobs and the remaining 80 percent have little room for maneuvering.[4] The second problem is a widening of the income gap through a system that allows for the concentration of wealth in the hands of a minority. It is a trend that by all indications undercuts inclusive growth and most certainly is antithetic to sustainable development. Even thus said, the impact of this process will be far more profound in developing countries.

The traditional path of economic development for most poor countries has always been to leverage their comparative advantage in low wages and natural resource endowments. Many are yet to generate the capacity to attract foreign technology and capital to complement their low-wage labor and, in most cases, are still behind the curve in terms of developing a solid industrial base. The process is made further complex by the interlocking and unbridled competitive forces of globalization.

It used to be the case that labor played a central role in dictating the forms of North–South cooperation, particularly as Northern transnational corporations were keen on taking advantage of cheap labor in the Global South. With the advent of industrial-level automation, the incentive of cheap labor has been losing its luster. It is being replaced by an increasing emphasis on a North–North centered cooperation. Consequently, the old case for cheap labor as an incentive for foreign direct investment inflows into the Global South is becoming increasingly tenuous. In times past, it made sense to leverage this aspect, but cheap labor in its crude form without any corresponding high value skills and technological base do not offer irresistible attractiveness to multinational corporations (MNCs) and in any case, most foreign investors believe it is not worth their while. Without properly addressing these lingering questions, there is usually a rush to roll the carpet for foreign labor-intensive industries to take advantage of the cheap labor through unsustainable foreign direct investment (FDI) arrangements. In no time, the utility of this move comes in for serious questioning, with the onset of automation and industrial scale automation only to perpetuate the existing problem of employment and poverty reduction.

Moreover, the importance of products that were produced in the Global South has decreased due to an increased capacity of supply and to changes in consumption mode in favor of fluff rather than stuff, as was previously mentioned. Thus, local firms in developing countries have very limited access to international markets. Besides, preferences of local consumers have in many instances been crafted to favor the consumption of foreign products at the expense of locally produced ones. In other words, domestic markets have literally been saturated with foreign brands and thereby squeezed out local enterprises. It is not unusual to find assorted catalogues of foreign-brand products in some of the remotest parts of Africa. A situation of this sort makes it nearly impossible to implement import-barrier policies aimed at protecting their local markets. It also raises critical questions about the viability of providing subsidies to boost their infant industries. Granted that were even possible, it ultimately boils down to whether any of such industries can competitively enter the international market in the long run.

Globalization has ushered in a winner-takes-all dispensation where only globally competitive products stay on the market. And in most cases, it becomes near impossible for enterprises born in developing countries to break the stranglehold of the most competitive products on the market. It speaks to a situation in which developing countries become consigned to looking from outside despite their best efforts to join the fray. The real concern is how to go beyond the dependence on resource exports to developing globally competitive products that can propel them into the heart of international commerce.

Natural resource endowments do not offer a comprehensive growth solution. The finite nature of natural resources alongside price fluctuations makes them an unreliable source of long-term growth. Reliance on commodity exports stifles growth in other important sectors of the economy, inasmuch as the concept of the Dutch disease is becoming a cliché. Interests are growing toward diversification in some resource-endowed economies. That means creating an environment to foster the growth of local enterprises with an eye for making them competitive in the long term. Without a determination for long-term international competitiveness, many local enterprises will be destined for stillbirth.

An alternative source of growth to support industrial development can come from leveraging cheap labor and commodity export may be the domestic market. The case of China is the best example. For China, its huge market of 1.3 billion, which is very attractive for MNCs and international investors, is a strong driver of economic growth. Chinese economic policy has for many years been premised on exchanging its market of 1.3 billion with foreign advanced technology. For instance, the Chinese government's main condition for foreign corporations seeking access to the Chinese market is a transfer of such technologies as express railroads and desalination technology. Given the scale and potential rewards of accessing that market, corporations with the requisite technology have often proved willing to cut such deals. China, thus, can combine its cheap labor with access to advanced technology to enter the international market on a relatively stronger footing against the original producers of the technology. As enticing as this approach may be, it is fair to say it best fits the case of China and its huge population and is less promising for countries lacking China's sort of advantages of a huge domestic market endowment and hybrid state-led capitalism.

In this regard, developing countries face real difficulties in pursuing economic development under the environment of globalization. As if to make an already bad situation worse, developing countries are further constrained by a host of domestic factors that are adversarial to industrial growth. For industries to take root, four prerequisites need to be met: financial accessibility, market availability, efficient public service and strong institutions.

First, with respect to financial accessibility, the flow of money in the economy is similar to the flow of blood in the human body to guarantee survival. Top on the list of constraints is the limited access to financial resources to invest in start-ups or expand existing operations, mostly by domestic financial institutions. High interest rates bog down the few funding outlets. In the few instances where foreign financial institutions are operating, they usually tend to be more obsessed with their bottom lines and can scarcely come through with any meaningful contribution for a country's industrial development. Foreign financial institutions might be in favor of low-risk short-term businesses rather than high-risk long-term businesses. It was for this reason that when confronted with this challenge, the government of Korea heavily intervened in the financial sector to align it with its national development priorities. Specialized banks to finance SMEs and provide long-term development financing and agriculture were also set up for this explicit purpose.

Second, when it comes to the market situation, any corporations born under such an environment is thrust into this asymmetric competition against the established global behemoths of the industries they operate in. That will mean dealing with a flood of foreign-produced cheap goods from places as far afield as China, Mexico and Bangladesh. Lax enforcement of excise policies creates incentives for smuggling and tax evasion in the worst-case scenario. Because of the saturation of the markets by foreign products in developing countries, mentioned earlier, even the least of products such as a matchbox are not locally produced but imported. Under such pervasive conditions of dependence, it is inconceivable to see how a firm is expected to do well. Let us remember that there is an intricate connection between the growth of local industries and poverty reduction in the long run. One is tempted to ask the obvious question of what then is the best way out of the trap of poverty by developing countries? Is it possible that without any attempt at intervening, the current conditions will be self-corrected over time? Is there any role for external financial assistance through aid? As was emphasized, the treatment of a chronic disease, overcoming poverty requires a determined and consistent commitment.

Third, limited fiscal capacity limits public services in the government's traditional turf. In most developing countries, tax revenues generally come from a narrow tax base often against a huge demand for public expenditure. Without prudence, the huge expenditure leads to a slippery road of deficits. To make up for the deficits, or in some cases to meet the high expenditure, governments arbitrarily increase taxes in ways that undermine the incentives to invest. Developing countries tend to levy very high taxes on their narrow tax pool in an environment where value added tax (VAT) and income taxes are already too high. There is therefore little maneuver room for government to provide financing for industrial development.

Fourth, there is also a conspicuous weakness in the institutional capacity to execute effective poverty-reduction programs. In this respect, many post-war new republics had experienced many trials and errors. Based on those institutions, leaders are chosen, and development policies are formed and carried out by them. Since their foundation, many developing countries fell prey to the lure of socialism at the early stages of their development and, in the process, created systems that stifled industriousness, dynamism and economic vibrancy. While the strength of capitalism has proven to be superior to the socialist milieu of economic grayness, there has also been an inclination to perpetuate an overly simplistic narrative of the market-economy model. So often, we are made to believe in the omnipotence of market principles without due regard for the idiosyncrasies of each country, not least for developing countries.

With the failure of the socialist experiment, there is currently hardly any credible competitor to economic liberalism. While on the surface, it appears to be true, it must be tinkered with the fact that it does not always hold true for all situations all the time. The market principles that served today's industrial powerhouses do not fit the specific contexts of many of today's developing countries. Francis Fukuyama contends that supply-and-demand conditions of institutional building are critical to its success. He points to bottlenecks that can easily stymie some of the rather benign or otherwise well-intentioned attempts at engaging in a wholesale transplanting of Western institutions to developing countries, often oblivious of the differences in social and cultural contexts involved. It is what he rightly describes as the supply side of the institutional process. Internal demand for the establishment of such institutions should be at the heart of such initiatives, rather than the other way around.

The problem is that the conditions of developing countries are too immature to accommodate the liberal model. For institutional building, we need to consider two factors of the supply side and demand side. As to the former of the supply side, we question what institutions are critical for economic development and how they ought to be designed. In some institutions, transferability is recommended while in some others simply inappropriate.[5] Regarding the demand side, institutional development and institutional reform will not take place without demand. Even if society as a whole is better off with good institutions, every new institutional arrangement produces winners and losers, and the latter can rely on to protect their relative positions. In other cases, society may not understand relative efficiency or inefficiency of alternative institutions.[6] Institutional reform occurs when a society has generated strong domestic demand for institutions and then creates them wholesale or import them from the outside, or adapted foreign models to local conditions as was witnessed in Japan and Turkey in the nineteenth century, or South Korea and Taiwan in the 1960s.[7]

In this respect, there is a very weak case for external agents to create demand for institutions and the wisdom to transfer, as Fukuyama states:

> The international community is not simply limited to the amount of capacity it can build; it is complicit in the destruction of institutional capacity in many developing countries. . . . Since independence, the ability of African governments to design and implement policies has deteriorated. In the words

of the World Bank's African governors, "Almost every African country has witnessed a systematic retrogression in capacity in the last thirty years; the majority had better capacity at independence than they now possess." This deterioration in capacity has happened precisely during a period of accelerating external aid flows to the point where more than 10 percent of the GDP of the entire region comes from foreign assistance in various forms.[8]

He further elaborated his argument:

> The United States has intervened and/or acted as an occupation authority in many other countries, including Cuba, the Philippines, Haiti, the Dominican Republic, Mexico, Panama, Nicaragua, South Korea and South Vietnam. In each of these countries it pursued what amounted to nation-building activities – holding elections, trying to stamp out warlords and corruption and promoting economic development. South Korea was the only country to achieve long-term economic growth, which came about more through the Koreans' own efforts than those of the United States. Lasting institutions were few and far between.[9]

A corollary to the institutional incapacity is linked to the leadership question, as it pertains to being able to lay the foundational blocks for formidable development. Effective leadership should invoke a visionary spirit that can provide the momentum toward this end. Evidence of this weak trend is found in the wobbly start and transient leadership in many developing economies, culminating in what is dubbed the lost decades of the 1970s going into the 1980s into most parts of the mid-1990s as was witnessed in Latin American. There was a generation of leaders who pandered to populist whims and shied away from taking the necessary sacrificial long-term investment decisions that could have bolstered their economic fortunes. Understandably, such long-term decisions can hardly be taken under the all too common cyclical and volatile electoral systems that are currently in vogue. On the flip side, absolutist authoritarian regimes are also quite prone to go for the low-hanging fruit if that advances the leadership of the day's personal vanities. If we consider all these handicaps of developing economies, global economic competition is a game of unequal players. In this regard, Ha-Joon Chang argues that it is only fair that we "tilt the playing field" in favor of the weaker countries.[10]

Considering the foregoing situation, there has been an increasing consensus among economists that the industrialization-based model of development is on its way out.[11] Emerging economies are being cautioned against trying to emulate China's success by arguing that current technological transformations are materially changing the path to development. China, it is argued, is among the last wave of economies to successfully ride the tide of industrialization to achieve middle-income status. Much of the emerging world is facing a problem that Dani Rodrik calls "premature de-industrialization."[12] China was lucky to avoid the de-industrialization environment with its unique hybrid socialist political system and market economy and huge domestic market. Its authoritarian political system allowed it to maintain a rigid grip on the economic levers during economic growth.

However, no matter how harsh and thorny the path to development, the resolve to push the envelope ought to be sustained. It is a must for any countries to be able to provide the people with sufficient human needs and enlarged freedom. Korea has shown the example that in its quest for progress it realized not only economic development but also national security and the dividends of democracy. The challenge is then how to reach the goal under globalization. It requires identification of the right path toward it, and then taking the path in practice, not going astray.

Regarding the right path to take, in the circumstance that the world is merged to one market, it seems almost impossible at a first glance for poverty countries with no industrial base to develop industry and foster enterprises for getting out of the poverty. If progress is underway of deindustrialization at a stage that even industrialization was not taken place yet, it will be no ordinary problem. However hard environment globalization creates, as a developing country we cannot reverse it. Such being the case, we have to find a way for survival adapting ourselves to the rule of games of globalization.

The starting point in my view is to secure access to the global value chain. If we cannot be producers of final goods and services in the globalized market, then there should be a way for us to plug into the share of the value chain that generates them. For instance, IT companies in Silicon Valley have been able to nurture a huge IT value chain in the global market. Business imperatives drew Silicon Valley firms to come up with ways of providing around-the-clock services to their global clientele in a way that cancels out the time differences across the different regions of the world. India was found to be an ideal destination to outsource services that could not be carried out at headquarters. The corresponding boom in the call center services in India is a testament to its distinct advantage in English proficiency and convenient time differences to plug into a section of the global value chain. By tapping into the global value chain this way, Indian firms were given a critical platform upon which its domestic IT companies entered the global market. This then leads to my conviction that developing countries have what it takes to discover a niche in the global market that can suitably reflect their unique endowments. It doesn't necessarily have to be grand, just a way of getting a foot in the door.

The second point to discovering the way is to concede that it will be simply unrealistic to pursue global competitiveness on a national scale. I say so taking into consideration that at this stage of weak development capacity it will rather be foolhardy to expect realistic gains from competing with the existing captains of global industry. The wisdom here lies in concentrating national capacity on a specific region or field in a way that allows for accumulation of the latent capacity to project global competitiveness down the road. Creating one success story could potentially provide a rippling effect on other sectors of the economy, thus leading to long-term development.

Third, it is imperative to have a system in place that can attract, retain and train highly skilled personnel. That requires having the most ideal conditions for recruitment of specialists in the respective expertise to be able to lead the charge. In other words, putting together a comprehensive human resource program that can facilitate the creation of this pool of highly skilled personnel will go very far.

Regarding the latter issue of how to reach the goal in safety not going astray on its way, we need to embrace the principle of economic development. Economic development requires a commitment to sacrificing today for tomorrow, or a sense of delayed gratification. That means sacrificing consumption for savings and frugality for diligence. Admittedly, sacrificing consumption in an atmosphere of extreme poverty is a hard sell. For this reason, it is easy for any countries on their path to economic development to go astray. A visionary leadership that can marshal the collective will of the people to travel down a path will ultimately serve the best interest of the collective.

First of all, for effective leadership, the need to also constitute a core development-oriented cadre of leadership cannot be overemphasized at the early phase of national economic development. This core should be the fulcrum that leads the charge of visionary programs and able to resist needless political meddling in its quest to efficiently carryout its mandate. Surely, leadership can be well exercised with the support of an efficient bureaucratic system. Indeed, the indispensable role of leadership is a fact borne out by the recent trend of world economic history. Many of the successful economies of our day benefited immensely from effective leadership and those lagging have had to pay the price for inept leadership.[13]

In saying this, there is the need to guard against pandering to cheap populist critics seeking to maliciously exploit political pluralism to achieve self-serving ends. It is important that legitimate opposition should never be morphed into such retrogressive tendencies. When confronted with such uncouth opposition, President Park could pass that test through a consistent strategy premised on entrusting the policy management and implementation into the hands of the executive and state bureaucracy. The citizenry will be more inclined to make important sacrifices toward overcoming poverty and back a government if they are given enough proof of the efficiency of the state's management acumen.

You will recall that the early development phase of South Korea was characterized by severe gridlock at the behest of rabble-rousing parochial politicians. The government was denounced for, among other things, exploiting the country's young female labor force, regional discrimination and being overly dependent on foreign capital. Standing its ground, the government pressed on with its quest to develop the country's industrial base to become globally competitive. From Korea's experience, 80 percent of the citizenry will be inclined to follow the lead of just 10 percent of a leadership whose integrity is beyond reproach. Then, there will be no room for the remaining 10 percent who are rabble-rousers.[14] Development policies must be practical and realistic. Just as it is inconceivable to wage a war without a comprehensive battle plan, so it is with trying to pursue poverty reduction without meeting the requirements of practicality. This requires being able to analyze the prevailing conditions and changes in the environment to inform the required policy intervention measures. Not having such a plan in place will be like embarking on a voyage without a compass to guide the voyage.

Second, even if the best of plans is put together, it will still count for nothing if there is no corresponding and effective implementation. Effective implementation remains one of the major challenges in developing countries. The reasons they are not making significant progress in development is that in many cases they do not lack decent development plans, but that those plans are not implemented.[15] The Economic Planning Board (EPB) of Korea was charged with the explicit responsibility of overseeing this aspect of development policies. The minister of the agency, who doubled as the deputy prime minister, was the main go-to when it came to streamlining, leading and coordinating various development policies related to macro-economic management, industrial development, human resource development (HRD), development of science and technology, fiscal management and the banking industry. Most critical policy decisions were coordinated between the presidency, his chief economic advisor and the deputy prime minister. Effective policy implementation also requires steadfast coordination and collaboration between the different ministries within the national development policy framework. It goes to underscore the importance of clearly defining authority and responsibility within the bureaucracy toward this end.

Third, strategic allocation of resources is yet another critical dimension of the policy mix. Mobilization of resources requires an extensive level of commitment. The treatment of poverty cannot be effective without understanding its diverse manifestation. Limited financial resources and administrative capacity make it even more imperative to be frugal and prudent in state spending. Ideally, it is far more prudent to defer immediate consumption in favor of investment in long term programs, a lesson that Korea learned earlier in its growth.

Finally, the last stage ought to be aimed at rebalancing development structures. Strategic development can result in unintended imbalances in the economic growth trajectory and, if left unaddressed, can trigger long-term social instability and ultimately undermine sustainable development. It becomes imperative to shift gears to incorporate inclusive growth in ways that narrow the inter-sectoral development gap that may arise because of the strategic development policies.

If these wisdoms are put into practice with consistency, developing economies sometimes will be able to transform their societies. In a marathon, the order of the athletes regularly changes along the full course of the race. This possibility comes from a few factors.

The first factor is particularly true in the era of rapid technological innovation. The economies with sunk costs with past technology will not be flexible in making transformations for adopting new technology. No one ever expected to hear Nokia's CEO's parting words: "we didn't do anything wrong, but somehow, we lost," as he announced the takeover of his company by Microsoft. Once the dominant force in the global cell phone market, Nokia never fully braced for the resolve, speed and power of its rivals; consequently, as history has painfully demonstrated to the Finnish corporation, it failed to learn and evolve to respond to the dynamism of the global economy and with that its very own existence. As the once-omnipresent Nokia cell phone has now been taken over and renamed Microsoft Mobile, it is hard to envisage what the future holds.

The second factor is the aging of the population. As economic development proceeds, fertility rates will fall and eventually lead to an aging population with enhanced health care services. Economic vitality largely depends upon the age of the population.

The third factor is the change in human value and attitude. Human value and attitude regarding the value of money and attitude toward work are subject to change in the course of rise in income and standards of living. As earnings and standards of living rise, people are less motivated to work for money and material satisfaction. Thomas L. Friedman argues that the world is flat, and flatteners are proliferations of computers, emergence of the internet and Web browsers, workflow revolutions, and geopolitical flatteners symbolized by the collapse of Communism.[16] I think that for the world to be flat, it requires additional factors of will and efforts for development by the people of developing economies.

Notes

1 Makhtar Diop, "Securing Africa's Land for Shared Prosperity," World Bank, July 22, 2013, accessed August 10, 2017, www.worldbank.org/en/news/opinion/2013/07/22/securing-africa-s-land-for-shared-prosperity
2 Kevin Sieff, "Zimbabwe's White Farmers Find Their Services in Demand Again," *Guardian Weekly*, September 25, 2015, accessed August 10, 2017, www.theguardian.com/world/2015/sep/25/zimbabwe-land-reforms-mugabe-white-farmers
3 Special Report, "The Third Great Wave," *The Economist*, October 4, 2014, p. 11.
4 This is called the Pareto Principle, and is applied to many social such as wealth distribution, value creation and employment.
5 Francis Fukuyama, *State-Building* (New York: Cornell University Press, 2004), 21–23, 31–32.
6 *Ibid.*, 32–33.
7 *Ibid.*, 35.
8 *Ibid.*, 39–40.
9 *Ibid.*, 39.
10 Chang Ha-Joon, *Bad Samaritans* (New York: Bloomsbury Press, 2008), 219.
11 Dani Rodrik of the Institute for Advanced Study in Princeton and Arvind Subramanian of the Peterson Institute for International Economics support this argument. See Special Report, "The Third Great Wave," *The Economist*.
12 "The Third Great Wave," *The Economist*.
13 For inept leadership, Felon of Argentina and the Kim family in North Korea may be illustrated. For good leadership, Lee Kwan Yew of Singapore named Yoshida Sikeru, Deng Xiaoping and Park Chung-hee as great leaders of Asia who saved their countries in crisis. Seol Bong-sik, *Bakjeonghuiwa hangukgyeongje* [Park Chung-hee and the Korean Economy] (Seoul, Korea: Chung-Ang University Press, 2006), 253.
14 The ratio of polls in general elections by the leftist progressive parties has been changed from 13.2 percent in 2004, 12.6 percent in 2008, 12 percent in 2012 and to 8.95 percent in 2016.
15 Most aid recipient countries have decent poverty reduction strategies in collaboration of the World Bank. If these strategies are well implemented as was planned, most countries should have witnessed considerable economic progress.
16 Thomas L. Friedman, *The World Is Flat* (New York: Farrar, Straus and Giroux, 2005), 50–200.

Bibliography

Acemoglu, Daron and Robinson, James A. (2012), *Why Nations Fail*, Crown Business, New York

Administration of Forestry Management (2007), *The Mountain of Korea: The World Calls It a Miracle* [in Korean], Daejun: Korea Forestry Newspaper, Korea

Ban, Sung Hwan, Moon, Pal Yong and Perkis, Dwight H. (1982), *Studies in the Modernization of the Republic of Korea 1945–1975: Rural Development*, Harvard University Press, Cambridge, MA

Chang, Ha-Joon (2008), *Bad Samaritans*, Bloomsbury Press, New York

Cho, Hye-young (2012), *Modularization of Korea's Development Experience: Industrial Park Development Strategy and Management Practices*, Ministry of Knowledge Economy and KICOX

Cho, Kap-jae (2007), *Park Chung Hee, Jeon 13 Kwon* [Park Chung-hee, Series 1–13], Jaeil Printing, Seoul, Korea

Cho, Lee-jay et al. (2005), *Hankuk Geundaehwa: Kyjuckui Kwajung* [Modernization of the Republic of Korea: A Process of Miracle], Chosunilbosa, Seoul, Korea

Cho, Sang-haeng (2012), *Chung Ju-yung, Himangul Gyongyunghada* [Chung Ju-yung, Manage the Hope], ByBooks, Seoul, Korea

Cho, Soon (1994), *The Dynamics of Korean Economic Development*, Institute for International Economics, Washington, DC

Choi, Hyung-sup (1994), "Kwahak Kisului Gaebal (1960–1980)" [Development of Science and Technology (1960–1980), in *Park Chung-hee Sidae: Uriegae Muatinga* [The Park Chung-hee Era: What Was It to Us], edited by Kim, Sung-jin, Chosunilbosa, Seoul, Korea

——— (1995), *Buli Geojijiannun Yonkuso* [The Institute, the Light Never Goes Off], Chosunilbosa, Seoul, Korea

Choi, Kwang (2004), *Tax Policy and Tax System in Korea*, Korea Institute of Public Finance, Seoul Korea

Chun, Seung-hun (2004), *Mikukui Gyongjaejeok Tumyungsungui Ihae* [Understanding of Economic Transparency System in the U.S], Korea Institute of Public Finance, Seoul, Korea

Chun, Seung-hun et al. (2008), *Building the Foundation for the Development of SMEs in Ghana*, Ministry of Strategy and Finance and KDI

——— (2014), *Tax Administration and System Reforms in the Democratic Republic of the Congo*, Ministry of Strategy and Finance and KDI

Chung, Gap-jin (2015), *Hankuk Saemaulundongui Sunggongyoin Bunseok* [The Analysis of Success Factors of the Saemaul Undong], Korea Rural Development Corporation

Dedijer, Stevan (1963), *Underdeveloped Science in Underdeveloped Countries*, Minerva, Springer

Economic Planning Board (1982), *Gaebalsidaeui Gyungjaejungchack* [Economic Policy During the Development Age], Miraesa, Seoul, Korea

The Economist, "Special Report, the Third Great Wave," October 4, 2014

Fanon, Frantz (1963), *The Wretched of the Earth*, Grove Press

Feeney, Griffith and Andrew Mason (1998), "Population in East Asia," Population Series 88–2, East-West Center, Honolulu, HI

Fukuyama, Francis (2004), *State-Building*, Cornell University Press, Ithaca, NY

Garraty, John A. and Gay, Peter (1981), *The Columbia History of the World*, Harper and Row

Gerschenkron, A. (1962), *Economic Backwardness in Historical Perspective: A Book of Essays*, Harvard University Press, Belknap Press, Cambridge, MA

Han, Yung-u (1998), *Hankukui Yeoksa* [*The History of Korea*], Saekyungwon, Seoul, Korea

Henry, Peter Blair and Conrad Miller (2009), "Institutions vs. Policies: A Tale of Two Islands." *American Economic Review*, 99(2): 261–267.

Henteges, Harriet Ann (1975), *The Repatriation and Utilization of High-Level Manpower: A Case Study of the Korea Institute of Science and Technology*, Johns Hopkins University, Baltimore, MD

Hoffmann, Walther (1931), *Stadien und Typen der Industialisierung: Ein Beitrag zur quantitativen Analyse historischer Wirtschaftsprozesse*, Jena Fischer, Berlin, Germany

Hong, Eun-ju and Lee, Eun-hyung (2015), *Korean Miracle 3: Junghwahakgongup, Jichukdul Heundulda* [The Korean Miracle III: Heavy and Chemical Industry Shakes the Axis of the Earth], Nanam, Seoul, Korea

Hong, Eun-ju, Lee, Eun-hyung and Yang, Jae-chan (2013), *Korean Miracle 1* [in Korean], Nanam, Seoul, Korea

Hwang, Byung-tae (2011), *Park Chung-hee Paradigm* [Park Chung-hee Paradigm], Chosunilbosa, Seoul, Korea

Kang, Kwang-ha (2005), *Gyungjaegaebal 5 Gaenyun Gaehoik: Mokpyo mit Jiphaengui Pyungga* [Five Year Economic Development Plan: Evaluation of Goals and Implementation], Seoul National University Press, Seoul, Korea

Kim, Chung-yum (2011), *From Despair to Hope: Economic Policymaking in Korea 1945–1979*, Korea Development Institute, Seoul, Korea

Kim, Eun-mee (1997), *Big Business, Strong State: Collusion and Conflict in South Korean Development, 1960–1990*, State University of New York Press, Albany

Kim, Hak-jun (2010), *Seoyangindului Kwanchalhan Hugi Chosun* [Observation by the Western People on the Latter Period of Chosun], Seogang University, Korea

Kim, Jun-kyung et al. (2012), *Hankuk Gaebalgyunghumui Modyulhwa: Haeoiwonjoui Hankuk Gaebal Younghyang* [Modularization of Korea's Development Experience: Impact of Foreign Aid on Korea's Development], Ministry of Strategy and Finance and KDI School

Kim, Kwang-suk and Kim, Joon-kyung (1997), *Korean Economic Development: An Overview, in the Korean Economy 1945–1995: Performance and Vision for the 21st Century*, edited by Cha Dong-Se, Kim Kwang-Suk, Dwight H. Perkins, KDI

Kim, Sok-Dong et al. (2012), *Hankuk Gaebalgyunghumui Modyulhwa: Loksaekhyungmyung, Tongilbyo Pumjongui Gaebalkwa Bogeup* [Modularization of Korea's Development Experience: The Green Revolution in Korea, Development and

Dissemination of Tongil-type Rice Varieties], RDA and Northern Agriculture Research Institute Inc.

Kim, Sung-jin (2006), *Park Chung-heereul Malhada: Geo Jongchigaehyuckkwa Kwaingchungsung* [Speak of Park Chung-hee: His Political Reform and Excessive Loyalty], Life and Dream, Seoul, Korea

Kim, Yong-hwan (2002), *Imja, Janega Saryunggwananinga* [Aren't You Commander?], Maeil Business Newspaper, Seoul, Korea

Kim, Yong-suh et al. (2006), *Park Chung-hee Sidaeui Jaejomyung* [The Reflection of Park Chung-hee Era], Tradition and Modern Days, Seoul, Korea

Korea Engineering Club (2014), *Jokukgeundaehwaui Juyeokdul* [The Heroes of "Quantum Jump"], Quiparang Press, Seoul, Korea

Korea Institute for Health and Social Affairs (1990), *Jungbuui Gajockgaehoikui Pyongga* [Evaluation of Government's Family Planning Program], KIHASA Publications, Seoul, Korea

——— (1991), *Ingujungchaekui 30 Nyon* [The 30 Years of Population Policy], KIHASA Publications, Seoul, Korea

Kwon, Sun-jik (2015), *Korean Miracle 3: Nongchongeundaehwaundong project, Saemaul Undong* [The Korean Miracle III: Rural Modernization Project, Saemaul Undong], Nanam, Seoul, Korea

Lee, Dae-hwan (2012), *Chungam Park Tae-jun* [Park Tae-jun: A Memorial Issue], ASIA Publishers

Lee, Hyung-koo and Chun, Seung-hun (2003), *Josae Jaejung Jungchack 50 Nyon Jungeon mit Jungchaeckpyungga* [The Evaluation of 50 Year Tax and Fiscal Policy of Korea], Korea Institute of Public Finance, Seoul, Korea

Lee, Kye-min (2015), *Korean Miracle 3: Supui Yuksarul Saerossuda* [The Korean Miracle III: Rewrite the History of Forest], Nanam, Seoul, Korea

Lee, Kye-min, Lee, Hyun-rak, Kim, Kang-jung and Hong, Eun-ju (2014), *Korean Miracke 2: Dojeonkwa Bisang* [The Korean Miracle II: Challenge and Flight], Nanam, Seoul, Korea

Lee, Kyung-yun (2013), *Park Tae-jun Ceorum: Moksumul Geolmyun Saegyega Naesonane* [Like Park Tae-jun: If Taking One's Life, the World Will Be in My Hands], FKI Media Co., Seoul, Korea

Lucas, Robert E., Jr. (1993), "Making a Miracle," *Econometrica*, Vol. 61, No. 2, March

Ma, Tay-Cheng and Ouyang, Lishu (2016), "Democracy and Growth: A Perspective From Democratic Experience," *Economic Inquiry*, 54(4), 1790–1804

Min, Seok-ki (2012), *Ho-Am Lee Byung-chull* [in Korean], ReadersBook, Seoul, Korea

Moyo, Dambisa (2009), *Dead Aid*, Farrar, Straus and Giroux, New York

Nam, Duk-woo (2009), *Gungjaegaebalui Gilmokaeseo* [At a Corner of Economic Development], Samsung Economic Research Institute, Seoul, Korea

Nicholas, Van de Walle (2001), *African Economies and the Politics of Permanent Crisis*, Cambridge University Press, Cambridge

O, Won-chol (1995), *Hankukhyung Gyungjae Geonsul 1* [Korean Type Economic Construction 1: An Engineering Approach], Korea Type Economic Policy Institute, Seoul, Korea

——— (1996), *Hankukhyung Gyungjae Geonsul 2* [Korean Type Economic Construction 2: An Engineering Approach], Korea Type Economic Policy Institute, Seoul, Korea

——— (1996), *Hankukhyung Gyungjae Geonsul 3* [Korean Type Economic Construction 3: An Engineering Approach], Korea Type Economic Policy Institute, Seoul, Korea

—— (1996), *Hankukhyung Gyungjae Geonsul 4* [Korean Type Economic Construction 4: An Engineering Approach], Korea Type Economic Policy Institute Seoul, Korea

—— (1996), *Hankukhyung Gyungjae Geonsul 5* [Korean Type Economic Construction 5: An Engineering Approach], Korea Type Economic Policy Institute, Seoul, Korea

—— (1997), *Hankukhyung Gyungjae Geonsul 6* [Korean Type Economic Construction 6: An Engineering Approach], Korea Type Economic Policy Institute, Seoul, Korea

—— (1999), *Hankukhyung Gyungjae Geonsul 7* [Korean Type Economic Construction 7: An Engineering Approach], Korea Type Economic Policy Institute, Seoul, Korea

—— (2002), *Construction of the Shipbuilding Industry: A Model for Korean Industrialization*, KDI, Seoul, Korea

—— (2003), *The Construction of Pyramid Type Export Oriented Industries* [in Korean], Korea Type Economic Policy Institute, Seoul, Korea

—— (2006), *Park Chung-heenun Eoddukhae Gyungjaegangkuk Mandulotna* [How Park Chung-hee Made Economic Power], Dongsuh Press, Seoul, Korea

—— (2009), *The Korea Story*, Wisdom Tree, Seoul, Korea

Paik, Young-hun (2014), *Jokuk Geundaehwaui Undockassso* [At a Hill of Modernization of My Fatherland], Mind and Thinking, Seoul, Korea

Park, Hun (2004), *Hankuk Sokyuhwahakgongup 30 Nyonui Hoigo* [Reflection of 40 Years of Petrochemical Industry of Korea], Korea Petrochemical Industry Association, Seoul, Korea

Park, Jin-hwan (1997), *The Saemaul Movement: Korea's Approach to Rural Modernization in 1970s*, Korea Rural Economic Institute, Seoul, Korea

Park, Myung Ho (2013), *2012 Modularization of Korea's Development Experience: Land Reform in Korea*, Ministry of Strategy and Finance and Hankuk University of Foreign Studies

Park, Sang-ha (2010), *Igginun Chung Ju-young, Jijiannus Lee Byung-chull* [Winning Chung Ju-yung, Not Losing Lee Byung-chull], Muhan, Seoul, Korea

Park, Tae-jun (2004), "Park Tae-jun Hoigorok" [The Memoir of Park Tae-jun], *Jungangilbo*, August 2–December 9, Seoul, Korea

Riddell, Roger C. (2008), *Does Foreign Aid Really Work?* Oxford University Press, Oxford

Sachs, Jeffrey D. (2005), *The End of Poverty*, The Wiylic Agency (UK) Ltd.

Seo, Gab-kyung (2011), *The Steel King: The Story of Park Tau-jun* [in Korean], Haneon, Seoul, Korea

Seol, Bong-sik (2006), *Park Chung-heewa Hankukgyungjae* [Park Chung-hee and Korean Economy], Chung-Ang University Press, Seoul, Korea

Song, Bok et al. (2012), *Park Tae-jun Sasang, Miraerul Youlda* [The Thought of Park Tae-jun, Open the Future], Asia, Seoul, Korea

Song, Byung Nam (1997), *The Rise of The Korean Economy*, Oxford University Press, Hong Kong

Song, Jang-June, Lee, Jae-Hoon and Chun, Seung-Hun (2006), *National Strategy for the Development of Small-and Medium-Sized Enterprises in the Republic of Mozambique*, The African Development Bank

Soto, Hernando de (2000), *The Mystery of Capital*, Basic Books, New York

Steinberg, David I. (2001), *Burma: The State of Myanmar*, Georgetown University Press, Washington, DC

Stiglitz, Joseph E. (2002), *Globalization and Its Discontents*, Penguin Books

—— (2012), *The Price of inequality: How Today's Divided Society Endangers Our Future*, W.W. Norton

Todaro, Michael P. and Smith, Stephen C. (2007), *Economic Development*, 10th ed., Pearson, New York

Toffler, Alvin (1980), *The Third Wave*, Bantam Books

UN (2005), *In Larger Freedom: Towards Development, Security and Human Rights for All*, Report of the Secretary-General of the United Nations

Walle, Van de (1996), *Partnership for Capacity Building in Africa: Strategy and Program of Action*, World Bank

Whang, In-joung (1974), *Economic Transformation of Korea, 1945–95: Issues and Responses*, The Sejong Institute, Seoul, Korea

—— (1974), *Integration and Coordination of Population Policies in Korea, Asian Survey*, University of California Press, Berkeley

—— (1986), *Social Development in Action: The Korean Experience*, KDI, Seoul, Korea

The World Bank (1998), *Assessing Aid – What Works, What Doesn't, and Why?* Oxford University Press, New York

—— (2003), *Better Governance for Development in the Middle East and North Africa – Enhancing Inclusiveness and Accountability.* World Bank Publications, New York

Yoo, Jung-Ho (1989), *The Government in Korean Economic Growth*, Korea Development Institute, Seoul, Korea

Yoo, Young-mi (2010), *Oae Saegueui Jolbandun Gumjurinunga?* [Translated into Korean from *Wie kommt der Hunger in die Welt?* by Joan Ziegler], Galapagos, Seoul, Korea

Index